Kaplan Publishing are constantly finding new
difference to your studies and our exciting o
offer something different to students lookin

This book comes with free MyKaplan online
study anytime, anywhere. **This free online r...
separately and is included in the price of the book.**

Having purchased this book, you have access to the following online study materials:

CONTENT	ACCA (including FBT, FMA, FFA)		FIA (excluding FBT, FMA, FFA)	
	Text	Kit	Text	Kit
Electronic version of the book	✓	✓	✓	✓
Knowledge checks with instant answers	✓		✓	
Material updates	✓	✓	✓	✓
Latest official ACCA exam questions*		✓		
Pocket Notes (digital copy)	✓		✓	
Study Planner	✓			
Progress Test including questions and answers	✓		✓	
Syllabus recap Videos		✓		✓
Revision Planner		✓		✓
Question Debrief and Walkthrough Videos		✓		
Mock Exam including questions and answers		✓		

* Excludes BT, MA, FA, FBT, FMA, FFA; for all other papers includes a selection of questions, as released by ACCA

How to access your online resources

Received this book as part of your Kaplan course?
If you have a MyKaplan account, your full online resources will be added automatically, in line with the information in your course confirmation email. If you've not used MyKaplan before, you'll be sent an activation email once your resources are ready.

Bought your book from Kaplan?
We'll automatically add your online resources to your MyKaplan account. If you've not used MyKaplan before, you'll be sent an activation email.

Bought your book from elsewhere?
Go to **www.mykaplan.co.uk/add-online-resources**
Enter the ISBN number found on the title page and back cover of this book.
Add the unique pass key number contained in the scratch panel below.
You may be required to enter additional information during this process to set up or confirm your account details.

This code can only be used once for the registration of this book online. This registration and your online content will expire when the examinations covered by this book have taken place. Please allow one hour from the time you submit your book details for us to process your request.

Please scratch the film to access your unique code.

Please be aware that this code is case-sensitive and you will need to include the dashes within the passcode, but not when entering the ISBN.

ACCA

Applied Skills

Financial Reporting (FR)

EXAM KIT

British Library Cataloguing-in-Publication Data

A catalogue record for this book is available from the British Library.

Published by:
Kaplan Publishing UK
Unit 2 The Business Centre
Molly Millar's Lane
Wokingham
Berkshire
RG41 2QZ

ISBN: 978-1-83996-389-6

Acknowledgements

These materials are reviewed by the ACCA examining team. The objective of the review is to ensure that the material properly covers the syllabus and study guide outcomes, used by the examining team in setting the exams, in the appropriate breadth and depth. The review does not ensure that every eventuality, combination or application of examinable topics is addressed by the ACCA Approved Content. Nor does the review comprise a detailed technical check of the content as the Approved Content Provider has its own quality assurance processes in place in this respect.

We are grateful to the Association of Chartered Certified Accountants and the Chartered Institute of Management Accountants for permission to reproduce past examination questions. The answers have been prepared by Kaplan Publishing.

CONTENTS

	Page
Index to questions and answers	P.5
Analysis of past examinations	P.10
Exam technique	P.12
Exam specific information	P.14
Kaplan's recommended revision approach	P.15
Kaplan's detailed revision plan	P.19
Technical update	P.23

Section

1	Objective Test Questions – Section A	1
2	Objective Case Questions – Section B	69
3	Constructed Response Questions – Section C	121
4	Answers to Objective Test Questions – Section A	221
5	Answers to Objective Case Questions – Section B	271
6	Answers to Constructed Response Questions – Section C	307
7	Specimen exam questions	495
8	Answers to specimen exam questions	515
9	References	527

This document references IFRS® Standards and IAS® Standards, which are authored by the International Accounting Standards Board (the Board), and published in the 2022 IFRS Accounting Standards Red Book.

Features in this edition

In addition to providing a wide-ranging bank of exam-standard questions, we have also included in this edition:

- Details of the examination format.
- Examples of objective-test, objective-test case and constructed response questions that will form part of the examination format.
- Exam-specific information and advice on exam technique.
- An analysis of all of the recent published examinations.
- Our recommended approach to make your revision for this particular subject as effective as possible. This includes step-by-step guidance on how best to use our Kaplan material (study text, pocket notes and exam kit) at this stage in your studies.
- Enhanced tutorial answers packed with specific key answer tips, technical tutorial notes and exam technique tips from our experienced tutors.

You will find a wealth of other resources to help you with your studies on the following sites:

www.mykaplan.co.uk and www.accaglobal.com/students/

Quality and accuracy are of the utmost importance to us so if you spot an error in any of our products, please send an email to mykaplanreporting@kaplan.com with full details.

Our Quality Co-ordinator will work with our technical team to verify the error and take action to ensure that it is corrected in future editions.

INDEX TO QUESTIONS AND ANSWERS

INTRODUCTION

A number of the previous ACCA exam questions within this kit have been adapted to reflect updated standards, and the revised exam format. If changed in any way from the original version, whether due to updates in the IFRS® Standards or due to changes in exam format, this is indicated in the end column of the index below with the mark (A).

The specimen examination is included at the end of the kit.

KEY TO THE INDEX

ENHANCEMENTS

We have added the following enhancements to the answers in this exam kit:

Key answer tips

Answers include key answer tips to help your understanding of each question.

Tutorial note

Answers include more tutorial notes to explain some of the technical points in more detail.

Top tutor tips

For selected questions, we 'walk through the answer' giving guidance on how to approach the questions with helpful 'tips from a top tutor', together with technical tutor notes.

These answers are indicated with the 'footsteps' icon in the index.

ONLINE ENHANCEMENTS

Answer debrief

For selected questions, we recommend that they are to be completed in full exam conditions (i.e. properly timed in a closed book environment).

In addition to the examining team's technical answer, enhanced with key answer tips and tutorial notes in this exam kit, online you can find an answer debrief by a top tutor that:

- works through the question in full
- explains key elements of the answer
- ensures that the easy marks are obtained as quickly as possible.

These questions are indicated with the 'video' icon in the index.

Answer debriefs will be available on MyKaplan at:

www.mykaplan.co.uk

	Page number		
	Question	Answer	Past exam

SECTION A – OBJECTIVE TEST QUESTIONS

	Question	Answer
Conceptual framework/IFRS Accounting Standards	1	221
Consolidated financial statements	45	253
Interpretation of financial statements	58	263
Statement of cash flows	65	268

SECTION B – OBJECTIVE CASE QUESTIONS

	Question	Answer
Conceptual framework/IFRS Accounting Standards	69	271
Consolidated financial statements	111	297
Interpretation of financial statements	115	301
Statement of cash flows	118	303

SECTION C – CONSTRUCTED RESPONSE QUESTIONS

PREPARATION OF SINGLE ENTITY FINANCIAL STATEMENTS

No.	Name	Question	Answer	Past exam
401	Pricewell	121	307	Jun 09 (A)
402	Keystone	123	311	Dec 11 (A)
403	Fresco	125	314	Jun 12 (A)
404	Quincy	126	317	Dec 12 (A)
405	Atlas	128	320	Jun 13 (A)
406	Moby	129	323	Dec 13 (A)
407	Xtol	131	327	Jun 14 (A)
408	Dune	132	330	Jun 10 (A)
409	Kandy	134	335	Dec 14(A)
410	Clarion	135	338	Jun 15 (A)
411	Moston	137	340	Sep/Dec 15 (A)
412	Triage	138	343	Sep 16
413	Haverford	140	348	Mar/Jun 18 (A)
414	Duggan Co	141	351	Sep/Dec 18
415	Vernon Co	143	355	Mar/Jun 19
416	Loudon Co	144	358	Sep/Dec 20
417	Mims Co	146	360	Sep/Dec 21
418	Print Co	147	365	Mar/Jun 22

			Page number		
			Question	Answer	Past exam

BUSINESS COMBINATIONS

419	Premier		149	371	Dec 10 (A)
420	Pandar		150	374	Dec 09 (A)
421	Prodigal		152	377	Jun 11 (A)
422	Paladin		153	381	Dec 11 (A)
423	Pyramid		155	384	Jun 12 (A)
424	Viagem		156	387	Dec 12 (A)
425	Paradigm		158	389	Jun 13 (A)
426	Penketh		160	392	Jun 14 (A)
427	Palistar		161	394	Sep/Dec 15(A)
428	Laurel		163	397	Dec 16
429	Dargent Co		164	399	Mar/Jun 17
430	Party Co		166	402	Sep/Dec 17
431	Runner Co		167	406	Sep/Dec 19
432	Plank Co		169	409	Mar/Jul 20
433	Gold Co		170	413	Mar/Jun 21
434	Chang Co		172	417	–
435	Zeffer Co		173	419	–
436	Perd Co		174	421	Sep/Dec 22
437	Dobry Co		176	425	–

ANALYSING FINANCIAL STATEMENTS

		Page number Question	Answer	Past exam
438	Woodbank	177	428	Jun 14 (A)
439	Hydan	179	431	Dec 14(A)
440	Yogi	181	433	Jun 15 (A)
441	Xpand	183	435	Sep/Dec 15 (A)
442	Pitcarn	186	438	–
443	Gregory	187	440	Sep 16
444	Landing	189	444	Dec 16
445	Funject Co	191	446	Mar/Jun 17
446	Flash Co	193	449	–
447	Mowair Co	195	451	Sep/Dec 17
448	Perkins	197	455	Mar/Jun 18
449	Duke Co	199	457	Sep/Dec 18
450	Pirlo	200	461	Mar/Jun 19
451	Bun Co	202	464	Sep/Dec 19
452	Parul Co	203	467	–
453	Fit Co	205	469	Mar/Jul 20
454	Karl Co	206	472	Sep/Dec 20
455	Pastry Co	208	474	Mar/Jun 21
456	Pinardi Co	210	478	Sep/Dec 21
457	Venus Co	212	482	Mar/Jun 22
458	Treats Co	213	485	Sep/Dec 22
459	Souttar Co	215	489	–
460	Marvell Co	217	491	–

ANALYSIS OF PAST EXAMINATIONS

The table summarises the key topics that have been published by ACCA as tested in recent Financial Reporting exams. The information only relates to constructed response questions released by ACCA, as objective-test questions have not usually been published.

	Mar/ Jun 2018	Sep/ Dec 2018	Mar/ Jun 2019	Sep/ Dec 2019	Mar/ Jul 2020	Sep/ Dec 2020	Mar/ Jun 2021	Sep/ Dec 2021	Mar/ Jun 2022	Sep/ Dec 2022
Group financial statements										
Consolidated statement of profit or loss and other comprehensive income					✓		✓			✓
Consolidated statement of financial position		✓		✓						
Associates				✓	✓		✓			
Disposal	✓		✓			✓		✓		
Single entity financial statements										
Full trial balance	✓								✓	
Trial balance extract		✓	✓			✓		✓		
Adjusted profit	✓					✓				
Statement of profit or loss		✓	✓					✓	✓	
Statement of financial position	✓					✓			✓	
Statement of changes in equity	✓	✓						✓		
Cash flow extract								✓		
Performance appraisal										
Single entity	✓	✓		✓	✓		✓			✓
Groups	✓	✓	✓			✓		✓	✓	

Framework/IFRS										
IASB Framework										
Not for profit/ specialised entities										
IAS 2	✓								✓	
IAS 7										
IAS 8		✓	✓					✓		
IAS 10			✓							
IAS 12		✓	✓			✓		✓	✓	
IAS 16	✓		✓			✓			✓	✓
IAS 20										
IAS 21			✓					✓		
IAS 23										
IAS 28										
IAS 32 / IFRS 7/ IFRS 9	✓	✓	✓			✓	✓		✓	
IAS 33		✓	✓							
IAS 36			✓							
IAS 37		✓	✓			✓		✓	✓	
IAS 38							✓	✓		
IAS 40			✓				✓	✓		
IAS 41										
IFRS 3		✓								
IFRS 5								✓	✓	
IFRS 10		✓								
IFRS 13										
IFRS 15	✓	✓	✓							
IFRS 16										

EXAM TECHNIQUE

Computer-based exams (CBE)

- Do not attempt a CBE until you have **completed all study material** relating to it.
- On the ACCA website there are Financial Reporting CBE past exams as well as a full specimen CBE. It is **ESSENTIAL** that you attempt a few of these before your real CBE. You will become familiar with how to move around the screens and the way that questions are formatted, increasing your confidence and speed in the actual exam.
- Be sure you understand how to use the **software** before you start the exam. Ensure that you use the resources on the ACCA website to practise, **especially the ACCA Practice Platform**. If in doubt, ask the assessment centre staff to explain it to you.

Time management

- The examination is 3 hours long.
- This equates to 1.8 minutes per mark, so you need to allow 36 minutes per Constructed Response (CR) question and an average of 3.6 minutes per objective-test (OT) question.
- Decide whether you want to attempt the OTs first, or after completion of the CR questions. Whichever you choose to do first, ensure that you leave enough time to tackle the remainder.
- Whatever happens, always keep your eye on the clock and **do not over-run on any part of any question**!

Objective-test questions

- **Do not skip any of the material** in the syllabus during revision.
- No credit for workings will be given in these questions. The answer will either be correct (2 marks) or incorrect (0 marks).
- Read each question **very carefully**, as the alternative answer choices will be given based on common mistakes that could be made in attempting the question.
- **Double-check your answer** before committing yourself to it.
- Answer **every** question – if you do not know an answer, you don't lose anything by guessing, but think carefully before you **guess**.
- Remember that there is **only one correct answer to a multiple-choice question**. After you have eliminated the ones that you know to be wrong, if you are still unsure, guess. Only guess after you have **double-checked** that you have only eliminated answers that are **definitely** wrong.
- If you are **completely stuck** with a question, choose your best answer, flag the question for review and **return to it later** if you have time.

- The objective –test question types are as follows:
  - **Multiple choice** – choose one answer from a number of given options
  - **Multiple response** – choose more than one an answer from a number of given options
  - **Fill in the blank** – type an answer into a box
  - **Drag and drop** – drag an answer and drop it into place
  - **Drop down list** – choose one answer from a drop down list
  - **Hot spot** – choose one point on an image
  - **Hot area** – choose an area in an image

Constructed Response questions

- There will be a computational financial statements preparation question and a written analysis question. The workspace provided for response will be determined by the marks available. So, for example, if a question has a computational element for 6 marks (e.g. ratios) and a written element for 14 marks (e.g. interpretation) then the response area provided would be a word document rather than a spreadsheet.
- **Computational questions** require the use of a standard format, e.g. statement of profit or loss and other comprehensive income. Be sure that you know all the formats thoroughly before the exam and use the layouts that you see in the answers given in this book and in model answers.
- It is essential to show all your workings in your answer, especially if using a word document.
- For the **written question** consider how to structure the response and lay it out to articulate the answer clearly.
- Stick to the question and **ensure that you explain the reasons** why the numbers have changed.
- Your response should have:
  - a clear structure
  - a brief introduction, a main section and a conclusion.

  It is better to write a little about a lot of different points than a great deal about one or two points.
- You should do everything you can to make things easy for the marker. Cross-reference answers to workings in computational questions and use headings and sub-headings in written answers.
- For some computational questions, such as the calculation of ratios, the response area will contain a pre-formatted area to encourage and enable you to set out your workings easily. Please ensure that you use it!

  A typical pre-formatted area might look like this:

Ratio	**Working**	**20X7**	**Working**	**20X6**
Gross profit margin				
Operating profit margin				
Interest cover				
Inventory turnover days				

EXAM SPECIFIC INFORMATION

THE EXAM

FORMAT OF THE EXAM

The exam will be in **THREE sections**, and will be a mix of narrative and computational answers. Section A will be 15 objective test questions, each worth 2 marks. Section B will consist of 3 objective case questions, each worth 10 marks and containing 5 questions. Section C will consist of two 20-mark questions

		Number of marks
Section A:	Fifteen 2-mark objective test questions	30
Section B:	Three 10-mark objective case questions	30
Section C:	Two 20-mark constructed response questions, covering the interpretation and preparation of financial statements for a single entity or a group	40
		100

Note that the FR exam will have both a discursive and computational element. The questions will therefore include a mix of calculation-based and explanations-based questions.

PASS MARK

The pass mark for all ACCA Qualification examinations is 50%.

DETAILED SYLLABUS, STUDY GUIDE AND CBE SPECIMEN EXAM

The detailed syllabus and study guide written by the ACCA, along with the specimen exam, can be found at https://www.accaglobal.com/in/en/student/exam-support-resources/fundamentals-exams-study-resources/f7.html

Within the main accaglobal.com website this is accessed within the Study Support Resources area.

KAPLAN'S RECOMMENDED REVISION APPROACH

QUESTION PRACTICE IS THE KEY TO SUCCESS

Success in professional examinations relies upon you acquiring a firm grasp of the required knowledge at the tuition phase. In order to be able to answer the questions, knowledge is essential.

However, the difference between success and failure often hinges on your exam technique on the day and making the most of the revision phase of your studies.

The **Kaplan study text** is the starting point, designed to provide the underpinning knowledge to tackle all questions. However, in the revision phase, poring over textbooks is not the answer.

Kaplan Online knowledge check tests help you consolidate your knowledge and understanding, and are a useful tool to check whether you remember key topic areas.

Kaplan pocket notes are designed to help you quickly revise a topic area, but you then need to practise questions. There is a need to progress to full exam standard questions as soon as possible, and to tie your exam technique and technical knowledge together.

The **ACCA Practice Platform** provides an essential practice area for you to become familiar with the software available on the examination day. Use this to practise answering Constructed Response questions from this Exam Kit wherever possible.

The importance of question practice cannot be over-emphasised.

The recommended approach below is designed by expert tutors in the field, in conjunction with their knowledge of the examiner.

The approach taken for the Applied Skills exams is to revise by topic area.

You need to practise as many questions as possible in the time you have left before the exam.

OUR AIM

Our aim is to get you to the stage where you can attempt exam standard questions confidently, to time, in a closed book environment, with no supplementary help (i.e. to simulate the real examination experience).

Practising your exam technique on exam standard examination questions, in timed conditions, is also vitally important for you to assess your progress and identify areas of weakness that may need more attention in the final run up to the examination.

In order to achieve this we recognise that initially you may feel the need to practise some questions with open book help and exceed the required time.

The approach below shows you which questions you should use to build up to coping with exam standard question practice, and references to the sources of information available should you need to revisit a topic area in more detail.

Remember that in the real examination, all you have to do is:

- attempt all questions required by the exam
- only spend the allotted time on each question, and
- get them at least 50% right!

Try to practise this approach on every question you attempt from now to the real exam.

EXAMINER COMMENTS

We have included some of the examiner's comments to the examination questions in this kit for you to see the main pitfalls that students fall into with regard to technical content.

However, too many times in the general section of the report, the examiner comments that students had failed due to poor time management where students had shown signs of 'spending too much time on an earlier question and clearly rushing the answer to a subsequent question'.

Ensure that you read the examiner's comments from recent exams on the ACCA website.

Good exam technique is vital.

ACCA SUPPORT

For additional support with your studies please also refer to the ACCA Global website.

THE KAPLAN FINANCIAL REPORTING REVISION PLAN

Stage 1: Assess areas of strengths and weaknesses

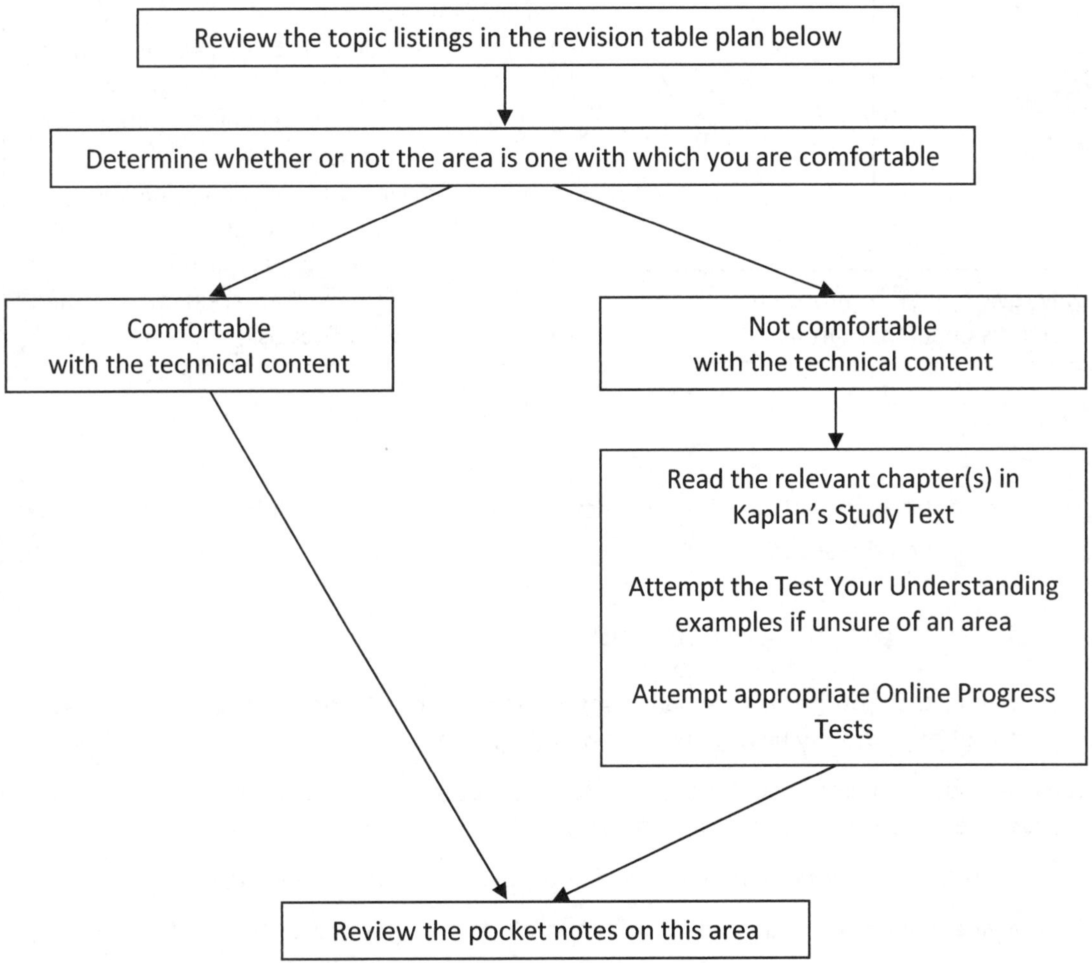

Stage 2: Practise questions

Follow the order of revision of topics as recommended in the revision table plan below and attempt the questions in the order suggested.

Try to avoid referring to textbooks, notes or the model answer until you have completed your attempt.

Try to answer the question in the allotted time.

Review your attempt with the model answer and assess how much of the answer you achieved in the allocated exam time.

Use the self-assessment box below to decide on your best course of action.

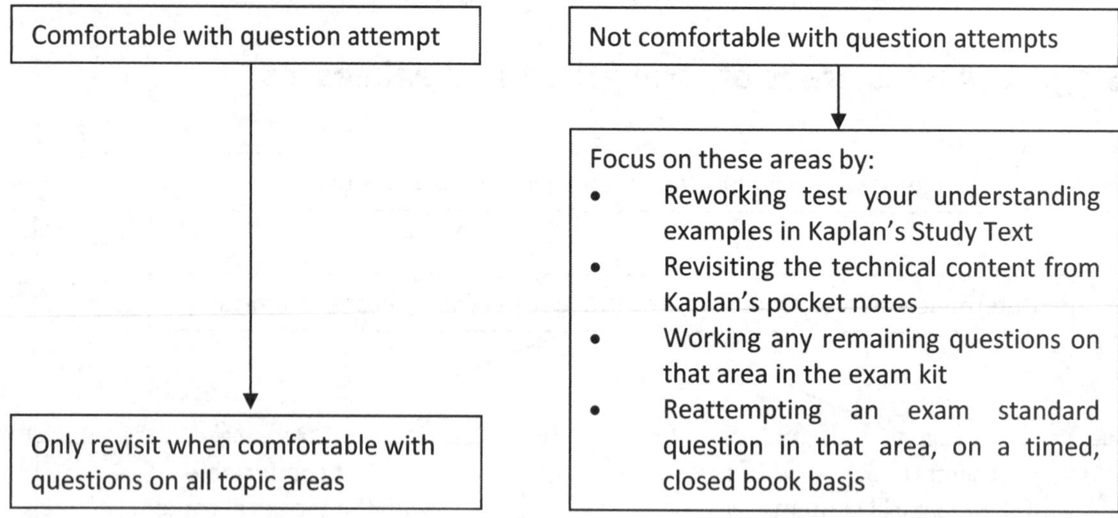

Note that:

The 'footsteps questions' give guidance on exam techniques and how you should have approached the question.

Stage 3: Final pre-exam revision

We recommend that you **attempt at least one three-hour mock computer-based examination** containing a set of previously unseen exam standard questions.

It is important that you get a feel for the breadth of coverage of the real exam without advanced knowledge of the topic areas covered – just as you will see on the real exam day.

Ideally this mock should be sat in timed, closed book, real exam conditions and could be:

- an online mock examination offered by your tuition provider and/or
- the examinations in the back of this exam kit (answered using ACCA CR Workspace) and/or
- the latest released examination Constructed Response questions (available shortly afterwards on MyKaplan with enhanced walk-through answers and a full tutor debrief). Ensure that you use the ACCA Practice Platform to attempt these.

KAPLAN'S DETAILED REVISION PLAN

Topic	Study Text Chapter	Pocket Note Chapter	Questions to attempt	Tutor guidance	Date attempted	Self-assessment
Consolidated statement of financial position	18	18	143–152 361–365 420, 423, 424, 426, 428, 430, 432, 433, 434	Practise using the Kaplan 5-working approach. Ensure you get the easy marks available in the question from adding the parent and subsidiary assets and liabilities together.		
Consolidated statement of profit or loss and other comprehensive income	19	19	158–164 366–370 421, 422, 425, 427, 428, 429, 431, 435, 436, 437, 438, 439	Watch the dates carefully – is there a mid-year acquisition? If so you have to time apportion the subsidiary company results when adding the parent and subsidiary together.		
Associates	20	20	165–169 374 421, 434, 435	Make sure that you understand the equity method of accounting, and the different treatments of PUP dependent upon the seller.		
Disposal of subsidiaries	21	21	186–189 375 438	Ensure you familiarise yourself with the workings related to calculating a profit/loss on disposal.		

Topic	Study Text Chapter	Pocket Note Chapter	Questions to attempt	Tutor guidance	Date attempted	Self-assessment
Accounting standards:						
Non-current assets (IAS 16, IAS 20, IAS 23, IAS 38, IAS 40, IFRS 5)	2	2	1–22, 30–36 226–245	Be clear on initial recognition rules and subsequent measurement for property, plant and equipment, intangible assets and investment properties. Ensure you know the definition of borrowing costs and the three recognition and two derecognition criteria. Ensure you understand how to deal with assets held for sale.		
IAS 36	4	4	23–29 256–285	Learn the impairment test proforma and the cash generating unit write down rules.		
Framework	6/7	6/7	37–59 64–66	Learn the key definitions and be able to apply them to various situations		
IAS 2, IAS 8, IAS 41, IFRS 13	8	8	60–63 67–76 286–295	Each standard is relatively small, but it is key that you learn definitions and the specific rules relating to each.		

Topic	Study Text Chapter	Pocket Note Chapter	Questions to attempt	Tutor guidance	Date attempted	Self-assessment
IAS 32/IFRS 7/IFRS 9	9	9	88–97 306–325	Amortised cost is the core area of financial liabilities here. Make sure you can deal with loans issued at a discount & redeemed at a premium. You will also need an awareness of the categories of financial asset in accordance with IFRS 9 and the accounting treatment for them.		
IAS 21	10	10	98–102 326–328	Examine the initial and subsequent treatment, in addition to the rules for unsettled transactions.		
IFRS 15	11	11	103–115 331–340	Different revenue scenarios should be looked at, in particular where revenue is recognised over time.		
IFRS 16	12	12	77–87 296–305	Be sure that you are able to construct a liability table.		
IAS 12	13	13	116–120 329–330	Learn the definition of a temporary difference and practise its application.		
IAS 33	14	14	121–130 341–345	Learn the formula and apply to share issues.		
IAS 37, IAS 10	15	15	131–142 346–365	For IAS 37 the recognition rules are very clear – learn the 3 recognition rules. Learn the differences between adjusting and non-adjusting events.		

Topic	Study Text Chapter	Pocket Note Chapter	Questions to attempt	Tutor guidance	Date attempted	Self-assessment
Statement of cash flows	16	16	216–225 391–400	Learn the proforma. Start with calculations in questions 201, 203, and 204 before moving on to analysing cash flows in 221 and 226.		
Preparation of individual company financial statements	1, 23	1	401–418	You have to learn the accounting standards examinable first and then apply your knowledge to these recommended questions.		
Ratio interpretation – single entity	22	22	190–215 381–390 440-443, 446-449, 451, 453, 455, 457, 460	Learn the ratio calculations and practise identifying where you pull the information for the formula out of the financial statements.		
Ratio interpretation – groups	22	22	444, 445, 450, 452, 454, 456, 458, 459	Focus on the impact of any acquisition/disposal of a subsidiary within the scenario.		

TECHNICAL UPDATE

There were minor changes to the Financial Reporting syllabus from 2022/23 to 2023/24. In addition to changes for the purpose of clarification, changes were as follows:

- Introduced a requirement to explain the purpose and role of the International Sustainability Standards Board (ISSB™)
- Deferred tax assets will now be examinable in addition to deferred tax liabilities
- Clarified that sales proceeds in a sale and leaseback transaction will always be equal to fair value in the FR exam.

Section 1

OBJECTIVE TEST QUESTIONS – SECTION A

CONCEPTUAL FRAMEWORK/INTERNATIONAL FINANCIAL REPORTING STANDARDS

1 IAS 16 *Property, Plant and Equipment* requires an asset to be measured at cost on its original recognition in the financial statements. EW used its own staff, assisted by contractors when required, to construct a new warehouse for its own use.

Identify whether the costs listed below should be capitalised or expensed.

	Capitalise	Expense
Clearance of the site prior to commencement of construction		
Professional surveyor fees for managing the construction work		
EW's own staff wages for time spent working on construction		
A proportion of EW's administration costs, based on staff time spent		

2 On 1 July 20X4, Experimenter opened a chemical reprocessing plant. The plant was due to be active for five years until 30 June 20X9, when it would be decommissioned. At 1 July 20X4, the costs of decommissioning the plant were estimated to be $4 million in 5 years' time. Experimenter considers that a discount rate of 12% is appropriate for the calculation of a present value, and the discount factor at 12% for five years is 0.567.

What is the total charge to the statement of profit or loss in respect of the decommissioning for the year ended 30 June 20X5?

A $453,600

B $725,760

C $800,000

D $2,268,000

3 An entity purchased property for $6 million on 1 July 20X3. The land element of the purchase was $1 million. The expected life of the building was 50 years and its residual value nil. On 30 June 20X5 the property was revalued to $7 million, of which the land element was $1.24 million and the buildings $5.76 million. On 30 June 20X7, the property was sold for $6.8 million.

What is the gain on disposal of the property that would be reported in the statement of profit or loss for the year to 30 June 20X7?

A Gain $40,000

B Loss $200,000

C Gain $1,000,000

D Gain $1,240,000

4 A manufacturing entity receives a grant of $1m towards the purchase of a machine on 1 January 20X3. The grant will be repayable if the entity sells the asset within 4 years, which it does not intend to do. The asset has a useful life of 5 years.

What is the deferred income liability balance at 30 June 20X3?

$____________,000

5 On 1 January 20X1 Sty received $1m from the local government on the condition that they employ at least 100 staff each year for the next 4 years. Due to an economic downturn and reduced consumer demand on 1 January 20X2, Sty no longer needed to employ any more staff and the conditions of the grant required full repayment.

What should be recorded in the financial statements on 1 January 20X2?

A Reduce deferred income balance by $750,000

B Reduce deferred income by $750,000 and recognise a loss of $250,000

C Reduce deferred income by $1,000,000

D Reduce deferred income by $1,000,000 and recognise a gain of $250,000

6 **Which of the following properties owned by Scoop would be classified as an investment property?**

A A property that had been leased to a tenant but which is no longer required and is now being held for resale

B Land purchased for its investment potential. Planning permission has not been obtained for building construction of any kind

C A new office building used as Scoop's head office, purchased specifically in order to exploit its capital gains potential

D A stately home used for executive training

7 During the current year an entity had in place $1 million of 6% loan finance and $2 million of 9% loan finance.

It constructed a new factory which cost $600,000 and this was funded out of the existing loan finance. The factory took 8 months to complete.

To the nearest thousand, what borrowing costs should be capitalised?

$_____________ ,000

8 **Which of the following statements is correct?**

Statement 1 If the revaluation model is used for property, plant and equipment, revaluations must subsequently be made with sufficient regularity to ensure that the carrying amount does not differ materially from the fair value at each reporting date.

Statement 2 When an item of property, plant and equipment is revalued, there is no requirement that the entire class of assets to which the item belongs must be revalued.

	Statement 1	**Statement 2**
True		
False		

9 Pootle Co received a government grant of $60,000 on 1 September 20X4. The conditions of the grant State that Pootle Co must employ a local worker on a full-time contract over a five-year period. Pootle Co expects to meet the conditions of the grant.

The full grant has been recorded as other income for the year ended 31 December 20X4.

What is the adjustment required to account correctly for the grant as at 31 December 20X4?

	Account name	**Value**
Debit		
Credit		

Select your answer from the following options:

Account name
Bank
Other income
Total accrued income
Total deferred income

Value
$4,000
$48,000
$56,000
$57,000

10 Tibet acquired a new office building on 1 October 20X4. Its initial carrying amount consisted of:

	$000
Land	2,000
Building structure	10,000
Air conditioning system	4,000
	16,000

The estimated lives of the building structure and air conditioning system are 25 years and 10 years respectively.

When the air conditioning system is due for replacement, it is estimated that the old system will be dismantled and sold for $500,000.

Depreciation is time-apportioned where appropriate.

At what amount will the office building be shown in Tibet's statement of financial position as at 31 March 20X5?

A $15,625,000

B $15,250,000

C $15,585,000

D $15,600,000

11 The following trial balance extract relates to a property which is owned by Veeton as at 1 April 20X4.

	Dr	Cr
	$000	$000
Property at cost (20 year original life)	12,000	
Accumulated depreciation as at 1 April 20X4		3,600

On 1 October 20X4, following a sustained increase in property prices, Veeton revalued its property to $10.8 million.

What will be the depreciation charge in Veeton's statement of profit or loss for the year ended 31 March 20X5?

$____________ ,000

12 **Which TWO of the following statements about IAS 20 *Accounting for Government Grants and Disclosure of Government Assistance* are true?**

A A government grant related to the purchase of an asset must be deducted from the carrying amount of the asset in the statement of financial position.

B A government grant related to the purchase of an asset should be recognised in profit or loss over the life of the asset.

C Free marketing advice provided by a government department is excluded from the definition of government grants.

D Any required repayment of a government grant received in an earlier reporting period is treated as prior period adjustment.

13 Smithson Co purchased a new building with a 50-year life for $10 million on 1 January 20X3. On 30 June 20X5, Smithson Co moved out of the building and rented it out to third parties on a short-term lease. Smithson Co uses the fair value model for investment properties. At 30 June 20X5 the fair value of the property was $11 million and at 31 December 20X5 it was $11.5 million.

What is the total net amount to be recorded in the statement of profit or loss in respect of the office for the year ended 31 December 20X5?

A Net income $400,000

B Net income $500,000

C Net income $1,900,000

D Net income $2,000,000

14 Gilbert took out a $7.5 million 10% loan on 1 January 20X6 to build a new warehouse during the year. Construction of the warehouse began on 1 February 20X6 and was completed on 30 November 20X6. As not all the funds were needed immediately, Gilbert invested $2 million in 4.5% bonds from 1 January to 1 May 20X6.

What are the total borrowing costs to be capitalised in respect of the warehouse?

$______________

15 Croft acquired a building with a 40-year life for its investment potential for $8 million on 1 January 20X3. At 31 December 20X3, the fair value of the property was estimated at $9 million with costs to sell estimated at $200,000.

If Croft Co uses the fair value model for investment properties, what gain should be recorded in the statement of profit or loss for the year ended 31 December 20X3?

$______________,000

16 Which of the following CANNOT be recognised as an intangible non-current asset in GHK's consolidated statement of financial position at 30 September 20X1?

A GHK spent $132,000 developing a new type of product. In June 20X1 management worried that it would be too expensive to fund. The finances to complete the project came from a cash injection from a benefactor received in November 20X1.

B GHK purchased a subsidiary during the year. During the fair value exercise, it was found that the subsidiary had a brand name with an estimated value of $50,000, but had not been recognised by the subsidiary as it was internally generated.

C GHK purchased a brand name from a competitor on 1 November 20X0, for $65,000.

D GHK spent $21,000 during the year on the development of a new product, after management concluded it would be viable in November 20X0. The product is being launched on the market on 1 December 20X1 and is expected to be profitable.

17 Which of the following could be classified as development expenditure in M's statement of financial position as at 31 March 20Y0 according to IAS 38 *Intangible Assets?*

A $120,000 spent on developing a prototype and testing a new type of propulsion system. The project needs further work on it as the system is currently not viable.

B A payment of $50,000 to a local university's engineering faculty to research new environmentally friendly building techniques.

C $35,000 developing an electric bicycle. This is near completion and the product will be launched soon. As this project is first of its kind it is expected to make a loss.

D $65,000 developing a special type of new packaging for a new energy-efficient light bulb. The packaging is expected to reduce M's distribution costs by $35,000 a year.

18 Which TWO of the following factors are reasons why key staff cannot be capitalised as an intangible asset by an entity?

A They do not provide expected future economic benefits

B They cannot be controlled by an entity

C Their value cannot be measured reliably

D They are not separable from the business as a whole

19 Amco Co carries out research and development. In the year ended 30 June 20X5 Amco Co incurred total costs in relation to project X of $750,000, spending the same amount each month up to 30 April 20X5, when the project was completed. The product produced by the project went on sale from 31 May 20X5.

The project had been confirmed as feasible on 1 January 20X5, and the product produced by the project was expected to have a useful life of five years.

What is the carrying amount of the development expenditure asset as at 30 June 20X5?

A $295,000

B $725,000

C $300,000

D $0

20 Sybil has acquired a subsidiary Basil in the current year.

Basil has a brand which has been reliably valued by Sybil at $500,000, and a customer list which Sybil has been unable to value.

Which of these describes how Sybil should treat these intangible assets of Basil in their consolidated Financial Statements?

A They should be included in goodwill.

B The brand should be capitalised as a separate intangible asset, whereas the customer list should be included within goodwill.

C Both the brand and the customer list should be capitalised as separate intangible assets.

D The customer list should be capitalised as a separate intangible asset, whereas the brand should be included within goodwill.

21 Dempsey Co owns a pharmaceutical business with a year-end of 30 September 20X4. Dempsey Co commenced the development stage of a new drug on 1 January 20X4. $40,000 per month was incurred until the project was completed on 30 June 20X4, when the drug went into immediate production. The directors became confident of the project's success on 1 March 20X4. The drug has an estimated life span of five years and time-apportionment is used by Dempsey where applicable.

What amount will Dempsey charge to profit or loss for development costs, including any amortisation, for the year ended 30 September 20X4?

A $12,000

B $98,667

C $48,000

D $88,000

22 **Which of the following statements relating to intangible assets is/are true?**

	True	**False**
All intangible assets must be carried at amortised cost or at an impaired amount, they cannot be revalued upwards.		
The development of a new process which is not expected to increase sales revenues may still be recognised as an intangible asset.		

23 A division of an entity has the following balances in its financial statements:

	$
Goodwill	700,000
Plant	950,000
Building	2,300,000
Intangibles	800,000
Other net assets	430,000

Following a period of losses, the recoverable amount of the division is deemed to be $4 million. A recent valuation of the building showed that the building has a market value of $2.5 million. The other net assets are at their recoverable amount. The entity uses the cost model for valuing building and plant.

To the nearest thousand, what is the balance on the building following the impairment review?

A $2,300,000

B $2,500,000

C $2,027,000

D $1,776,000

24 A division of an entity has the following balances in its financial statements:

	$
Goodwill	700,000
Plant	950,000
Building	2,300,000
Intangibles	800,000
Other net assets	430,000

Following a period of losses, the recoverable amount of the division is deemed to be $4 million. A recent valuation of the building showed that the building has a market value of $2.5 million. The other net assets are at their recoverable amount. The entity uses the cost model for valuing building and plant.

To the nearest thousand, what is the balance on plant following the impairment review?

$_______________,000

25 A vehicle was involved in an accident exactly halfway through the year. The vehicle cost $10,000 and had a remaining life of 10 years at the start of the year. Following the accident, the expected present value of cash flows associated with the vehicle was $3,400 and the fair value less costs to sell was $6,500.

What is the recoverable amount of the vehicle following the accident?

$_______________

26 The net assets of Fyngle, a cash generating unit (CGU), are:

	$
Property, plant and equipment	200,000
Allocated goodwill	50,000
Product patent	20,000
Net current assets (at net realisable value)	30,000
	300,000

As a result of adverse publicity, Fyngle has a recoverable amount of only $200,000.

What would be the value of Fyngle's property, plant and equipment after the allocation of the impairment loss?

A $154,545

B $170,000

C $160,000

D $133,333

27 **Which of the following is NOT an indicator of impairment?**

A Advances in the technological environment in which an asset is employed have an adverse impact on its future use.

B An increase in interest rates which increases the discount rate an entity uses.

C The carrying amount of an entity's net assets is higher than the entity's number of shares in issue multiplied by its share price.

D The estimated net realisable value of inventory has been reduced due to fire damage although this value is greater than its carrying amount.

28 Riley acquired a non-current asset on 1 October 20X9 at a cost of $100,000 which had a useful life of ten years and a nil residual value. The asset had been correctly depreciated up to 30 September 20Y4. At that date the asset was damaged and an impairment review was performed. On 30 September 20Y4, the fair value of the asset less costs to sell was $30,000 and the expected future cash flows were $8,500 per annum for the next five years. The current cost of capital is 10% and a five year annuity of $1 per annum at 10% would have a present value of $3.79.

What amount would be charged to profit or loss for the impairment of this asset for the year ended 30 September 20Y4?

$____________

29 Metric owns an item of plant which has a carrying amount of $248,000 as at 1 April 20X3. It is being depreciated at 12.5% per annum on a reducing balance basis.

The plant is used to manufacture a specific product which has been suffering a slow decline in sales. Metric has estimated that the plant will be retired from use on 31 March 20X7.

The estimated net cash flows from the use of the plant and their present values are:

	Net cash flows	Present values
	$	$
Year to 31 March 20X5	120,000	109,200
Year to 31 March 20X6	80,000	66,400
Year to 31 March 20X7	52,000	39,000
	252,000	214,600

On 1 April 20X4, Metric had an offer from a rival to purchase the plant for $200,000.

At what value should the plant appear in Metric's statement of financial position as at 31 March 20X4?

$______________

30 As at 30 September 20X3 the value of Dune's property in its statement of financial position comprised:

Cost (useful life 15 years)	$45 million
Accumulated depreciation	$6 million

On 1 April 20X4, Dune decided to sell the property. The property is being marketed by a property agent at a price of $42 million, which was considered a reasonably achievable price at that date. The expected costs to sell have been agreed at $1 million. Recent market transactions suggest that actual sale prices achieved for this type of property in the current market conditions are 10% less than the price at which they are marketed.

At 30 September 20X4 the property has not been sold.

At what value should the property be reported in Dune's statement of financial position as at 30 September 20X4?

A $36 million

B $37.5 million

C $36.8 million

D $42 million

31 BN has an asset that was classified as held for sale at 31 March 20X2. The asset had a carrying amount of $900 and a fair value of $800. The cost of disposal was estimated to be $50.

According to IFRS 5 *Non-current Assets Held for Sale and Discontinued Operations*, which value should be used for the asset as at 31 March 20X2?

A $750

B $800

C $850

D $900

32 **According to IFRS 5 *Non-current Assets Held for Sale and Discontinued Operations* which of the following represent criteria for an asset to be classified as held for sale?**

(i) Available for immediate sale in its present condition.

(ii) Sale is highly probable.

(iii) The sale is expected to be completed within the next month.

(iv) The asset is being marketed at a reasonable price.

A All of the above

B (i), (ii) and (iii)

C (i), (ii) and (iv)

D (ii), (iii) and (iv)

33 **According to IFRS 5 *Non-current Assets Held for Sale and Discontinued Operations* which of the following amounts in respect of a discontinued operation must be shown on the face of the statement of profit or loss?**

	Shown on the face of the statement of profit or loss	**Not shown**
Revenue		
Gross profit		
Profit after tax		

34 Rural has the following two lines of business that have been disposed of in the year:

Sector X operated in Country A. Rural has no other operations in Country A, and Sector X produced 0.5% of the total revenue of Rural.

Sector Y operated in the same country as the Rural head office. It sold a different product from the other components of Rural, and contributed 10% of the total revenue of Rural Co.

Which of these sectors, if either, should be disclosed as a discontinued operation in the current year?

	Discontinued operation Yes/No
Sector X	
Sector Y	

35 **What is the primary reason why discontinued operations are presented separately within financial statements?**

A To show an accurate valuation of the business

B To enhance the predictive nature of financial statements

C To make the financial statements easier to understand

D So the financial statements are verifiable

36 At 1 April 20X4, Tilly owned a property with a carrying amount of $800,000 which had a remaining estimated life of 16 years, and was carried under the cost model. On 1 October 20X4, Tilly decided to sell the property and correctly classified it as being 'held-for-sale'. A property agent reported that the property's fair value less costs to sell at 1 October 20X4 was expected to be $790,500 which had not changed at 31 March 20X5.

What should be the carrying amount of the property in Tilly's statement of financial position as at 31 March 20X5?

A $775,000

B $790,500

C $765,000

D $750,000

37 **Which of the following gives the best description of the objective of financial statements as set out by the International Accounting Standards Board's (The Board's) Conceptual Framework for Financial Reporting?**

A To provide all information about the reporting entity that users need.

B To fairly present the financial position, performance and changes in financial position of an enterprise.

C To provide information about the value of the reporting entity to the users.

D To provide financial information about the reporting entity that is useful to users in making decisions relating to providing resources to the entity.

38 **Which of the following statements relating to regulatory frameworks is/are true?**

	True	**False**
Accounting standards on their own provide a complete regulatory framework.		
A regulatory framework is required to ensure that financial reporting meets the needs of primary users.		

39 The International Accounting Standards Board's Conceptual Framework for Financial Reporting lists two fundamental qualitative characteristics of financial statements, relevance and faithful representation.

Place the qualities listed alongside the appropriate qualitative characteristic.

	Faithful representation	**Relevance**
Completeness		
Predictive value		
Neutrality		

40 The International Accounting Standards Board's Conceptual Framework for Financial Reporting identifies qualitative characteristics of financial statements.

Which TWO of the following characteristics are NOT fundamental qualitative characteristics according to the *IASB's The Conceptual Framework for Financial Reporting?*

A Relevance

B Reliability

C Faithful representation

D Comparability

41 **Match the element to the correct definition according to the International Accounting Standards Board's Conceptual Framework for Financial Reporting?**

Element
Expense
Liability
Asset
Equity

Definition
A present economic resource controlled by the entity as a result of past events
The residual interest in the assets of the entity after deducting all its liabilities.
A present obligation of the entity to transfer an economic resource as a result of past events
Decreases in assets or increases in liabilities, that result in decreases in equity, other than those relating to distributions to holders of equity claims

42 **Which of the following explains the value that relevant information contains?**

A Instructive value

B Fair value

C Confirmatory value

D Approximate value

43 Which of the following is an example of following the principle of faithful representation?

A Showing lease payments as a rental expense

B Being prudent by recording the entire amount of a convertible loan as a liability

C Creating a provision for staff relocation costs as part of a planned restructuring

D Recording a sale and repurchase transaction with a bank as a loan rather than a sale

44 A forum for consultation with parties affected by the work of the International Accounting Standards Board is provided by:

A The International Financial Reporting Interpretations Committee

B The IFRS Advisory Council

C The IFRS Foundation

D The IFRS Consulting Committee

45 Which of the following criteria need to be satisfied in order for an element to be recognised within the financial statements?

(i) It meets the definition of an element of the financial statements.

(ii) Recognition provides relevant information.

(iii) Recognition provides a reliable measure.

(iv) The element has fair value.

(v) Recognition provides faithful representation of the element.

A (i), (ii) and (v)

B (i), (iii) and (v)

C (i), (ii) and (iv)

D (i), (iii) and (iv)

46 Which description defines information that is relevant to users of financial information?

A Information that is free from error, bias and is a faithful representation of events

B Information that has been prudently prepared

C Information that is comparable from one period to the next

D Information that influences the decisions of users

47 Which description is most representative of the accounting framework used under IFRS Standards?

	True	False
It is a principles-based framework		
It is a legal obligation		

48 Which of the advantages below is/are likely advantage(s) of the global harmonisation of accounting standards?

	Advantage	**Not advantage**
Greater comparability between different firms		
Greater compatibility with legal systems		
Easier for large international accounting firms		

49 Which THREE of the following are advantages of applying a principles-based framework of accounting rather than a rules-based framework?

A It avoids 'fire-fighting', where standards are developed in responses to specific problems as they arise

B It allows preparers and auditors to deal with complex transactions which may not be specifically covered by an accounting standard

C Principles-based standards are thought to be harder to circumvent

D A set of rules is given which attempts to cover every eventuality

E It is easier to prove non-compliance

50 Which of the following is NOT a purpose of the International Accounting Standards Board's (the Board's) Conceptual Framework?

A To assist the Board in the preparation and review of IFRS Standards.

B To assist auditors in forming an opinion on whether financial statements comply with IFRS Standards.

C To assist in determining the treatment of items not covered by an existing IFRS Standards.

D To be authoritative where a specific IFRS Standard conflicts with the Conceptual Framework.

51 Which of the following bodies is responsible for funding the other bodies, as well as aiming for convergence between national and international standards?

A IFRS Foundation

B International Accounting Standards Board (The Board)

C IFRS Advisory Council

D IFRS Interpretations Committee

52 Faithful representation is a fundamental characteristic of useful information within the International Accounting Standards Board's Conceptual Framework for financial reporting.

Which of the following treatments applies the principle of faithful representation?

A Reporting a transaction based on its legal status rather than its economic substance.

B Excluding a subsidiary from consolidation because its activities are not compatible with those of the rest of the group.

C Recording the whole of the net proceeds from the issue of a loan note which is potentially convertible to equity shares as a liability.

D Allocating part of the sales proceeds of a motor vehicle to interest received even though it was sold with interest-free finance.

53 The International Accounting Standards Board's Conceptual Framework for Financial Reporting defines recognition as the process of incorporating within the financial statements an item which meets the definition of an element and satisfies certain criteria.

Which of the following elements should be recognised in the financial statements of an entity in the manner described?

A As a non-current liability: a provision for possible hurricane damage to property for an entity located in an area which experiences a high incidence of hurricanes.

B In equity: irredeemable preference shares.

C As a trade receivable: an amount of $10,000 due from a customer which has been sold (factored) to a finance company with no recourse to the seller.

D In revenue: the whole of the proceeds from the sale of an item of manufactured plant which has to be maintained by the seller for three years as part of the sale agreement.

54 **Which of the following is NOT included in the International Accounting Standards Board's (IASB) definition of an asset in the Conceptual Framework for Financial Reporting?**

A The asset is controlled by the entity

B The asset is a present economic resource

C The economic resource can be reliably measured

D The asset exists as a result of past events

55 Increasingly the International Accounting Standards Board is requiring or allowing current cost to be used in many areas of financial reporting.

Drexler acquired an item of plant on 1 October 20X2 at a cost of $500,000. It is being depreciated over five years, using straight-line depreciation and an estimated residual value of 10% of its historical cost or current cost as appropriate. As at 30 September 20X4, the manufacturer of the plant still makes the same item of plant and its current price is $600,000.

What is the correct carrying amount to be shown in the statement of financial position of Drexler as at 30 September 20X4 under historical cost and current cost? Select the correct value in each column.

Historical cost	✓	Current cost	✓
$300,000		$384,000	
$320,000		$600,000	

56 Tynan's year end is 30 September 20X4 and a number of potential liabilities have been identified.

Which TWO of the following should Tynan recognise as liabilities as at 30 September 20X4?

	Liability	**Not a liability**
The signing of a non-cancellable contract in September 20X4 to supply goods in the following year on which, due to a pricing error, a loss will be made.		
The cost of a reorganisation which was approved by the board in August 20X4 but has not yet been implemented, communicated to interested parties or announced publicly.		
An amount of deferred tax relating to the gain on the revaluation of a property during the current year. Tynan has no intention of selling the property in the foreseeable future.		
The balance on the warranty provision which relates to products for which there are no outstanding claims and whose warranties had expired by 30 September 20X4.		

57 Which of the following items should be recognised as an asset in the statement of financial position of an entity?

A A skilled and efficient workforce which has been very expensive to train. Some of these staff are still employed by the entity.

B A highly lucrative contract signed during the year which is due to commence shortly after the year-end.

C A government grant relating to the purchase of an item of plant several years ago which has a remaining life of four years.

D A receivable from a customer which has been sold (factored) to a finance company. The finance company has full recourse to the entity for any losses.

58 Comparability is identified as an enhancing qualitative characteristic in the International Accounting Standards Board's Conceptual Framework for Financial Reporting.

Which of the following does NOT improve comparability?

A Restating the financial statements of previous years when there has been a change of accounting policy.

B Prohibiting changes of accounting policy unless required by an IFRS Standard or to give more relevant and reliable information.

C Disclosing discontinued operations separately in financial statements.

D Applying an entity's current accounting policy to a transaction which an entity has not engaged in before.

59 Which of the following criticisms does NOT apply to historical cost financial statements during a period of rising prices?

A They contain mixed values, some items are at current values, some at out-of-date values

B They are difficult to verify as transactions could have happened many years ago

C They understate assets

D They overstate profits

60 According to IAS 8 *Accounting Policies, Changes in Accounting Estimates and Errors*, how should a material error in the previous financial reporting period be accounted for in the current period?

A By making an adjustment in the financial statements of the current period through the statement of profit or loss, and disclosing the nature of the error in a note.

B By making an adjustment in the financial statements of the current period as a movement on reserves, and disclosing the nature of the error in a note.

C By restating the comparative amounts for the previous period at their correct value, and disclosing the nature of the error in a note.

D By restating the comparative amounts for the previous period at their correct value, but without the requirement for a disclosure of the nature of the error in a note.

61 Which of the following statements regarding IFRS 13 *Fair Value Measurement* is not true?

A Level 1 inputs are likely to be used without adjustment.

B Level 3 inputs are based on the best information available to market participants and are therefore regarded as providing the most reliable evidence of fair value.

C Level 2 inputs may include quoted prices for similar (but not identical) assets and liabilities in active markets.

D Level 1 inputs comprise quoted prices in active markets for identical assets and liabilities at the reporting date.

62 Which of these changes would be classified as 'a change in accounting policy' as determined by IAS 8 *Accounting Policies, Changes in Accounting Estimates and Errors*?

A Increased the allowance for irrecoverable receivables from 5% to 10% of outstanding debts

B Changed the method of valuing inventory from FIFO to average cost

C Changed the depreciation of plant and equipment from straight line depreciation to reducing balance depreciation

D Changed the useful life of motor vehicles from six years to four years

63 In which TWO of the following situations can a change in accounting policy be made by an entity?

A If the change is required by an IFRS Standard

B If the entity thinks that a new accounting policy would be easier to report

C If a new accounting policy would show more favourable results

D If a new accounting policy results in more reliable and relevant presentation of events or transactions

64 According to the International Accounting Standards Board's Conceptual Framework for Financial Reporting which of the measurement bases below can be used by an entity for measuring assets and liabilities shown in its statement of financial position?

	Can be used	**Cannot be used**
Historical cost		
Present value		
Realisable value		

65 Which of the following statements is true about historical cost financial statements in times of rising prices?

A Profits will be overstated and assets will be understated

B The asset values will be overstated

C Unrecognised gains will be recorded incorrectly

D Depreciation will be overstated

66 The International Accounting Standards Board's Conceptual Framework for Financial Reporting identifies qualitative characteristics of financial statements.

Which TWO of the following characteristics are enhancing qualitative characteristics according to the *IASB's The Conceptual Framework for Financial Reporting?*

A Relevance

B Reliability

C Understandability

D Comparability

67 **Which of the following is a change in accounting policy and which a change in accounting estimate in accordance with IAS 8 *Accounting Policies, Changes in Accounting Estimates and Errors*?**

	Change in accounting policy	**Change in accounting estimate**
Classifying commission earned as revenue in the statement of profit or loss, having previously classified it as other operating income		
Revising the remaining useful life of a depreciable asset		

68 **Which of the following would be a change in accounting policy in accordance with IAS 8 *Accounting Policies, Changes in Accounting Estimates and Errors*?**

A Adjusting the financial statements of a subsidiary prior to consolidation as its accounting policies differ from those of its parent.

B A change to reporting depreciation charges as cost of sales rather than as administrative expenses.

C Depreciation method changed to reducing balance method rather than straight line.

D Reducing the value of inventory from cost to net realisable value due to a valid adjusting event after the reporting period.

69 Bouani Co manufactures cycling equipment. It has a number of specialised frames in inventory which cost $20,000 to manufacture. These frames were manufactured following an order from a customer at an agreed selling price of $30,000. Due to recent technological advances, the current cost of manufacturing such frames is estimated to be $15,000. Bouani Co also has inventory of 3,000 pedals with a cost of $20 each. These have become damaged. If Bouani Co spends $5,000 to repair all of them, these could be sold for $21 each.

Which TWO of the following statements regarding Bouani Co's inventory are true?

A The frames should be valued at $15,000

B The frames should be valued at $20,000

C The frames should be valued at $30,000

D The pedals should be valued at $60,000

E The pedals should be valued at $58,000

F The pedals should be valued at $65,000

70 **To which of the following items does IAS 41 *Agriculture* apply?**

(i) A change in fair value of a herd of animals relating to the unit price of the animals.

(ii) Logs held in a wood yard.

(iii) Farm land which is used for growing vegetables.

(iv) The cost of developing a new type of crop seed which is resistant to tropical diseases.

A All four

B (i) only

C (i) and (ii) only

D (ii) and (iii) only

71 IAS 2 Inventories specifies expenses that should be included in year-end inventory values. **Which THREE of the expenses below are allowable by IAS 2 as expenses that should be included in the cost of finished goods inventories?**

A Marketing and selling overhead

B Variable production overhead

C General management overhead

D Factory management overhead allocated to production

E Cost of delivering raw materials to the factory

F Abnormal increase in overhead charges caused by unusually low production levels due to the exceptionally hot weather.

72 Neville has only two items of inventory on hand at its reporting date.

Item 1 – Materials costing $24,000 bought for processing and assembly for a customer under a 'one off' order which is expected to produce a high profit margin. Since buying this material, the cost price has fallen to $20,000.

Item 2 – A machine constructed for another customer for a contracted price of $36,000. This has recently been completed at a cost of $33,600. It has now been discovered that in order to meet certain health and safety regulations modifications at an extra cost of $8,400 will be required. The customer has agreed to meet half of the extra cost.

What should be the total value of these two items of inventory in the statement of financial position?

$__________

73 Mario has incurred the following costs in relation to a unit of inventory:

	$
Raw materials cost	1.50
Import duties	0.40
Direct labour	0.50
Subcontracted labour costs	0.80
Recoverable sales tax	0.20
Storage costs	0.05
Production overheads (per unit)	0.25

There was a problem with the first batch of items produced, so abnormal wastage costs of $0.10 per unit have also been incurred by Mario.

At what cost should Mario value this inventory in its financial statements?

A $3.50

B $3.45

C $3.80

D $3.70

74 On 30 September 20X4 Razor's closing inventory was counted and valued at its cost of $1 million.

This included some items of inventory which had cost $210,000 and had been damaged in a flood on 15 September 20X4. These are not expected to achieve their normal selling price which is calculated to achieve a gross profit margin of 30%.

The sale of these goods will be handled by an agent who sells them at 80% of the normal selling price and charges Razor a commission of 25%.

At what value will the closing inventory of Razor be reported in its statement of financial position as at 30 September 20X4?

$__________

75 **Identify whether the following items would be accounted for under IAS 41 *Agriculture* or not.**

	Accounted for under IAS 41 *Agriculture*	**Outside the scope of IAS 41 *Agriculture***
Dairy cattle		
Milk		
Cheese		

76 Magna owned cattle recorded in the financial statements at $10,500 on 1 January 20X4. At 31 December 20X4 the cattle have a fair value of $13,000. If Magna sold the cattle, commission of 2% would be payable.

What is the correct accounting treatment for the cattle at 31 December 20X4 according to IAS 41 *Agriculture*?

A Hold at cost of $10,500

B Revalue to $13,000, taking gain of $2,500 to the statement of profit or loss

C Revalue to $13,000, taking gain of $2,500 to the revaluation surplus

D Revalue to $12,740, taking gain of $2,240 to the statement of profit or loss

77 During the year ended 30 September 20X4 Hyper entered into two lease transactions.

On 1 October 20X3, Hyper made a payment of $90,000 being the first of five equal annual payments under a lease for an item of plant. The lease has an implicit interest rate of 10% and the present value of the total lease payments on 1 October 20X3 was $340,000.

On 1 January 20X4, Hyper made a payment of $18,000 for a one-year lease of an item of equipment.

What amount in total would be charged to Hyper's statement of profit or loss for the year ended 30 September 20X4 in respect of the above transactions?

A $108,000

B $111,000

C $106,500

D $115,500

78 Z entered into a five year lease agreement on 1 November 20X2, paying $10,975 per annum, commencing on 31 October 20X3. The present value of the lease payments was $45,000 and the interest rate implicit in the lease was 7%.

What is the amount to be shown within non-current liabilities at 31 October 20X3?

A $26,200

B $28,802

C $37,175

D $36,407

79 IFRS 16 *Leases* permits certain assets to be exempt from the recognition treatment for right-of-use assets. Which of the following assets leased to an entity would be permitted to be exempt?

A A used motor vehicle with an original cost of $15,000 and a current fair value of $700, leased for 24 months

B A new motor vehicle with a cost of $15,000, leased for 24 months

C A new motor vehicle with a cost of $15,000, leased for 24 months, to be rented to customers on a daily rental basis

D A new motor vehicle with a cost of $15,000, leased for 12 months

80 On 1 January 20X3 Rabbit acquires a new machine with an estimated useful life of 6 years under the following agreement:

An initial payment of $13,760 will be payable immediately

5 further annual payments of $20,000 will be due, commencing 1 January 20X3

The interest rate implicit in the lease is 8%

The present value of the lease payments, excluding the initial payment, is $86,240

What will be recorded in Rabbit's financial statements at 31 December 20X4 in respect of the lease liability?

	Finance cost	**Non-current liability**	**Current liability**
A	4,123	35,662	20,000
B	5,299	51,539	20,000
C	5,312	51,712	20,000
D	5,851	43,709	15,281

81 **On 1 April 20X7 Pigeon entered into a five-year lease agreement for a machine with an estimated life of 7 years. Which of the following conditions would require the machine to be depreciated over 7 years?**

A Pigeon has the option to extend the lease for two years at a market-rate rental

B Pigeon has the option to purchase the asset at market value at the end of the lease

C Ownership of the asset passes to Pigeon at the end of the lease period

D Pigeon's policy for purchased assets is to depreciate over 7 years

82 On 1 January 20X4 Badger entered into a lease agreement to lease an item of machinery for 4 years with rentals of $210,000 payable annually in arrears. The asset has a useful life of 5 years and at the end of the lease term legal ownership will pass to Badger. The present value of the lease payments at the inception of the lease was $635,000 and the interest rate implicit in the lease is 12.2%. For the year ended 31 December 20X4 Badger accounted for this lease by recording the payment of $210,000 as an operating expense. This treatment was discovered during 20X5, after the financial statements for 20X4 had been finalised.

In the statement of changes in equity for the year ended 31 December 20X5 what adjustment will be necessary to retained earnings brought forward?

A $5,530 credit

B $132,530 credit

C $210,000 debit

D $Nil

83 Owl leases an asset with an estimated useful life of 6 years for an initial period of 5 years, and an optional secondary period of 2 years during which a nominal rental will be payable. The present value of the initial period lease payments is $87,000.

What will be the carrying amount of the right-of-use asset in Owl's statement of financial position at the end of the second year of the lease?

$__________

84 On 1 January 20X6, Sideshow sold a property for its fair value of $2 million, transferring title to the property on that date. Sideshow then leased it back under a 5-year lease, paying $150,000 per annum on 31 December each year. The present value of rentals payable was $599,000 and the interest rate implicit in the lease was 8%. The carrying amount of the property on 1 January 20X6 was $1.6 million and it had a remaining useful life of 20 years.

What entries would be made in Sideshow's statement of profit or loss for the year ended 31 December 20X6?

A Profit on disposal of $280,200, depreciation of $95,840, finance cost of $47,920

B Profit on disposal of $400,000, rental expense of $150,000

C Profit on disposal of $400,000, depreciation expense of $95,840, finance cost of $47,920

D Profit on disposal of $280,200, depreciation of $119,800, finance cost of $47,920

85 On 1 October 20X3, Fresco acquired an item of plant under a five-year lease agreement. The agreement had an implicit interest rate of 10% and required annual rentals of $6 million to be paid on 30 September each year for five years. The present value of the annual rental payments was $23 million.

What would be the current lease liability in Fresco's statement of financial position as at 30 September 20X4?

A $19,300,000

B $4,070,000

C $5,000,000

D $3,850,000

86 **Which of the following would not be included within the initial cost of a right-of-use asset?**

A Installation cost of the asset

B Estimated cost of dismantling the asset at the end of the lease period

C Payments made to the lessor before commencement of the lease

D Total lease rentals payable under the lease agreement

87 On 1 January 20X4, Stark entered into a sale and leaseback of its property. When it was sold, the asset had a carrying amount of $6 million and a remaining life of 10 years. Stark sold the asset for $7 million and leased it back on a 10 year lease, paying $1 million on 31 December each year. The lease carried an implicit interest rate of 7%.

What is the total expense that should be recorded in the statement of profit or loss for the year ended 31 December 20X4?

$______________ ,000

88 Viking issues $100,000 5% loan notes on 1 January 20X4, incurring issue costs of $3,000. These loan notes are redeemable at a premium, meaning that the effective rate of interest is 8% per annum.

What is the finance cost to be shown in the statement of profit or loss for the year ended 31 December 20X5?

A $8,240

B $7,981

C $7,760

D $8,000

89 An entity issues 3,000 convertible bonds at the start of year 1 at par. They have a three year term and a face value of $1,000 per bond. Interest is payable annually in arrears at 7% per annum. Each bond is convertible at any time up to maturity into 250 common shares. When the bonds are issued the prevailing market interest rate for similar debt without conversion options is 9%. The relevant discount factors are shown below.

Discount factors	7%	9%
Year 1	0.933	0.914
Year 2	0.871	0.837
Year 3	0.813	0.766

How is this initially recorded between the debt and equity elements?

	Debt element	Equity element
A	$2,988,570	$11,430
B	$2,826,570	$173,430
C	$528,570	$2,471,430
D	$3,000,000	$Nil

90 For a debt investment to be held under amortised cost, it must pass two tests. One of these is the contractual cash flow characteristics test.

What is the other test which must be passed?

A The business model test

B The amortised cost test

C The fair value test

D The purchase agreement test

91 On 1 July 20X7, an entity purchased a five-year loan note investment with a par value of $7m. The investment was purchased at a 12% discount. The loan note has a coupon rate of 5% and an effective interest rate of 7%. Interest is receivable annually in arrears. The entity has the intention of holding the loan note to receive the contractual cash flows.

How much finance income should be reported in the statement of profit or loss of the entity for the year ended 30 June 20X9 (to the nearest $000)?

$ ____________,000

92 ABC purchased 10,000 shares on 1 September 20X4, making the election to use the alternative treatment under IFRS 9 *Financial Instruments*. The shares cost $3.50 each. Transaction costs associated with the purchase were $500.

At 31 December 20X4, the shares are trading at $4.50 each.

What is the gain to be recognised on these shares for the year ended 31 December 20X4?

$____________

93 DEF purchased 15,000 shares in KMH Co on 1 August 20X6 at a cost of $6.50 each. Transaction costs on the purchase amounted to $1,500.

At the year-end 30 September 20X6, these shares are now worth $7.75 each.

Select the correct gain and the place it will be recorded.

Gain
$17,250
$18,750

Where recorded
Other comprehensive income
Statement of profit or loss

94 **For which category of financial instruments are transaction costs excluded from the initial value, and instead expensed to profit or loss?**

A Financial liabilities at amortised cost

B Financial assets at fair value through profit or loss

C Financial assets at fair value through other comprehensive income

D Financial assets at amortised cost

95 On 1 October 20X3, Bertrand issued $10 million convertible loan notes which carry a coupon rate of 5% per annum. The loan notes are redeemable on 30 September 20X6 at par for cash or can be exchanged for equity shares. A similar loan note, without the conversion option, would have required Bertrand to pay an interest rate of 8%.

The present value of $1 receivable at the end of each year, based on discount rates of 5% and 8%, can be taken as:

	5%	8%
End of year 1	0.95	0.93
2	0.91	0.86
3	0.86	0.79

How much would be recorded in equity in relation to the loan notes?

$____________,000

96 Wonder issued $20 million 5% loan notes on 1 January 20X9, incurring issue costs of $600,000. The loan notes are redeemable at a premium, giving them an effective interest rate of 7%.

What expense should be recorded in relation to the loan notes for the year ended 31 December 20X9?

$____________,000

97 For each of the financial instruments below, match them to the appropriate accounting treatment.

Instrument
Convertible loan notes
Equity investments where the entity has an intention to hold long-term and has chosen to apply the alternative treatment
Financial liability, not held for trading
Equity investments (default position)

Treatment
Fair value through profit or loss
Amortised cost
Split accounting
Fair value through other comprehensive income

98 IAS 21 *The Effects of Changes in Foreign Exchange Rates* defines the term 'functional currency'.

Which of the following is the correct definition of 'functional currency'?

A The currency in which the financial statements are presented

B The currency of the country where the reporting entity is located

C The currency that mainly influences sales prices and operating costs

D The currency of the primary economic environment in which an entity operates

99 Sunshine is an entity with a reporting date of 31 December 20X1 and a functional currency of dollars ($). On 30 June 20X1, it purchased land from overseas at a cost of 30 million dinars. The land is an item of property, plant and equipment and is measured using the cost model.

Exchange rates are as follows:

	Dinars: $1
As at 30 June 20X1	3.0
As at 31 December 20X1	2.0
Average rate for year-ended 31 December 20X1	2.5

The fair value of the land at 31 December 20X1 was 32 million dinars.

What is the carrying amount of the land as at 31 December 20X1?

A $10 million

B $15 million

C $12 million

D $16 million

100 In relation to IAS 21 *The Effects of Changes in Foreign Exchange Rates*, which of the following statements are true?

(i) Exchange gains and losses arising on the retranslation of monetary items are recognised in other comprehensive income in the period.

(ii) Non-monetary items measured at historical cost in a foreign currency are not retranslated at the reporting date.

(iii) An intangible asset is a non-monetary item.

A All of the above

B (ii) and (iii) only

C (i) and (iii) only

D (i) and (ii) only

101 An entity took out a bank loan for 12 million dinars on 1 January 20X1. It repaid 3 million dinars to the bank on 30 November 20X1. The entity has a reporting date of 31 December 20X1 and a functional currency of dollars ($). Exchange rates are as follows:

	Dinars: $1
1 January 20X1	6.0
30 November 20X1	5.0
31 December 20X1	5.6

What is the total loss arising (to the nearest $000) on the above transactions in the year ended 31 December 20X1?

$_______________,000

102 A manufacturing entity buys a machine (an item of property, plant and equipment) for 20 million dinars on 1 January 20X1. The machine is held under the cost model and has a useful life of 20 years. The entity has a reporting date of 31 December 20X1 and a functional currency of dollars ($). Exchange rates are as follows:

	Dinars: $1
1 January 20X1	2.0
31 December 20X1	3.0
Average rate for year-ended 31 December 20X1	2.5

What is the carrying amount of the machine as at 31 December 20X1?

A $9.7 million

B $9.6 million

C $9.5 million

D $6.3 million

103 Mango sold an item of maturing inventory to a bank on 1 January 20X3 for $500,000. At this date the inventory had cost $200,000 to produce but had a fair value of $900,000, which was expected to increase over the next 3 years. At the end of 3 years, Mango have the option to repurchase the inventory at $665,500, giving an effective interest rate of 10%.

What items should be recorded in the statement of profit or loss for the year ended 31 December 20X3?

A Revenue $500,000, cost of sales $200,000

B Profit on disposal $300,000

C Deferred income $500,000

D Finance cost $50,000

104 Repro has prepared its draft financial statements for the year ended 30 September 20X4. It has included the following transactions in revenue at the amounts stated below.

Which of these has been correctly included in revenue according to IFRS 15 *Revenue from Contracts with Customers*?

A Agency sales of $250,000 on which Repro is entitled to a commission of 10%.

B Sale proceeds of $20,000 for motor vehicles which were no longer required by Repro.

C Sales of $150,000 on 30 September 20X4. The amount invoiced to and received from the customer was $180,000, which includes $30,000 for ongoing servicing work to be done by Repro over the next two years.

D Sales of $200,000 on 1 October 20X3 to an established customer who (with the agreement of Repro) will make full payment on 30 September 20X5. Repro has a cost of capital of 10%.

105 Yling entered into a contract to construct an asset for a customer on 1 January 20X4 which is expected to last 24 months. The agreed price for the contract is $5 million. At 30 September 20X4, the costs incurred on the contract were $1.6 million and the estimated remaining costs to complete were $2.4 million. On 20 September 20X4, Yling received a payment from the customer of $1.8 million which was equal to the full amount billed. Yling calculates contract progress using the input method, on the basis of costs incurred compared to the estimated total costs.

What amount would be reported as a contract asset in Yling's statement of financial position as at 30 September 20X4?

$__________

106 CN started a three-year contract to build a new university campus on 1 April 20X4. The contract had a fixed price of $90 million. CN will satisfy the performance obligation over time. CN incurred costs to 31 March 20X5 of $77 million and estimated that a further $33 million would need to be spent to complete the contract.

CN measures the progress of contracts using work completed compared to contract price. At 31 March 20X5, a surveyor valued the work completed to date at $63 million.

Select the correct amounts to be shown in revenue and cost of sales in the statement of profit or loss for the year ended 31 March 20X5?

Revenue	Cost of sales
$63 million	$77 million
$57 million	$83 million

107 Locke sells machines, and also offers installation and technical support services. The individual selling prices of each product are shown below.

Sale price of goods	$75
Installation	$30
One year service	$45

Locke sold a machine on 1 May 20X1, charging a reduced price of $100, including installation and one year's service.

Locke only offers discounts when customers purchase a package of products together.

According to IFRS 15 *Revenue from Contracts with Customers*, how much should Locke record in revenue for the year ended 31 December 20X1? Workings should be rounded to the nearest $.

$___________

108 **Place the following steps for recognising revenue in order in accordance with IFRS 15 *Revenue from Contracts with Customers*.**

Step
Identify the separate performance obligations within a contract
Identify the contract
Determine the transaction price
Recognise revenue when (or as) a performance obligation is satisfied
Allocate the transaction price to the performance obligations in the contract

Correct order

109 BL entered into a contract with a customer on 1 November 20X4. The contract was scheduled to run for two years and has a sales value of $40 million. BL will satisfy the performance obligations over time.

At 31 October 20X5, the following details were obtained from BL's records:

	$m
Costs incurred to date	16
Estimated costs to completion	18
Progress at 31 October 20X5	45%

Applying IFRS 15 *Revenue from Contracts with Customers*, how much revenue and cost of sales should BL recognise in its statement of profit or loss for the year ended 31 October 20X5?

	Revenue	Cost of sales
A	$40 million	$16 million
B	$40 million	$34 million
C	$18 million	$16 million
D	$18 million	$15.3 million

110 Malik is a construction business, recognising progress based on work certified as a proportion of total contract value. Malik will satisfy the performance obligation over time. The following information relates to one of its long-term contracts as at 31 May 20X4, Malik's year-end.

	$
Contract price	200,000
Costs incurred to date	135,000
Estimated cost to complete	15,000
Invoiced to customer	120,000
Work certified to date	180,000

In the year to 31 May 20X3 Malik had recognised revenue of $60,000 and profit of $15,000 in respect of this contract.

What profit should appear in Malik's statement of profit or loss as at 31 May 20X4 in respect of this contract?

$__________

111 Which of the following items has correctly been included in Hatton's revenue for the year to 31 December 20X1?

A $2 million in relation to a fee negotiated for an advertising contract for Rees, one of Hatton's clients. Hatton acted as an agent during the deal and is entitled to 10% commission.

B $500,000 relating to a sale of specialised equipment on 31 December 20X1. The full sales value was $700,000 but $200,000 relates to servicing that Hatton will provide over the next 2 years, so Hatton has not included that in revenue this year.

C $800,000 relating to a sale of some surplus land owned by Hatton.

D $1 million in relation to a sale to a new customer on 31 December 20X1. Control passed to the customer on 31 December 20X1. The $1 million is payable on 31 December 20X3. Interest rates are 10%.

112 Sugar has entered into a long-term contract to build an asset for a customer, Hewer. Sugar will satisfy the performance obligation over time and has measured the progress towards satisfying the performance obligation at 45% at the year-end.

The price of the contract is $8 million. Sugar has spent $4.5 million to date, but the estimated costs to complete are $5.5 million. To date, Hewer has paid Sugar $3 million.

What is the net liability that should be recorded in Sugar's statement of financial position?

$______________,000

113 Ratten commenced a contract to build an asset for a customer in the year ended 30 September 20X4. The contract price was agreed at $1.5m, and the total expected costs of the contract are $800,000. Ratten will satisfy the performance obligation over time.

The following figures were correctly recognised in the profit or loss account for the year ended 30 September 20X4:

	$000
Revenue	450
Cost of sales	(240)
Profit	210

The following figures are also relevant in relation to this contract:

	20X4	20X5
	$000	$000
Work certified to date	450	1,050

Ratten recognises progress on the basis of work certified compared to contract price.

What should Ratten include in its statement of profit or loss for the year ended 30 September 20X5 for revenue in respect of the contract?

A $600,000

B $1,050,000

C $1,500,000

D $450,000

114 Sawyer entered into a contract to construct an asset for a customer during the year, and identified the performance obligation as one which is satisfied over time. Sawyer recognises progress towards completion using an input method, based on costs to date compared to total costs. The following information is relevant to the contract.

	$
Contract price	1,000,000
Costs incurred to date	500,000
Estimated cost to complete	300,000
Work invoiced to date	600,000

What is the value of the contract asset to be recorded in Sawyer's statement of financial position?

A $25,000

B $100,000

C $375,000

D $625,000

115 Hindberg is a car retailer. On 1 April 20X4, Hindberg sold a car to Latterly on the following terms:

The selling price of the car was $25,300. Latterly paid $12,650 (half of the cost) on 1 April 20X4 and will pay the remaining $12,650 on 31 March 20X6 (two years after the sale). Latterly can obtain finance at 10% per annum.

What is the total amount which Hindberg should credit to profit or loss in respect of this transaction in the year ended 31 March 20X5?

A $23,105

B $23,000

C $20,909

D $24,150

116 Tamsin Co's accounting records shown the following:

	$
Income tax payable for the year	60,000
Over provision in relation to the previous year	4,500
Opening provision for deferred tax	2,600
Closing provision for deferred tax	3,200

What is the income tax expense that will be shown in the statement of profit or loss for the year?

A $54,900

B $67,700

C $65,100

D $56,100

117 The following information has been extracted from the accounting records of Clara Co:

	$
Estimated income tax for the year ended 30 September 20X0	$75,000
Income tax paid for the year ended 30 September 20X0	$80,000
Estimated income tax for the year ended 30 September 20X1	$83,000

What figures will be shown in the statement of profit or loss for the year ended 30 September 20X1 and the statement of financial position as at that date in respect of income tax?

Statement of profit or loss	Statement of financial position

Options:

$75,000
$80,000
$83,000
$88,000

118 Hudson has the following balances included on its trial balance at 30 June 20X4.

	$	
Taxation	4,000	Credit
Deferred taxation	12,000	Credit

The taxation balance relates to an overprovision from 30 June 20X3.

At 30 June 20X4, the directors estimate that the provision necessary for taxation on current year profits is $15,000.

The carrying amount of Hudson's non-current assets exceeds the tax written-down value by $30,000. The rate of tax is 30%.

What is the charge for taxation that will appear in the statement of profit or loss for the year to 30 June 20X4?

A $23,000

B $28,000

C $8,000

D $12,000

119 The information below relates to the financial statements of an entity as at 30 September 20X7.

	$
Carrying amount:	
Plant (cost less depreciation)	110,000
Land (original cost $200,000)	280,000
Tax base:	
Plant	90,000
Land	200,000
Tax rate	20%
Deferred tax liability	20,000
Revaluation surplus	64,000

The amount of the deferred tax liability is: CORRECT/INCORRECT

The amount of the revaluation surplus is: CORRECT/INCORRECT

120 Holmes has the following balances included on its trial balance at 30 June 20X4:

	$	
Taxation	7,000	Credit
Deferred taxation	16,000	Credit

The taxation balance relates to an overprovision from 30 June 20X3.

At 30 June 20X4, the directors estimate that the provision necessary for taxation on current year profits is $12,000. The balance on the deferred tax account needs to be increased to $23,000, which includes the impact of the increase in property valuation below.

During the year Holmes revalued its property for the first time, resulting in a gain of $10,000. The rate of tax is 30%.

What is the charge for taxation that will appear in the statement of profit or loss for the year to 30 June 20X4?

A $9,000

B $12,000

C $23,000

D $1,000

121 Garfish had profits after tax of $3 million in the year ended 31 December 20X7. On 1 January 20X7, Garfish had 2.4 million ordinary shares in issue. On 1 April 20X7 Garfish made a one for two rights issue at a price of $1.40 when the market price of Garfish's shares was $2.00.

What is the basic earnings per share (to one decimal place) for the year ended 31 December 20X7, according to IAS 33 *Earnings Per Share*?

_____________ cents.

122 On 1 January 20X4, Sam Co had 3 million ordinary shares in issue. On 1 June 20X4, Sam Co made a 1 for 3 bonus issue. On 30 September 20X4, Sam Co issued a further 1 million shares at full market price. Sam Co had profits attributable to ordinary equity holders of $2 million for the year ended 31 December 20X4.

What is the basic earnings per share figure for the year ended 31 December 20X4, according to IAS 33 *Earnings Per Share*?

A 47.1¢

B 52.2¢

C 56.8¢

D 50.0¢

123 During the year, Mac made a 1 for 3 rights issue at $1.60 when the market price was $2.20. Last year's EPS was 81 cents. There were no other issues of shares during the year.

What is the restated earnings per share figure for comparative purposes?

_______________ cents.

124 Coral Co has net profit for the year ended 30 September 20X5 of $10,500,000. Coral has had 6 million shares in issue for many years. On 1 October 20X4 Coral issued a convertible bond. It had an initial liability element of $2,500,000, and the market interest rate for non-convertible instruments is 8%. The bond is convertible in five years, with 50 shares issued for every $100 nominal of convertible bond held. Coral Co pays tax at a rate of 28%

What is the Diluted Earnings per Share figure?

A 177.4¢

B 175.0¢

C 147.6¢

D 146.8¢

125 Isco's financial statements show a profit for the year to 31 December 20X5 of $2 million. On 1 January 20X5 Isco had 4 million shares in issue and made no further issues of shares during the year. At 31 December 20X5 there were 1 million outstanding options to buy shares at $3 each. For the year to 31 December 20X5, the average market value of Isco's shares was $5.

What is Isco's diluted earnings per share for the year ended 31 December 20X5?

A 50.0¢

B 28.6¢

C 45.5¢

D 43.4¢

126 Gromit Co has the following extract from its consolidated profit or loss account:

	$000
Profit for the period	2,800
Other comprehensive income: revaluation gain	500
Total comprehensive income	3,300
Profit for the period attributable to:	
Parent	2,250
Non-controlling Interest	550
	2,800
Total comprehensive income attributable to:	
Parent	2,600
Non-controlling interest	700
	3,300

What figure should be used as earnings by Gromit in its earnings per share (EPS) calculation?

$__________ ,000

127 Which TWO of the following do NOT need to be removed from an entity's net profit in a statement of profit or loss in order to calculate the earnings figure to be used in the earnings per share calculation?

A Redeemable preference share dividends

B Irredeemable preference share dividends

C Profit attributable to the non-controlling interest

D An error in expenses discovered after the financial statements have been authorised for issue

E Ordinary dividends

128 Aqua has correctly calculated its basic earnings per share (EPS) for the current year.

Allocate the items to the appropriate category.

Included within Diluted EPS calculation	Included within Basic EPS calculation

Options:

A 1 for 5 rights issue of equity shares during the year at $1.20 when the market price of the equity shares was $2.00
The issue during the year of a loan note, convertible into ordinary shares
The granting of directors' share options during the year, exercisable in three years' time
Equity shares issued during the year as the purchase consideration for the acquisition of a new subsidiary

129 Many commentators believe that the trend of earnings per share (EPS) is a more reliable indicator of underlying performance than the trend of the net profit for the year.

Which of the following statements supports this view?

A Net profit can be manipulated by the choice of accounting policies but EPS cannot be manipulated in this way.

B EPS takes into account the additional resources made available to earn profit when new shares are issued for cash, whereas net profit does not.

C The disclosure of a diluted EPS figure is a forecast of the trend of profit for future periods.

D The comparative EPS is restated where a change in accounting policy affects the previous year's profits.

130 On 1 October 20X3, Hoy had $2.5 million of equity shares of 50 cents each in issue.

No new shares were issued during the year ended 30 September 20X4, but on that date there were outstanding share options to purchase 2 million equity shares at $1.20 each. The average market value of Hoy's equity shares during the year was $3 per share.

Hoy's profit after tax for the year ended 30 September 20X4 was $1,550,000.

What is Hoy's diluted earnings per share for the year ended 30 September 20X4?

A 25.0¢

B 31.0¢

C 26.7¢

D 22.1¢

131 AP has the following two legal claims outstanding:

- A legal action claiming compensation of $500,000 filed against AP in March 20X4.
- A legal action taken by AP against a third party, claiming damages of $200,000, which was started in January 20X3 and is nearing completion.

In both cases, it is more likely than not that the amount claimed will have to be paid.

How should AP report these legal actions in its financial statements for the year ended 31 March 20X5?

Allocate the correct treatment against each of the cases.

Legal action against AP	Legal action by AP

Options:

Contingent Liability
Contingent Asset
Provision
Asset

132 Which of the following would require a provision for a liability to be created by BW at its reporting date of 31 October 20X5?

A The government introduced new laws on data protection which come into force on 1 January 20X6. BW's directors have agreed that this will require a large number of staff to be retrained. At 31 October 20X5, the directors were waiting on a report they had commissioned that would identify the actual training requirements.

B At the year-end BW is negotiating with its insurance provider about an outstanding insurance claim. On 20 November 20X5, the provider agreed to pay $200,000.

C BW makes refunds to customers for any goods returned within 30 days of sale, and has done so for many years.

D A customer is suing BW for damages alleged to have been caused by BW's product. BW is contesting the claim and at 31 October 20X5 the directors have been advised by BW's legal advisers that it is very unlikely to lose the case.

133 Using the requirements set out in IAS 10 *Events after the Reporting Period*, which of the following would be classified as an adjusting event after the reporting period in financial statements ended 31 March 20X4 that were approved by the directors on 31 August 20X4?

A A reorganisation of the enterprise, proposed by a director on 31 January 20X4 and agreed by the Board on 10 July 20X4.

B A strike by the workforce which started on 1 May 20X4 and stopped all production for 10 weeks before being settled.

C The receipt of cash from a claim on an insurance policy for damage caused by a fire in a warehouse on 1 January 20X4. The claim was made in January 20X4 and the amount of the claim had not been recognised at 31 March 20X4 as it was uncertain that any money would be paid. The insurance enterprise settled with a payment of $1.5 million on 1 June 20X4.

D The enterprise had made large export sales to the USA during the year. The year-end receivables included $2 million for amounts outstanding that were due to be paid in US dollars between 1 April 20X4 and 1 July 20X4. By the time these amounts were received, the exchange rate had moved in favour of the enterprise.

134 Target is preparing its financial statements for the year ended 30 September 20X7. Target is facing a number of legal claims from its customers with regards to a faulty product sold. The total amount being claimed is $3.5 million. Target's lawyers say that the customers have an 80% chance of being successful.

According to IAS 37 *Provisions, Contingent Liabilities and Contingent Assets*, what amount, if any, should be recognised in respect of the above in Target's statement of financial position as at 30 September 20X7?

$_____________,000

135 ABC has a year end of 31 December 20X4. On 15 December 20X4 the directors publicly announced their decision to close an operating unit and make a number of employees redundant. Some of the employees currently working in the unit will be transferred to other operating units within ABC.

The estimated costs of the closure are as follows:

	$000
Redundancy costs	800
Lease termination costs	200
Relocation of continuing employees to new locations	400
Retraining of continuing employees	300
	1,700

What is the closure provision that should be recognised?

A $800,000

B $1,000,000

C $1,400,000

D $1,700,000

136 On 1 October 20X3, Xplorer commenced drilling for oil in an undersea oilfield. The extraction of oil causes damage to the seabed which has a restorative cost (ignore discounting) of $10,000 per million barrels of oil extracted. Xplorer extracted 250 million barrels of oil in the year ended 30 September 20X4.

Xplorer is also required to dismantle the drilling equipment at the end of its five-year licence. This has an estimated cost of $30 million on 30 September 20X8. Xplorer's cost of capital is 8% per annum and $1 has a present value of 68 cents in five years' time.

What is the total provision (extraction plus dismantling) which Xplorer would report in its statement of financial position as at 30 September 20X4 in respect of its oil operations?

A $34,900,000

B $24,532,000

C $22,900,000

D $4,132,000

137 Which TWO of the following events which occur after the reporting date of an entity but before the financial statements are authorised for issue are classified as ADJUSTING events in accordance with IAS 10 *Events after the Reporting Period*?

A A change in tax rate announced after the reporting date, but affecting the current tax liability

B The discovery of a fraud which had occurred during the year

C The determination of the sale proceeds of an item of plant sold before the year end

D The destruction of a factory by fire

138 Each of the following events occurred after the reporting date of 31 March 20X5, but before the financial statements were authorised for issue.

Identify whether the events would represent adjusting or non-adjusting events.

	Adjusting	**Non-adjusting**
A public announcement in April 20X5 of a formal plan to discontinue an operation which had been approved by the board in February 20X5.		
The settlement of an insurance claim for a loss sustained in December 20X4.		

139 In a review of its provisions for the year ended 31 March 20X5, Cumla's assistant accountant has suggested the following accounting treatments:

(i) A provision for one third of the cost of replacing an oven lining, which requires replacing every three years for technical reasons, and was last replaced on 1 April 20X4.

(ii) The partial reversal (as a credit to the statement of profit or loss) of the accumulated depreciation provision on an item of plant because the estimate of its remaining useful life has been increased by three years.

(iii) Providing $1 million for deferred tax at 25% relating to a $4 million revaluation of property during March 20X5 even though Cumla has no intention of selling the property in the near future.

Which of the above suggested treatments of provisions is/are permitted by IFRS Standards?

A (i) only

B (i) and (ii)

C (ii) and (iii)

D (iii) only

140 **Identify whether the statements below are true or false:**

	True	**False**
IAS 10 *Events After the Reporting Period* covers the period from the reporting date to the annual general meeting		
According to IAS 10 *Events After the Reporting Period*, any non-adjusting event should be disclosed as a note in the financial statements		

141 Fauberg owns a number of offices in country Y and is in the process of finishing its financial statements for the year ended 31 December 20X4. In December 20X4, country Y announced changes to health and safety regulations, meaning that Fauberg's air conditioning units will have to be replaced by 30 June 20X5.

This is estimated to cost Fauberg $500,000. Fauberg has a history of compliance with regulations and intends to do the work by June 20X5.

Which of the conditions for a provision will be met at 31 December 20X4?

	Yes/No
There is a present obligation from a past event	
A reliable estimate can made	
There is a probable outflow of economic benefits	

142 Which TWO of the following statements about provisions are true?

A Future operating losses cannot be provided for

B Changes in provisions should be applied retrospectively, adjusting the prior year financial statements

C Provisions should be accounted for prudently, reflecting the maximum that could possibly be paid out

D Provisions should be discounted to present value if the effect of the time value of money is material

CONSOLIDATED FINANCIAL STATEMENTS

143 Petre owns 100% of the share capital of the following companies. The directors are unsure of whether the investments should be consolidated into the group financial statements of not.

Identify whether the following companies should be consolidated or not.

	Consolidated	**Not to be consolidated**
Beta is a bank and its activity is so different from the engineering activities of the rest of the group that it would be meaningless to consolidate it.		
Delta is located in a country where local accounting standards are compulsory and these are not compatible with IFRS Standards used by the rest of the group.		
Gamma is located in a country where a military coup has taken place and Petre has lost control of the investment for the foreseeable future.		

144 Tazer acquired Lowdown, an unincorporated entity, for $2.8 million. A fair value exercise performed on Lowdown's net assets at the date of purchase showed:

	$000
Property, plant and equipment	3,000
Identifiable intangible asset	500
Inventory	300
Trade receivables less payables	200
	4,000

How would the purchase be reflected in the consolidated statement of financial position?

A Record the net assets at their above values and credit profit or loss with $1.2 million

B Record the net assets at their above values and credit goodwill with $1.2 million

C Ignore the intangible asset ($500,000), recording the remaining net assets at their values shown above and crediting profit or loss with $700,000

D Record the purchase as a financial asset investment at $2.8 million

145 **Which of the following definitions is not included within the definition of control per IFRS 10 *Consolidated Financial Statements*?**

A Having power over the investee

B Having exposure, or rights, to variable returns from its investment with the investee

C Having the majority of shares in the investee

D Having the ability to use its power over the investee to affect the amount of the investor's returns

146 Pamela acquired 80% of the share capital of Samantha on 1 January 20X1. Part of the purchase consideration was $200,000 cash to be paid on 1 January 20X4. The applicable cost of capital is 10%.

What will the deferred consideration liability be at 31 December 20X2?

A $150,262

B $165,288

C $200,000

D $181,818

147 Philip acquired 85% of the share capital of Stanley on 1 October 20X1. The profit for the year ended 31 December 20X1 for Stanley was $36,000. Profits are deemed to accrue evenly over the year. At 31 December 20X1 Stanley's statement of financial position showed:

Equity share capital	$200,000
Retained earnings	$180,000

What were the net assets of Stanley on acquisition?

$__________,000

148 On 30 June 20X4 GHI acquired 800,000 of JKL's 1 million shares.

GHI issued 3 shares for every 4 shares acquired in JKL. On 30 June 20X4 the market price of a GHI share was $3.80 and the market price of a JKL share was $3.

GHI agreed to pay $550,000 in cash to the existing shareholders on 30 June 20X5. GHI's borrowing rate was 10% per annum.

GHI paid professional fees of $100,000 for advice on the acquisition.

What is the cost of investment that will be used in the goodwill calculation in the consolidated financial statements of GHI?

$__________,000

149 MNO has a 75% owned subsidiary PQR. During the year MNO sold inventory to PQR for an invoiced price of $800,000. PQR have since sold 75% of that inventory on to third parties. The sale was at a mark-up of 25% on cost to MNO. PQR is the only subsidiary of MNO.

What is the adjustment to inventory that would be included in the consolidated statement of financial position of MNO at the year-end resulting from this sale?

A $120,000

B $40,000

C $160,000

D $50,000

150 West has a 75% subsidiary Life, and is preparing its consolidated statement of financial position as at 31 December 20X6. The carrying amount of property, plant and equipment in the two companies at that date is as follows:

West $300,000

Life $60,000

On 1 January 20X6 Life had transferred some property to West for $40,000. At the date of transfer the property, which had cost $42,000, had a carrying amount of $30,000 and a remaining useful life of five years.

What is the carrying amount of property, plant and equipment in the consolidated statement of financial position of West as at 31 December 20X6?

$____________ ,000

151 Which TWO of the following situations are unlikely to represent control over an investee?

A Owning 55% and being able to elect 4 of the 7 directors

B Owning 51%, but the constitution requires that decisions need the unanimous consent of shareholders

C Having currently exercisable options which would take the shareholding in the investee to 55%

D Owning 40% of the shares but having majority of voting rights within the investee

E Owning 35% of the ordinary shares and 80% of the preference shares of the investee

152 Identify if the following will be recognised as part of the cost of an investment in a subsidiary.

	Include in cost of investment	**Do not include in the cost of investment**
An agreement to pay a further $30,000 if the subsidiary achieves an operating profit of over $100,000 in the first 3 years after acquisition		
Professional fees of $10,000 in connection with the investment		

153 Peter acquires 80% of the share capital of Paul on 1 August 20X6 and is preparing its group financial statements for the year ended 31 December 20X6.

How will Paul's results be included in the group statement of profit or loss?

A 80% of Paul's revenue and expenses for the year ended 31 December 20X6

B 100% of Paul's revenue and expenses for the year ended 31 December 20X6

C 80% of Paul's revenue and expenses for the period 1 August 20X6 to 31 December 20X6

D 100% of Paul's revenue and expenses for the period ended 1 August 20X6 to 31 December 20X6

154 Which of the following would result in an unrealised profit within a group scenario?

A A parent sells a building originally costing $800,000 to its subsidiary for $900,000. The subsidiary still holds this asset at the date of consolidation.

B A parent sells a building originally costing $800,000 to its subsidiary for $900,000. The subsidiary has sold this asset before the date of consolidation.

C A parent sells goods which originally cost $14,000 to its subsidiary for $18,000. The subsidiary has sold all of these goods at the date of consolidation.

D A parent sells goods which originally cost $14,000 to an associate for $18,000. The associate has sold all of these goods at the date of consolidation.

155 Identify whether the following facts about goodwill impairment are true or false.

	True	**False**
Goodwill impairment will always be deducted in full from the parent's retained earnings		
Goodwill impairment will be apportioned between the parent and the non-controlling interest (NCI) when the NCI is valued at fair value		

156 Which of the following is not a condition which must be met for the parent to be exempt from producing consolidated financial statements?

A The activities of the subsidiary are significantly different to the rest of the group and to consolidate them would prejudice the overall group position

B The ultimate parent produces consolidated financial statements that comply with IFRS Standards and are publicly available

C The parent's debt or equity instruments are not traded in a public market

D The parent itself is a wholly owned subsidiary or a partially owned subsidiary whose owners do not object to the parent not producing consolidated financial statements

157 On 1 January 20X1, Branch purchased 75% of Leaf's 80 million shares. At this date, Leaf's retained earnings were $60 million. The consideration paid for Leaf was 2 Branch shares for every 3 Leaf shares purchased, plus a cash payment of $1 per purchased share. At the date of acquisition, the value of a Branch share was $2.50.

What is the consideration paid for Branch on 1 January 20X1?

$___________

158 STU has an 80% subsidiary VWX, which has been a subsidiary of STU for the whole of the current year. VWX reported a profit after tax of $600,000 in its own financial statements. You ascertain that at the year-end there was unrealised profit of $60,000 on sales by VWX to STU.

What is the non-controlling interest in VWX that would be reported in the consolidated statement of profit or loss and other comprehensive income of STU for the year?

$___________

159 Harry acquired an 80% holding in Style on 1 April 20X6. From 1 April 20X6 to 31 December 20X6 Style sold goods to Harry for $4.3m at a mark-up of 10%. Harry's inventory at 31 December 20X6 included $2.2m of such inventory. The statements of profit or loss for each entity for the year to 31 December 20X6 showed the following in respect of cost of sales:

Harry $14.7m

Style $11.6m

What is the cost of sales figure to be shown in the consolidated statement of profit or loss for the year to 31 December 20X6?

A $18,900,000

B $20,200,000

C $19,100,000

D $19,300,000

160 Heel acquired a 60% holding in Sock on 1 January 20X6. At this date Sock owned a building with a fair value $200,000 in excess of its carrying amount, and a remaining life of 10 years. All depreciation is charged to operating expenses. Goodwill had been impaired by $55,000 in the year to 31 December 20X6. The balances on operating expenses for the year to 31 December 20X7 are shown below:

Heel $600,000

Sock $350,000

What are consolidated operating expenses for the year to 31 December 20X7?

$___________,000

161 A acquired a 60% holding in B on 1 July 20X6. At this date, A gave B a $500,000 8% loan. The interest on the loan has been accounted for correctly in the individual financial statements. The totals for finance costs for the year to 31 December 20X6 in the individual financial statements are shown below.

A $200,000

B $70,000

What are consolidated finance costs for the year to 31 December 20X6?

A $215,000

B $225,000

C $230,000

D $250,000

162 Identify whether the following would affect the profit attributable to the non-controlling interest in the consolidated statement of profit or loss if the non-controlling interest is measured at fair value

	Affects the NCI share of profit	**Does not affect the NCI share**
Goodwill impairment		
The parent selling inventory to the subsidiary at a profit of $10,000, all of which remains in the subsidiary's inventory at the year end		
The subsidiary having an item of plant with a fair value of $500,000 above its carrying amount at acquisition, and a remaining life of 10 years		

163 AB has owned 80% of CD for many years. In the current year ended 30 June 20X3, AB has reported total revenues of $5.5 million, and CD of $2.1 million. AB has sold goods to CD during the year with a total value of $1 million, earning a margin of 20%. Half of these goods remain in year-end inventories.

What is the consolidated revenue figure for the AB group for the year ended 30 June 20X3?

$____________,000

164 Burridge bought 30% of Allen on 1 July 20X4. Allen's statement of profit or loss for the year shows a profit of $400,000. Allen paid a dividend to Burridge of $50,000 on 1 December 20X4. At the year end, the investment in Allen was judged to have been impaired by $10,000.

What will be the share of profit from associate shown in the consolidated statement of profit or loss for the year ended 31 December 20X4?

A $57,000

B $50,000

C $60,000

D $110,000

165 Beasant bought 30% of Arnie on 1 January 20X8, when Arnie had share capital of 100,000 $1 shares and $400,000 retained earnings. The consideration comprised one Beasant share for every 3 shares bought in Arnie. At the date of acquisition, Beasant's shares had a market value of $4.50 and Arnie's had a market value of $2. At 31 December 20X8, Arnie's net assets were $460,000.

What is the value of investment in associate shown in the consolidated statement of financial position as at 31 December 20X8?

A $8,000

B $33,000

C $63,000

D $123,000

166 Identify which concept each of the following transactions is applying

	Single entity concept	**Going concern concept**
Removing unrealised profits on group sales		
Removing intra-group balances		

167 Identify the correct treatments for the following investments in the consolidated financial statements of the Nicol group.

30% of the share capital of Hansen. The other 70% is owned by Lawro, another listed entity, whose directors make up Hansen's board.	Subsidiary
80% of the share capital of Kennedy, whose activities are significantly different from the rest of the Nicol group.	Associate
30% of the share capital of Bruce. The Nicol group have appointed 2 of the 5 board members of Bruce, with the other board members coming from three other entities.	Investment

168 Badger acquired 30% of Eagle on 1 July 20X3 at a cost of $5.5 million. Badger has classified Eagle as an associate undertaking. For the year ended 30 September 20X3, Eagle has reported a net profit of $625,000.

What is the value of the associate investment in the group statement of financial position of Badger as at 30 September 20X3?

A $5,546,875

B $5,500,000

C $6,125,000

D $5,968,750

169 Green is an associate undertaking of Purple. Purple owns 30% of the shares in Green, and has done so for many years.

During the year ended 31 December 20X4, Green made a net profit of $1.5 million. Green sold goods to Purple during the year with a value of $2 million, and half are still in Purple's inventories at year end. All the goods were sold at a margin of 30%.

Purple has recognised previous impairments in relation to its investment in Green of $225,000. In the current year, Purple wishes to recognise an additional impairment charge of $35,000.

What is the share of profit of associate to be shown in Purple's consolidated statement of profit or loss?

$__________,000

170 **Which of the following statements regarding consolidated financial statements is correct?**

A For consolidation, it may be acceptable to use financial statements of the subsidiary where the year-end differs from the parent by 2 months.

B For consolidation, all companies within the group must have the same year end.

C All companies within a group must have the same accounting policy in their individual financial statements.

D The profit made on all intra-group sales in the year must be removed from the consolidated financial statements.

171 **'An associate is an entity over which the investor has significant influence'** (IAS28, para 3).

Which TWO of the following indicate the presence of significant influence?

A The investor owns 330,000 of the 1,500,000 equity voting shares of the investee

B The investor has representation on the board of directors of the investee

C The investor is able to insist that all of the sales of the investee are made to a subsidiary of the investor

D The investor controls the votes of a majority of the board members

172 Consolidated financial statements are presented on the basis that the companies within the group are treated as if they are a single economic entity.

Which TWO of the following are requirements of preparing consolidated financial statements?

A All subsidiaries must adopt the accounting policies of the parent in their individual financial statements

B Subsidiaries with activities which are substantially different to the activities of other members of the group should not be consolidated

C All assets and liabilities of subsidiaries should be included at fair value

D Unrealised profits within the group must be eliminated from the consolidated financial statements

173 Alpha Co acquired 80% of the ordinary share capital of Bravo Co on 1 September 20X4 and 40% of the ordinary share capital of Charlie Co a number of years ago. On 30 November 20X4, Alpha Co sold goods to Bravo Co making a profit of $2,000. Half of these items remained in inventory at the year end. The profit for the year ended 31 December 20X4 for each entity is:

	Profit for the year
	$
Alpha Co	80,200
Bravo Co	51,900
Charlie Co	86,800

What is the amount of profit attributable to the equity shareholders of Alpha Co in the consolidated statement of profit or loss for the year ended 31 December 20X4?

$ ___________

174 Platinum Co acquired 80% of the ordinary share capital of Palladium Co on 1 April 20X0 by means of cash and contingent consideration. At this date, Platinum Co assessed the fair value of contingent consideration at $250,000. Platinum Co calculates non-controlling interest, using the fair value at the date of acquisition, which was estimated to be $100,000 and the goodwill arising on acquisition was $300,000.

The following figures for Palladium Co are relevant:

	$'000
Ordinary shares of $1 each at acquisition	500
Retained earnings at 1 January 20X0	(300)
Profit for the year ended 31 December 20X0	120

The profits for Palladium Co have accrued evenly throughout the year.

What was the cash consideration paid by Platinum Co for the investment in Palladium Co?

$ ___________

175 Indicate whether the following statements are true or false in relation to accounting for the acquisition of a subsidiary.

	True ✓	**False** ✓
Where a parent company is satisfied that there has been a gain on a bargain purchase (negative goodwill), it should be recognised in the consolidated statement of profit or loss immediately.		
If the liabilities of the acquired entity are overstated, then goodwill will also be overstated.		

176 On 1 January 20X4, Viagem acquired 80% of the equity share capital of Greca.

Extracts of their statements of profit or loss for the year ended 30 September 20X4 are:

	Viagem	**Greca**
	$000	$000
Revenue	64,600	38,000
Cost of sales	(51,200)	(26,000)

Sales from Viagem to Greca throughout the year to 30 September 20X4 had consistently been $800,000 per month.

Viagem made a mark-up on cost of 25% on these sales.

Greca had $1.5 million of these goods in inventory as at 30 September 20X4.

What would be the cost of sales in Viagem's consolidated statement of profit or loss for the year ended 30 September 20X4?

$__________,000

177 Pact acquired 80% of the equity shares of Sact on 1 July 20X4, paying $3 for each share acquired. This represented a premium of 20% over the market price of Sact's shares at that date.

Sact's equity at 31 March 20X5 comprised:

	$	$
Equity shares of $1 each		100,000
Retained earnings at 1 April 20X4	80,000	
Profit for the year ended 31 March 20X5	40,000	
		120,000
		220,000

The only fair value adjustment required to Sact's net assets on consolidation was a $20,000 increase in the value of its land.

Pact's policy is to value non-controlling interests at fair value at the date of acquisition.

For this purpose the market price of Sact's shares at that date can be deemed to be representative of the fair value of the shares held by the non-controlling interest.

What would be the carrying amount of the non-controlling interest of Sact in the consolidated statement of financial position of Pact as at 31 March 20X5?

A $54,000

B $50,000

C $56,000

D $58,000

178 Germane has a number of relationships with other companies.

In which of the following relationships is Germane necessarily the parent?

(i) Foll has 50,000 non-voting and 100,000 voting equity shares in issue with each share receiving the same dividend. Germane owns all of Foll's non-voting shares and 40,000 of its voting shares.

(ii) Kipp has 1 million equity shares in issue of which Germane owns 40%. Germane also owns $800,000 out of $1 million 8% convertible loan notes issued by Kipp. These loan notes may be converted on the basis of 40 equity shares for each $100 of loan note, or they may be redeemed in cash at the option of the holder.

(iii) Germane owns 49% of the equity shares in Polly and 52% of its non-redeemable preference shares. As a result of these investments, Germane receives variable returns from Polly and has the ability to affect these returns through its power over Polly.

A (i) only

B (i) and (ii) only

C (ii) and (iii) only

D All three

179 Wilmslow acquired 80% of the equity shares of Zeta on 1 April 20X4 when Zeta's retained earnings were $200,000. During the year ended 31 March 20X5, Zeta purchased goods from Wilmslow totalling $320,000. At 31 March 20X5, one quarter of these goods were still in the inventory of Zeta. Wilmslow applies a mark-up on cost of 25% to all of its sales.

At 31 March 20X5, the retained earnings of Wilmslow and Zeta were $450,000 and $340,000 respectively.

What would be the amount of retained earnings in Wilmslow's consolidated statement of financial position as at 31 March 20X5?

$___________,000

180 IFRS Standards require extensive use of fair values when recording the acquisition of a subsidiary.

Which TWO of the following comments, regarding the use of fair values on the acquisition of a subsidiary, are correct?

A The use of fair value to record a subsidiary's acquired assets does not comply with the historical cost principle.

B The use of fair values to record the acquisition of plant always increases consolidated post-acquisition depreciation charges compared to the corresponding charge in the subsidiary's own financial statements.

C Cash consideration payable one year after the date of acquisition needs to be discounted to reflect its fair value.

D When acquiring a subsidiary, the fair value of liabilities and contingent liabilities must also be considered.

E Patents must be included as part of goodwill because it is impossible to determine the fair value of an acquired patent, as, by definition, patents are unique.

181 Identify whether the following statements are true or false

	True	False
The profit made by a parent on the sale of goods to a subsidiary is only realised when the subsidiary sells the goods to a third party		
Eliminating intra-group unrealised profits never affects non-controlling interests		
The profit element of goods supplied by the parent to an associate and held in year-end inventory must be eliminated in full		

182 Johnson paid $1.2 million for a 30% investment in Treem's equity shares on 1 August 20X4.

Treem's profit after tax for the year ended 31 March 20X5 was $750,000. On 31 March 20X5, Treem had $300,000 goods in its inventory which it had bought from Johnson in March 20X5. These had been sold by Johnson at a mark-up on cost of 20%.

Treem has not paid any dividends.

On the assumption that Treem is an associate of Johnson, what would be the carrying amount of the investment in Treem in the consolidated statement of financial position of Johnson as at 31 March 20X5?

$_______________ ,000

183 On 1 January 20X4, Pigagem acquired 80% of the equity share capital of Streca.

Extracts of their statements of financial position for the year ended 31 December 20X4 are:

	Pigagem	Streca
	$000	$000
Receivables	64,600	38,000

At 31 December 20X4, Streca recorded a payable to Pigagem of $3 million which did not agree to Pigagem's receivable balance due to $1 million cash in transit.

What is the value of receivables in the consolidated statement of financial position as at 31 December 20X4?

$_______________ ,000

184 Identify whether the following statements are true or false.

	True	False
If a subsidiary is disposed of on the last day of the reporting period then its assets and liabilities must still be included in the consolidated statement of financial position.		
The gain or loss arising on the disposal of a subsidiary in the consolidated financial statements is recorded in other comprehensive income.		

185 Johanna acquired 100% of Sidney on 1 January 20X4, paying $5 million cash, including $200,000 professional fees. Johanna also agreed to pay $10 million on 1 January 20X6. Johanna Co has a cost of capital of 10%

Identify the components to be included within the calculation of goodwill for the acquisition of Sidney Co for the year ended 31 December 20X4.

Consideration	To be included in goodwill
Cash consideration of $5 million	
Cash consideration of $4.8 million	
Deferred cash consideration of $8.3 million	
Deferred cash consideration of $9.1 million	

186 The Garden group has a reporting date of 31 December 20X3. On 30 September 20X3, the group disposed of its 80% holding in the ordinary shares of Shed for $10 million in cash. The disposal of Shed constitutes a discontinued operation. The following information relates to Shed:

	$m
Goodwill at disposal	2
Net assets at disposal	9
Non-controlling interest at disposal	3

What should be recorded as the profit (or loss) on disposal in the consolidated statement of profit or loss for the year ended 31 December 20X3?

A Loss of $2 million

B Profit of $2 million

C Profit of $4 million

D Loss of $4 million

187 Wind purchased 80% of the ordinary shares of Snow for $4 million many years ago and holds the investment in its individual statement of financial position at cost. On 30 September 20X3, Wind disposed of its shares in Snow for $10 million in cash

What is the profit arising on the disposal of the shares that will be reported in Wind's individual statement of profit or loss for the year ended 30 September 20X3?

$__________

188 On 30 June 20X4, the Winter group disposed of its 70% holding in the ordinary shares of Spring for $9 million in cash. Winter originally purchased the shares for $6 million. At the acquisition date, the goodwill was $4.6 million, and has not been impaired. Spring's net assets at the disposal date were $5 million. The non-controlling interest in Spring at the disposal date was $3.1 million.

What is the profit arising on the disposal of Spring that will be recorded in the consolidated statement of profit or loss for the year ended 31 December 20X4?

$__________,000

189 On 30 June 20X4, the Tea group disposed of its 60% holding in the ordinary shares of Coffee for $15 million in cash. The non-controlling interest at the acquisition date was measured at its fair value of $2.2 million.

Coffee's net assets at the acquisition and the disposal date were $5 million and $8 million respectively. Goodwill arising on the acquisition of Coffee of $1 million had been fully impaired by the disposal date.

What is the profit arising on the disposal of Coffee that will be recorded in the consolidated statement of profit or loss for the year ended 31 December 20X4?

A Profit of $10.0 million

B Profit of $9.2 million

C Profit of $10.4 million

D Profit of $10.2 million

INTERPRETATION OF FINANCIAL STATEMENTS

190 Which of the following statements about a not-for-profit entity is valid?

A There is no requirement to calculate an earnings per share figure as it is not likely to have shareholders who need to assess its earnings performance.

B The current value of its property is not relevant as it is not a commercial entity.

C Interpretation of its financial performance using ratio analysis is meaningless.

D Its financial statements will not be closely scrutinised as it does not have investors.

191 Which of the following ratios is likely to be most relevant for a local charity?

A Operating profit margin

B Current ratio

C Earnings per share

D Return on capital employed

192 Identify whether each of the following is a limitation of applying ratio analysis to published financial statements or not.

	Limitation	Not a limitation
Different ways of calculating certain ratios exist		
Accounting policy choices can limit comparability between different companies		

193 The following information has been taken from Preston's financial statements:

Preston has inventory turnover of six times.

The year-end receivables collection period is 42 days.

Cost of sales for the year was $1,690,000. Credit purchases for the year were $2,150,000.

Preston's cash cycle at 31 December 20X7 was 68 days

All calculations should be made to the nearest full day, and the trading year has 365 days.

What is Preston's trade payables collection period as at 31 December 20X7?

___________ days

194 Which TWO of the following explanations are unlikely to lead to an increase in receivables collection period?

A A new contract with a large customer has been won following a competitive tender

B A large one-off credit sale has been completed just before the year end

C The entity has recently expanded into a number of high street retail units

D Difficult economic conditions have led to some customers struggling to pay on time

E A website has been opened in the year for trade direct to the public

195 The following extracts of the financial statements of Wiggo have been obtained:

Revenue	$980,000
Cost of sales	($530,000)
Operating expenses	($210,000)
Equity	$600,000
Loan	$300,000
Deferred tax	$44,000
Payables	$46,000

What is the return on capital employed of Wiggo?

A 24.2%

B 25.4%

C 26.7%

D 50%

196 The following extracts of the financial statements of Wiggo have been obtained:

	20X5
Inventories	$130,000
Receivables	$80,000
Cash	$10,000
Loan repayable 20X8	$90,000
Deferred tax	$14,000
Payables	$70,000
Overdraft	$34,000

What is the quick ratio of Wiggo?

____________:1

197 **Which of the following items is unlikely to be considered a 'one-off' item which would impact the comparability of ratios?**

A A new website selling direct to the public has meant that deliveries are now made to more diverse geographical areas, increasing delivery costs

B A closure of a department has led to redundancies

C Sale of surplus property leading to a profit on disposal

D A storm in the year led to significant damage to the warehouse

198 **Which of the following is not a valid reason for a decrease in gross profit margin?**

A A major customer renewed their contract during the year following a competitive tender process

B New plant and equipment used in the manufacturing process has been purchased in the year, which has increased the depreciation expense

C Delivery costs to customers have risen following an increase in the rates charged by couriers

D A national recession has led to sales prices being cut in response

199 KRL manufactures pharmaceuticals, and is investigating a proposed takeover of another entity which is based overseas.

Identify which sources of information will be available for KRL to use in relation to the acquisition.

	Available to KRL to use	**Not available to KRL to use**
Details of the overseas country in which the target entity operates		
Recent financial statements of the entity		
Internal business plans of the takeover target		

200 Marcel has calculated that its current year Price Earnings (P/E) ratio is 12.6.

The sector average P/E ratio is 10.5

Which of the following would be an explanation of the difference between Marcel's P/E ratio and the sector average?

A Marcel is seen as a less risky investment than the sector average, and there is higher confidence about the future prospects of Marcel.

B Marcel is seen as a more risky investment than the sector average, however there is higher confidence about the future prospects of Marcel.

C Marcel is seen as a less risky investment than the sector average, however there is low confidence about the future prospects of Marcel.

D Marcel is seen as a more risky investment than the sector average, and there is low confidence about the future prospects of Marcel.

201 **Identify whether the statements about diluted earnings per share below are true or false.**

	True	**False**
It acts as a prediction of the future Earnings Per Share figure		
It discloses that Earnings Per Share could have been higher		

202 Apollo took out a new loan on 1 January 20X6. This loan carries an effective interest rate of 8%. The initial proceeds of the loan are $2.5m, which is after paying issue costs of $250k. The coupon rate on the loan is 6%. Apollo must keep to an interest cover ratio of 9 times under the arrangements made with the bank.

What operating profit must be maintained by Apollo in the year ended 31 December 20X6, in order to meet the minimum interest cover ratio specified by the bank?

A $1,350,000

B $1,800,000

C $450,000

D $1,980,000

203 Rodgers has just completed its financial statements for the year ended 30 June 20X6. It is reporting a net profit of $1,250,000 for the current year, and has $1 million of 50 cent shares in issue. The current market price of Rodgers' shares is $3.50.

What is the Price Earnings (P/E) ratio of Rodgers for the year ended 30 June 20X6?

______________ times

204 Puel has just completed its financial statements for the year ended 30 June 20X6. It has $1 million of 50 cent shares in issue, and the current market price per share is $3.50.

Puel has paid total dividends during the year ended 30 June 20X6 of $1,500,000.

What is the dividend yield (to one decimal place) for the year ended 30 June 20X6?

______________ %

205 Alco and Saleco are both food retailers. They are both showing a return on capital employed (ROCE) figure of 10% for the current year. Both companies have the same financial year end. Alco has reported a net profit (based on profit before interest and tax) of 25% and Saleco has reported a net profit of 2%.

What, if any, is the difference between these two companies, even though they are showing the same ROCE calculation?

A The companies are identical

B Alco operates at the high end of the market, and Saleco at the lower end

C Alco operates at the lower end of the market, and Saleco at the high end

D There is not enough information in the question to determine the difference

206 Identify whether each of the following is a limitation of applying ratio analysis to published financial statements or not.

	Limitation	Not a limitation
Financial statements often use historic cost, meaning that inflation is not taken into account		
Complex items may not fit into any accounting standards and therefore may be omitted from the financial statements		

207 Lepchem is a pharmaceutical business which was launched in September 20X1. Lepchem have been funded through bank loans and equity investment. Lepchem's aim is to develop new pharmaceuticals which could then be sold for a high margin. So far, Lepchem have not managed to successfully develop or sell any pharmaceuticals.

Which ratio is likely to be the most relevant for Lepchem for the year to 31 December 20X1?

A Current ratio

B Gross profit margin

C Operating profit margin

D Receivables collection period

208 Identify whether the following criteria could be used to assess the performance of a not-for-profit entity.

	Could be used to assess	Will not be used
The return given to investors		
The success in achieving the organisation's stated aims		
How well costs are being managed		

209 Which of the following measures is likely to be the least relevant to a property management business which rents out commercial properties?

A Non-current asset turnover

B Return on capital employed

C Average rent earned

D Inventory turnover period

210 Quartile is in the jewellery retail business which can be assumed to be highly seasonal. For the year ended 30 September 20X4, Quartile assessed its operating performance by comparing selected accounting ratios with those of its business sector average as provided by an agency. You may assume that the business sector used by the agency is an accurate representation of Quartile's business.

Which TWO of the following circumstances may invalidate the comparison of Quartile's ratios with those of the sector average?

A In the current year, Quartile has experienced significant rising costs for its purchases

B The sector average figures are compiled from companies whose year-end is between 1 July 20X4 and 30 September 20X4

C Quartile does not revalue its properties, but is aware that others in this sector do

D During the year, Quartile discovered an error relating to the inventory count at 30 September 20X3. This error was correctly accounted for in the financial statements for the current year ended 30 September 20X4

211 The following information has been taken or calculated from Fowler's financial statements for the year ended 30 September 20X4.

Fowler's cash cycle at 30 September 20X4 is 70 days. Its inventory turnover is six times.

Year-end trade payables are $230,000.

Purchases on credit for the year were $2 million.

Cost of sales for the year was $1.8 million.

What is Fowler's trade receivables collection period as at 30 September 20X4?

$_____________ days

212 Trent uses the formula (year-end trade receivables/credit sales for the year) × 365 to calculate how many days on average its customers take to pay.

Which TWO of the following would NOT affect the correctness of the above calculation of the average number of days a customer takes to pay?

A Trent experiences considerable seasonal trading

B Trent makes a number of cash sales through retail outlets

C Revenue does not include a 15% sales tax whereas the receivables do include the tax

D Trent factors with recourse the receivable of its largest customer

213 At 31 March 20X5 Jasim had equity of $200,000 and debt of $100,000.

Which of the following transactions, considered separately, would increase Jasim's gearing?

A During the year a property was revalued upwards by $20,000

B A bonus issue of equity shares of 1 for 4 was made during the year using other components of equity

C A provision for estimated damages was reduced during the year from $21,000 to $15,000 based on the most recent legal advice

D An asset was acquired under a lease with a present value of lease payments of $23,000

214 Which of the following current year events would explain a fall in an entity's operating profit margin compared to the previous year?

A An increase in gearing leading to higher interest costs

B A reduction in the allowance for uncollectable receivables

C A decision to value inventory on the average cost basis from the first in first out (FIFO) basis. Unit prices of inventory had risen during the current year

D A change from the amortisation of development costs being included in cost of sales to being included in administrative expenses

215 Which of the following ratios are likely to DECREASE due to a significant revaluation gain on a depreciating asset at the start of the year?

(1) Return on capital employed (ROCE)

(2) Gearing (debt/equity)

(3) Operating profit margin

(4) Net asset turnover

A 1, 2, 3 and 4

B 1, 2 and 3 only

C 2, 3 and 4 only

D 1 and 4 only

STATEMENT OF CASH FLOWS

216 The following information is available for the property, plant and equipment of Fry as at 30 September:

	20X4	**20X3**
	$000	$000
Carrying amounts	23,400	14,400

The following items were recorded during the year ended 30 September 20X4:

(i) Depreciation charge of $2.5 million

(ii) An item of plant, with a carrying amount of $3 million, was sold for $1.8 million

(iii) A property was revalued upwards by $2 million

(iv) Environmental provisions of $4 million relating to property, plant and equipment were capitalised during the year

What amount would be shown in Fry's statement of cash flows for purchase of property, plant and equipment for the year ended 30 September 20X4?

$____________'000

217 At 1 October 20X4, BK had accrued interest payable of $12,000.

During the year ended 30 September 20X5, BK charged finance costs of $41,000 to its statement of profit or loss, including unwinding a discount relating to a provision stated at its present value of $150,000 at 1 October 20X4. The closing balance on accrued interest payable account at 30 September 20X5 was $15,000, and BK has a discount rate of 6%.

How much interest paid should BK show on its statement of cash flows for the year ended 30 September 20X5?

A $38,000

B $29,000

C $35,000

D $41,000

218 The following balances were extracted from N's statement of financial position as at 31 December.

	20X9	**20X8**
	$000	$000
Deferred taxation	38	27
Current tax payable	119	106

Extract from statement of profit or loss for the year ended 31 December 20X9.

	$000
Income tax expense	122

The amount of tax paid that should be included in N's statement of cash flows for the year ended 31 December 20X9 is:

$____________,000

219 Which item would be NOT be shown in a statement of cash flows using the indirect method?

A Cash paid to employees

B Cash paid to purchase machinery

C Cash paid to shareholders as dividend

D Cash paid to redeem loan notes

220 IAS 7 *Statement of Cash Flows* sets out the three main headings to be used in a statement of cash flows.

Which TWO of the items below would be included under the heading 'Cash flows from operating activities' according to IAS 7?

A Tax paid

B Purchase of investments

C Loss on disposal of machinery

D Purchase of equipment

221 During the year to 31 July 20X7 Smartypants made a profit of $37,500 after accounting for depreciation of $2,500.

During the year non-current assets were purchased for $16,000, receivables increased by $2,000, inventories decreased by $3,600 and trade payables increased by $700.

What was the increase in cash and bank balances during the year?

A $21,300

B $30,300

C $24,900

D $26,300

222 Identify the correct treatment in the calculation of net cash from operating activities under the indirect method.

	Add to profit before tax	**Deduct from profit before tax**
Decrease in trade receivables		
Increase in inventories		
Profit on sale of non-current assets		
Depreciation		

223 Butcher had the following balances in its statement of financial position as at 30 June 20X0 and 20X1:

	20X1	**20X0**
Share capital	$170,000	$150,000
Share premium	$105,000	$95,000
10% debentures	$170,000	$190,000

How much will appear in the statement of cash flows for the year ended 30 June 20X1 under the heading 'cash flows from financing activities'?

$_________,000

224 At 1 January 20X0 Casey had property, plant and equipment with a carrying amount of $180,000. In the year ended 31 December 20X0 Casey disposed of assets with a carrying amount of $60,000 for $50,000. Casey revalued a building from $75,000 to $100,000 and charged depreciation for the year of $20,000. At the end of the year, the carrying amount of property, plant and equipment was $250,000.

How much will be reported in the statement of cash flows for the year ended 31 December 20X0 under the heading 'cash flows from investing activities'?

A $75,000 outflow

B $125,000 outflow

C $135,000 outflow

D $50,000 inflow

225 At 1 January 20X0 Casey had government grants held in deferred income of $900,000. During the year, Casey released $100,000 to the statement of profit or loss. At 31 December 20X0, the remaining deferred income balance was $1,100,000.

Select the TWO amounts to be included in the statement of cash flows for Casey.

Amortisation of government grant	**Receipt of grant**
Increase of $100,000 to cash generated from operations	Cash received from grant $300,000 in investing activities
Decrease of $100,000 to cash generated from operations	Cash received from grant $100,000 in investing activities

Section 2

OBJECTIVE CASE QUESTIONS – SECTION B

CONCEPTUAL FRAMEWORK/INTERNATIONAL FINANCIAL REPORTING STANDARDS

The following scenario relates to questions 226–230

Flightline is an airline which treats its aircraft as complex non-current assets, accounted for under the historical cost model. The cost and other details of an aircraft are:

	$000	Estimated life
Interior cabin fittings – installed 1 April 20X5	25,000	5 years
Engine - installed 1 April 20X5	9,000	36,000 flying hours

In the year ended 31 March 20X9, the aircraft flew for 1,200 hours for the six months to 30 September 20X8.

On 1 October 20X8 the aircraft suffered a 'bird strike' accident which damaged the engine beyond repair. This was replaced by a new engine with a life of 36,000 hours at cost of $10.8 million.

Flightline's year end is 31 March 20X9.

---

226 What is the depreciation to be charged in respect of the engine for the 6-month period to 1 October 20X8?

$__________,000

227 Which of the following explains the correct accounting treatment of the engine?

A Write off the damaged engine, capitalise the new engine and depreciate over 24,000 hours

B Treat the $10.8 million as a repair to the damaged engine and continue to depreciate the engine as in the first 6 months

C Capitalise $6 million to replace the damaged engine, expense the other $4.8 million

D Write off the damaged engine, capitalise the new engine and depreciate over 36,000 hours

228 A wing was also damaged, but was repaired at a cost of $3 million. The accident also caused cosmetic damage to the exterior of the aircraft which required repainting at a cost of $2 million.

Identify the correct treatment for the $3 million repair costs to the wing and the $2 million repainting of the aircraft

	Capitalise	Expense
$3 million repair of the wing		
$2 million repainting of the exterior		

229 As the aircraft was out of service for some weeks due to the accident, Flightline took the opportunity to upgrade its cabin facilities at a cost of $4.5 million. This did not increase the estimated remaining life of the cabin fittings, but the improved facilities enabled Flightline to substantially increase the airfares on this aircraft.

What is the carrying amount of the cabin fittings as at 31 March 20X9?

A $8,600,000

B $8,000,000

C $5,000,000

D $7,250,000

230 The 'bird strike' accident represents an indication of impairment.

Complete the following sentence from the choice below.

The aircraft will be impaired if its ________________ exceeds its recoverable amount.

Options: Replacement cost, Fair value less costs to sell, Carrying amount, Value in use

---

The following scenario relates to questions 231–235

Speculate owns two properties and uses fair value accounting where possible.

Property A: An office building used by Speculate for administrative purposes. At 1 April 20X2 it had a carrying amount of $2 million and a remaining life of 20 years. On 1 October 20X2, the property was let to a third party and reclassified as an investment property. The property had a fair value of $2.3 million at 1 October 20X2, and $2.34 million at 31 March 20X3.

Property B: Another office building let on a 12-month lease to a subsidiary of Speculate. At 1 April 20X2, it had a fair value of $1.5 million which had risen to $1.65 million at 31 March 20X3.

---

231 What is the correct treatment when Property A is reclassified as an investment property?

A Take $350,000 gain to other comprehensive income

B Take $350,000 gain to the statement of profit or loss

C Take $400,000 gain to other comprehensive income

D Take $400,000 gain to the statement of profit or loss

232 Which of the following models can Speculate use to account for investment properties in its individual financial statements?

(i) Cost model

(ii) Revaluation model

(iii) Fair value model

A (i) and (ii) only

B (i) and (iii) only

C (ii) and (iii) only

D All three

233 What is the total gain for investment properties to be included in Speculate's individual statement of profit or loss for the year ended 31 March 20X3? Enter your answer to the nearest dollar ($).

$ ________________

234 In the individual and consolidated financial statements of Speculate, how would Property B be accounted for?

Individual	✓	**Consolidated**	✓
Investment property		Investment property	
Property, plant & equipment		Property, plant & equipment	
Within goodwill		Cancelled as an intra-group item	

235 What would the carrying amount of Property A be at 31 March 20X3 if Speculate used the cost model for investment properties?

A $1,950,000

B $1,900,000

C $2,185,000

D $2,182,051

The following scenario relates to questions 236–240

The following issues relating to Chestnut Co's non-current assets are outstanding for the year ended 31 December 20X7:

Factory

At 1 January 20X7, Chestnut Co's factory had a carrying amount of $5m. It has a remaining useful life of ten years at that date. On 31 December 20X7 there was an impairment review of the factory and the recoverable amount was deemed to be $2.5m. Chestnut Co's factory had previously been revalued upwards and the revaluation surplus has a credit balance of $1m relating to this factory.

Head Office

Chestnut Co's head office cost $12m on 1 January 20X1 and is being depreciated over a 40-year life. On 31 December 20X4, there was an impairment review of the head office and the recoverable amount was deemed to be $9m. A more recent valuation, at 31 December 20X7, has estimated that the recoverable amount of the head office is $11m.

Machinery

On 1 April 20X7, Chestnut Co received a grant of $2.6m towards new production machinery. The machinery cost $4m and is expected to have a useful life of five years. Depreciation is charged on a straight-line proportionate basis. Chestnut Co uses the cost model when accounting for its head office, and the deferred income method in relation to government grants

236 Which of the following assets belonging to Chestnut Co require an annual impairment review?

A The head office only

B The machinery only

C Both the head office and the machinery

D Neither the head office nor the machinery

237 In accordance with IAS 36 Impairment of Assets, what is the correct journal entry to reflect the depreciation and the impairment of Chestnut Co's factory for the year ended 31 December 20X7?

A Dr Statement of profit or loss $1.5m, Dr Revaluation surplus $1m, Cr Non-current assets $2.5m

B Dr Statement of profit or loss $2.5m, Cr Non-current assets $2.5m

C Dr Non-current assets $2.5m, Cr Statement of profit or loss $1.5m, Cr Non-current assets $1m

D Dr Non-current assets $2.5m, Cr Statement of profit or loss $2.5m

238 What is the carrying amount of Chestnut Co's head office in the statement of financial position as at 31 December 20X7?

A $8.25m

B $9.9m

C $10.8m

D $11m

239 Which of the following statements relating to government grants is correct?

A The deferred income method should always be used for grants related to assets

B Grants related to income must be disclosed separately in the statement of profit or loss as other income

C The deferred income method should only be used if the grant is repayable

D Grants related to assets can be accounted for using either the deferred income method or by deducting from the asset's carrying amount

240 What is the carrying amount of the non-current liability in respect of the government grant in Chestnut Co's statement of financial position as at 31 December 20X7?

A $2.08m

B $1.69m

C $2.21m

D $1.56m

The following scenario relates to questions 241–245

Wilrob Co has the following research projects at 31 March 20X7:

Project 324 – The project commenced on 1 April 20X6 and incurred total costs of $15m during the period to 31 December 20X6 on a pro-rata basis. On 30 June 20X6, the directors were confident that the project met the capitalisation criteria of IAS 38 Intangible Assets. The project was completed and began to generate revenue from 1 January 20X7. It is estimated that the project will generate revenue for five years.

Project 325 – The project commenced on 1 September 20X6. Costs of $20,000 per month were incurred until 31 January 20X7 when the project was abandoned. The specialist equipment that had been purchased for Project 325 was transferred for use in another of Wilrob Co's research projects.

Project 326 – The project commenced on 1 January 20X7. Costs of $40,000 per month were incurred until 31 August 20X7 when the directors increased the spend to $60,000 to complete the project quickly as a potential buyer had been identified on 20 July 20X7. The directors had not been confident of the success of the project until this point.

---

241 Which TWO of the following are required by IAS 38 *Intangible Assets* in relation to the amortisation of intangible assets (excluding goodwill)?

A Intangible assets should be amortised over the expected useful life or not at all if the useful life is deemed to be indefinite

B Intangible assets should not be amortised but instead reviewed for impairment losses only

C Intangible assets should be amortised on the basis of the expected pattern of consumption of the expected future economic benefits

D Intangible assets should not be amortised or impaired and instead simply carried forward at their original cost until sold or scrapped

242 **Which TWO of the following statements are true in relation to IAS 38 *Intangible Assets*?**

A IAS 38 requires the revaluation of intangible assets where an entity has chosen to revalue its tangible non-current assets

B IAS 38 does not permit the revaluation of any intangible assets in any circumstances

C IAS 38 permits the revaluation of intangible assets only if there is an active market for such assets

D IAS 38 requires that the initial recognition of intangibles must be at cost

243 **In accordance with IAS 38 *Intangible Assets*, what is charged to the statement of profit or loss for the year ended 31 March 20X7 in respect of project 324?**

A $5.5m

B $6.5m

C $7m

D $10m

244 **In accordance with IAS 38 *Intangible Assets*, which of the following is/are true or false in respect of the accounting treatment of projects 325 and 326?**

	True ✓	False ✓
The cost for project 325 should be expensed in the statement of profit or loss for the year ended 31 March 20X7		
The specialist equipment which was purchased for project 325 should not be depreciated as it has been used in abandoned or research projects		
The costs for project 326 should be included as an asset in the statement of financial position as at 31 March 20X7		

245 During the year ended 31 March 20X8, Wilrob Co incurred the following costs:

(1) $400,000 in staff costs incurred in updating a computerised record of potential customers

(2) $800,000 for the purchase of a domain name for the website of an entity making substantial online sales

(3) $4m for a patent purchased to improve the production process, with an expected useful life of three years

Which of the above costs would be capitalised as intangible assets in accordance with IAS 38 *Intangible Assets*?

A 1 only

B 3 only

C 2 and 3 only

D 1, 2 and 3

The following scenario relates to questions 246–250

Apex received a $10 million 6% loan on 1 April 20X7. The loan will be redeemable at a premium which means the loan has an effective finance cost of 7.5% per annum. The loan was specifically issued to finance the building of a new store.

Construction of the store commenced on 1 May 20X7 and it was completed and ready for use on 28 February 20X8, but did not open for trading until 1 April 20X8.

246 How should the loan be treated in the financial statements of Apex for the year ended 31 March 20X8?

A Present value

B Fair value through other comprehensive income

C Fair value through profit or loss

D Amortised cost

247 Which TWO of the statements below regarding IAS 23 *Borrowing Costs* are correct?

A Borrowing costs must be capitalised if they are directly attributable to qualifying assets

B Borrowing costs should cease to be capitalised once the related asset is substantially complete

C Borrowing costs must be capitalised if they are directly attributable to non-current assets

D Borrowing costs may be capitalised if they are directly attributable to qualifying assets

E Borrowing costs should commence to be capitalised once expenditure is being incurred on the construction of the asset

248 How much should be recorded as finance costs in the statement of profit or loss for the year ended 31 March 20X8?

$__________,000

249 How much interest should be capitalised as part of property, plant and equipment as at 31 March 20X8?

$__________,000

250 Apex decided that not all of the funds raised were needed immediately and temporarily invested some of the funds in April 20X7, earning $40,000 interest.

How should the $40,000 be accounted for in the financial statements of Apex?

A Net off the amount capitalised in property, plant and equipment

B Taken to the statement of profit or loss as investment income

C Taken as other comprehensive income

D Deducted from the outstanding loan amount in the statement of financial position

The following scenario relates to questions 251–255.

Abena Co prepares financial statements to 30 June each year.

During the year to 30 June 20X5, the company spent $550,000 on new plant as follows:

	$000
Plant cost	525
Delivery to site	3
Building alterations to accommodate the plant	12
Costs of initial testing of the new plant	2
Plant operator training costs	8

Abena Co's fixtures and fittings were purchased on 1 July 20X2 at a cost of $50,000. The directors have depreciated them on a straight-line basis over an estimated useful life of eight years assuming a $5,000 residual value. At 1 July 20X4, the directors realise that the remaining useful life of the fixtures is five years. There is no change to the estimated residual value.

Abena Co began a research project in October 20X3 with the aim of developing a new type of machine. If successful, Abena Co will manufacture the machines and sell them to customers as well as using them in their own production processes. During the year ended 30 June 20X4, costs of $25,000 were incurred on conducting feasibility studies and some market research. During the year ended 30 June 20X5, a further $80,000 was incurred on constructing and testing a prototype of the machine.

251 In accordance with IAS 16 Property, Plant and Equipment, what is the value of additions to plant for Abena Co for the year ended 30 June 20X5?

A $525,000

B $542,000

C $550,000

D $540,000

252 Which of the following is TRUE in relation to the change in the remaining useful life of the fixtures and fittings?

A It is a change of accounting policy which should be retrospectively applied

B It is a change of accounting policy which should be disclosed in the notes to the financial statements

C It is a change of accounting estimate which should be retrospectively applied

D It is a change of accounting estimate which should be prospectively applied

253 In accordance with IAS 16, what is the depreciation charge for the fixtures and fittings for Abena Co for the year ended 30 June 20X5?

A $7,500

B $9,000

C $7,750

D $6,750

254 In accordance with IAS 38 Intangible Assets, what is the correct treatment of the $25,000 costs incurred on the research project by Abena Co during the year ended 30 June 20X4?

A They should be recognised as an intangible non-current asset as future economic benefits are expected from the use and sale of the machinery

B They should be written off to profit or loss as an expense as they are research costs at this date

C They should be included in tangible non-current assets as machinery which will be put into use once completed

D They should be set against a provision made for the estimated total cost of the project which was set up at the start of the research

255 In accordance with IAS 38, which of the following is true when Abena Co moves to the production and testing stage of the prototype during the year ended 30 June 20X5?

A The project has moved to the development stage. If the IAS 38 development expenditure criteria are met, Abena Co can choose whether to recognise the $80,000 costs as an intangible non-current asset

B The project is still in its research stage and the $80,000 costs incurred by Abena Co cannot be recognised as an intangible non-current asset until a product is ready for sale

C The project has moved to the development stage. If the IAS 38 development expenditure criteria are met, Abena Co must recognise the $80,000 costs as an intangible non-current asset

D The project is still in its research stage and so Abena Co must expense the $80,000 costs to profit or loss

---

The following scenario relates to questions 256–260

Shawler constructed a furnace on 1 April 20X3, causing significant environmental damage which must be repaired at the end of the asset's useful life of ten years. The present value of this is estimated to be $4 million. Shawler has a cost of capital of 8%.

On 1 October 20X3, Shawler received a government grant of $1.2 million relating to the cost of plant with a five-year life. Shawler accounts for grants using the deferred credit method.

On 1 October 20X3, Shawler also acquired land for 12 million dinars. The land was used to construct a factory during the year. Shawler's functional currency is the dollar ($).

On 1 October 20X3 the exchange rate was 4 Dinars: $1. At 31 March 20X4 the exchange rate was 2 Dinars:$1 and the average rate for the year was 3 Dinars:$1.

---

256 What is the total finance cost (to the nearest thousand) to be recorded in the statement of profit or loss in respect of the environmental damage caused by the furnace for the year ended 31 March 20X4?

$__________,000

257 **What is the non-current liability in respect of the government grant to be shown in Shawler's statement of financial position as at 31 March 20X4?**

A $840,000

B $1,080,000

C $960,000

D $720,000

258 **What is the carrying amount of the land to be shown in the statement of financial position of Shawler as at 31 March 20X4? Give your answer to the nearest $000.**

$__________,000

259 The costs below are the costs associated with the construction of the factory.

Which of the following can NOT be capitalised?

A Legal fees relating to the site purchase

B Health and safety training for new construction workers

C Direct labour costs associated with the construction

D Costs of site preparation

260 In the following year it was discovered that Shawler had breached the conditions relating to the government grant and therefore the grant had to be repaid.

Which TWO of the following describe the correct accounting treatment to record the repayment of the grant?

A Remove all deferred income balances

B Record an expense in the statement of profit or loss

C Increase the cost of plant

D Make an adjustment to the prior year financial statements

The following scenario relates to questions 261–265.

During the year ended 31 December 20X8, Linetti Co built an extension to its head office. The costs associated with the construction of the head office extension are as follows:

	$m
Land acquisition	10.0
Fees for environmental certifications and building permits	0.5
Architect and engineer fees	1.0
Construction material and labour costs (including unused materials)	6.6

At 30 September 20X8, the date when the head office extension became available for use, the cost of unused materials on site amounted to $0.5m. At that date, the total borrowing costs incurred on a loan which was used to specifically finance the head office extension amounted to $0.8m.

Linetti Co also acquired 100% of a subsidiary, Scully Co, on 1 January 20X8. The carrying amount of the assets of Scully Co in the consolidated financial statements of the Linetti group at 31 December 20X8, immediately before an impairment review, were as follows:

	$m
Goodwill	1.4
Brand name	2.0
Property, plant and equipment	6.0
Current assets (at recoverable amount)	2.4
	11.8

The recoverable amount of Scully Co was estimated at $9.6m at 31 December 20X8 and the impairment of the investment in Scully Co was deemed to be $2.2m.

261 For the year ended 31 December 20X8, how much should be capitalised in respect of the construction of the extension to the head office building?

A $18.4m

B $17.6m

C $18.9m

D $18.1m

262 Linetti Co incurred further expenditure on the head office extension after it had been completed.

Which of the following would qualify as capital expenditure?

A Property insurance premiums incurred

B Installation of new office fixtures and fittings

C Marketing costs telling the public that the head office extension is operational

D Maintenance and relocation of computers and related office equipment

263 At 31 December 20X9, the directors of Linetti Co decide to adopt the revaluation model of IAS® 16 *Property, Plant and Equipment* for Linetti Co's property.

In accordance with IAS 16, which of the following statements is FALSE?

A In subsequent years, the depreciation will be based on the revalued amount of the head office building as opposed to its cost

B Any revaluation gain on the head office building is recognised in other comprehensive income and any revaluation loss is recognised in profit or loss

C Each component part of the head office building is revalued separately

D The residual value and the useful life of the head office building must be reviewed each year

264 Assuming Scully Co represents a cash generating unit, what is the carrying amount of the brand at 31 December 20X8 following the impairment review?

A $1.2m

B $1.45m

C $1.73m

D $1.8m

265 Which, if any, of the following statements regarding impairment reviews is/are correct?

1 At the end of each reporting period, an entity should assess if there is any indication that assets have been impaired

2 Annual impairment reviews are required on all intangible assets with indefinite lives

A 1 only

B 2 only

C Both 1 and 2

D Neither 1 nor 2

The following scenario relates to questions 266–270

NovAir Co is an airline and prepares its financial statements to 31 December each year.

NovAir Co purchased a new aircraft for $15m on 1 January 20X5 with the following details:

Aircraft components	Cost ($'000)	Residual value ($'000)	Useful life (years)
Airframe	8,000	500	20
Engines	5,000	600	8
Engine testing costs	600		8
Interior of aircraft	1,400		5
Total	**15,000**		

NovAir Co depreciates its assets on a straight-line basis.

To fund the purchase of the aircraft, NovAir Co borrowed 10 million euros on 1 January 20X5. The interest on the loan is insignificant and should be ignored. The loan was due to be repaid in four annual equal instalments with the first repayment being made on 1 January 20X6.

Information relating to the exchange rate is as follows:

1 January 20X5	1 euro = $1.00
31 December 20X5 and 1 January 20X6	1 euro = $1.25
Average rate for the year ended 31 December 20X5	1 euro = $1.20
31 December 20X6 and 1 January 20X7	1 euro = $1.10
31 December 20X7	1 euro = $1.00

NovAir Co's functional currency is the $.

On 31 December 20X5, a significant engine malfunction was discovered. As a result of this malfunction, the aircraft was grounded. NovAir Co cannot reliably estimate a recoverable amount for the engines. The aircraft, including the engines, can be treated as a cash-generating unit.

266 In accordance with IAS 16 *Property, Plant and Equipment* (PPE), which TWO of the following statements are correct?

A The depreciation charge should be recognised in profit or loss unless it is included in the carrying amount of another asset

B When fair value is used to measure PPE then all other assets must be measured using the same principle

C The costs of safety inspections that are legally required to operate PPE can never be capitalised as part of the cost of an asset

D At the very least, the residual value and useful life of an asset should be reviewed at the end of each financial year

267 In accordance with IAS 16 *Property, Plant and Equipment*, what is the total aircraft depreciation to be charged to profit or loss for the year ended 31 December 20X5 (to the nearest $000)?

$ ___________ ,000

268 In accordance with IAS 21 *The Effect of Changes in Foreign Exchange Rates*, what is the total balance of the loan liability at 31 December 20X5?

A $10m

B $12m

C $8m

D $12.5m

269 At 31 December 20X6, the balance on the liability for the loan is 7.5 million euros. At 31 December 20X7, the balance is 5 million euros.

In accordance with IAS 21 *The Effects of Changes in Foreign Exchange Rates*, which TWO of the following correctly reflect how the foreign currency transaction should be reflected in the financial statements of NovAir Co for the year ended 31 December 20X7?

A The liability at 31 December 20X7 should be stated at $5m

B A foreign currency exchange gain of $500,000 should be reported

C The liability at 31 December 20X7 should be stated at $4.545m

D A foreign currency exchange loss of $455,000 should be reported

270 In accordance with IAS 36 *Impairment of Assets*, which of the following statements is correct?

A NovAir Co must not recognise an impairment loss for the engines since the recoverable amount cannot be estimated reliably

B NovAir Co must determine the recoverable amount of the engines using the depreciated replacement cost method

C NovAir Co must write the carrying amount of the engines down to the residual value since the recoverable amount cannot be estimated reliably

D NovAir Co must determine the recoverable amount of the aircraft and allocate a proportion of any impairment losses to the engines based on their carrying amount

The following scenario relates to questions 271–275

During the year Darby started research work on a new processor chip. Darby has a past history of being particularly successful in bringing similar projects to a profitable conclusion. In addition to this, Darby spent $200,000 training staff to use new equipment.

Darby also developed a new online platform during the year, spending $100,000 a month evenly from 1 February 20X5 to 31 October 20X5. Darby was unsure of the outcome of the project, but doubts were resolved on 1 May, following successful testing. The platform launched on 1 November 20X5 and was expected to last 5 years.

271 Darby's accounting assistant has read something which states that intangible assets are identifiable, non-monetary items without physical substance.

Which TWO of the following relate to items being classed as identifiable?

A Items must have probable future economic benefits

B Items must arise from legal or contractual rights

C Items must have a measurable cost

D Items must be separable

272 Identify the correct accounting treatment for items below.

	Capitalise	**Expense**
Training for staff		
Expenditure on processor chip		

273 How much should be recorded in Darby's statement of profit or loss for the year ended 31 December 20X5 in relation to the development of the online platform?

$__________,000

274 Which of the facts relating to the online platform is/are correct?

(i) The online platform will be subject to annual impairment review due to the judgemental nature of the project.

(ii) Once capitalised, the development costs should be held at fair value at each year end.

(iii) Depreciation on any plant used to develop the platform would be capitalised as part of the development costs.

A (i) only

B (ii) and (iii) only

C (iii) only

D (i) and (ii) only

275 Darby acquired a patent with a 10-year life for $500,000 on 1 January 20X5. On 31 December 20X5, management believed that the patent was less fully utilised than expected and determined the following information as part of their impairment review:

	$000
Potential sale proceeds of the patent	400
Estimated disposal costs	20
Value in use of the asset	480

What is the value of the impairment loss in the year ended 31 December 20X5?

A $70,000

B $30,000

C $20,000

D Nil

The following scenario relates to questions 276–280

Aphrodite has a year end of 31 December and operates a factory which makes computer chips for mobile phones. It purchased a machine on 1 July 20X3 for $80,000 which had a useful life of ten years and is depreciated on the straight-line basis, time apportioned in the years of acquisition and disposal. The machine was revalued to $81,000 on 1 July 20X4. There was no change to its useful life at that date.

A fire at the factory on 1 October 20X6 damaged the machine, leaving it with a lower operating capacity. The accountant considers that Aphrodite will need to recognise an impairment loss in relation to this damage and has ascertained the following information at 1 October 20X6:

(1) The carrying amount of the machine is $60,750.

(2) An equivalent new machine would cost $90,000.

(3) The machine could be sold in its current condition for a gross amount of $45,000. Dismantling costs would amount to $2,000.

(4) In its current condition, the machine could operate for three more years which gives it a value in use figure of $38,685.

276 In accordance with IAS 16 *Property, Plant and Equipment*, what is the depreciation charged to Aphrodite's statement of profit or loss in respect of the machine for the year ended 31 December 20X4?

A $9,000

B $8,000

C $8,263

D $8,500

277 IAS 36 *Impairment of Assets* contains a number of examples of internal and external events which may indicate the impairment of an asset.

In accordance with IAS 36, which TWO of the following would definitely NOT be an indicator of the potential impairment of an asset (or group of assets)?

A A reduction in Aphrodite's cost of capital

B Adverse changes in the economic performance of one or more assets

C A significant change in the technological environment in which an asset is employed making its software effectively obsolete

D The carrying amount of an entity's net assets being below the entity's market capitalisation

E An unexpected fall in the market value of one or more assets

278 What is the total impairment loss associated with Aphrodite's machine at 1 October 20X6?

A $nil

B $17,750

C $22,065

D $15,750

279 The accountant has decided that it is too difficult to reliably attribute cash flows to this one machine and that it would be more accurate to calculate the impairment on the basis of the factory as a cash-generating unit.

In accordance with IAS 36 *Impairment of Assets*, which TWO of the following are TRUE regarding cash generating units?

A A cash-generating unit to which goodwill has been allocated should be tested for impairment every five years.

B A cash-generating unit must be a subsidiary of the parent.

C There is no need to consistently identify cash-generating units based on the same types of asset from period to period.

D A cash-generating unit is the smallest identifiable group of assets for which independent cash flows can be identified.

E Assets in a cash-generating unit should never be impaired below their recoverable amount.

280 On 1 July 20X7, it is discovered that the damage to the machine is worse than originally thought. The machine is now considered to be worthless and the recoverable amount of the factory as a cash-generating unit is estimated to be $950,000.

At 1 July 20X7, the cash-generating unit comprises the following assets:

	$000
Building	500
Plant and equipment (including the damaged machine at a carrying amount of $35,000)	335
Goodwill	85
Net current assets (at recoverable amount)	250
	1,170

In accordance with IAS 36 *Impairment of Assets*, what will be the carrying amount of Aphrodite's plant and equipment when the impairment loss has been allocated to the cash-generating unit?

$____________

The following scenario relates to questions 281–285

Radar's directors made the following decisions during the year ended 31 March 20X3:

- it disposed of all of its outlets in country A
- it rebranded all of its outlets in country B to target the tourism market. The previous target market in country B had been aimed at business clients.

At a board meeting on 1 January 20X3, Pulsar's directors decided sell an item of plant, which had a carrying value of $4 million at 1 April 20X2 and a remaining life of 20 years. The plant is expected to sell for $3.9 million within 12 months.

A decision was also made to close down a regional office, which was communicated to the employees before the year end. 50 employees would be retrained and kept within Radar at a cost of $100,000, the others took redundancy and will be paid $300,000.

$75,000 is to be spent on marketing materials directing customers of the existing factory to other production facilities operated by Radar.

281 **Which THREE of the following criteria need to be satisfied in order to recognise an asset as held for sale in accordance with IFRS 5 *Non-Current Assets Held for Sale and Discontinued Operations*?**

A Asset is no longer in use

B Asset is being actively marketed

C Sale of the asset has been agreed

D The plan to sell the asset is unlikely to be withdrawn

E Asset is likely to be sold within twelve months

282 Identify whether the change in operations in countries A and B represent a discontinued operation in accordance with IFRS 5 *Non-Current Assets Held for Sale and Discontinued Operations*.

A Only country A represents a discontinued operation

B Only country B represents a discontinued operation

C Both countries will be regarded as discontinued operations

D Neither country will be regarded as a discontinued operation

283 At what value should the plant be held at 31 March 20X3 according to IFRS 5 *Non-Current Assets Held for Sale and Discontinued Operations?*

A $3,800,000

B $3,900,000

C $4,000,000

D $3,850,000

284 What provision should be recorded in relation to the office closure?

A $300,000

B $475,000

C $375,000

D $400,000

285 On 30 June 20X3, before the financial statements were authorised for issue, the plant was sold at a loss of $100,000 and the redundancies were settled at $50,000 more than expected.

Identify whether each item represents an adjusting or non-adjusting event according to IAS 10 Events After the Reporting Period

	Adjusting event	Non-adjusting event
Disposal of plant		
Redundancy settlement		

The following scenario relates to questions 286–290

Tunshill has an item of plant with an estimated five-year life. The plant is wearing well and at 1 October 20X8 the production manager believed that the plant was likely to last 5 more years.

Tunshill wishes to change its method of inventory valuation from first-in/first-out (FIFO) to average cost (AVCO). The value of Tunshill's inventory at 30 September 20X9 (on the FIFO basis) is $20 million. However, on the AVCO basis it would be valued at $18 million. Tunshill's inventory at 30 September 20X8 was $15 million, but on the AVCO basis it would have been reported as $13.4 million.

Tunshill also has two items of inventory that require review. Item A cost $50 per unit. Tunshill has struggled to sell the item and has 2,000 units still in inventory. Tunshill has agreed a contract with a distributor to sell the items for $55 each, but will charge commission of 20%.

Item B relates to a one-off purchase of rare metal for a profitable contract costing $80,000. No work has yet been done, but after further costs of $20,000 it will be converted into a product and sold for an agreed price of $150,000. Since buying the metal, the cost price has fallen to $50,000.

286 Which TWO circumstances are outlined in IAS 8 *Accounting Policies, Changes in Accounting Estimates and Errors* as acceptable reasons to change accounting policy?

A To provide greater comparison with competitors

B If a change results in providing more reliable and relevant information to users

C If required by an International Financial Reporting Standard

D If tax law in a country changes

E To show the best possible results for the investors

287 Fill in the blanks in the sentence below with the correct option.

The change in useful life of the plant will be a change in accounting ____________ and should be applied ______________.

Options: Policy, Estimate, Error, Retrospectively, Prospectively, Prudently

288 Which of the options below outline the correct treatment for the change in valuation method from FIFO to AVCO?

A Profit would be reduced by $400,000

B Profit would be reduced by $2,000,000

C Opening retained earnings would increase by $1,600,000

D Opening retained earnings would decrease by $400,000

289 At what value should item A be included in Tunshill's statement of financial position as at 30 September 20X9?

$______________,000

290 At what value should item B be included in Tunshill's statement of financial position as at 30 September 20X9?

A $50,000

B $80,000

C $130,000

D $100,000

The following scenario relates to questions 291–295

Schrute owns a herd of cattle, which produce milk. Schrute then turns this into cheese.

On 1 April 20X5, Shrute purchased a flock of sheep for $100,000, which included transaction costs of $5,000. At 31 March 20X6, the flock was valued at $120,000. Every time animals are sold there is a 5% commission fee payable to the national farming agency.

Shrute uses the historical cost model and charges all depreciation as an operating expense.

In addition to this, Schrute uses a number of items of specialised farm machinery. This machinery cost Schrute $200,000 on 1 April 20X2 and has a 10-year useful life. At 31 March 20X6, there is only one supplier who still sells this machinery and the current price of new machinery is $300,000.

---

291 Which of the following items held by Schrute will be accounted for under the provisions of IAS 41 *Agriculture*?

(i) Herd of cattle

(ii) Milk

(iii) Cheese

A (i) only

B (ii) and (iii) only

C (i) and (ii) only

D All three items

292 What gain should be taken to Shrute's statement of profit or loss for the year ended 31 March 20X6 in respect of the flock of sheep?

$____________

293 Using current cost accounting, what is the value of the machinery at 31 March 20X6?

A $120,000

B $180,000

C $200,000

D $300,000

294 At 31 March 20X6, a valuations expert informed the directors of Schrute that the property owned and used by Shrute for farming had significantly increased in value. This had been decided by looking at the price per square metre at similar properties in the area and concluded that this could be used to value Schrute's farm with no adjustments necessary.

Which of the following inputs within IFRS 13 *Fair Value Measurement* describes the method used to value the farm?

A Level 1 input

B Level 2 input

C Level 3 input

D Level 4 input

295 If Schrute chooses to value the farm at the market value, which TWO of the following ratios will NOT be affected?

A Current ratio

B Return on capital employed

C Gross profit margin

D Gearing

E Net profit (before tax) margin

The following scenario relates to questions 296–300

On 1 October 20X6 Fino entered into an agreement to lease twenty telephones for its team of sales staff. The telephones are to be leased for a period of 24 months at a cost of $240 per telephone per annum, payable annually in advance. The present value of the lease payments at 1 October 20X6 is $9,164.

On 1 April 20X7, Fino entered into an agreement to lease an item of plant from the manufacturer. The lease required four annual payments in advance of $100,000 each commencing on 1 April 20X7. The plant would have a useful life of four years and would be scrapped at the end of this period. The present value of the total lease payments is $350,000.

Fino has a cost of capital of 10%.

---

296 Which of the following applies the principle of faithful representation to the above plant lease agreement?

A Recording an annual rent expense in Fino's statement of profit or loss

B Expensing any interest on a straight-line basis over 4 years

C Recording an asset in Fino's statement of financial position to reflect control

D Record the $100,000 paid as a prepayment to be released over 4 years

297 How much would be charged to Fino's statement of profit or loss for the year ended 30 September 20X7 in respect of the telephones if Fino applied the exemption permitted under IFRS 16 *Leases*?

A $4,800

B $4,582

C $4,364

D $5,498

298 What would be the carrying amount of the right-of-use plant asset as at 30 September 20X7?

$__________

299 What interest would be charged to Fino's statement of profit or loss for the year ended 30 September 20X7 in respect of the plant lease?

A $12,500

B $25,000

C $17,500

D $35,000

300 Applying the principles of IFRS 16 *Leases* to capitalise the plant and recognise the lease liability would have what impact upon the following ratios?

	Increase	**Decrease**
Return on Capital Employed		
Gearing		
Interest cover		

The following scenario relates to questions 301–305

On 1 January 20X6 Lotso entered into an agreement to lease new machinery under a 5-year lease, with $300,000 payable on 31 December each year. The asset has a useful life of 6 years, and ownership transfers to Lotso at the end of the lease. The interest rate implicit in the lease is 6% and the present value of the lease payments is $1,263,000.

On 1 January 20X6 Lotso sold its head office to a finance company, but continued to use the head office for the remainder of its 20-year estimated useful life under a lease agreement. The carrying amount of the head office on 1 January 20X6 was $10 million and the fair value of the asset and sale proceeds received on 1 January 20X6 were $11.5 million.

301 What would be the finance cost in respect of the machinery lease for the year ended 31 December 20X6?

$____________

302 What current liability (to the nearest thousand) will be recorded in Lotso's statement of financial position as at 31 December 20X6 in relation to the machinery lease?

A $300,000

B $238,000

C $1,039,000

D $801,000

303 What is the carrying amount of the right-of-use machinery asset as at 31 December 20X6?

A $1,039,000

B $1,263,000

C $1,052,500

D $1,010,400

304 What would be the carrying amount of the head office at 31 December 20X6?

A Nil

B $9,500,000

C $8,075,000

D $10,925,000

305 Identify if the statements below are true or false

Statement 1: In a sale and leaseback transaction, no profit will be recognised by the lessee.

Statement 2: In a sale and leaseback transaction, the sale proceeds will usually be treated as a loan to the lessee.

	True	**False**
Statement 1		
Statement 2		

The following scenario relates to questions 306–310

On 1 September 20X3, Laidlaw factored (sold) $2 million of trade receivables to Finease. Laidlaw received an immediate payment of $1.8 million. Under the factoring agreement any receivables not collected after four months will be sold back to Laidlaw.

On 1 October 20X2, Laidlaw sold some maturing inventory which had a cost of $4.5 million to a bank for its fair value of $5 million. Under the terms of the sale agreement Laidlaw has the option to repurchase the inventory after a period of ten years at a price of $7.4 million. At this date the fair value of the inventory is expected to be $11 million, and the repurchase price reflects an equivalent annual rate of interest of 4%

Laidlaw issued $10 million convertible loan notes on 1 October 20X2 that carry a nominal (coupon) interest rate of 5% per annum, and are redeemable on 1 October 20X5. A similar loan note, without the conversion option, would have required Laidlaw to pay an interest rate of 8%.

Relevant discount rates are shown below:

		5%	8%
End of year	1	0.95	0.93
	2	0.91	0.86
	3	0.86	0.79

306 Which of the following is correct regarding Laidlaw's factoring of trade receivables for the year ended 30 September 20X3?

A $200,000 should be recorded as an administrative expense for the disposal of the receivables

B The receivables should be removed from the statement of financial position

C This represents a 'without recourse' factoring agreement

D The receipt of $1.8 million should be treated as a loan

307 What amount should be recorded in equity (to the nearest thousand) in respect of the convertible loan notes issued by Laidlaw?

$__________000

308 Which TWO of the following items should be recorded in Laidlaw's financial statements for the year ended 30 September 20X3 in respect of the maturing inventory sale?

A $200,000 finance cost

B $50,000 release of deferred income

C $5 million revenue

D $5.2 million loan

E $450,000 deferred income liability

F $500,000 gross profit

309 Which of the following statements regarding the convertible loan notes is NOT true?

A The convertible loan notes will affect gearing due to the liability component being different to the equity component

B The equity amount will remain fixed until the date of conversion

C The liability at 30 September 20X5 will be $10 million

D 5% interest will be charged to the statement of profit or loss as a finance cost

310 Applying the principle of split accounting to convertible loan notes is important to satisfy which of the following qualitative characteristics?

A Faithful representation

B Timeliness

C Verifiability

D Relevance

The following scenario relates to questions 311–315

The following trial balance extract relates to Howard at 30 September 20X5:

	$000	$000
Convertible loan notes – Liability component at 1 Oct X4 (note (i))		28,508
5% loan notes (note (ii))		10,000
Equity investments (note (iii))	6,000	

The following notes are relevant:

(i) The convertible loan notes are 8% $30 million convertible loan notes issued on 1 October 20X4 at par. An equivalent loan without the conversion would carry an interest rate of 10%. Howard's finance director correctly split the instrument into its equity and liability components at 1 October 20X4, but has done nothing else.

(ii) The 5% loan notes were issued at par of $10 million, but Howard incurred $400,000 issue costs. The loan notes have an effective interest rate of 8%.

(iii) The equity investments relate to 1 million shares in Kapoor, an unrelated entity. During the year, Kapoor paid a dividend of 10 cents per share. At 30 September 20X5 the fair value of each Kapoor share was $7.

311 Which of the items included in the trial balance extract will be classified as financial instruments?

A Convertible loan notes and equity investments only

B Loan notes and equity investments only

C Convertible loan notes and loan notes only

D All three items

312 What should the value of the liability element of the convertible loan note be at 30 September 20X5, to the nearest thousand?

A $28,508,000

B $28,389,000

C $28,959,000

D $30,000,000

313 What finance cost should be shown in the statement of profit or loss in respect of the loan notes?

$___________

314 What income should be recorded in the statement of profit or loss in relation to the equity investments?

A $600,000

B $1,100,000

C $1,600,000

D $1,000,000

315 Howard is uncertain of how to treat professional fees. For which of the following investments should professional fees be capitalised as part of initial value of the asset?

	Capitalised	**Not capitalised**
Fair value through other comprehensive income investments		
Fair value through profit or loss investments		
Amortised cost investments		

The following scenario relates to questions 316–320.

Sachi Co issued $2m 6% convertible loan notes on 1 April 20X2. The convertible loan notes are redeemable on 31 March 20X5 at par for cash or can be exchanged for equity shares in Sachi Co on that date. Similar loan notes without the conversion option carry an interest rate of 9%.

The following table provides information about discount rates:

	6%	9%
Year 1	0.943	0.917
Year 2	0.890	0.842
Year 3	0.840	0.772

On 1 April 20X3, Sachi Co purchased 50,000 $1 equity shares in Speedi Co at $4 per share, incurring transaction costs of $4,000. The intention is to hold the shares for trading. By 31 March 20X4 the shares are trading at $7 per share. In addition to the gain on investment, Sachi Co also received a dividend from Speedi Co during the year to 31 March 20X4.

316 In accordance with IAS 32 *Financial Instruments: Presentation*, which of the following describes an equity instrument?

A A contractual obligation to deliver cash or another financial asset to another entity

B A contract which is evidence of a residual interest in the assets of an entity after deducting all of its liabilities

C A contractual right to exchange financial instruments with another entity under potentially favourable conditions

D A contract which gives rise to both a financial asset of one entity and a financial liability of another

317 In accordance with IAS 32, how should the issue of the convertible loan notes be recognised in Sachi Co's financial statements?

A As debt. Interest should be charged at 6% because it cannot be assumed that loan note holders will choose the equity option

B As equity because the loan notes are convertible to equity shares

C As debt and equity because the convertible loan notes contain elements of both

D As debt. Interest should be charged at 9% to allow for the conversion of the loan notes

318 What amount in respect of the convertible loan notes will be shown under non-current liabilities in Sachi Co's statement of financial position as at 1 April 20X2 (to the nearest $000)?

A $2,000,000

B $1,848,000

C $1,544,000

D $2,701,000

319 In accordance with IFRS 9 Financial Instruments, at what amount will the Speedi Co shares be shown under 'investments in equity instruments' in Sachi Co's statement of financial position as at 31 March 20X4?

A $204,000

B $354,000

C $346,000

D $350,000

320 Where should the gain on the investment in Speedi Co and its dividend be recognised in Sachi Co's financial statements for the year ended 31 March 20X4?

A Both in profit or loss

B Gain on investment in other comprehensive income and the dividend in profit or loss

C Gain on investment in profit or loss and the dividend in other comprehensive income

D Both in other comprehensive income

The following scenario relates to questions 321–325.

The following is an extract from Diaz Co's trial balance as at 31 December 20X8:

	Debit	**Credit**
	$m	$m
Inventory at 31 December 20X8	8.6	
Trade receivables	6.2	
5% loan notes		9.0

The inventory count was completed on 31 December 20X8, but two issues have been noted. First, products with a sales value of $0.6m had been incorrectly excluded from the count. Second, items costing $0.2m which had been included in the count were damaged and could only be sold for 50% of the normal selling price. Diaz Co makes a mark-up of 50% on both of these items.

Diaz Co entered into a factoring agreement with Finaid Co on 31 December 20X8. In accordance with the agreement, Diaz Co sold trade receivables with a carrying amount of $6.2m to Finaid Co for $6m. Under the terms of the factoring agreement, after six months Finaid Co will return any unpaid receivables to Diaz Co for collection. Finaid Co will also charge Diaz Co a fee of 5% of any uncollected balances at the end of each month.

The 5% loan notes were issued for $9m on 1 July 20X8. Diaz Co incurred issue costs of $0.5m associated with this, which have been expensed within finance costs. The loan note interest is payable each 30 June and the loan note is repayable at a premium, giving them an effective interest rate of 8%.

---

321 In accordance with IAS 32 *Financial Instruments: Presentation*, which of the items in the trial balance would be classified as financial instruments?

A Closing inventory and trade receivables only

B 5% loan notes only

C Trade receivables and 5% loan notes only

D Closing inventory, trade receivables and 5% loan notes

322 What is the correct carrying amount of inventory to be recognised in Diaz Co's financial statements as at 31 December 20X8?

A $8.95m

B $9.0m

C $8.9m

D $9.15m

323 In an attempt to improve reported profit, the directors of Diaz Co want to change the valuation method of inventory from first in first out (FIFO) to an average cost method.

Which, if any, of the following statements regarding the potential change in inventory valuation is/are correct?

1 The change will represent a change in accounting estimate

2 The financial statements will be adjusted prospectively

A 1 only

B 2 only

C Both 1 and 2

D Neither 1 nor 2

324 Which of the following statements regarding the factoring arrangement is NOT true?

A $6m received should be recorded in the liabilities of Diaz Co at 31 December 20X8

B $0.2m should be expensed in Diaz Co's statement of profit or loss for the year ended 31 December 20X8

C A total of the 5% monthly fee should be expensed in Diaz Co's statement of profit or loss for the year ended 31 December 20X9

D The receivables will remain as an asset in the financial statements of Diaz Co at 31 December 20X8

325 In respect of the 5% loan notes, how much should be expensed within Diaz Co's statement of profit or loss for the year ended 31 December 20X8?

A $0.68m

B $0.45m

C $0.72m

D $0.34m

The following scenario relates to questions 326–330

Vance buys and sells goods in Kromits (Kr), but has a functional currency of dollars ($).

Vance purchased goods for Kr 10,000 on 1 September 20X1. At Vance's year end of 31 December 20X1 this amount remains unpaid.

Vance sold goods on 1 September 20X1 for Kr 60,000. On 1 October 20X1 Vance received Kr 30,000. The remaining Kr 30,000 is unpaid at 31 December 20X1.

Vance's assistant accountant estimated the tax expense for the year ended 31 December 20X1 at $43,000. However, he had ignored deferred tax. At 1 January 20X1 Vance had a deferred tax liability of $130,000. At 31 December 20X1 Vance had temporary taxable differences of $360,000. Vance pays tax at 25%. All movements in deferred tax are taken to the statement of profit or loss.

Relevant exchange rates are:

1 September	Kr10:$1
1 October	Kr10.5:$1
31 December	Kr8:$1
Average rate	Kr9:$1

326 What gain or loss should be recorded in the statement of profit or loss for the year ended 31 December 20X1 in relation to the payable recorded for the purchase of goods?

A Loss of $111

B Gain of $111

C Loss of $250

D Gain of $250

327 What gain or loss should be recorded in the statement of profit or loss for the year ended 31 December 20X1 in relation to the sale of goods?

A Loss of $607

B Gain of $607

C Loss of $893

D Gain of $893

328 Which of the statements below is/are true?

Statement 1: The inventory purchased on 1 October 20X1 should be retranslated at the closing rate if the goods remain in inventory at 31 December 20X1.

Statement 2: The foreign exchange gains will be added to the revenue for the year.

	True	**False**
Statement 1		
Statement 2		

329 What will be recorded as the tax expense in the statement of profit or loss for the year ended 31 December 20X7?

$__________

330 Vance's assistant accountant has discovered that there is a debit balance on the trial balance of $3,000 relating to the over/under-provision of tax from the prior year.

What impact will this have on Vance's current year financial statements?

A Increase the tax liability by $3,000 in the statement of financial position

B Decrease the tax liability by $3,000 in the statement of financial position

C Increase the tax expense by $3,000 in the statement of profit or loss

D Decrease the tax expense by $3,000 in the statement of profit or loss

---

The following scenario relates to questions 331–335

Bailey constructs buildings for customers that can take many years to complete. Bailey has three contracts in progress at 30 September 20X7, which are detailed below. All of the contracts below began in the current year.

	Contract 1	**Contract 2**	**Contract 3**
	$000	$000	$000
Price	10,000	8,000	4,000
Costs incurred to date	(6,000)	(4,000)	(500)
Costs to complete	(1,000)	(6,000)	(2,000)
Progress	80%	60%	25%
Amount billed to date	7,000	3,000	800

---

331 What revenue should be recorded (to the nearest thousand) in relation to contract 1?

$__________,000

332 What cost of sales should be recorded (to the nearest thousand) in relation to contract 2?

A $4,200,000

B $9,400,000

C $5,640,000

D $6,800,000

333 What should be recorded in the statement of financial position (to the nearest thousand) in relation to contract 3?

A Nil

B $200,000 contract liability

C $200,000 contract asset

D $500,000 contract asset

334 Bailey's assistant accountant is unsure about how to deal with a brand new contract where the progress and overall profit cannot yet be ascertained.

Which of the statements below is/are true?

Statement 1 – Where the progress and overall profit are unknown, no contract asset or liability can be recognised.

Statement 2 – Where the progress and overall profit are unknown, revenue should be recognised to the level of recoverable costs.

	True	**False**
Statement 1		
Statement 2		

335 Bailey's assistant has also enquired about changing the way of measuring the progress of contracts.

Complete the following to show how the change should be applied.

As a change in accounting ____________, applied ____________.

Options: prospectively, retrospectively, estimate, policy

The following scenario relates to questions 336–340

Creg sold and installed a large item of machinery for $800,000 on 1 November 20X7. Included within the price was a 2 year servicing contract which has a value of $240,000 and a fee for installation of $50,000.

Creg works as an agent for a number of smaller contractors, earning commission of 10%. Creg's revenue includes $6 million received from clients under these agreements with $5.4 million in cost of sales representing the amount paid to the contractors.

Creg sold a large number of vehicles to a new customer for $10 million on 1 July 20X7. The customer paid $990,000 up front and agreed to pay the remaining balance on 1 July 20X8. Creg has a cost of capital of 6%.

---

336 **How much should be recorded in Creg's revenue in its statement of profit or loss for the year ended 31 December 20X7 in relation to the large machinery sale?**

A $530,000

B $680,000

C $560,000

D $580,000

337 Creg's sales director is close to selling another large machine, offering free service, therefore selling the entire machine for $560,000. Creg never sells servicing separately.

How should this discount be applied in relation to the sale of the machinery?

Sales element	Discount applied	Discount not applied
Machine		
Installation		
Service		

338 What adjustment needs to be made to revenue in respect of the commission sales?

A Reduce revenue by $6 million

B Reduce revenue by $5.4 million

C Increase revenue by $600,000

D No adjustment is required

339 How much should initially be recorded in revenue in respect of the sale of vehicles in the statement of profit or loss for the year ended 31 December 20X7? Answer to the nearest $000.

$__________,000

340 On 31 December 20X7 Creg sold some maturing goods to a bank for $3 million. The estimated value of the goods at that date was $5 million, which is expected to keep rising. Creg keeps the goods on its premises and has the option to repurchase the goods on 31 December 20X9 for $3.63 million.

Which of the following outlines the correct treatment for the maturing inventory?

A Record a loss on disposal of $2 million in the statement of profit or loss

B Take $3 million to revenue, disclosing the repurchase option

C Leave the inventory in current assets, increasing in value as the goods mature

D Treat the $3 million as a loan with 10% compound interest accruing over the 2 years

The following scenario relates to questions 341–345

The profit after tax for Barstead for the year ended 30 September 20X7 was $15 million. At 1 October 20X6 Barstead had in issue 36 million equity shares. On 1 January 20X7 Barstead made a fully subscribed rights issue of one new share for every four shares held at a price of $2.80 each. The market price of the equity shares of Barstead immediately before the issue was $3.80.

The profit after tax for Cabott for the year ended 30 September 20X7 was $15 million. At 1 October 20X6 Cabott had in issue 43.25 million equity shares and a $10 million convertible loan note which has an effective interest rate of 8%. The loan note will mature in 20X8 and will be redeemed at par or converted to equity shares on the basis of 25 shares for each $100 of loan note at the loan-note holders' option. The loan interest is tax deductible. Cabott's tax rate is 25%.

The profit after tax for Dunstan for the year ended 30 September 20X7 was $12 million. On 1 October 20X6 Dunstan had 34 million shares in issue. On 1 February 20X7 Dunstan made a market issue of 3 million shares at full price. On 1 July 20X7 Dunstan made a bonus issue of one new share for every five shares held.

341 What is the basic earnings per share for Barstead for the year ended 30 September 20X7?

A 41.7¢

B 35.5¢

C 33.2¢

D 34.7¢

342 What is the diluted earnings per share for Cabott for the year ended 30 September 20X7?

A 34¢

B 35¢

C 36¢

D 33¢

343 What is the basic earnings per share for Dunstan for the year ended 30 September 20X7?

A 26¢

B 32¢

C 28¢

D 31¢

344 Which of the three companies will have to restate the prior year comparative earnings per share figure?

Company	Comparative restated	No restatement
Barstead		
Cabott		
Dunstan		

345 Which, if any, of the statements below regarding diluted earnings per share is/are correct?

Statement 1: Diluted earnings per share is a forecast of a future trend in profit, showing the expected earnings in the next period to improve the relevance of information for users.

Statement 2: Diluted earnings per share acts as a warning to shareholders and shows how the current earnings per share could fall based on items currently in existence.

	Correct	**Incorrect**
Statement 1		
Statement 2		

The following scenario relates to questions 346–350

On 7 January 20X5, Hermione was informed that it was being sued by an employee in respect of a workplace accident that took place in October 20X4. Legal advisors advise that Hermione is certain to lose the case. They have provided the following information:

Estimated pay-out	**Probability of payment occurring**
$1 million	30%
$2 million	60%
$3 million	10%

Hermione has sold 100,000 machines that are covered by a warranty agreement as at 31 December 20X4. If a machine develops a major fault then the average cost to Hermione of repairing it is $100. If a machine develops a minor fault then the average cost to Hermione of repairing it is $30. It is believed that 6% of the machines under warranty will develop major faults and that 8% will develop minor faults. The time value of money can be ignored.

On 15 December 20X4, the directors of Hermione decided to restructure the business and created a detailed and formal plan. On that date, an announcement was made to the employees who were informed that they would be made redundant in March 20X5. The directors estimate that the restructuring exercise will involve the following costs:

Type of cost	$m
Redundancy payments	1.2
Staff relocation	0.8
Investment in new systems	2.0

346 Which of the following are outlined in IAS 37 *Provisions, Contingent Liabilities and Contingent Assets* as criteria required for recognising a provision?

(i) An entity has a present obligation from a past event.

(ii) It is possible that an outflow of resources will be required.

(iii) A reliable estimate can be made of the amount of the obligation.

A (i), (ii) and (iii)

B (i) and (ii) only

C (i) and (iii) only

D (ii) and (iii) only

347 **What amount should be recognised as a provision in respect of the workplace accident claim in the year ended 31 December 20X4?**

A Nil

B $1.8 million

C $2 million

D $3 million

348 **What amount should be recognised as a warranty provision in the year ended 31 December 20X4?**

$________ ,000

349 **What amount should be recognised as a restructuring provision in the year ended 31 December 20X4?**

A $1.2 million

B $2.0 million

C $3.2 million

D $4.0 million

350 The following situations have arisen in the year ended 31 December 20X4:

Situation 1: A law was introduced in November 20X4 requiring Hermione to fit new smoke filters in its factory by February 20X5 at an estimated cost of $500,000. By the reporting date, Hermione had not fitted the smoke filters.

Situation 2: The management accountant of Hermione has reliably forecast an operating loss of $4 million for the year ended 31 December 20X5.

Which, if any, of the situations require a provision to be recognised?

	Provision	**No provision**
Situation 1		
Situation 2		

The following scenario relates to questions 351–355

Promoil's financial statements for the year ended 30 September 20X8 were authorised for issue by its directors on 6 November 20X8 and the Annual General Meeting will be held on 6 December 20X8.

On 1 October 20X7, Promoil acquired an oil platform at a cost of $30 million. The estimated cost of removing the platform at the end of the asset's life on 30 September 20Y7 will be $15 million. The present value of $1 in 10 years using Promoil's cost of capital of 8% is $0.46.

On 12 October 20X8 a fire destroyed Promoil's largest warehouse. The carrying amount of the warehouse was $10 million. Promoil expects to be able to recover $9 million from its insurers and its going concern is not in doubt.

A single class of inventory held at another warehouse was valued at its cost of $460,000 and sold for $280,000 on 10 October 20X8.

351 There is no legal obligation for Promoil to remove the oil platform, but Promoil has a published environmental policy which it has a history of honouring.

Which of the following is correct regarding Promoil's proposed accounting treatment?

A No provision should be recorded as there is no legal obligation

B Promoil should recognise a provision as there is a constructive obligation

C No provision should be made but a contingent liability should be recorded

D If Promoil make a provision, the present value of the costs will be expensed in the statement of profit or loss for the year to 30 September 20X8

352 **If Promoil makes the provision, what liability (to the nearest thousand) will be shown in its statement of financial position as at 30 September 20X8?**

$__________ ,000

353 **Select the correct category for the events listed below in relation to IAS 10 *Events After the Reporting Period.***

	Adjusting	Non-adjusting
Fire in the warehouse		
Sale of inventory		

354 On 18 November 20X8 the government announced tax changes which have the effect of increasing Promoil's deferred tax liability by $650,000 as at 30 September 20X8.

Which of the following is correct in respect of IAS 10 *Events After the Reporting Period* regarding the tax changes?

A This is a non-adjusting event and no disclosure is required

B This is an adjusting event

C This is neither an adjusting or non-adjusting event

D This is an adjusting event and the financial statements should be reissued

355 Promoil owns the whole of the equity share capital of its subsidiary Hamlet. Hamlet's statement of financial position includes a loan of $25 million that is repayable in five years' time. $15 million of this loan is secured on Hamlet's property and the remaining $10 million is guaranteed by Promoil in the event of a default by Hamlet. It is possible that Hamlet will be unable to repay the loan, but not likely.

How should this be treated in the financial statements of Promoil?

A A contingent liability

B A provision

C Not included in Promoil's financial statements

D A reduction to property, plant and equipment

The following scenario relates to questions 356–360.

Manda Co prepares its financial statements to 30 September each year. Manda Co's draft financial statements were finalised on 20 October 20X3. They were authorised for issue on 15 December 20X3 and the annual general meeting of shareholders took place on 23 December 20X3.

On 30 September 20X3, Manda Co moved out of one of its properties and put it up for sale. The property met the criteria as held for sale on 30 September 20X3. On 1 October 20X2, the property had a carrying amount of $2.6m and a remaining life of 20 years. The property is held under the revaluation model. The property was expected to sell for a gross amount of $2.5m with selling costs estimated at $50,000.

Manda Co decided to sell an item of plant during the year ended 30 September 20X3. On 1 October 20X2, the plant had a carrying amount of $490,000 and a remaining useful life of seven years. The plant met the held for sale criteria on 1 April 20X3. At 1 April 20X3, the plant had a fair value less costs to sell of $470,000, which had fallen to $465,000 at 30 September 20X3.

---

356 In accordance with IAS 10 Events after the Reporting Period, which of the following statements is/are CORRECT for Manda Co?

(1) All events which occur between 30 September 20X3 and 15 December 20X3 should be considered as events occurring after the reporting period

(2) An event which occurs between 30 September 20X3 and 15 December 20X3 and which provides evidence of a condition which existed at 30 September 20X3 should be considered as an adjusting event

A 1 only

B Both 1 and 2

C 2 only

D Neither 1 nor 2

357 In accordance with IAS 10, which of the following events would be classed as a non-adjusting event in Manda Co's financial statements for the year ended 30 September 20X3?

A During October 20X3, there was evidence of a permanent diminution in the carrying amount of a property held at 30 September 20X3

B On 1 December 20X3 the acquisition of a subsidiary was completed, following lengthy negotiations which began in September 20X3

C The sale of inventory during October 20X3 at a value less than its cost. This inventory was included in the financial statements at cost on 30 September 20X3

D The insolvency of a major customer during October 20X3, whose balance was included within receivables at 30 September 20X3

358 What is the total amount charged to Manda Co's profit or loss in respect of the property for the year ended 30 September 20X3?

A $130,000

B $180,000

C $150,000

D $100,000

359 In accordance with IFRS 5 Non-current Assets Held for Sale and Discontinued Operations, what is the carrying amount of the plant in Manda Co's statement of financial position as at 30 September 20X3?

A $420,000

B $470,000

C $455,000

D $465,000

360 Which of the following items should be classed as an asset held for sale under IFRS 5?

A Manda Co's head office building is to be demolished, at which point the land will be put up for sale. A number of prospective bidders have declared an interest and the land is expected to sell within a few months of the demolition.

B An item of plant was put up for sale at the start of the year for $500,000. Six parties have made a bid to Manda Co for the plant but none of these bids has been above $200,000.

C A chain of retail outlets are currently advertised for sale. Manda Co has provisionally accepted a bid, subject to surveys being completed. The surveys are not expected to highlight any problems. The outlets are currently empty.

D A brand name which Manda Co purchased in 20X2 is associated with the sale of potentially harmful products. Manda Co has decided to stop producing products under this brand, which is currently held within intangible assets.

The following scenario relates to questions 361–365.

Jeffers Co prepares financial statements for the year ended 31 December 20X8. The financial statements are expected to be authorised for issue on 15 March 20X9.

The following three events have occurred in January 20X9:

1 Health and safety fine

A health and safety investigation of an incident which occurred in 20X8 was concluded in January 20X9, resulting in a $1.5m fine for Jeffers Co. A provision for $1m had been recognised in Jeffers Co's financial statements for the year ended 31 December 20X8.

2 Customer ceased trading

Notice was received on 10 January 20X9 that a customer owing $1.2m at 31 December 20X8 had ceased trading. It is unlikely that the debt will be recovered in full.

3 Acquisition of a competitor

The acquisition of a competitor was finalised on 10 January 20X9, being the date Jeffers Co obtained control over the competitor. Negotiations in respect of the acquisition commenced in May 20X8.

In addition to this, there is an outstanding court case at 31 December 20X8 relating to faulty goods supplied by Jeffers Co. Legal advice states that there is a small chance that they will have to pay out $6m, but the most likely outcome is believed to be a payout of $5m. Either way, Jeffers Co will have to pay legal fees of $0.2m. All payments are expected to be made on 31 December 20X9. Jeffers Co has a cost of capital of 10% (discount factor 0.909).

Jeffers Co believes the fault lies with the supplier, and is pursuing a counter-claim. Legal advice states that it is possible, but not likely, that this action will succeed.

361 Which, if any, of the following statements regarding IAS *Events after the Reporting Period* 10 is/are correct?

1 'Events after the reporting period' are deemed to be all events from the date the financial statements are authorised for issue up until the date of the annual meeting with the shareholders

2 Non-adjusting events do not need to be reflected in any part of an entity's financial statements or annual report

A 1 only

B 2 only

C Both 1 and 2

D Neither 1 nor 2

362 Which of the three events which occurred in January 20X9 would be classified as adjusting events in accordance with IAS 10?

1 Health and safety fine

2 Customer ceased trading

3 Acquisition of a competitor

A 1 and 2 only

B 1 and 3 only

C 2 and 3 only

D 1, 2 and 3

363 What amount should be recorded as a provision in respect of the outstanding court case against Jeffers Co as at 31 December 20X8 (to the nearest hundred thousand)?

A $5.6m

B $5.5m

C $4.7m

D $4.5m

364 At 31 December 20X8, which of the following represents the correct accounting treatment of the counter-claim made by Jeffers Co against the supplier?

A Nothing is recognised or disclosed in the financial statements

B Disclose as a contingent asset

C Recognise a receivable from the supplier

D Net the possible counter-claim proceeds from the supplier against the provision for legal claim

365 In February 20X9, a major fire broke out in Jeffers Co's property and warehouse. Jeffers Co has no insurance, and now the management of the company believes it is unable to continue trading.

How should this be reflected in Jeffers Co's financial statements for the year ended 31 December 20X8?

A No adjustment should be made to the figures in the financial statements, however, this event must be disclosed in the notes

B The financial statements can no longer be prepared on a going concern basis

C No disclosure is required in the financial statements, however, this event must be reflected in the financial statements for the year ended 31 December 20X9

D The financial statements should continue to be prepared using the going concern basis, with an impairment loss recognised against the non-current assets

CONSOLIDATED FINANCIAL STATEMENTS

The following scenario relates to questions 366–370

On 1 April 20X4 Penfold acquired 80% of Superted's equity shares in a share for share exchange. Penfold issued 2 shares for every 5 acquired in Superted. Penfold's share price on 1 April 20X4 was $5.30. The share exchange has not yet been recorded.

Extracts from the individual financial statements of Penfold and Superted as at 30 September 20X4 are shown below.

	Penfold	**Superted**
	$000	$000
Property, plant and equipment	345,000	141,000
Trade receivables	32,400	38,000
Equity shares of $1 each	170,000	15,000
Other components of equity (share premium)	6,000	2,000

(i) During the year, Penfold traded with Superted, and had a payable of $6 million at 30 September 20X4. Superted's receivable balance differed from this due to a $2 million payment from Penfold not being received until October 20X4.

(ii) Penfold measures the non-controlling interest at fair value. At the date of acquisition this was $7.2 million.

(iii) Superted made a profit of $24 million for the year ended 30 September 20X4.

(iv) Penfold sold an item of plant to Superted on 1 April 20X4 for $25 million when its carrying amount was $20 million. It had a remaining useful life of 5 years at this date.

(v) Penfold also owns 30% of Arnold, an unrelated entity. Penfold are not able to appoint any members of the board of Arnold as the other 70% is held by another investor who is able to appoint all members of the board.

366 What will be reported as other components of equity on the consolidated statement of financial position as at 30 September 20X4?

A $31,440,000

B $26,640,000

C $28,640,000

D $33,440,000

367 What will be reported as receivables on the consolidated statement of financial position as at 30 September 20X4?

$____________,000

368 What will be reported as non-controlling interest on the consolidated statement of financial position as at 30 September 20X4?

A $9,700,000

B $9,500,000

C $7,200,000

D $9,600,000

369 What will be reported as property, plant and equipment on the consolidated statement of financial position as at 30 September 20X4?

$___________,000

370 How should the investment in Arnold be recorded in the consolidated statement of financial position of Penfold?

A A subsidiary

B An associate

C A financial instrument

D A contingent asset

The following scenario relates to questions 371–375.

On 1 October 20X4, Popper purchased 70% of the share capital of Stopper. Popper agreed to pay $6 million on 30 September 20X6. Popper has a cost of capital of 8%.

Extracts from the statements of profit or loss for the year ended 31 March 20X5 for both Popper and Stopper are shown below.

	Popper	Stopper
	$000	$000
Cost of sales	(319,200)	(176,400)
Operating expenses	(50,610)	(33,120)

The following notes are relevant:

(i) Since acquisition, Popper sold goods to Stopper totalling $1 million per month, making a margin of 20%. At the year end, Stopper held 30% of these goods.

(ii) On acquisition, Stopper's net assets were equal to their carrying amount, with the exception of Stopper's head office, which had a fair value of $4 million in excess of its carrying amount and a remaining life at acquisition of 20 years. All depreciation is charged to operating expenses.

(iii) At 31 March 20X5, goodwill is impaired by $600,000. Goodwill impairment is included within operating expenses. Popper measures the non-controlling interest using the fair value method.

---

371 What liability (to the nearest thousand) should be recorded in respect of the deferred consideration in Popper's consolidated statement of financial position as at 31 March 20X5?

$___________,000

372 What is the cost of sales figure to be included in the consolidated statement of profit or loss for the year ended 31 March 20X5?

A $402,600,000

B $401,760,000

C $395,760,000

D $396,400,000

373 What is the operating expenses figure to be included in the consolidated statement of profit or loss for the year ended 31 March 20X5?

A $67,970,000

B $67,670,000

C $67,570,000

D $67,870,000

374 Which of the items in the scenario would affect the profit attributable to the non-controlling interest?

A Notes (i) and (ii) only

B Notes (i) and (iii) only

C Notes (ii) and (iii) only

D Notes (i), (ii) and (iii)

375 Which, if any, of the following statements about fair values is/are correct?

Statement 1: Popper must include all of Stopper's assets, liabilities and contingent liabilities at fair value in the consolidated financial statements.

Statement 2: Professional fees associated with the acquisition of Stopper can be included within the goodwill because the non-controlling interest is measured at fair value.

	Correct	**Incorrect**
Statement 1		
Statement 2		

The following scenario relates to questions 376–380

On 1 January 20X5, Prunier acquired 80% of Sheringham's two million $1 ordinary shares. At this date, Sheringham had retained earnings of $4 million and a revaluation surplus of $2 million. Prunier had retained earnings of $10 million and a revaluation surplus of $5 million.

The fair value of Sheringham's net assets at acquisition were equal to their carrying amounts with the exception of Sheringham's property which had a fair value of $800,000 in excess of its carrying amount and a remaining life of 20 years.

At 31 December 20X5, Prunier and Sheringham both revalued their assets. Prunier's assets increased by a further $2 million while Sheringham's increased by $500,000. At this date, Prunier's retained earnings were $11 million and Sheringham's were $3.5 million.

376 What will the consolidated retained earnings be at 31 December 20X5?

A $11,432,000

B $10,560,000

C $11,368,000

D $10,568,000

377 What will be the other comprehensive income attributable to the parent for the year ended 31 December 20X5?

$__________,000

378 Identify whether or not the following items should be recognised as assets in the consolidated financial statements of Prunier.

	Recognised	**Not to be recognised**
Sheringham's brand name, which was internally generated so not shown in Sheringham's financial statements but has a fair value of $3 million		
A research project in progress, which was one of the main reasons Prunier purchased Sheringham and has a fair value of $2 million		
An intangible asset related to an encryption process which has now been deemed illegal. This is included within intangibles at $1.5 million		

379 Prunier has also owned 30% of Anderson for many years, and uses equity accounting to account for the investment. During the year Prunier sold $3 million of goods to Anderson at a mark-up of 20%. Anderson has a quarter of the goods left in inventory at the year end.

What is the value of the unrealised profit adjustment as at 31 December 20X5?

A $150,000

B $37,500

C $125,000

D $45,000

380 On 31 December 20X9, Prunier disposed of its entire holding of Sheringham for $9 million. At this date, the remaining goodwill was $1 million. The fair value of the non-controlling interest was $2.5 million and the fair value of the net assets (including the fair value adjustment) was $10.6 million.

What is the profit/loss on the disposal of Sheringham to be shown in the consolidated financial statements of Prunier?

A $100,000 loss on disposal

B $1,900,000 gain on disposal

C $5,100,000 loss on disposal

D $2,020,000 gain on disposal

INTERPRETATION OF FINANCIAL STATEMENTS

The following scenario relates to questions 381–385

LOP is looking to expand overseas by acquiring a new subsidiary.

Two geographical areas have been targeted, Frontland and Sideland.

Entity A operates in Frontland and entity B operates in Sideland. Both entities are listed on their local exchanges.

Figures for entities A, B and LOP are provided below for the last trading period.

	A	**B**	**LOP**
Revenue	\$160m	\$300m	\$500m
Gross profit margin	26%	17%	28%
Profit from operations margin	9%	11%	16%
Gearing	65%	30%	38%
Average rate of interest expensed in profit or loss	4%	9%	8%
Price/Earnings (P/E) ratio	11.6	15.9	16.3

381 Which of the following statements is a realistic conclusion that could be drawn from the above information?

A A appears to be benefiting from economies of scale.

B B has lower operating expenses than A.

C A has attracted a lower rate of interest on its borrowings than B because its gearing level would suggest that is a lower risk to lenders than B.

D Acquisition of either entity would lead to an improvement in LOP's gross margin due to the increased revenue that would be achieved.

382 Which TWO of the following statements are true, based on the information provided?

A A would be a riskier investment than B because it has higher gearing.

B A would give LOP greater benefit in terms of additional borrowing capacity.

C The market is more confident about the future performance of B than LOP.

D The market is more confident about the future performance of LOP than A or B.

E LOP's P/E ratio would definitely fall if it acquired either A or B.

383 Which of the following statements concerning the use of ratio analysis to make a decision about investing in A or B is FALSE?

A A and B may use different accounting standards when preparing their financial statements and this would reduce the comparability of their profit margins.

B A and B may target different types of customer, meaning that comparison between the two is difficult.

C A and B may apply different accounting policies, such as cost model v revaluation model for property, plant and equipment. This would reduce comparability of their gearing ratios.

D A and B are listed on different stock exchanges which reduces comparability of their P/E ratios.

384 If LOP acquired B, it has assessed that combining the two companies would lead to an overall saving in cost of sales of $5 million.

If this was taken into account, what would be the gross margin of LOP combined with B to one decimal place?

__________%

385 Your assistant has raised concerns about B, having heard that they may have treated lease payments as operating expenses instead of capitalising the right-of-use assets as required by IFRS 16 *Leases*.

Which, if any, of the following statements is/are true in relation to this?

Statement 1: If B has incorrectly treated the leases, gearing will be overstated.

Statement 2: If B has incorrectly treated the leases, the average rate of interest calculated could be inaccurate.

	Correct	**Incorrect**
Statement 1		
Statement 2		

The following scenario relates to questions 386–390

Key figures from Franck's financial statements for the year ended 30 September 20X2 are shown below.

	$000
Revenue	9,400
Profit from operations	1,500
Share capital	15,000
Retained earnings	3,000
Loans	2,000

Franck has operated in the computer software industry for many years, gaining a reputation for steady growth. It is interested in acquiring Duik, which has recently been put up for sale. Extracts from Duik's financial statements can be seen below.

	$000
Revenue	1,200
Loss from operations	(600)
Share capital	24,000
Retained losses	(1,200)
Loans	4,000

386 Calculate Franck's return on capital employed (based on profit from operations) without the acquisition of Duik to one decimal place.

__________%

387 What is the combined operating margin if Franck and Duik are combined?

A 9.6%

B 19.8%

C 14.2%

D 8.5%

388 Which, if any, of the following statements is/are correct?

Statement 1: If Duik is acquired, gearing will increase.

Statement 2: If Duik is acquired, return on capital employed will decrease.

	Correct	**Incorrect**
Statement 1		
Statement 2		

389 Which of the following is NOT a factor to consider in respect of Duik being a subsidiary of another entity?

A Sales or purchases between the parent and Duik may not be at market rates

B Duik may get the benefit of shared assets with the parent

C Duik's individual financial statements may contain errors

D Loans made from Duik's parent may carry lower interest than market rates

390 What other information is NOT likely to be available to Franck before entering into negotiations for the acquisition of Duik?

A A breakdown of dividends paid by Duik historically

B Duik's statement of cash flows

C A breakdown of Duik's upcoming projects which are in progress

D The directors' report outlining the performance for the year

STATEMENT OF CASH FLOWS

The following scenario relates to questions 391–395

The assistant accountant of Cooper has started work on the statement of cash flows for the year ended 31 December 20X8, completing a draft of the cash generated from operations as shown below.

	$000
Profit from operations	3,500
Depreciation	4,600
Release of government grant	1,400
Profit on disposal of property	(3,700)
Increase in inventories	(400)
Decrease in trade and other receivables	(300)
Increase in trade and other payables	900
Cash generated from operations	**13,400**

In addition to this, the assistant has seen that the balance of property was $39.5 million at 1 January 20X8 and $29 million at 31 December 20X8. There were no additions of property in the year.

There was also a deferred income balance relating to government grants of $6 million at 1 January 20X8. The closing deferred income balance was $8 million.

391 What method has Cooper's assistant accountant used to calculate the cash generated from operations?

A Classification by function

B Classification by nature

C Indirect method

D Direct method

392 In relation to the calculation of cash generated from operations, select the TWO cells which contain errors made by the assistant.

	$000
Profit from operations	3,500
Depreciation	4,600
Release of government grant	1,400
Profit on disposal of property	(3,700)
Increase in inventories	(400)
Decrease in trade and other receivables	(300)
Increase in trade and other payables	900
Cash generated from operations	6,000

393 How much would be recorded in Cooper's statement of cash flows in relation to the sale of property?

A $9,600,000

B $2,200,000

C $3,700,000

D $5,900,000

394 What will be recorded as the receipt of government grants in the year?

$__________,000

395 Cooper's assistant accountant has been studying statements of cash flows and is unsure whether the information contained in the study material is true.

Which, if any, of the following statements is/are true?

Statement 1: Intangible assets will have no impact on the statement of cash flow as they have no physical substance.

Statement 2: A rights issue of shares will increase the cash flows from financing activities.

A Statement 1 is correct

B Statement 2 is correct

C Both statements are correct

D Neither statement is correct

The following scenario relates to questions 396–400

Extracts from Depay's financial statements for the year ended 30 September 20X2 are shown below.

Statement of profit or loss extract:	$000
Finance costs	(60)
Profit before tax	142
Income tax expense	(57)
Profit for the year	85

Statement of financial position extract:	**20X2**	**20X1**
	$000	$000
Retained earnings	900	940
5% loan notes	515	500
Deferred tax liability	150	125
Tax payable	30	40
Lease liabilities	300	310

The following information is relevant:

(i) Depay disposed of some land during the year, which had a remaining revaluation surplus at disposal of $20,000.

(ii) $40,000 of the finance costs relate to the loan notes which are repayable at a premium, making the effective rate of interest 8%. The remaining interest relates to the lease liabilities.

(iii) During the year, Depay received a dividend from a subsidiary.

(iv) Depay acquired $70,000 of new assets under lease agreements during the year. Depay makes annual payments under leases on 30 September each year.

---

396 What will be recorded in Depay's statement of cash flows under dividends paid?

A $145,000

B $105,000

C $40,000

D $125,000

397 What will be recorded in Depay's statement of cash flows under interest paid?

A $20,000

B $25,000

C $45,000

D $60,000

398 What will be recorded in Depay's statement of cash flows under tax paid?

$__________

399 Where should the dividend received be shown in Depay's statement of cash flows?

A Operating activities

B Investing activities

C Financing activities

D It should not be recorded

400 How much should be shown within financing activities in respect of lease liabilities repaid?

$__________

Section 3

CONSTRUCTED RESPONSE QUESTIONS – SECTION C

Please note that the following icons will be used in this section

💻 = word processing
▦ = spreadsheet

PREPARATION OF SINGLE ENTITY FINANCIAL STATEMENTS

401 PRICEWELL

The following trial balance relates to Pricewell at 31 March 20X9:

	$000	$000
Leasehold property – at valuation 31 March 20X8 (note (1))	25,200	
Plant and equipment (owned) – at cost (note (1))	46,800	
Right-of-use assets – at cost (note (1))	20,000	
Accumulated depreciation at 31 March 20X8:		
Owned plant and equipment		12,800
Right-of-use plant		5,000
Lease payment (paid on 31 March 20X9) (note (1))	6,000	
Lease liability at 1 April 20X8 (note (1))		15,600
Contract with customer (note (2))	14,300	
Inventory at 31 March 20X9	28,200	
Trade receivables	33,100	
Bank	5,500	
Trade payables		33,400
Revenue (note (3))		310,000
Cost of sales (note (3))	234,500	
Distribution costs	19,500	
Administrative expenses	27,500	
Equity dividend paid	8,000	
Equity shares of 50 cents each		40,000
Retained earnings at 31 March 20X8		44,100
Current tax (note (4))	700	
Deferred tax (note (4))		8,400
	469,300	469,300

The following notes are relevant:

(1) **Non-current assets:**

The 15-year leasehold property was acquired on 1 April 20X7 at a cost of $30 million. The accounting policy is to revalue the property at fair value at each year end. The valuation in the trial balance of $25.2 million as at 31 March 20X8 led to an impairment charge of $2.8 million which was reported in the statement of profit or loss and other comprehensive income in the year ended 31 March 20X8. At 31 March 20X9 the property was valued at $24.9 million.

Owned plant is depreciated at 25% per annum using the reducing balance method.

The right-of-use plant was acquired on 1 April 20X7. The rentals are $6 million per annum for four years payable in arrears on 31 March each year. The interest rate implicit in the lease is 8% per annum. Right-of-use plant is depreciated over the lease period.

No depreciation has yet been charged on any non-current assets for the year ended 31 March 20X9. All depreciation is charged to cost of sales.

(2) On 1 October 20X8 Pricewell entered into a contract to construct a bridge over a river. The performance obligation will be satisfied over time. The agreed price of the bridge is $50 million and construction was expected to be completed on 30 September 20Y0. The $14.3 million in the trial balance is:

	$000
Materials, labour and overheads	12,000
Specialist plant acquired 1 October 20X8	8,000
Payment from customer	(5,700)
	14,300

The sales value of the work done at 31 March 20X9 has been agreed at $22 million and the estimated cost to complete (excluding plant depreciation) is $10 million. The specialist plant will have no residual value at the end of the contract and should be depreciated on a monthly basis. Pricewell recognises progress towards satisfaction of the performance obligation on the outputs basis as determined by the agreed work to date compared to the total contract price.

(3) Pricewell's revenue includes $8 million for goods it sold acting as an agent for Trilby. Pricewell earned a commission of 20% on these sales and remitted the difference of $6.4 million (included in cost of sales) to Trilby.

(4) The directors have estimated the provision for income tax for the year ended 31 March 20X9 at $4.5 million. The required deferred tax provision at 31 March 20X9 is $5.6 million. All adjustments to deferred tax should be taken to the statement of profit or loss. The balance of current tax in the trial balance represents the under/over provision of the income tax liability for the year ended 31 March 20X8.

Required:

(a) Prepare the statement of profit or loss and other comprehensive income for the year ended 31 March 20X9. (10 marks)

(b) Prepare the statement of financial position as at 31 March 20X9. (10 marks)

Note: A statement of changes in equity and notes to the financial statements are not required.

(Total: 20 marks)

402 KEYSTONE

The following trial balance relates to Keystone at 30 September 20X1:

	$000	$000
Revenue		377,600
Material purchases (note (1))	64,000	
Production labour (note (1))	124,000	
Factory overheads (note (1))	80,000	
Distribution costs	14,200	
Administrative expenses (note (2))	46,400	
Finance costs	350	
Investment income		800
Property – at cost (note (1))	50,000	
Plant and equipment – at cost (note (1))	44,500	
Accumulated amortisation/depreciation at 1 October 20X0		
– property		10,000
– plant and equipment		14,500
Inventory at 1 October 20X0	46,700	
Trade receivables	31,150	
Trade payables		27,800
Bank		2,300
Equity shares of 20 cents each		50,000
Retained earnings at 1 October 20X0		15,600
Deferred tax (note (4))		2,700
	501,300	501,300

The following notes are relevant:

(1) During the year Keystone manufactured an item of plant for its own use. The direct materials and labour were $3 million and $4 million respectively. Production overheads are 75% of direct labour cost and Keystone determines the final selling price for goods by adding a mark-up on total cost of 40%. These manufacturing costs are included in the relevant expense items in the trial balance. The plant was completed and put into immediate use on 1 April 20X1.

All plant and equipment is depreciated at 20% per annum using the reducing balance method with time apportionment in the year of acquisition.

The directors decided to revalue the property in line with recent increases in market values. On 1 October 20X0 an independent surveyor valued the property at $48 million, which the directors have accepted. The property was being amortised over an original life of 20 years which has not changed. Keystone does not make a transfer to retained earnings in respect of excess amortisation. The revaluation gain will create a deferred tax liability (see note (4)).

All depreciation and amortisation is charged to cost of sales. No depreciation or amortisation has yet been charged on any non-current asset for the year ended 30 September 20X1.

(2) On 15 August 20X1, Keystone's share price stood at $2.40 per share. On this date Keystone paid a dividend (included in administrative expenses) that was calculated to give a dividend yield of 4%.

(3) The inventory at 30 September 20X1 was valued at $56.6 million.

(4) A provision for income tax for the year ended 30 September 20X1 of $24.3 million is required. At 30 September 20X1, the tax base of Keystone's net assets was $15 million less than their carrying amounts. This excludes the effects of the revaluation of the leased property. The income tax rate of Keystone is 30%.

Required:

(a) Prepare the statement of profit or loss and other comprehensive income for Keystone for the year ended 30 September 20X1. (12 marks)

(b) Prepare the statement of financial position for Keystone as at 30 September 20X1. (8 marks)

A statement of changes in equity is not required.

(Total: 20 marks)

403 FRESCO

The following trial balance **extract** relates to Fresco at 31 March 20X2:

	$000	$000
Equity shares of 50 cents each (note (1))		45,000
Share premium (note (1))		5,000
Retained earnings at 1 April 20X1		5,100
Equity financial asset investments (note (5))	6,000	
Leased property (12 years) – at cost (note (2))	48,000	
Plant and equipment – at cost (note (2))	47,500	
Accumulated amortisation of leased property at 1 April 20X1		16,000
Accumulated depreciation of plant and equipment at 1 April 20X1		33,500
Deferred tax (note (4))		3,200
Revenue		350,000
Cost of sales	298,700	
Lease payments (note (2))	8,000	
Distribution costs	16,100	
Administrative expenses	26,900	
Bank interest	300	
Current tax (note (4))	800	
Suspense account (note (1))		13,500

The following notes are relevant:

(1) The suspense account represents the corresponding credit for cash received for a fully subscribed rights issue of equity shares made on 1 January 20X2. The terms of the share issue were one new share for every five held at a price of 75 cents each.

(2) Non-current assets:

To reflect a marked increase in property prices, Fresco decided to revalue its leased property on 1 April 20X1. The directors accepted the report of an independent surveyor who valued the leased property at $36 million on that date. Fresco has not yet recorded the revaluation. The remaining life of the leased property is eight years at the date of the revaluation. Fresco makes an annual transfer to retained profits to reflect the realisation of the revaluation surplus. In Fresco's tax jurisdiction the revaluation does not give rise to a deferred tax liability.

On 1 April 20X1, Fresco acquired an item of plant under a lease agreement that had an implicit finance cost of 10% per annum. The lease payments in the trial balance represent an initial deposit of $2 million paid on 1 April 20X1 and the first annual rental of $6 million paid on 31 March 20X2. The lease agreement requires further annual payments of $6 million on 31 March each year for the next four years. The present value of the lease payments, excluding the initial deposit, was $23 million.

Plant and equipment (other than the leased plant) is depreciated at 20% per annum using the reducing balance method.

No depreciation or amortisation has yet been charged on any non-current asset for the year ended 31 March 20X2. Depreciation and amortisation are charged to cost of sales.

(3) In March 20X2, Fresco's internal audit department discovered a fraud committed by the credit controller who did not return from a foreign business trip. The outcome of the fraud is that $4 million of the trade receivables have been stolen by the credit controller and are not recoverable. Of this amount, $1 million relates to the year ended 31 March 20X1 and the remainder to the current year. Fresco is not insured against this fraud.

(4) Fresco's income tax calculation for the year ended 31 March 20X2 shows a tax refund of $2.4 million. The balance on current tax in the trial balance represents the under/over provision of the tax liability for the year ended 31 March 20X1. At 31 March 20X2, Fresco had taxable temporary differences of $12 million requiring a deferred tax liability. The income tax rate of Fresco is 25%.

(5) The investments had a fair value of $7.2 million as at 31 March 20X2. There were no acquisitions or disposals of these investments during the year ended 31 March 20X2.

Required:

(a) Prepare the statement of profit or loss and other comprehensive income for Fresco for the year ended 31 March 20X2. (13 marks)

(b) Prepare the statement of changes in equity for Fresco for the year ended 31 March 20X2. (7 marks)

(Total: 20 marks)

404 QUINCY

The following trial balance relates to Quincy as at 30 September 20X2:

	$000	$000
Revenue (note (1))		213,500
Cost of sales	136,800	
Distribution costs	12,500	
Administrative expenses (note (2))	19,000	
Loan note interest (note (2))	1,500	
Dividend paid	19,200	
Investment income		400
Equity shares of 25 cents each		60,000
6% loan note (note (2))		25,000
Retained earnings at 1 October 20X1		6,500
Plant and equipment at cost (note (3))	83,700	
Accumulated depreciation at 1 October 20X1: plant and equipment		33,700
Equity financial asset investments (note (4))	17,000	
Inventory at 30 September 20X2	24,800	
Trade receivables	28,500	
Bank	2,900	
Current tax (note (5))	1,100	
Deferred tax (note (5))		1,200
Trade payables		6,700
	347,000	347,000

The following notes are relevant:

(1) On 1 October 20X1, Quincy sold one of its products for $10 million (included in revenue in the trial balance). As part of the sale agreement, Quincy is committed to the ongoing servicing of this product until 30 September 20X4 (i.e. three years from the date of sale). The value of this service has been included in the selling price of $10 million. The estimated cost to Quincy of the servicing is $600,000 per annum and Quincy's normal gross profit margin on this type of servicing is 25%. The service performance obligation will be satisfied over time. Ignore discounting.

(2) Quincy issued a $25 million 6% loan note on 1 October 20X1. Issue costs were $1 million and these have been charged to administrative expenses. The loan will be redeemed on 30 September 20X4 at a premium which gives an effective interest rate on the loan of 8%.

(3) Plant and equipment is depreciated at 15% per annum using the reducing balance method.

No depreciation has yet been charged for the year ended 30 September 20X2. All depreciation is charged to cost of sales.

(4) The investments had a fair value of $15.7 million as at 30 September 20X2. There were no acquisitions or disposals of these investments during the year ended 30 September 20X2.

(5) The balance on current tax represents the under/over provision of the tax liability for the year ended 30 September 20X1. A provision for income tax for the year ended 30 September 20X2 of $7.4 million is required. At 30 September 20X2, Quincy had taxable temporary differences of $5 million, requiring a provision for deferred tax. Any deferred tax adjustment should be reported in the statement of profit or loss. The income tax rate of Quincy is 20%.

Required:

(a) Prepare the statement of profit or loss and other comprehensive income for Quincy for the year ended 30 September 20X2. (10 marks)

(b) Prepare the statement of financial position for Quincy as at 30 September 20X2.

(10 marks)

Notes to the financial statements are not required.

(Total: 20 marks)

405 ATLAS

The following trial balance relates to Atlas at 31 March 20X3:

	$000	$000
Equity shares of 50 cents each		50,000
Retained earnings at 1 April 20X2		11,200
Land and buildings – at cost (land $10 million) (note (2))	60,000	
Plant and equipment – at cost (note (2))	94,500	
Accumulated depreciation at 1 April 20X2: – buildings		20,000
– plant and equipment		24,500
Inventory at 31 March 20X3	43,700	
Trade receivables	42,200	
Bank		6,800
Deferred tax (note (4))		6,200
Trade payables		35,100
Revenue (note (1))		550,000
Cost of sales	411,500	
Distribution costs	21,500	
Administrative expenses	30,900	
Bank interest	700	
Current tax (note (4))		1,200
	705,000	705,000

The following notes are relevant:

(1) Revenue includes the sale of $10 million of maturing inventory made to Xpede on 1 October 20X2. The cost of the goods at the date of sale was $7 million and Atlas has an option to repurchase these goods at any time within three years of the sale at a price of $10 million plus accrued interest from the date of sale at 10% per annum. At 31 March 20X3 the option had not been exercised, but it is highly likely that it will be before the date it lapses.

(2) Non-current assets:

On 1 October 20X2, Atlas terminated the production of one of its product lines. From this date, the plant used to manufacture the product has been actively marketed at an advertised price of $4.2 million which is considered realistic. It is included in the trial balance at a cost of $9 million with accumulated depreciation (at 1 April 20X2) of $5 million.

On 1 April 20X2, the directors of Atlas decided that the financial statements would show an improved position if the land and buildings were revalued to market value. At that date, an independent valuer valued the land at $12 million and the buildings at $35 million and these valuations were accepted by the directors. The remaining life of the buildings at that date was 14 years. Atlas does not make a transfer to retained earnings for excess depreciation. Ignore deferred tax on the revaluation surplus.

Plant and equipment is depreciated at 20% per annum using the reducing balance method and time apportioned as appropriate.

All depreciation is charged to cost of sales, but none has yet been charged on any non-current asset for the year ended 31 March 20X3.

(3) At 31 March 20X3, a provision is required for directors' bonuses equal to 1% of revenue for the year.

(4) Atlas estimates that an income tax provision of $27.2 million is required for the year ended 31 March 20X3 and at that date the liability to deferred tax is $9.4 million. The movement on deferred tax should be taken to profit or loss. The balance on current tax in the trial balance represents the under/over provision of the tax liability for the year ended 31 March 20X2.

Required:

(1) Prepare the statement of profit or loss and other comprehensive income for Atlas for the year ended 31 March 20X3. (9 marks)

(2) Prepare the statement of financial position of Atlas as at 31 March 20X3. (11 marks)

Notes to the financial statements and a statement of changes in equity are not required.

(Total: 20 marks)

406 MOBY

Answer debrief

After preparing a draft statement of profit or loss for the year ended 30 September 20X3 and adding the year's profit (before any adjustments required by notes (1) to (5) below) to retained earnings, the summarised trial balance of Moby as 30 September 20X3 is:

	$000	$000
Contract to construct asset (note (1))	1,000	
Lease rental paid on 30 September 20X3 (note (2))	9,200	
Land ($12 million) and building ($48 million) at cost (note (2))	60,000	
Leased plant at initial carrying amount (note (2))	35,000	
Accumulated depreciation at 1 October 20X2:		
building		10,000
leased plant		7,000
Inventory at 30 September 20X3	56,600	
Trade receivables	38,500	
Bank		7,300
Insurance provision (note (3))		150
Deferred tax (note (4))		8,000
Lease liability at 1 October 20X2 (note (2))		29,300
Trade payables		18,300
Equity shares of $1 each		27,000
Loan note (note (5))		40,000
Retained earnings at 30 September 20X3		53,250
	200,300	200,300

The following notes are relevant:

(1) During the year, Moby entered into a contract to construct an asset for a customer. The performance obligation is satisfied over time. The balance in the trial balance represents:

Cost incurred to date	$8 million
Value of contract billed and cash received	$7 million

The contract commenced on 1 October 20X2 and is for a fixed price of $25 million. The costs to complete the contract at 30 September 20X3 are estimated at $12 million. Moby's policy is to measure progress based on the work certified as a percentage of the contract price. The value of work certified at 30 September 20X3 is $10 million.

(2) Non-current assets:

Moby decided to revalue its land and building, for the first time, on 1 October 20X2. A qualified valuer determined the relevant revalued amounts to be $16 million for the land and $38.4 million for the building. The building's remaining life at the date of the revaluation was 16 years. This revaluation has not yet been reflected in the trial balance figures. Moby does not make a transfer from the revaluation surplus to retained earnings in respect of the realisation of the revaluation surplus. Deferred tax is applicable to the revaluation surplus at 25%.

The leased plant was acquired on 1 October 20X1 under a five-year lease which has an implicit interest rate of 10% per annum. The rentals are $9.2 million per annum payable on 30 September each year.

No depreciation has yet been charged on any non-current asset for the year ended 30 September 20X3. All depreciation is charged to cost of sales.

(3) On 1 October 20X2, Moby received a renewal quote of $400,000 from their property insurer. The directors were surprised at how much it had increased and believed it would be less expensive to 'self-insure'. Accordingly, they charged $400,000 to operating expenses and credited the same amount to the insurance provision. During the year expenses of $250,000 were incurred, relating to previously insured property damage which Moby has debited to the provision.

(4) A provision for income tax for the year ended 30 September 20X3 of $3.4 million is required. At 30 September 20X3, the tax base of Moby's net assets was $24 million less than their carrying amounts. This does not include the effect of the revaluation in note (2) above. The income tax rate of Moby is 25%.

(5) The $40 million loan note was issued at par on 1 October 20X2. No interest will be paid on the loan. However, it will be redeemed on 30 September 20X5 for $53,240,000 which gives an effective finance cost of 10% per annum.

Required:

(a) Prepare a schedule of adjustments required to the retained earnings of Moby as at 30 September 20X3 as a result of the information in notes (1) to (5) above.

(8 marks)

(b) Prepare the statement of financial position for Moby as at 30 September 20X3.

(12 marks)

Note: A statement of changes in equity and notes to the financial statements are not required.

(Total: 20 marks) ⊞

407 XTOL

The following trial balance relates to Xtol at 31 March 20X4:

	$000	$000
Revenue		490,000
Cost of sales	290,600	
Operating costs	70,300	
Loan note interest (note (2))	2,500	
Bank interest	900	
Plant and equipment at cost (note (1))	155,500	
Accumulated depreciation at 1 April 20X3:		
plant and equipment		43,500
Inventory at 31 March 20X4	96,000	
Trade receivables	103,000	
Trade payables		32,200
Bank		5,500
Equity shares of $1 each (note (4))		66,000
Share premium (note (4))		15,000
Retained earnings at 1 April 20X3		15,200
5% convertible loan note (note (2))		50,000
Current tax (note (3))	3,200	
Deferred tax (note (3))		4,600
	722,000	722,000

The following notes are relevant:

(1) Plant and equipment is depreciated at 12½% per annum on the reducing balance basis. All amortisation/depreciation of non-current assets is charged to cost of sales.

(2) On 1 April 20X3, Xtol issued a 5% $50 million convertible loan note at par. Interest is payable annually in arrears on 31 March each year. The loan note is redeemable at par or convertible into equity shares at the option of the loan note holders on 31 March 20X6. The interest on an equivalent loan note without the conversion rights would be 8% per annum.

The present values of $1 receivable at the end of each year, based on discount rates of 5% and 8%, are:

	5%	8%
End of year 1	0.95	0.93
2	0.91	0.86
3	0.86	0.79

(3) The balance on current tax represents the under/over provision of the tax liability for the year ended 31 March 20X3. A provision of $28 million is required for current tax for the year ended 31 March 20X4 and at this date the deferred tax liability was assessed at $8.3 million.

(4) The equity shares and share premium balances in the trial balance above include a fully subscribed 1 for 5 rights issue at $1.60 per share which was made by Xtol on 1 October 20X3. The market value of Xtol's shares was $2.50 on 1 October 20X3.

Required:

(a) Prepare Xtol's statement of profit or loss for the year ended 31 March 20X4. (6 marks)

(b) Prepare the statement of financial position for Xtol as at 31 March 20X4. (9 marks)

(c) Calculate the basic earnings per share of Xtol for the year ended 31 March 20X4.

(5 marks)

Note: Answers and workings (for parts (a) to (b)) should be presented to the nearest $000. A statement of changes in equity is not required.

(Total: 20 marks)

408 DUNE

The following trial balance relates to Dune at 31 March 20X4:

	$000	$000
Equity shares of $1 each		40,000
Other components of equity		20,000
5% loan note (note (1))		20,000
Retained earnings at 1 April 20X3		38,400
Leasehold (15 years) property – at cost (note (2))	45,000	
Plant and equipment – at cost (note (2))	67,500	
Accumulated depreciation – 1 April 20X3 – leasehold property		6,000
– plant and equipment		23,500
Investments at fair value through profit or loss (note (3))	26,500	
Inventory at 31 March 20X4	48,000	
Trade receivables	40,700	
Bank	15,500	
Deferred tax (note (4))		6,000
Trade payables		52,000
Revenue		400,000
Cost of sales	294,000	
Distribution costs	26,400	
Administrative expenses (note (1))	34,200	
Dividend paid	10,000	
Loan note interest paid (six months)	500	
Bank interest	200	
Investment income		1,200
Current tax (note (4))		1,400
	608,500	608,500

The following notes are relevant:

(1) The 5% loan note was issued on 1 April 20X3 at its nominal (face) value of $20 million. The direct costs of the issue were $500,000 and these have been charged to administrative expenses. The loan note will be redeemed on 31 March 20X6 at a substantial premium. The effective finance cost of the loan note is 10% per annum.

(2) Non-current assets:

In order to fund a new project, on 1 October 20X3 Dune decided to sell its leasehold property. From that date it commenced a short-term rental of an equivalent property. The leasehold property is being marketed by a property agent at a price of $40 million, which was considered a reasonably achievable price at that date. The expected costs to sell have been agreed at $500,000. Recent market transactions suggest that actual selling prices achieved for this type of property in the current market conditions are 15% less than the value at which they are marketed. At 31 March 20X4 the property had not been sold.

Plant and equipment is depreciated at 15% per annum using the reducing balance method.

No depreciation/amortisation has yet been charged on any non-current asset for the year ended 31 March 20X4. Depreciation, amortisation and impairment charges are all charged to cost of sales.

(3) The investments at fair value through profit or loss had a fair value of $28 million on 31 March 20X4. There were no purchases or disposals of any of these investments during the year.

(4) A provision for income tax for the year ended 31 March 20X4 of $12 million is required. The balance on current tax represents the under/over provision of the tax liability for the year ended 31 March 20X3. At 31 March 20X4 the tax base of Dune's net assets was $14 million less than their carrying amounts. The income tax rate of Dune is 30%.

(5) Dune has accounted for a fully subscribed rights issue of equity shares made on 1 January 20X4 of one new share for every four in issue at 42 cents each, when the market value of a Dune share was 82 cents.

Required:

(a) Prepare the statement of profit or loss for Dune for the year ended 31 March 20X4, and the statement of financial position for Dune as at 31 March 20X4.

Notes to the financial statements and a statement of changes in equity are not required. (15 marks)

(b) Using the information in note (5), calculate earnings per share for Dune for the year ended 31 March 20X4. Also, calculate the re-stated figure for 20X3 if the EPS figure in the original 20X3 financial statements was 68¢ per share. (5 marks)

(Total: 20 marks)

409 KANDY

Answer debrief: calculate your allowed time, allocate the time to the separate parts

After preparing a draft statement of profit or loss for the year ended 30 September 20X4 and adding the year's profit (before any adjustments required by notes (1) to (3) below) to retained earnings, the summarised trial balance of Kandy as at 30 September 20X4 is:

	$000	$000
Equity shares of $1 each		40,000
Retained earnings as at 30 September 20X4		19,500
Proceeds of 6% loan (note (1))		30,000
Land ($5 million) and buildings – at cost (note (2))	55,000	
Plant and equipment – at cost (note (2))	58,500	
Accumulated depreciation at 1 October 20X3: buildings		20,000
plant and equipment		34,500
Current assets	68,700	
Current liabilities		38,400
Deferred tax (note (3))		2,500
Interest payment (note (1))	1,800	
Investments (note (4))	2,000	
Current tax (note (3))		1,100
	184,000	184,000

The following notes are relevant:

(1) The loan note was issued on 1 October 20X3 and incurred issue costs of $1 million which were charged to profit or loss. Interest of $1.8 million ($30 million at 6%) was paid on 30 September 20X4. The loan is redeemable on 30 September 20X8 at a substantial premium which gives an effective interest rate of 9% per annum. No other repayments are due until 30 September 20X8.

(2) Non-current assets:

The price of property has increased significantly in recent years and on 1 October 20X3, the directors decided to revalue the land and buildings. The directors accepted the report of an independent surveyor who valued the land at $8 million and the buildings at $39 million on that date. The remaining life of the buildings at 1 October 20X3 was 15 years. Kandy does not make an annual transfer to retained earnings to reflect the realisation of the revaluation gain. However the revaluation will give rise to a deferred tax liability. The income tax rate of Kandy is 20%.

Plant and equipment is depreciated at 12½% per annum using the reducing balance method.

No depreciation has been charged for the year ended 30 September 20X4.

(3) A provision of $2.4 million is required for current income tax on the profit of the year to 30 September 20X4. The balance on current tax in the trial balance is the under/over provision of tax for the previous year. In addition to the temporary differences relating to the information in note (2), Kandy has further taxable temporary differences of $10 million as at 30 September 20X4.

(4) The investments in the trial balance are held at their fair value at 1 October 20X3. At 30 September 20X4 the value had risen to $2.6 million.

Required:

(a) Prepare a schedule of adjustments required to the retained earnings of Kandy as at 30 September 20X4 as a result of the information in notes (1) to (4) above.

(9 marks)

(b) Prepare the statement of financial position of Kandy as at 30 September 20X4.

(11 marks)

Note: The notes to the statement of financial position are not required.

(Total: 20 marks)

410 CLARION

After preparing a draft statement of profit or loss for the year ended 30 September 20X4 and adding the year's profit (before any adjustments required by notes (1) to (5) below) to retained earnings, the summarised trial balance of Clarion as at 31 March 20X5 is:

	$000	$000
Equity shares of $1 each		35,000
Retained earnings – 31 March 20X5		33,100
8% loan notes (note (1))		20,000
Plant and equipment at cost (note (2))	77,000	
Right-of-use plant (note (3))	8,000	
Accumulated depreciation plant and equipment – 1 April 20X4		19,000
Investments through profit or loss – value at 1 April 20X4 (note (4))	6,000	
Inventory at 31 March 20X5	11,700	
Trade receivables	20,500	
Bank		1,900
Deferred tax (note (5))		2,700
Trade payables		9,400
Environmental provision (note (2))		4,000
Lease liability (note (3))		4,200
Loan note interest paid (note (1))	800	
Suspense account (note (1))	5,800	
Investment income (note (4))		500
	129,800	129,800

The following notes are also relevant.

(1) On 31 March 20X5, one quarter of the 8% loan notes were redeemed at par and six months' outstanding loan interest was paid. The suspense account represents the debit entry corresponding to the cash payment for the capital redemption and the outstanding interest.

(2) Property, plant and equipment

Included in property, plant and equipment is an item of plant with a cost of $14 million purchased on 1 April 20X4. However, the plant will cause environmental damage which will have to be rectified when it is dismantled at the end of its five year life. The present value (discounting at 8%) on 1 April 20X4 of the rectification is $4 million. The environmental provision has been correctly accounted for, however, no finance cost has yet been charged on the provision.

No depreciation has yet been charged on plant and equipment which should be charged to cost of sales on a straight-line basis over a five-year life. No plant is more than four years old.

(3) The right-of-use plant was acquired on 1 April 20X4 under a five-year lease with an initial deposit of $2.3 million and annual payments of $1.5 million on 31 March each year. The present value of the annual payments under the lease (**excluding the initial deposit**) at 1 April 20X4 was $5.7 million, the lease has an implicit rate of interest of 10%, and the right-of-use plant has been correctly capitalised. The lease liability in the trial balance above represents the initial liability less the first annual payment.

(4) The investments through profit or loss are those held at 31 March 20X5 (after the sale below). They are carried at their fair value as at 1 April 20X4, however, they had a fair value of $6.5 million on 31 March 20X5. During the year an investment which had a carrying amount of $1.4 million was sold for $1.6 million. Investment income in the trial balance above includes the profit on the sale of the investment and dividends received during the year.

(5) A provision for current tax for the year ended 31 March 20X5 of $3.5 million is required. At 31 March 20X5, the tax base of Clarion's net assets was $12 million less than their carrying amounts. The income tax rate of Clarion is 25%.

Required:

(a) Prepare Clarion's statement of financial position as at 31 March 20X5. (15 marks)

(b) Prepare extracts from the statement of cash flows for Clarion for the year ended 31 March 20X5 in respect of cash flows from investing and financing activities. (5 marks)

Notes to the financial statements are not required.

(Total: 20 marks)

411 MOSTON  Walk in the footsteps of a top tutor

The following trial balance **extracts** (i.e. it is not a complete trial balance) relate to Moston as at 30 June 20X5:

	$000	$000
Revenue		113,500
Cost of sales	88,500	
Research and development costs (note (1))	7,800	
Distribution costs	2,800	
Administrative expenses (note (3))	6,800	
Loan note interest and dividends paid (notes (3) and (5))	5,000	
Investment income		300
Equity shares of $1 each (note (5))		30,000
5% loan note (note (3))		20,000
Retained earnings as at 1 July 20X4		6,200
Revaluation surplus as at 1 July 20X4		3,000
Other components of equity		9,300
Property at valuation 1 July 20X4 (note (2))	28,500	
Plant and equipment at cost (note (2))	27,100	
Accumulated depreciation plant and equipment 1 July 20X4		9,100

The following notes are relevant:

(1) Moston commenced a research and development project on 1 January 20X5. It spent $1 million per month on research until 31 March 20X5, at which date the project passed into the development stage. From this date it spent $1.6 million per month until the year end (30 June 20X5), at which date development was completed. However, it was not until 1 May 20X5 that the directors of Moston were confident that the new product would be a commercial success.

Expensed research and development costs should be charged to cost of sales.

(2) Non-current assets:

Moston's property is carried at fair value which at 30 June 20X5 was $29 million. The remaining life of the property at the beginning of the year (1 July 20X4) was 15 years. Moston does not make an annual transfer to retained earnings in respect of the revaluation surplus. Ignore deferred tax on the revaluation.

Plant and equipment is depreciated at 15% per annum using the reducing balance method.

No depreciation has yet been charged on any non-current asset for the year ended 30 June 20X5. All depreciation is charged to cost of sales.

(3) The 5% loan note was issued on 1 July 20X4 at its nominal value of $20 million incurring direct issue costs of $500,000 which have been charged to administrative expenses. The loan note will be redeemed after three years at a premium which gives the loan note an effective finance cost of 8% per annum. Annual interest was paid on 30 June 20X5.

(4) A provision for current tax for the year ended 30 June 20X5 of $1.2 million is required, together with an increase to the deferred tax provision to be charged to profit or loss of $800,000.

(5) Moston paid a dividend of 20 cents per share on 30 March 20X5, which was followed the day after by an issue of 10 million equity shares at their full market value of $1.70. The share premium on the issue was recorded in other components of equity.

Required:

(a) Prepare the statement of profit or loss and other comprehensive income for Moston for the year ended 30 June 20X5. (10 marks)

(b) Prepare the statement of changes in equity for Moston for the year ended 30 June 20X5. (5 marks)

(c) Prepare extracts from the statement of cash flows for Moston for the year ended 30 June 20X5 in respect of cash flows from investing and financing activities. (5 marks)

Note: The statement of financial position and notes to the financial statements are NOT required.

(Total: 20 marks)

412 TRIAGE

After preparing a draft statement of profit or loss (before interest and tax) for the year ended 31 March 20X6 (before any adjustments which may be required by notes (1) to (4) below), the summarised trial balance of Triage Co as at 31 March 20X6 is:

	$000	$000
Equity shares of $1 each		50,000
Retained earnings as at 1 April 20X5		3,500
Draft profit before interest and tax for year ended 31 March 20X6		30,000
6% convertible loan notes (note (1))		40,000
Property (original life 25 years) – at cost (note (2))	75,000	
Plant and equipment – at cost (note (2))	72,100	
Accumulated amortisation/depreciation at 1 April 20X5:		
leased property		15,000
plant and equipment		28,100
Trade receivables (note (3))	28,000	
Other current assets	9,300	
Current liabilities		17,700
Deferred tax (note (4))		3,200
Interest payment (note (1))	2,400	
Current tax (note (4)	700	
	187,500	187,500

The following notes are relevant:

(1) Triage Co issued 400,000 $100 6% convertible loan notes on 1 April 20X5. Interest is payable annually in arrears on 31 March each year. The loans can be converted to equity shares on the basis of 20 shares for each $100 loan note on 31 March 20X8 or redeemed at par for cash on the same date. An equivalent loan without the conversion rights would have required an interest rate of 8%.

The present value of $1 receivable at the end of each year, based on discount rates of 6% and 8%, are:

		6%	8%
End of year	1	0.94	0.93
	2	0.89	0.86
	3	0.84	0.79

(2) Non-current assets:

The directors decided to revalue the property at $66.3m on 1 October 20X5. Triage Co does not make an annual transfer from the revaluation surplus to retained earnings to reflect the realisation of the revaluation gain. However, the revaluation will give rise to a deferred tax liability at a tax rate of 20%.

The property is depreciated on a straight-line basis and plant and equipment at 15% per annum using the reducing balance method.

No depreciation has yet been charged on any non-current assets for the year ended 31 March 20X6.

(3) In September 20X5, the directors of Triage Co discovered a fraud. In total, $700,000 which had been included as receivables in the above trial balance had been stolen by an employee. $450,000 of this related to the year ended 31 March 20X5, the rest to the current year. The directors are hopeful that 50% of the losses can be recovered from their insurers.

(4) A provision of $2.7m is required for current income tax on the profit of the year to 31 March 20X6. The balance on current tax in the trial balance is the under/over provision of tax for the previous year. In addition to the temporary differences relating to the information in note (2), at 31 March 20X6 the carrying amounts of Triage Co's net assets are $12m more than their tax base.

Required:

(a) Prepare a schedule of adjustments required to the draft profit before interest and tax (in the above trial balance) to give the profit or loss of Triage Co for the year ended 31 March 20X6 as a result of the information in notes (1) to (4) above. (5 marks)

(b) Prepare the statement of financial position of Triage Co as at 31 March 20X6. (12 marks)

(c) The issue of convertible loan notes can potentially dilute the basic earnings per share (EPS).

Calculate the diluted earnings per share for Triage Co for the year ended 31 March 20X6 (there is no need to calculate the basic EPS). (3 marks)

Note: A statement of changes in equity and the notes to the statement of financial position are not required.

(Total: 20 marks)

413 HAVERFORD CO

Below is the trial balance for Haverford Co at 31 December 20X7:

	$000	$000
Property – carrying amount 1 January 20X7 (note (4))	18,000	
Ordinary shares $1 at 1 January 20X7 (note (3))		20,000
Other components of equity (Share premium) at 1 January 20X7 (note (3))		3,000
Revaluation surplus at 1 January 20X7 (note (4))		800
Retained earnings at 1 January 20X7		6,270
Draft profit for the year ended 31 December 20X7		2,250
4% Convertible loan notes (note (1))		8,000
Dividends paid	3,620	
Cash received from contract customer (note (2))		3,100
Cost incurred on contract to date (note (2))	3,600	
Inventories (note (5))	4,310	
Trade receivables	5,510	
Cash	10,320	
Current liabilities		1,940
	45,360	45,360

The following notes are relevant:

(1) On 1 January 20X7, Haverford Co issued 80,000 $100 4% convertible loan notes. The loan notes can be converted to equity shares on 31 December 20X9 or redeemed at par on the same date. An equivalent loan without the conversion rights would have required interest of 6%. Interest is payable annually in arrears on 31 December each year. The annual payment has been included in finance costs for the year. The present value of $1 receivable at the end of each year, based on discount rates of 4% and 6%, are:

	4%	6%
End of year 1	0.962	0.943
End of year 2	0.925	0.890
End of year 3	0.889	0.840

(2) During the year, Haverford Co entered into a contract to construct an asset for a customer, satisfying the performance obligation over time. The contract had a total price of $14m. The costs to date of $3.6m are included in the above trial balance. Costs to complete the contract are estimated at $5.4m.

At 31 December 20X7, the contract is estimated to be 40% complete. To date, Haverford Co has received $3.1m from the customer and this is shown in the above trial balance.

(3) Haverford Co made a 1 for 5 bonus issue on 31 December 20X7, which has not yet been recorded in the above trial balance. Haverford Co intends to utilise the share premium as far as possible in recording the bonus issue.

(4) Haverford Co's property had previously been revalued upwards, leading to the balance on the revaluation surplus at 1 January 20X7. The property had a remaining life of 25 years at 1 January 20X7.

At 31 December 20X7, the property was valued at $16m.

No entries have yet been made to account for the current year's depreciation charge or the property valuation at 31 December 20X7. Haverford Co does not make an annual transfer from the revaluation surplus in respect of excess depreciation.

(5) It has been discovered that inventory totalling $0.39m had been omitted from the final inventory count in the above trial balance.

Required:

(a) Calculate the adjusted profit for Haverford Co for the year ended 31 December 20X7. (6 marks)

(b) Prepare the statement of changes in equity for Haverford Co for the year ended 31 December 20X7. (6 marks)

(c) Prepare the statement of financial position for Haverford Co as at 31 December 20X7. (8 marks)

(Total: 20 marks)

414 DUGGAN CO

The following **extracts** from the trial balance have been taken from the accounting records of Duggan Co as at 30 June 20X8:

	$000	$000
Convertible loan notes (note (4))		5,000
Cost of sales	21,700	
Finance costs (note (4))	1,240	
Investment income		120
Operating expenses (notes (2) and (5))	13,520	
Retained earnings at 1 July 20X7		35,400
Revenue (note (1))		43,200
Equity share capital ($1 shares) at 1 July 20X7		12,200
Tax (note (3))		130

The following notes are relevant:

(1) Duggan Co entered into a contract where the performance obligation is satisfied over time. The total price on the contract is $9m, with total expected costs of $5m.

Progress towards completion was measured at 50% at 30 June 20X7 and 80% on 30 June 20X8.

The correct entries were made in the year ended 30 June 20X7, but no entries have been made for the year ended 30 June 20X8.

(2) On 1 January 20X8, Duggan Co was notified that an ex-employee had started court proceedings against them for unfair dismissal. Legal advice was that there was an 80% chance that Duggan Co would lose the case and would need to pay an estimated $1.012m on 1 January 20X9.

Based on this advice, Duggan Co recorded a provision of $800k on 1 January 20X8, and has made no further adjustments. The provision was recorded in operating expenses.

Duggan Co has a cost of capital of 10% per annum and the discount factor at 10% for one year is 0.9091.

(3) The balance relating to tax in the trial balance relates to the under/over provision from the prior period. The tax estimate for the year ended 30 June 20X8 is $2.1m.

In addition to this, there has been a decrease in taxable temporary differences of $2m in the year. Duggan Co pays tax at 25% and movements in deferred tax are to be taken to the statement of profit or loss.

(4) Duggan Co issued $5m 6% convertible loan notes on 1 July 20X7. Interest is payable annually in arrears. These bonds can be converted into one share for every $2 on 30 June 20X9. Similar loan notes, without conversion rights, incur interest at 8%. Duggan Co recorded the full amount in liabilities and has recorded the annual payment made on 30 June 20X8 of $0.3m in finance costs.

Relevant discount rates are as follows:

Present value of $1 in:	6%	8%
1 year	0.943	0.926
2 years	0.890	0.857

(5) Duggan Co began the construction of an item of property on 1 July 20X7 which was completed on 31 March 20X8. A cost of $32m was capitalised. This included $2.56m, being a full 12 months' interest on a $25.6m 10% loan taken out specifically for this construction. On completion, the property has a useful life of 20 years.

Duggan Co also recorded $0.4m in operating expenses, representing depreciation on the asset for the period from 31 March 20X8 to 30 June 20X8.

(6) It has been discovered that the previous financial controller of Duggan Co engaged in fraudulent financial reporting. Currently, $2.5m of trade receivables has been deemed to not exist and requires to be written off. Of this, $0.9m relates to the year ended 30 June 20X8, with $1.6m relating to earlier periods.

(7) On 1 November 20X7, Duggan Co issued 1.5 million shares at their full market price of $2.20. The proceeds were credited to a suspense account.

Required:

(a) Prepare a statement of profit or loss for Duggan Co for the year ended 30 June 20X8. (12 marks)

(b) Prepare a statement of changes in equity for Duggan Co for the year ended 30 June 20X8. (5 marks)

(c) Calculate the basic earnings per share for Duggan Co for the year ended 30 June 20X8. (3 marks)

Note: All workings should be done to the nearest $000.

(Total: 20 marks)

415 VERNON CO

The following **extract** is from the trial balance of Vernon Co at 31 December 20X8:

	$000	$000
Cost of sales	46,410	
Finance costs	4,050	
Investment income (note (3))		1,520
Operating expenses (note (3))	20,640	
Revenue (notes (1) and (2))		75,350
Tax (note (6))	130	

The following notes are relevant:

(1) Vernon Co made a large sale of goods on 1 July 20X8, which was also the date of delivery. Under the terms of the agreement, Vernon Co will receive payment of $8m on 30 June 20X9. Currently, Vernon Co has recorded $4m in revenue and trade receivables. The directors intend to record the remaining $4m revenue in the year ended 31 December 20X9. The costs of this sale have been accounted for correctly in the financial statements for the year ended 31 December 20X8. Vernon Co has a cost of capital of 8% at which an appropriate discount factor would be 0.9259.

(2) Vernon Co also sold goods to an overseas customer on 1 December 20X8 for 12m Kromits (Kr). They agreed a 60-day payment term. No entries have yet been made to record this sale, although the goods were correctly removed from inventory and expensed in cost of sales. The amount remains unpaid at 31 December 20X8.

Relevant exchange rates are:

1 December 20X8: 6.4 Kr/$
31 December 20X8: 6.0 Kr/$

(3) Vernon Co acquired $9m 5% bonds at par value on 1 January 20X8 and intends to hold them to maturity. Interest is receivable on 31 December each year. Vernon Co incurred $0.4m broker fees when acquiring the bonds, which has been expensed to operating expenses. These bonds are repayable at a premium so have an effective rate of 8%. Vernon Co has recorded the interest received on 31 December 20X8 in investment income.

(4) During the year, Vernon Co revalued its head office for the first time, resulting in an increase in value of $12m at 31 December 20X8. Deferred tax is applicable to this gain at 25%.

(5) Vernon Co values its investment properties using the fair value model. The investment properties increased in value by $4m at 31 December 20X8.

(6) The tax figure in the trial balance represents the under/over provision from the previous year. The current tax liability for the year ended 31 December 20X8 is estimated to be $3.2m.

(7) At 1 January 20X8, Vernon Co had 30 million $1 equity shares in issue. On 1 April 20X8, Vernon Co issued an additional 5 million $1 equity shares at full market value. On 1 July 20X8, Vernon Co performed a 2 for 5 rights issue, at $2.40 per share. The market value of a Vernon Co share at 1 July 20X8 was $3.10 per share.

Required:

(a) Produce a statement of profit or loss and other comprehensive income for Vernon Co for the year ended 31 December 20X8. (15 marks)

(b) Calculate the earnings per share for Vernon Co for the year ended 31 December 20X8. (5 marks)

(Total: 20 marks)

416 LOUDON CO

Loudon Co has prepared a draft statement of profit or loss for the year ended 30 September 20X8 (before any adjustments required by notes (1) to (4) below). The draft profit has been added to retained earnings and the summarised trial balance of Loudon Co as at 30 September 20X8 is:

	$000	$000
Equity shares of $1 each		10,000
Retained earnings as at 30 September 20X8 (draft)		4,122
Office building at cost	20,000	
Factories cost 1 October 20X7 (note (2))	40,000	
Office building accumulated depreciation 1 October 20X7		4,000
Factories accumulated depreciation 1 October 20X7		11,100
Environmental provision 1 October 20X7 (note (3))		1,228
Current liabilities		34,500
Current assets	14,700	
Proceeds of 5% loan note (note (1))		5,000
Deferred Tax		1,500
Interest paid (note (1))	250	
Suspense account (note (2))		3,500
	74,950	74,950

The following notes are relevant:

(1) Loan note

A 5% loan note was issued on 1 October 20X7 at its face value of $5m. Direct costs of the issue amounted to $0.125m and were charged to profit or loss. The loan will be redeemed in five years' time at a substantial premium which gives an effective interest rate of 8%. The annual repayments of $250,000 ($5m at 5%) are paid on 30 September each year.

(2) Non-current assets

Loudon Co acquired an office building for $20m on 1 October 20X2 with an estimated useful life of 25 years. Depreciation is charged on a pro-rata basis. On 1 April 20X8, the building was deemed to be impaired as its recoverable amount was estimated to be $12m. At that date the estimated remaining life was revised to 12 years. Ignore the deferred tax consequences of this revaluation.

Loudon Co had ten factories. On 1 October 20X7 Loudon Co sold one of its factories with a carrying amount of $3m (cost $5m and accumulated depreciation $2m) for $3.5m. The only entry made in respect of the disposal is for the proceeds, which have been credited to suspense.

No depreciation has yet been charged on any non-current asset for the year ended 30 September 20X8. The factories are depreciated at 15% per annum using the reducing balance method.

(3) Environmental provision

Loudon Co has an obligation to clean-up environmental damage caused at one of its factory sites during 20X7. The clean-up is due to take place at the end of the factory's useful life. The liability has been accounted for appropriately and the balance at 1 October 20X7 represents the correct present value at that date. Loudon Co has a cost of capital of 5%.

(4) Deferred tax

At 30 September 20X8, the tax written down value of property, plant and equipment was $25m. The income tax rate applicable to Loudon Co is 20%.

Required:

(a) Prepare a schedule of adjustments required to the retained earnings of Loudon Co as at 30 September 20X8 as a result of the information in notes (1) to (4). (8 marks)

(b) Prepare the statement of financial position of Loudon Co as at 30 September 20X8. (12 marks)

Note: The notes to the statement of financial position are not required. All calculations should be rounded to the nearest $000.

(Total: 20 marks)

417 MIMS CO

The following is an **extract** from the trial balance of Mims Co for the year ended 31 December 20X5.

	$000	$000
Revenue		24,300
Cost of sales	11,600	
Administrative expenses	10,900	
Distribution costs	7,300	
Income tax (note 3)	140	
Deferred tax liability 1 January 20X5 (note 3)		7,700
Provision at 1 January 20X5 (note 2)		4,600
Retained earnings at 1 January 20X5		43,200
Equity share capital ($1) at 1 January 20X5		60,000
Intangible assets (note 6)	3,300	
Investment property (note 5)	19,000	
Finance costs	1,400	
Investment income		500
Suspense account		46,500

The following information is relevant:

(1) Mims Co noted there an error in the inventory count at 31 December 20X4, meaning that the closing inventory balance in the 20X4 financial statements was overstated by $0.7m. No entries have yet been made to correct this error.

(2) The provision relates to a court case in existence since December 20X4. Mims Co settled this case on 31 December 20X5 for $6m. The full amount was credited correctly to cash, with a corresponding debit entry being made in the suspense account.

(3) The income tax figure in trial balance relates to the under/over provision from the previous year. The current year tax is estimated to be a tax **refund** of $1.2m. In addition to this, the deferred tax liability at 31 December 20X5 is estimated to be $8.2m.

(4) On 30 September 20X5 Mims Co made a 1 for 4 rights issue. The exercise price was $3.50 per share. The proceeds were correctly accounted for in cash, with a corresponding credit entry being made in the suspense account.

(5) Mims Co acquired an investment property for $20m cash on January 20X5 and decided to use the fair value model to account for investment properties. As the property is expected to have a 20-year useful life, depreciation was recorded on this basis. The fair value of the property at 31 December 20X5 has been assessed at S22m but no accounting has taken place in relation to this. All depreciation and amortisation is charged on a pro-rata basis to administrative expenses. There were no other acquisitions or disposals of non-current assets.

(6) Mims Co incurred a number of expenses in relation to brands during the year and has capitalised the following costs as intangible assets:

$1.3m cash was paid on 1 April 20X5 to promote one of its major brands which is deemed to have an indefinite life.

$2m cash was paid on 1 October 20X5 to acquire a brand from one of its competitors. Mims Co expect the brand to have a useful life of five years. Mims Co intend to sell it after five years. At the point of sale it is estimated that the value of the brand will have increased, and so no amortisation has been accounted for in the current year.

(7) Mims Co paid a dividend of $0.04 per share on all existing shares on 31 December 20X5, recording the dividend paid in administrative expenses.

Required:

(a) Prepare the statement of profit or loss for Mims Co for the year ended 31 December 20X5. (12 marks)

(b) Prepare the statement of changes in equity for Mims Co for the year ended 31 December 20X5. (5 marks)

(c) Prepare the following extracts from the statement of cash flows for Mims Co for the year ended 31 December 20X5:

(i) Cash flows from investing activities

(ii) Cash flows from financing activities (3 marks)

(Total: 20 marks)

418 PRINT CO

Print Co is a manufacturing company and has the following trial balance at 30 June 20X2:

	$000	$000
Equity shares of $1 each		29,600
Other components of equity (share premium)		15,500
Retained earnings at 30 June 20X1		11,470
Plant and machinery (note (v))		
– Cost	16,200	
– Accumulated depreciation at 30 June 20X1		7,290
Land - at cost	45,000	
Bank loan (repayable 20X5) (note (i))		30,000
Trade and other receivables	25,010	
Trade and other payables		4,170
Cash at bank	4,700	
Revenue		97,400
Production costs	60,150	
Administrative expenses	29,570	
Distribution costs	7,200	
Finance costs	750	
Inventory at 30 June 20X1	6,850	
	195,430	195,430

The following additional information is available:

(i) On 1 January 20X2 Print Co raised funds of $30m. The full amount was recorded in the nominal ledger as a bank loan. The funds actually consisted of a bank loan of $16m and $14m from the issue of seven million $1 ordinary shares. Interest is payable on the loan at 5% per annum. An accrual for six months interest has been included in trade and other payables and recognised as a finance cost. However, the calculation of interest was incorrectly based on the nominal ledger loan balance at 30 June 20X2.

(ii) Inventories at 30 June 20X2 were initially valued at a total cost of $5.7m. This includes 700 units with a cost of $1,400 per unit. In order to sell these items they need an additional process that costs $400 per unit, at which point they can then be sold for $1,600 per unit.

(iii) At 30 June 20X2, Print Co has a contract to purchase 22,500 electrical components over the next three years at a cost of $450 each. These purchases are made at a constant rate. These components are no longer required for their initial purpose but do have an alternative use, which will require additional manufacturing costs of $600 per component. Thereafter, each component can then be sold for $900. Alternatively, Print Co could cancel the contract immediately by paying a penalty of $4m. Any adjustment resulting from this information should be made to administration expenses. Ignore discounting.

(iv) On 1 July 20X1 the directors of Print Co decided to sell a piece of machinery and the asset met the criteria to be classified as held for sale at that date. The machine, which cost $2.4m, had a carrying amount of $1.5m at 1 July 20X1. At that date its fair value less costs to sell was $1.14m. The machine was sold for $1.1m after selling costs on 1 July 20X2. No adjustments have been made to take account of classifying the machine as held for sale.

(v) Print Co's policy is to depreciate plant and machinery at 15% per annum on cost and to present the depreciation charge in cost of sales.

(vi) The income tax **refund** for the year has been estimated to be $2.53m.

Required:

(a) Prepare the statement of profit or loss for Print Co for the year ended 30 June 20X2.

(8 marks)

(b) Prepare the statement of financial position for Print Co as at 30 June 20X2.

(12 marks)

(Total: 20 marks)

BUSINESS COMBINATIONS

419 PREMIER  Walk in the footsteps of a top tutor

On 1 June 20X0, Premier acquired 80% of the equity share capital of Sanford. The consideration consisted of two elements: a share exchange of three shares in Premier for every five acquired shares in Sanford and $800,000 cash. The share issue has not yet been recorded by Premier. At the date of acquisition shares in Premier had a market value of $5 each. Below are the summarised draft financial statements of both entities.

Statements of financial position as at 30 September 20X0	**Premier**	**Sanford**
Assets	$000	$000
Non-current assets		
Property, plant and equipment	25,500	13,900
Investments	1,800	nil
	27,300	13,900
Current assets		
Inventory	5,300	500
Receivables	4,200	1,100
Bank	3,000	800
	12,500	2,400
Total assets	39,800	16,300
Equity and liabilities		
Equity shares of $1 each	12,000	5,000
Other equity reserve – 30 September 20W9 (note (4))	500	nil
Retained earnings	12,300	4,500
	24,800	9,500
Liabilities		
Current liabilities	15,000	6,800
Total equity and liabilities	39,800	16,300

The following information is relevant:

(1) At the date of acquisition, the fair values of Sanford's assets were equal to their carrying amounts with the exception of its property. This had a fair value of $1.2 million **below** its carrying amount, and had a remaining useful life of 8 years at the date of acquisition. Sanford has not incorporated this in its financial statements.

(2) Premier had $2 million (at cost to Premier) of inventory that had been supplied in the post-acquisition period by Sanford as at 30 September 20X0. Sanford made a mark-up on cost of 25% on these sales.

(3) Premier had a trade payable balance owing to Sanford of $350,000 as at 30 September 20X0. This did not agree with the corresponding receivable in Sanford's books due to a $130,000 payment made to Sanford, which Sanford has not yet recorded.

(4) Premier's investments include investments in shares which at the date of acquisition were classified as fair value through other comprehensive income (FVTOCI). The investments have increased in value by $300,000 during the year. The other equity reserve relates to these investments and is based on their value as at 30 September 20W9. There were no acquisitions or disposals of any of these investments during the year ended 30 September 20X0.

(5) Premier's policy is to value the non-controlling interest at fair value at the date of acquisition, deemed to be $3.5 million.

(6) Consolidated goodwill was impaired by $1.5 million at 30 September 20X0.

(7) Sanford's profit for the year ended 30 September 20X0 was $3.9 million.

Required:

Prepare the consolidated statement of financial position for Premier as at 30 September 20X0. **(20 marks)**

420 PANDAR  Walk in the footsteps of a top tutor

On 1 April 20X9 Pandar purchased 80% of the equity shares in Salva. On the same date Pandar acquired 40% of the 40 million equity shares in Ambra paying $2 per share.

The statement of profit or loss for the year ended 30 September 20X9 are:

	Pandar	**Salva**	**Ambra**
	$000	$000	$000
Revenue	210,000	150,000	50,000
Cost of sales	(126,000)	(100,000)	(40,000)
Gross profit	84,000	50,000	10,000
Distribution costs	(11,200)	(7,000)	(5,000)
Administrative expenses	(18,300)	(9,000)	(11,000)
Investment income (interest and dividends)	9,500		
Finance costs	(1,800)	(3,000)	Nil
Profit (loss) before tax	62,200	31,000	(6,000)
Income tax (expense) relief	(15,000)	(10,000)	1,000
Profit (loss) for the year	47,200	21,000	(5,000)

The following information is relevant:

(1) The fair values of the net assets of Salva at the date of acquisition were equal to their carrying amounts with the exception of an item of plant which had a carrying amount of $12 million and a fair value of $17 million. This plant had a remaining life of five years (straight-line depreciation) at the date of acquisition of Salva. All depreciation is charged to cost of sales.

The fair value of the plant has not been reflected in Salva's financial statements.

No fair value adjustments were required on the acquisition of the investment in Ambra.

(2) Immediately after its acquisition of Salva, Pandar invested $50 million in an 8% loan note from Salva. All interest accruing to 30 September 20X9 has been accounted for by both entities. Salva also has other loans in issue at 30 September 20X9.

(3) Salva paid a dividend of $8 million during the year.

(4) After the acquisition, Pandar sold goods to Salva for $15 million on which Pandar made a gross profit of 20%. Salva had one third of these goods still in its inventory at 30 September 20X9. Pandar also sold goods to Ambra for $6 million, making the same margin. Ambra had half of these goods still in inventory at 30 September 20X9.

(5) The non-controlling interest in Salva is to be valued at its (full) fair value at the date of acquisition.

(6) The goodwill of Salva has been impaired by $2 million at 30 September 20X9. Due to its losses, the value of Pandar's investment in Ambra has been impaired by $3 million at 30 September 20X9.

(7) All items in the above statement of profit or loss are deemed to accrue evenly over the year unless otherwise indicated.

Required:

(a) Calculate the carrying amount of the investment in Ambra to be included within the consolidated statement of financial position as at 30 September 20X9. (4 marks)

(b) Prepare the consolidated statement of profit or loss for the Pandar Group for the year ended 30 September 20X9. (16 marks)

(Total: 20 marks) 田

421 PRODIGAL

On 1 October 20X0 Prodigal purchased 75% of the equity shares in Sentinel. The summarised statements of profit or loss and other comprehensive income for the two entities for the year ended 31 March 20X1 are:

	Prodigal	Sentinel
	$000	$000
Revenue	450,000	240,000
Cost of sales	(260,000)	(110,000)
Gross profit	190,000	130,000
Distribution costs	(23,600)	(12,000)
Administrative expenses	(27,000)	(23,000)
Finance costs	(1,500)	(1,200)
Profit before tax	137,900	93,800
Income tax expense	(48,000)	(27,800)
Profit for the year	89,900	66,000
Other comprehensive income		
Gain on revaluation of land (note (1))	2,500	1,000
Total comprehensive income	92,400	67,000

The following extracts for the equity of the entities at 1 April 20X0 (before acquisition) is available:

	$000	$000
Revaluation surplus (land)	8,400	nil
Retained earnings	90,000	125,000

The following information is relevant:

(1) Prodigal's policy is to revalue the group's land to market value at the end of each accounting period. Prior to its acquisition by Prodigal, Sentinel's land had been valued at historical cost. During the post-acquisition period Sentinel's land had increased in value over its value at the date of acquisition by $1 million. Sentinel has recognised the revaluation within its own financial statements.

(2) Immediately after the acquisition of Sentinel on 1 October 20X0, Prodigal transferred an item of plant with a carrying amount of $4 million to Sentinel at an agreed value of $5 million. At this date the plant had a remaining life of two and half years. Prodigal had included the profit on this transfer as a reduction in its depreciation costs. All depreciation is charged to cost of sales.

(3) After the acquisition Sentinel sold goods to Prodigal for $40 million. These goods had cost Sentinel $30 million. $12 million of the goods sold remained in Prodigal's closing inventory.

(4) Prodigal's policy is to value the non-controlling interest of Sentinel at the date of acquisition at its fair value which the directors determined to be $100 million.

(5) The goodwill of Sentinel has not suffered any impairment.

(6) All items in the above statements of comprehensive income are deemed to accrue evenly over the year unless otherwise indicated.

Required:

(a) Prepare the consolidated statement of profit or loss and other comprehensive income of Prodigal for the year ended 31 March 20X1. (15 marks)

(b) Prepare extracts of the equity section (including the non-controlling interest) of the consolidated statement of financial position of Prodigal as at 31 March 20X1. (5 marks)

Note: you are NOT required to calculate consolidated goodwill or produce the statement of changes in equity.

(Total: 20 marks)

422 PALADIN

On 1 October 20X0, Paladin secured a majority equity shareholding in Saracen on the following terms:

– an immediate payment of $4 per share on 1 October 20X0.

– and a further amount deferred until 1 October 20X1 of $5.4 million.

The immediate payment has been recorded in Paladin's financial statements, but the deferred payment has not been recorded. Paladin's cost of capital is 8% per annum.

On 1 February 20X1, Paladin also acquired 25% of the equity shares of Augusta paying $10 million in cash. Augusta made a profit of $1.2 million for the year ended 30 September 20X1.

The summarised statements of financial position of the two entities at 30 September 20X1 are:

	Paladin	**Saracen**
Assets	$000	$000
Non-current assets		
Property, plant and equipment	40,000	31,000
Intangible assets	7,500	
Investments – Saracen (8 million shares at $4 each)	32,000	
– Augusta	10,000	nil
	89,500	31,000
Current assets	22,000	13,700
Total assets	111,500	44,700

Equity and liabilities		
Equity		
Equity shares of $1 each	50,000	10,000
Retained earnings – at 1 October 20X0	25,700	12,000
– for year ended 30 September 20X1	9,200	6,000
	84,900	28,000
Non-current liabilities		
Deferred tax	15,000	8,000
Current liabilities	11,600	8,700
Total equity and liabilities	111,500	44,700

The following information is relevant:

(1) Paladin's policy is to value the non-controlling interest at fair value at the date of acquisition. For this purpose the directors of Paladin considered a share price for Saracen of $3.50 per share to be appropriate.

(2) At the date of acquisition, the fair values of Saracen's property, plant and equipment was equal to its carrying amount with the exception of Saracen's plant which had a fair value of $4 million above its carrying amount. At that date the plant had a remaining life of four years. Saracen uses straight-line depreciation for plant assuming a nil residual value.

Also at the date of acquisition, Paladin valued Saracen's customer relationships as an intangible asset at fair value of $3 million. Saracen has not accounted for this asset. Trading relationships with Saracen's customers last on average for six years.

(3) At 30 September 20X1, Saracen's inventory included goods bought from Paladin (at cost to Saracen) of $2.6 million. Paladin had marked up these goods by 30% on cost.

(4) Impairment tests were carried out on 30 September 20X1 which concluded that consolidated goodwill was not impaired, but, due to disappointing earnings, the value of the investment in Augusta was impaired by $2.5 million.

(5) Assume all profits accrue evenly through the year.

Required:

Prepare the consolidated statement of financial position for Paladin as at 30 September 20X1.

(Total: 20 marks)

423 PYRAMID

On 1 April 20X1, Pyramid acquired 80% of Square's equity shares by means of an immediate share exchange and a cash payment of 88 cents per acquired share, deferred until 1 April 20X2. Pyramid has recorded the share exchange, but not the cash consideration. Pyramid's cost of capital is 10% per annum.

The summarised statements of financial position of the two entities as at 31 March 20X2 are:

	Pyramid	Square
Assets	$000	$000
Non-current assets		
Property, plant and equipment	38,100	28,500
Investments – Square	24,000	
– Other equity (note (3))	2,000	nil
	64,100	28,500
Current assets		
Inventory (note (2))	13,900	10,400
Trade receivables (note (2))	11,400	5,500
Bank (note (2))	9,400	600
Total assets	98,800	45,000
Equity shares of $1 each	25,000	10,000
Share premium	17,600	nil
Retained earnings – at 1 April 20X1	16,200	18,000
– for year ended 31 March 20X2	14,000	8,000
	72,800	36,000
Non-current liabilities (note (1))	16,500	4,000
Current liabilities (note (2))	9,500	5,000
Total equity and liabilities	98,800	45,000

The following information is relevant:

(1) At the date of acquisition, Pyramid conducted a fair value exercise on Square's net assets which were equal to their carrying amounts with the following exceptions:

- An item of plant had a fair value of $3 million above its carrying amount. At the date of acquisition it had a remaining life of five years. Ignore deferred tax relating to this fair value.
- Square had an unrecorded deferred tax liability of $1 million, which was unchanged as at 31 March 20X2.

Pyramid's policy is to value the non-controlling interest at fair value at the date of acquisition. For this purpose a share price for Square of $3.50 each is representative of the fair value of the shares held by the non-controlling interest.

(2) Pyramid sells goods to Square at cost plus 50%. Below is a summary of the recorded activities for the year ended 31 March 20X2 and balances as at 31 March 20X2:

	Pyramid	**Square**
	$000	$000
Sales to Square	16,000	
Purchases from Pyramid		14,500
Included in Pyramid's receivables	4,400	
Included in Square's payables		1,700

On 26 March 20X2, Pyramid sold and despatched goods to Square, which Square did not record until they were received on 2 April 20X2. Square's inventory was counted on 31 March 20X2 and does not include any goods purchased from Pyramid.

On 27 March 20X2, Square remitted to Pyramid a cash payment which was not received by Pyramid until 4 April 20X2. This payment accounted for the remaining difference on the current accounts.

(3) The other equity investments of Pyramid are carried at their fair values on 1 April 20X1. At 31 March 20X2, these had increased to $2.8 million.

Required:

Prepare the consolidated statement of financial position for Pyramid as at 31 March 20X2.

(Total: 20 marks)

424 VIAGEM

Answer debrief

On 1 January 20X2, Viagem acquired 90% of the equity share capital of Greca in a share exchange in which Viagem issued two new shares for every three shares it acquired in Greca. Additionally, on 31 December 20X2, Viagem will pay the shareholders of Greca $1.76 per share acquired. Viagem's cost of capital is 10% per annum. The deferred consideration has not yet been recorded by Viagem.

At the date of acquisition, shares in Viagem and Greca had a stock market value of $6.50 and $2.50 each, respectively.

Statements of profit or loss for the year ended 30 September 20X2

	Viagem	**Greca**
	$000	$000
Revenue	64,600	38,000
Cost of sales	(51,200)	(26,000)
Gross profit	13,400	12,000
Distribution costs	(1,600)	(1,800)
Administrative expenses	(3,800)	(2,400)
Investment income	500	nil
Finance costs	(420)	nil

Profit before tax	8,080	7,800
Income tax expense	(2,800)	(1,600)
Profit for the year	5,280	6,200
Equity as at 1 October 20X1		
Equity shares of $1 each	30,000	10,000
Retained earnings	54,000	35,000

The following information is relevant:

(1) At the date of acquisition, the fair values of Greca's assets were equal to their carrying amounts with the exception of two items:

- An item of plant had a fair value of $1.8 million above its carrying amount. The remaining life of the plant at the date of acquisition was three years. Depreciation is charged to cost of sales.
- Greca had a contingent liability which Viagem estimated to have a fair value of $450,000. This has not changed as at 30 September 20X2.

Greca has not incorporated these fair value changes into its financial statements.

(2) Viagem's policy is to value the non-controlling interest at fair value at the date of acquisition. For this purpose, Greca's share price at that date can be deemed to be representative of the fair value of the shares held by the non-controlling interest.

(3) Sales from Viagem to Greca throughout the year ended 30 September 20X2 had consistently been $800,000 per month. Viagem made a mark-up on cost of 25% on these sales. Greca had $1.5 million of these goods in inventory as at 30 September 20X2.

(4) Viagem's investment income is a dividend received from its investment in a 40% owned associate which it has held for several years. The underlying earnings for the associate for the year ended 30 September 20X2 were $2 million.

(5) Although Greca has been profitable since its acquisition by Viagem, the market for Greca's products has been badly hit in recent months and Viagem has calculated that the goodwill has been impaired by $2 million as at 30 September 20X2.

Required:

(a) Calculate the consolidated goodwill at the date of acquisition of Greca. (7 marks)

(b) Prepare the consolidated statement of profit or loss for Viagem for the year ended 30 September 20X2. (13 marks)

(Total: 20 marks)

425 PARADIGM

On 1 October 20X2, Paradigm acquired 75% of Strata's equity shares by means of a share exchange of two new shares in Paradigm for every five acquired shares in Strata. In addition, Paradigm issued to the shareholders of Strata a $100 10% loan note for every 1,000 shares it acquired in Strata. Paradigm has not recorded any of the purchase consideration, although it does have other 10% loan notes already in issue.

The market value of Paradigm's shares at 1 October 20X2 was $2 each.

The summarised statements of financial position of the two entities as at 31 March 20X3 are:

	Paradigm	Strata
Assets	$000	$000
Non-current assets		
Property, plant and equipment	47,400	25,500
Financial asset: equity investments (notes (1) and (3))	7,500	3,200
	54,900	28,700
Current assets		
Inventory (note (2))	20,400	8,400
Trade receivables	14,800	9,000
Bank	2,100	nil
Total assets	92,200	46,100
Equity and liabilities		
Equity		
Equity shares of $1 each	40,000	20,000
Retained earnings/(losses) – at 1 April 20X2	19,200	(4,000)
– for year ended 31 March 20X3	7,400	8,000
	66,600	24,000
Non-current liabilities		
10% loan notes	8,000	nil
Current liabilities		
Trade payables	17,600	13,000
Bank overdraft	nil	9,100
Total equity and liabilities	92,200	46,100

The following information is relevant:

(1) At the date of acquisition, Strata produced a draft statement of profit or loss which showed it had made a net loss after tax of $2 million at that date. Paradigm accepted this figure as the basis for calculating the pre- and post-acquisition split of Strata's profit for the year ended 31 March 20X3.

Also at the date of acquisition, Paradigm conducted a fair value exercise on Strata's net assets which were equal to their carrying amounts (including Strata's financial asset equity investments) with the exception of an item of plant which had a fair value of $3 million **below** its carrying amount. The plant had a remaining useful life of three years at 1 October 20X2.

Paradigm's policy is to value the non-controlling interest at fair value at the date of acquisition. For this purpose, a share price for Strata of $1.20 each is representative of the fair value of the shares held by the non-controlling interest.

(2) Each month since acquisition, Paradigm's sales to Strata were consistently $4.6 million. Paradigm had marked these up by 15% on cost. Strata had one month's supply ($4.6 million) of these goods in inventory at 31 March 20X3. Paradigm's normal mark-up (to third party customers) is 40%.

(3) The financial asset equity investments of Paradigm and Strata are carried at their fair values as at 1 April 20X2. As at 31 March 20X3, these had fair values of $7.1 million and $3.9 million respectively.

(4) There were no impairment losses within the group during the year ended 31 March 20X3.

Required:

(a) Prepare the consolidated statement of financial position for Paradigm as at 31 March 20X3. (15 marks)

(b) A financial assistant has observed that the fair value exercise means that a subsidiary's net assets are included at acquisition at their fair (current) values in the consolidated statement of financial position. The assistant believes that it is inconsistent to aggregate the subsidiary's net assets with those of the parent because most of the parent's assets are carried at historical cost.

Required:

Comment on the assistant's observation and explain why the net assets of acquired subsidiaries are consolidated at acquisition at their fair values. (5 marks)

(Total: 20 marks)

426 PENKETH

On 1 October 20X3, Penketh acquired 90 million of Sphere's 150 million $0.50 equity shares. Penketh will pay $1.54 cash on 30 September 20X4 for each share acquired. Penketh's finance cost is 10% per annum. Sphere's share price as at 1 October 20X3 was $1.25. The statements of profit or loss and other comprehensive income for the year ended 31 March 20X4 are:

	Penketh	Sphere
	$000	$000
Revenue	620,000	310,000
Cost of sales	(400,000)	(150,000)
Gross profit	220,000	160,000
Distribution costs	(40,000)	(20,000)
Administrative expenses	(36,000)	(25,000)
Investment income	5,000	1,600
Finance costs	(2,000)	(5,600)
Profit before tax	147,000	111,000
Income tax expense	(45,000)	(31,000)
Profit for the year	102,000	80,000
Other comprehensive income		
Gain/(loss) on revaluation of land (note (2))	(2,200)	1,000
Total comprehensive income for the year	99,800	81,000

The following information is relevant:

(1) A fair value exercise on 1 October 20X3 concluded that the carrying amounts of Sphere's net assets were equal to their fair values with the following exceptions:

- Plant with a remaining life of two years had a fair value of $6 million in excess of its carrying amount. Plant depreciation is charged to cost of sales.
- Penketh placed a value of $5 million on Sphere's good relationships with its customers. Penketh expected, on average, a customer relationship to last for a further five years. Amortisation is charged to administrative expenses.

(2) Sphere's land, valued using the revaluation model, increased by $1 million since the acquisition.

(3) After the acquisition Penketh sold goods to Sphere for $20 million at a 25% mark-up. Sphere had one fifth of these goods still in inventory at 31 March 20X4.

(4) All items accrue evenly over the year unless otherwise indicated. Sphere had retained earnings of $70 million at 1 April 20X3. There were no other components of equity at this date.

(5) Penketh measures the non-controlling interest at fair value at the date of acquisition. To calculate fair value, the share price of Sphere should be used.

Required:

(a) Calculate goodwill arising on the acquisition of Sphere as at 1 October 20X3. (5 marks)

(b) Prepare the consolidated statement of profit or loss and other comprehensive income of Penketh for the year ended 31 March 20X4. (15 marks)

(Total: 20 marks)

427 PALISTAR

On 1 January 20X5, Palistar acquired 75% of Stretcher's equity shares by means of an immediate share exchange of two shares in Palistar for five shares in Stretcher. The fair value of Palistar and Stretcher's shares on 1 January 20X5 were $4 and $3 respectively. In addition to the share exchange, Palistar will make a cash payment of $1.32 per acquired share, deferred until 1 January 20X6. Palistar has not recorded any of the consideration for Stretcher in its financial statements. Palistar's cost of capital is 10% per annum.

The summarised statements of financial position of the two entities as at 30 June 20X5 are:

	Palistar	**Stretcher**
	$000	$000
Assets		
Non-current assets (note (2))		
Property, plant and equipment	55,000	28,600
Financial asset equity investments (note (5))	11,500	6,000
	66,500	34,600
Current assets		
Inventory (note (4))	17,000	15,400
Trade receivables (note (4))	14,300	10,500
Bank	2,200	1,600
	33,500	27,500
Total assets	100,000	62,100
Equity and liabilities		
Equity		
Equity shares of $1 each	20,000	20,000
Other component of equity	4,000	nil
Retained earnings – at 1 July 20X4	26,200	14,000
– for year ended 30 June 20X5	24,000	10,000
	74,200	44,000
Current liabilities (note (4))	25,800	18,100
Total equity and liabilities	100,000	62,100

The following information is relevant:

(1) Stretcher's business is seasonal and 60% of its annual profit is made in the period 1 January to 30 June each year.

(2) At the date of acquisition, the fair value of Stretcher's net assets was equal to their carrying amounts with the following exceptions:

The fair value of Stretcher's financial asset equity investments, carried at a value of $6 million, was $7 million (see also note (5)).

Stretcher owned the rights to a popular mobile (cell) phone game. At the date of acquisition, a specialist valuer estimated that the rights were worth $12 million and had an estimated remaining life of five years.

(3) Following an impairment review, consolidated goodwill is to be written down by $3 million as at 30 June 20X5.

(4) Palistar sells goods to Stretcher at cost plus 30%. Stretcher had $1.8 million of goods in its inventory at 30 June 20X5 which had been supplied by Palistar. In addition, on 28 June 20X5, Palistar processed the sale of $800,000 of goods to Stretcher, which Stretcher did not account for until their receipt on 2 July 20X5. The in-transit reconciliation should be achieved by assuming the transaction had been recorded in the books of Stretcher before the year end. At 30 June 20X5, Palistar had a trade receivable balance of $2.4 million due from Stretcher which differed to the equivalent balance in Stretcher's books due to the sale made on 28 June 20X5.

(5) At 30 June 20X5, the fair values of the financial asset equity investments of Palistar and Stretcher were $13.2 million and $7.9 million respectively.

(6) Palistar's policy is to value the non-controlling interest at fair value at the date of acquisition. For this purpose the value given for Stretcher's shares may be used.

Required:

Prepare the consolidated statement of financial position for Palistar as at 30 June 20X5.

(Total: 20 marks)

428 LAUREL

On 1 January 20X6, Laurel acquired 60% of the equity share capital of Rakewood in a share exchange in which Laurel issued three new shares for every five shares it acquired in Rakewood. The share issue has not yet been recorded by Laurel. Additionally, on 31 December 20X6, Laurel will pay to the shareholders of Rakewood $1.62 per share acquired. Laurel's cost of capital is 8% per annum.

At the date of acquisition, shares in Laurel and Rakewood had a market value of $7 and $2 each respectively.

Statements of profit or loss for the year ended 30 September 20X6

	Laurel	**Rakewood**
	$000	$000
Revenue	84,500	52,000
Cost of sales	(58,200)	(34,000)
Gross profit	26,300	18,000
Distribution costs	(2,000)	(1,600)
Administrative expenses	(4,100)	(2,800)
Investment income (note (4))	500	400
Finance costs	(300)	nil
Profit before tax	20,400	14,000
Income tax expense	(4,800)	(3,600)
Profit for the year	15,600	10,400

Equity as at 1 October 20X5

	$000	$000
Equity shares of $1 each	20,000	15,000
Retained earnings	72,000	25,000

The following information is relevant:

(1) At the date of acquisition, Laurel conducted a fair value exercise on Rakewood's net assets which were equal to their carrying amounts with the following exceptions:

- an item of plant had a fair value of $4m above its carrying amount. At the date of acquisition it had a remaining life of two years.
- inventory of $800,000 had a fair value of $1m. All of this inventory had been sold by 30 September 20X6.

(2) Laurel's policy is to value the non-controlling interest at fair value at the date of acquisition. For this purpose Rakewood's share price at 1 January 20X6 can be deemed representative of the fair value of the shares held by the non-controlling interest.

(3) Laurel had traded with Rakewood for many years before the acquisition. Sales from Rakewood to Laurel throughout the year ended 30 September 20X6 were consistently $1.2m per month. Rakewood made a mark-up on cost of 20% on these sales. Laurel had $1.8m of these goods in inventory as at 30 September 20X6.

(4) Laurel's investment income consists of:

– its share of a dividend of $500,000 paid by Rakewood in August 20X6.

– a dividend of $200,000 received from Artic, a 25% owned associate which it has held for several years. The profit after tax of Artic for the year ended 30 September 20X6 was $2.4m.

(5) Assume, except where indicated otherwise, that all items of income and expense accrue evenly throughout the year.

(6) There were no impairment losses within the group during the year ended 30 September 20X6.

Required:

(a) Calculate the consolidated goodwill at the date of acquisition of Rakewood Co. (7 marks)

(b) Prepare the consolidated statement of profit or loss for Laurel Co for the year ended 30 September 20X6. (13 marks)

(Total: 20 marks)

429 DARGENT CO

On 1 January 20X6 Dargent Co acquired 75% of Latree Co's equity shares by means of a share exchange of two shares in Dargent Co for every three Latree Co shares acquired. On that date, further consideration was also issued to the shareholders of Latree Co in the form of a $100 8% loan note for every 100 shares acquired in Latree Co. None of the purchase consideration, nor the outstanding interest on the loan notes at 31 March 20X6, has yet been recorded by Dargent Co. At the date of acquisition, the share prices of Dargent Co and Latree Co are $3.20 and $1.80 respectively.

The summarised statements of financial position of the two companies as at 31 March 20X6 are:

	Dargent Co	Latree Co
	$000	$000
Assets		
Non-current assets		
Property, plant and equipment (note (1))	75,200	31,500
Investment in Amery Co at 1 April 20X5 (note (4))	4,500	nil
	79,700	31,500
Current assets		
Inventory (note (3))	19,400	18,800
Trade receivables (note (3))	14,700	12,500
Bank	1,200	600
	35,300	31,900
Total assets	115,000	63,400

Equity and liabilities		
Equity shares of $1 each	50,000	20,000
Retained earnings – at 1 April 20X5	20,000	19,000
– for year ended 31 March 20X6	16,000	8,000
	86,000	47,000
Non-current liabilities		
8% loan notes	5,000	nil
Current liabilities (note (3))	24,000	16,400
Total equity and liabilities	115,000	63,400

The following information is relevant:

(1) At the date of acquisition, the fair values of Latree Co's assets were equal to their carrying amounts. However, Latree Co operates a mine which requires to be decommissioned in five years' time. No provision has been made for these decommissioning costs by Latree Co. The present value (discounted at 8%) of the decommissioning is estimated at $4m and will be paid five years from the date of acquisition (the end of the mine's life).

(2) Dargent Co's policy is to value the non-controlling interest at fair value at the date of acquisition. Latree Co's share price at that date can be deemed representative of the fair value of the shares held by the non-controlling interest.

(3) The inventory of Latree Co includes goods bought from Dargent Co for $2.1m. Dargent Co applies a consistent mark-up on cost of 40% when arriving at its selling prices.

On 28 March 20X6, Dargent Co despatched goods to Latree Co with a selling price of $700,000. These were not received by Latree Co until after the year-end, and so have not been included in the above inventory at 31 March 20X6.

At 31 March 20X6, Dargent Co's records showed a receivable due from Latree Co of $3m. This differed to the equivalent payable in Latree Co's records due to the goods in transit.

The intra-group reconciliation should be achieved by assuming that Latree Co had received the goods in transit before the year-end.

(4) The investment in Amery Co represents 30% of its voting share capital and Dargent Co uses equity accounting to account for this investment. Amery Co's profit for the year ended 31 March 20X6 was $6m and Amery Co paid total dividends during the year ended 31 March 20X6 of $2m. Dargent Co has recorded its share of the dividend received from Amery Co in investment income (and cash).

(5) All profits and losses accrued evenly throughout the year.

(6) There were no impairment losses within the group for the year ended 31 March 20X6.

Required:

Prepare the consolidated statement of financial position for Dargent Co as at 31 March 20X6.

(Total: 20 marks)

430 PARTY CO

The following are the draft statements of financial position of Party Co and Streamer Co as at 30 September 20X5:

	Party Co	Streamer Co
	$000	$000
ASSETS		
Non-current assets		
Property, plant and equipment	392,000	84,000
Investments	120,000	Nil
	512,000	84,000
Current assets	94,700	44,650
Total assets	606,700	128,650
EQUITY AND LIABILITIES		
Equity		
Equity shares	190,000	60,000
Retained earnings	210,000	36,500
Revaluation surplus	41,400	4,000
	441,400	100,500
Non-current liabilities		
Deferred consideration	28,000	Nil
Current liabilities	137,300	28,150
Total equity and liabilities	606,700	128,650

The following information is relevant:

(1) On 1 October 20X4, Party Co acquired 80% of the share capital of Streamer Co. At this date the retained earnings of Streamer Co were $34m and the revaluation surplus stood at $4m. Party Co paid an initial cash amount of $92m and agreed to pay the owners of Streamer Co a further $28m on 1 October 20X6. The accountant has recorded the full amounts of both elements of the consideration in investments. Party Co has a cost of capital of 8%. The appropriate discount rate is 0.857.

(2) On 1 October 20X4, the fair values of Streamer Co's net assets were equal to their carrying amounts with the exception of some inventory which had cost $3m but had a fair value of $3.6m. On 30 September 20X5, 10% of these goods remained in the inventories of Streamer Co.

(3) During the year, Party Co sold goods totalling $8m to Streamer Co at a gross profit margin of 25%. At 30 September 20X5, Streamer Co still held $1m of these goods in inventory. Party Co's normal margin (to third party customers) is 45%.

(4) The Party group uses the fair value method to value the non-controlling interest. At acquisition the non-controlling interest was valued at $15m.

Required:

(a) **Prepare the consolidated statement of financial position of the Party group as at 30 September 20X5.** **(15 marks)**

(b) Party Co has a strategy of buying struggling businesses, reversing their decline and then selling them on at a profit within a short period of time. Party Co is hoping to do this with Streamer Co.

As an adviser to a prospective purchaser of Streamer Co, explain any concerns you would raise about making an investment decision based on the information available in the Party Group's consolidated financial statements in comparison to that available in the individual financial statements of Streamer Co. **(5 marks)**

(Total: 20 marks)

431 RUNNER CO

On 1 April 20X4, Runner Co acquired 80% of Jogger Co's equity shares when the retained earnings of Jogger Co were $19.5m. The consideration consisted of cash of $42.5m paid on 1 April 20X4 and a further cash payment of $21m, deferred until 1 April 20X5. No accounting entries have been made in respect of the deferred cash payment. Runner Co has a cost of capital of 8%. The appropriate discount rate is 0.926.

The draft, summarised statements of financial position of the two companies at 31 March 20X5 are shown below:

	Runner Co	**Jogger Co**
	$000	$000
ASSETS		
Non-current assets		
Property plant and equipment	455,800	44,700
Investments	55,000	–
	510,800	44,700
Current assets		
Inventory	22,000	16,000
Trade receivables	35,300	9,000
Bank	2,800	1,500
	60,100	26,500
Total assets	570,900	71,200

EQUITY AND LIABILITIES	$000	$000
Equity		
Equity shares of $1 each	202,500	25,000
Retained earnings	286,600	28,600
	489,100	53,600
Current liabilities		
Trade payables	81,800	17,600
Total equity and liabilities	570,900	71,200

(1) Runner Co's policy is to value the non-controlling interest at fair value at the date of acquisition. The fair value of the non-controlling interest in Jogger Co on 1 April 20X4 was estimated at $13m.

(2) The fair values of Jogger Co's other assets, liabilities and contingent liabilities at 1 April 20X4 were equal to their carrying amounts with the exception of a specialised piece of plant which had a fair value of $10m in excess of its carrying amount. This plant had a ten-year remaining useful life on 1 April 20X4.

(3) In December 20X4 Jogger Co sold goods to Runner Co for $6.4m, earning a gross margin of 15% on the sale. Runner Co still held $4.8m of these goods in its inventories at 31 March 20X5.

(4) Jogger Co still had the full invoice value of $6.4m in its trade receivables at 31 March 20X5. Runner Co's payables only showed $3.4m as it made a payment of $3m on 31 March 20X5 which was not recorded by Jogger Co until 3 April 20X5.

Required:

(a) **Prepare the consolidated statement of financial position for Runner Co as at 31 March 20X5.** **(16 marks)**

(b) Runner Co acquired 30% of Walker Co's equity shares on 1 April 20X5 for $13m, Walker Co had been performing poorly over the last few years and Runner Co hoped its influence over Walker Co would help to turn the company around. In the year ended 31 March 20X6 Walker Co made a loss of $30m. Runner Co has no contractual obligation to make good the losses relating to Walker Co.

Explain how Walker Co should be accounted for in the consolidated statement of financial position of Runner Co for the year ended 31 March 20X6. Your answer should also include a calculation of the carrying amount of the investment in the associate at that date. **(4 marks)**

(Total: 20 marks)

432 PLANK CO

Plank Co has owned 35% of Arch Co since 1 June 20X7 and it acquired 85% of Strip Co on 1 April 20X8. The statements of profit or loss and other comprehensive income for the year ended 31 December 20X8 are:

	Plank Co	Strip Co	Arch Co
	$000	$000	$000
Revenue	705,000	218,000	256,000
Cost of sales	(320,000)	(81,000)	(83,500)
Gross profit	385,000	137,000	172,500
Distribution costs	(58,000)	(16,000)	(18,500)
Administrative expenses	(92,000)	(28,000)	(29,000)
Investment income	46,000	2,000	-
Finance costs	(12,000)	(14,000)	(11,000)
Profit before tax	269,000	81,000	114,000
Income tax expense	(51,500)	(15,000)	(21,430)
Profit for the year	217,500	66,000	92,570
Other comprehensive income			
Gain on revaluation of land	2,800	3,000	–
Total comprehensive income for the year	220,300	69,000	92,570

The following information is relevant:

(i) A fair value exercise conducted on 1 April 20X8 concluded that the carrying amounts of Strip Co's net assets were equal to their fair values with the exception of an item of machinery which had a fair value of $8m in excess of its carrying amount. At 1 April 20X8, the machinery had a remaining life of three years. Depreciation is charged to cost of sales.

(ii) Since acquisition, Plank Co has sold goods to Strip Co totalling $39m. Strip Co had one quarter of these goods in inventory at 31 December 20X8. During the year, Plank Co also sold goods to Arch Co for $26m, all of which Arch Co held in inventory at 31 December 20X8. All of these goods had a mark-up on cost of 30%.

(iii) The investment income of Plank Co for the year ended 31 December 20X8 includes dividends from Strip Co and Arch Co (see note (4)). It also includes $5m interest receivable on a loan made to Strip Co on 1 April 20X8.

(iv) Strip Co paid a dividend to shareholders of $18m on 31 December 20X8. Arch Co paid a dividend on 31 December 20X8 of $35m.

(v) In Plank Co's consolidated statement of financial position at 31 December 20X7, the carrying amount of Plank Co's investment in Arch Co was $145,000. This was calculated using equity accounting.

(vi) All other comprehensive income occurred after 1 April 20X8. Unless otherwise indicated, all other items in the above statements of profit or loss and other comprehensive income are deemed to accrue evenly over the year.

Required:

(a) **Prepare the consolidated statement of profit or loss and other comprehensive income of Plank Co for the year ended 31 December 20X8. (18 marks)**

(b) **Calculate the carrying amount of the investment in Arch Co in the consolidated statement of financial position of Plank Co as at 31 December 20X8. (2 marks)**

(Total: 20 marks)

433 GOLD CO

On 1 January 20X2 Gold Co acquired 90% of the 16 million $1 equity share capital of Silver Co. Gold Co issued three new shares in exchange for every five shares it acquired in Silver Co. Additionally Gold Co will pay further consideration on 31 December 20X2 of $2.42 per share acquired. Gold Co's cost of capital is 10% per annum and the discount factor at 10% for one year is 0.9091. At the date of acquisition, shares in Gold Co and Silver Co had fair values of $8.00 and $3.50 respectively.

Statement of profit or loss for the year ended 30 September 20X2:

	Gold Co	**Silver Co**
	$000	$000
Revenue	103,360	60,800
Cost of sales	(81,920)	(41,600)
Gross profit	21,440	19,200
Distribution costs	(2,560)	(2,980)
Administrative expenses	(6,080)	(3,740)
Investment income	800	–
Finance costs	(672)	–
Profit before tax	12,928	12,480
Income tax expense	(4,480)	(2,560)
Profit for the year	8,448	9,920

The following information is relevant:

(1) At 1 October 20X1, the retained earnings of Silver Co were $56m.

(2) At the date of acquisition, the fair value of Silver Co's assets were equal to their carrying amounts with the exception of two items:

An item of plant had a fair value of $2.6m above its carrying amount. The remaining life of the plant at the date of acquisition was three years. Depreciation is charged to cost of sales.

Silver Co had a contingent liability which Gold Co estimated to have a fair value of $850,000. This has not changed as at 30 September 20X2.

Silver Co has not incorporated these fair value changes into its financial statements.

(3) Gold Co's policy is to value the non-controlling interest at fair value at the date of acquisition. For this purpose, Silver Co's share price at that date can be deemed to be representative of the fair value of the shares held by the non-controlling interest.

(4) Sales from Gold Co to Silver Co in the post-acquisition period had consistently been $600,000 per month. Gold Co made a mark-up on cost of 25% on these sales. Silver Co had $1.2m of these goods in inventory as at 30 September 20X2.

(5) Gold Co's investment income is a dividend received from its investment in a 40% owned associate which it has held for several years. The associate made a profit of $3m for the year ended 30 September 20X2.

(6) On 1 October 20X1 Gold Co issued 100,000 $100 6% convertible loan notes at par value, with interest payable annually in arrears over a five-year term. The equivalent rate for non-convertible loan notes was 8%. Gold Co has recorded the loan notes as a liability at par value and charged the annual 6% interest to finance costs.

	Discount factors in year 5:	**Annuity factors for 5 years:**
6%	0.747	4.212
8%	0.681	3.993

(7) At 30 September 20X2 no impairment to goodwill is required.

(8) Profits accrue evenly throughout the year unless otherwise stated.

Required:

(a) Calculate the goodwill arising on the acquisition of Silver Co. **(6 marks)**

(b) Prepare the consolidated statement of profit or loss for Gold Co for the year ended 30 September 20X2. **(14 marks)**

(Total: 20 marks)

Note: All workings should be done to the nearest $000.

434 CHANG CO

On 1 January 20X8 Chang Co acquired 80% of the 8 million $1 equity share capital of Sing Co. Chang Co issued three new shares in exchange for every five shares it acquired in Sing Co. Additionally Chang Co will pay further consideration on 31 December 20X8 of $2.20 per share acquired. Chang Co's cost of capital is 10% per annum and the discount factor at 10% for one year is 0.9091. At the date of acquisition, the fair value of Chang Co's shares was $9 each.

Statement of profit or loss for the year ended 30 September 20X8:

	Chang Co	**Sing Co**
	$000	$000
Revenue	51,680	30,400
Cost of sales	(30,960)	(20,800)
Gross profit	20,720	9,600
Distribution costs	(1,280)	(1,490)
Administrative expenses	(3,040)	(1,870)
Investment income	400	–
Finance costs	(336)	–
Profit before tax	16,464	6,240
Income tax expense	(2,240)	(1,280)
Profit for the year	14,224	4,960

The following information is relevant:

(1) At 1 October 20X7, the retained earnings of Sing Co were $28m.

(2) At the date of acquisition, the fair value of Sing Co's assets was equal to their carrying amounts with the exception of two items:

An item of plant had a fair value of $1.8m above its carrying amount. The remaining life of the plant at the date of acquisition was three years. Depreciation is charged to cost of sales.

Sing Co had a contingent liability which Chang Co estimated to have a fair value of $400,000. This has not changed as at 30 September 20X8.

Sing Co has not incorporated these fair value changes into its financial statements.

(3) Chang Co's policy is to value the non-controlling interest at acquisition as a proportion of the subsidiary's net assets.

(4) Sales from Sing Co to Chang Co in the post-acquisition period had consistently been $300,000 per month. Sing Co made a margin of 25% on these sales. Chang Co's inventory included $600,000 of these goods at 30 September 20X8.

(5) Chang Co's investment income is a dividend received from its investment in a 30% owned associate which it has held for several years. The associate made a profit after tax of $1m for the year ended 30 September 20X8.

(6) On 1 October 20X7 Chang Co issued 50,000 $100 6% convertible loan notes at par value, with interest payable annually in arrears over a five-year term. The equivalent rate for non-convertible loan notes was 8%. Chang Co has recorded the loan notes as a liability at par value and charged the annual 6% interest to finance costs.

	Year 5 discount factors	5 years annuity factors
6%	0.747	4.212
8%	0.681	3.993

(7) At 30 September 20X8 goodwill is to be impaired by $1 million.

(8) Profits accrue evenly throughout the year unless otherwise stated.

Required:

(a) Calculate the goodwill arising on the acquisition of Sing Co. (5 marks)

(b) Prepare the consolidated statement of profit or loss for Chang Co for the year ended 30 September 20X8. (15 marks)

(Total: 20 marks)

Note: All workings should be done to the nearest $000.

435 ZEFFER CO

On 1 October 20X0 Zeffer acquired 75% of the equity shares of Shem and 80% of the equity shares of Jaco. The fair value of the consideration paid was $3.5 million for Shem and $4.5 million for Jaco.

On 31 March 20X3 Zeffer sold its entire shareholding in Shem for $6.2 million. The summarised statements of profit or loss for the three entities for the year ended 30 September 20X3 are:

	Zeffer	Shem	Jaco
	$000	$000	$000
Revenue	70,000	24,000	15,000
Cost of sales	(34,000)	(14,000)	(8,800)
Gross profit	36,000	10,000	6,200
Operating expenses	(18,000)	(3,000)	(1,200)
Finance costs	(2,400)	(1,000)	(600)
Profit before tax	15,600	6,000	4,400
Income tax expense	(4,800)	(1,200)	(800)
Profit for the year	10,800	4,800	3,600

(1) At 1 October 20X0 the fair value of the net assets of Jaco were equal to their carrying amounts, with the exception of an item of plant whose fair value exceeded its carrying amount by $400,000. At this date the remaining life of the plant was five years. All depreciation is charged to cost of sales.

(2) During the year to 30 September 20X3 Jaco sold goods to Zeffer for $1.2 million, at a margin of 30%. $300,000 of these goods were in Zeffer's inventory at 30 September 20X3.

(3) At 1 October 20X0 the fair value of Shem's net assets was equal to their carrying amount of $3.8 million.

(4) Zeffer values the non-controlling interest in its subsidiaries as a proportion of that subsidiary's net assets.

(5) At 1 October 20X2 Shem's net assets had a value of $5 million, and goodwill in Shem had been impaired by $200,000. The goodwill of Jaco was deemed unimpaired.

(6) The disposal of Shem satisfies the conditions to be treated as a discontinued operation according to IFRS 5 *Non-current Assets Held for Sale and Discontinued Operations*. No entries have been made in respect of the disposal of Shem.

Required:

Prepare the consolidated statement of profit or loss of the Zeffer Group for the year ended 30 September 20X3. (20 marks)

436 PERD CO

Perd Co acquired 80% of Sebastian Co on 1 April 20X6. Non-controlling interest is valued at fair value.

Extracts from the draft financial statements of both entities are shown below:

Statement of profit or loss for the year ended 31 March 20X8:

	Perd Co	Sebastian Co
	$000	$000
Revenue	58,200	34,300
Cost of sales	(34,340)	(20,400)
Gross profit	**23,860**	**13,900**
Operating expenses	(18,040)	(7,130)
Profit from operations	**5,820**	**6,770**
Investment income	3,000	-
Finance costs	(3,240)	(1,600)
Profit before tax	**5,580**	**5,170**
Tax	(1,560)	(1,480)
Profit for the year	**4,020**	**3,690**

Statement of financial position as at 31 March 20X8:

	Perd Co	**Sebastian Co**
	$000	$000
Total assets	**297,310**	**110,540**

The following information is relevant:

(1) The cost of Perd Co's investment in Sebastian Co has been excluded from the total assets listed above. As part of the consideration for Sebastian Co, $8m is due to be paid on 1 April 20X8. Perd Co recorded a liability of $7.547m in its individual statement of financial position at 31 March 20X7 which correctly represents the liability at that date. No other accounting entries have been made in relation to this consideration for the year ended 31 March 20X8. Perd Co has a cost of capital of 6%.

(2) On acquisition of Sebastian Co, the goodwill was correctly calculated at $3.2m. In the year to 31 March 20X7, goodwill was deemed to have been impaired by $400,000. A further impairment of $300,000 is to be recognised for the year ended 31 March 20X8. Impairment losses are charged to operating expenses.

(3) At 1 April 20X6, Sebastian Co's property had a carrying amount of $11m but a fair value of $14m. At this date, the property had a remaining life of 15 years. Sebastian Co sold the property for $15m on 30 September 20X7. For the year ended 31 March 20X8, Sebastian Co has recorded the historic cost depreciation and the historic cost profit on disposal of the property in operating expenses. Depreciation is charged on a pro-rata basis.

(4) Perd Co made sales of $9m to Sebastian Co during the year ended 31 March 20X8. Sebastian Co had only paid for $2m of these goods at 31 March 20X8. These sales were made at a mark-up on cost of 25%, and Sebastian Co holds one third of these goods at 31 March 20X8.

(5) At 31 March 20X8, the Perd group decided to revalue its non-current assets for the first time. Perd Co's assets were deemed to have increased by $4.1m and Sebastian Co's assets by $0.7m. Neither company has recorded the revaluation in its individual financial statements. Ignore deferred tax.

(6) Sebastian Co paid a dividend of $1m in the year, which has been correctly recorded by both companies.

Required:

(a) Prepare the consolidated statement of profit or loss and other comprehensive income for the Perd group for the year ended 31 March 20X8. (15 marks)

(b) Calculate the total assets that would be recognised in the consolidated statement of financial position for the Perd group as at 31 March 20X8. (5 marks)

(Total: 20 marks)

437 DOBRY

Dobry Co purchased its 80% shareholding in Krol Co for cash five years ago when Krol Co's retained earnings were $30,000 and the balance on its revaluation surplus was $15,000.

Henz Co had retained earnings of $16,000 when Dobry Co acquired its 75% shareholding for cash of $100,000 on 1 January 20X6 with a further cash payment of $87,200 deferred until 1 January 20X7. No accounting entries have been made in respect of the deferred cash consideration. Dobry Co has a cost of capital of 9%.

The following are the summarised statements of financial position of the companies as at 31 December 20X6:

	Dobry Co	Krol Co	Henz Co
	$	$	$
Non-current assets:			
Property, plant and equipment	240,000	130,000	120,000
Investments:			
Krol Co	180,000	–	–
Henz Co	100,000	–	–
Current assets	526,000	170,000	80,000
	1,046,000	300,000	200,000
Ordinary $1 share capital	500,000	100,000	100,000
Revaluation surplus	–	30,000	–
Retained earnings	238,000	80,000	32,000
	738,000	210,000	132,000
Current liabilities	308,000	90,000	68,000
	1,046,000	300,000	200,000

(1) At the date of acquisition the fair value of Krol Co's net assets was equal to their carrying amount.

(2) At the date of acquisition the fair value of Henz Co's net assets was equal to their carrying amount, with the exception of some plant whose fair value was $24,000 greater than its carrying amount. At this date the plant had a remaining useful life of four years.

(3) At the end of 20X6, the goodwill impairment review revealed a loss of $8,000 in relation to the business combination with Krol Co. The goodwill in Henz was unimpaired.

(4) During November 20X6, Krol Co sold goods to Dobry Co for $18,000 at a mark-up on cost of 20%. Half of these goods were still held by Dobry Co at 31 December 20X6, and the balance payable was still outstanding.

(5) Dobry Co measures goodwill and the non-controlling interest using the fair value method for Krol Co, and the proportionate method for Henz Co. The fair value of the non-controlling interest of Krol Co at the date of acquisition was $39,000.

Required:

Prepare the consolidated statement of financial position of the Dobry group as at 31 December 20X6. **(Total: 20 marks)**

ANALYSING FINANCIAL STATEMENTS

438 WOODBANK

Shown below are the financial statements of Woodbank for its most recent two years.

Consolidated statements of profit or loss for the year ended 31 March:

	20X4	**20X3**
	$000	$000
Revenue	150,000	110,000
Cost of sales	(117,000)	(85,800)
Gross profit	33,000	24,200
Distribution costs	(6,000)	(5,000)
Administrative expenses	(9,000)	(9,200)
Finance costs – loan note interest	(1,750)	(500)
Profit before tax	16,250	9,500
Income tax expense	(5,750)	(3,000)
Profit for the year	10,500	6,500

Statements of financial position as at 31 March:

	20X4	**20X3**
	$000	$000
Assets		
Non-current assets		
Property, plant and equipment	118,000	85,000
Goodwill	30,000	nil
	148,000	85,000
Current assets		
Inventory	15,500	12,000
Trade receivables	11,000	8,000
Bank	500	5,000
	27,000	25,000
Total assets	175,000	110,000

Equity		
Equity shares of $1 each	80,000	80,000
Retained earnings	15,000	10,000
Retained earnings	15,000	10,000
	95,000	90,000
Non-current liabilities: 10% loan notes	55,000	5,000
Current liabilities		
Trade payables	21,000	13,000
Current tax payable	4,000	2,000
	25,000	15,000
Total equity and liabilities	175,000	110,000

The following information is available:

(1) On 1 January 20X4, Woodbank purchased the trading assets and operations of Shaw for $50 million and, on the same date, issued additional 10% loan notes to finance the purchase. Shaw was an unincorporated entity and its results (for three months from 1 January 20X4 to 31 March 20X4) and net assets (including goodwill not subject to any impairment) are included in Woodbank's financial statements for the year ended 31 March 20X4. There were no other purchases or sales of non-current assets during the year ended 31 March 20X4.

(2) Extracts of the results (for three months) of the previously separate business of Shaw, which are included in Woodbank's statement of profit or loss for the year ended 31 March 20X4, are:

	$000
Revenue	30,000
Cost of sales	(21,000)
Gross profit	9,000
Distribution costs	(2,000)
Administrative expenses	(2,000)

(3) The following six ratios have been correctly calculated for Woodbank for the year ended 31 March:

	20X3	20X4
Return on capital employed (ROCE) (profit before interest and tax/year-end total assets less current liabilities)	10.5%	12.0%
Net asset (equal to capital employed) turnover	1.16 times	1.0 times
Gross profit margin	22.0%	22.0%
Profit before interest and tax margin	9.1%	12.0%
Current ratio	1.7:1	1.08:1
Gearing (debt/(debt + equity))	5.3%	36.7%

Required:

(a) **Calculate for the year ended 31 March 20X4 equivalent ratios to the first FOUR only for Woodbank excluding the effects of the purchase of Shaw.**

Note: Assume the capital employed for Shaw is equal to its purchase price of $50 million. **(4 marks)**

(b) **Assess the comparative financial performance and position of Woodbank for the year ended 31 March 20X4. Your answer should refer to the effects of the purchase of Shaw.** **(12 marks)**

(c) **Discuss what further information specific to the acquisition of Shaw that would allow you to make a more informed assessment of Woodbank's performance and position.** **(4 marks)**

(Total: 20 marks)

439 HYDAN

Answer debrief

Xpand is a publicly listed entity which has experienced rapid growth in recent years through the acquisition and integration of other entities. Xpand is interested in acquiring Hydan, a retailing business, which is one of several entities owned and managed by the same family, of which Lodan is the ultimate parent.

The summarised financial statements of Hydan for the year ended 30 September 20X4 are:

Statement of profit or loss

	$000
Revenue	70,000
Cost of sales	(45,000)
Gross profit	25,000
Operating costs	(7,000)
Directors' salaries	(1,000)
Profit before tax	17,000
Income tax expense	(3,000)
Profit for the year	14,000

Statement of financial position

	$000	$000
Assets		
Non-current assets		
Property, plant and equipment		32,400
Current assets		
Inventory	7,500	
Bank	100	
		7,600
Total assets		40,000
Equity and liabilities		
Equity		
Equity shares of $1 each		1,000
Retained earnings		18,700
		19,700
Non-current liabilities		
Directors' loan accounts (interest free)		10,000
Current liabilities		
Trade payables	7,500	
Current tax payable	2,800	
		10,300
Total equity and liabilities		40,000

From the above financial statements, Xpand has calculated for Hydan the ratios below for the year ended 30 September 20X4. It has also obtained the equivalent ratios for the retail sector average which can be taken to represent Hydan's sector.

	Hydan	**Sector average**
Return on equity (ROE) (including directors' loan accounts)	47.1%	22.0%
Net asset turnover	2.36 times	1.67 times
Gross profit margin	35.7%	30.0%
Net profit margin	20.0%	12.0%

From enquiries made, Xpand has learned the following information:

(1) Hydan buys all of its trading inventory from another of the family entities at a price which is 10% less than the market price for such goods.

(2) After the acquisition, Xpand would replace the existing board of directors and need to pay remuneration of $2.5 million per annum.

(3) The directors' loan accounts would be repaid by obtaining a loan of the same amount with interest at 10% per annum.

(4) Xpand expects the purchase price of Hydan to be $30 million.

Required:

(a) **Recalculate the ratios for Hydan after making appropriate adjustments to the financial statements for notes (1) to (4) above. For this purpose, the expected purchase price of $30 million should be taken as Hydan's equity and net assets are equal to this equity plus the loan. You may assume the changes will have no effect on taxation.** **(6 marks)**

(b) **In relation to the ratios calculated in (a) above, and the ratios for Hydan given in the question, comment on the performance of Hydan compared to its retail sector average.** **(9 marks)**

(c) One of Xpand's directors has suggested that it would be wise to look at the Lodan group's consolidated financial statements rather than Hydan's individual financial statements.

As an adviser to Xpand, explain any concerns you would raise about basing an investment decision on the information available in Lodan's consolidated financial statements and Hydan's entity financial statements. **(5 marks)**

(Total: 20 marks)

 **Calculate your allowed time, allocate the time to the separate parts**

440 YOGI

Yogi is a public entity and extracts from its most recent financial statements are provided below:

Statements of profit or loss for the year ended 31 March

	20X5	**20X4**
	$000	$000
Revenue	36,000	50,000
Cost of sales	(24,000)	(30,000)
Gross profit	12,000	20,000
Profit from sale of division (see note (1))	1,000	nil
Distribution costs	(3,500)	(5,300)
Administrative expenses	(4,800)	(2,900)
Finance costs	(400)	(800)
Profit before taxation	4,300	11,000
Income tax expense	(1,300)	(3,300)
Profit for the year	3,000	7,700

Statements of financial position as at 31 March

	20X5		20X4	
	$000	$000	$000	$000
Property, plant and equipment		16,300		19,000
Intangible – goodwill		nil		2,000
		16,300		21,000
Inventory	3,400		5,800	
Trade receivables	1,300		2,400	
Bank	1,500		nil	
		6,200		8,200
Total assets		22,500		29,200
Equity shares of $1 each		10,000		10,000
Retained earnings		3,000		4,000
		13,000		14,000
Non-current liabilities				
10% loan notes		4,000		8,000
Current liabilities				
Bank overdraft	nil		1,400	
Trade payables	4,300		3,100	
Current tax payable	1,200		2,700	
		5,500		7,200
Total equity and liabilities		22,500		29,200

Notes

(1) On 1 April 20X4, Yogi sold the net assets (including goodwill) of a separately operated division of its business for $8 million cash, making a profit of $1 million. This transaction required shareholder approval and, to secure this, the management of Yogi offered shareholders a dividend of 40 cents for each share in issue out of the proceeds of the sale. The trading results of the division which are included in the statement of profit or loss for the year ended 31 March 20X4 above are:

	$000
Revenue	18,000
Cost of sales	(10,000)
Gross profit	8,000
Distribution costs	(1,000)
Administrative expenses	(1,200)
Profit before interest and tax	5,800

(2) The following selected ratios for Yogi have been calculated for the year ended 31 March 20X4 (as reported above):

Gross profit margin	40.0%
Operating profit margin	23.6%
Return on capital employed	
(profit before interest and tax/(total assets – current liabilities))	53.6%
Net asset turnover	2.27 times

Required:

(a) Calculate the equivalent ratios for Yogi:

(1) for the year ended 31 March 20X4, after excluding the contribution made by the division that has been sold, and

(2) for the year ended 31 March 20X5, excluding the profit on the sale of the division. (5 marks)

(b) Comment on the comparative financial performance and position of Yogi for the year ended 31 March 20X5. (10 marks)

(c) On a separate matter, you have been asked to advise on an application for a loan to build an extension to a sports club which is a not-for-profit organisation. You have been provided with the audited financial statements of the sports club for the last four years.

Required:

Identify and explain the ratios that you would calculate to assist in determining whether you would advise that the loan should be granted. (5 marks)

(Total: 20 marks)

441 XPAND

Xpand is a public entity which has grown in recent years by acquiring established businesses. The following financial statements for two potential target entities are shown below. They operate in the same industry sector and Xpand believes their shareholders would be receptive to a takeover. An indicative price for 100% acquisition of the entities is $12 million each.

Statements of profit or loss for the year ended 30 September 20X5

	Kandid	**Kovert**
	$000	$000
Revenue	25,000	40,000
Cost of sales	(19,000)	(32,800)
Gross profit	6,000	7,200
Distribution and administrative expenses	(1,250)	(2,300)
Finance costs	(250)	(900)
Profit before tax	4,500	4,000
Income tax expense	(900)	(1,000)
Profit for the year	3,600	3,000

Statements of financial position as at 30 September 20X5

	$000	$000
Non-current assets		
Property	nil	3,000
Owned plant	4,800	2,000
Right-of-use asset	nil	5,300
	4,800	10,300
Current assets		
Inventory	1,600	3,400
Trade receivables	2,100	5,100
Bank	1,100	200
	4,800	8,700
Total assets	9,600	19,000
Equity and liabilities		
Equity		
Equity shares of $1 each	1,000	2,000
Property revaluation surplus	nil	900
Retained earnings	1,600	2,700
	2,600	5,600
Non-current liabilities		
Lease liability	nil	4,200
5% loan notes (31 December 20X6)	5,000	nil
10% loan notes (31 December 20X6)	nil	5,000
	5,000	9,200
Current liabilities		
Trade payables	1,250	2,100
Lease liability	nil	1,000
Taxation	750	1,100
	2,000	4,200
Total equity and liabilities	9,600	19,000

Notes

(1) Carrying amount of plant:

	Kandid	Kovert
	$000	$000
Owned plant – cost	8,000	10,000
Less government grant	(2,000)	
	6,000	
Accumulated depreciation	(1,200)	(8,000)
	4,800	2,000
Right-of-use asset – initial value	nil	8,000

(2) The following ratios have been calculated:

	Kandid	Kovert
Return on year-end capital employed (ROCE)	62.5%	
Net asset (taken as same figure as capital employed) turnover	3.3 times	2.5 times
Gross profit margin	24.0%	18.0%
Profit margin (before interest and tax)	19.0%	
Current ratio	2.4:1	2.1:1
Closing inventory holding period	31 days	38 days
Trade receivables collection period	31 days	47 days
Trade payables payment period (using cost of sales)	24 days	
Gearing (debt/(debt + equity))	65.8%	

Required:

(a) **Calculate the missing ratios for Kovert. All lease liabilities are treated as debt, and profit before interest and tax should be used for the calculation of return on capital employed. (4 marks)**

(b) **Using the above information, assess the relative performance and financial position of Kandid and Kovert for the year ended 30 September 20X5 in order to assist the directors of Xpand to make an acquisition decision. (12 marks)**

(c) **Describe what further information may be useful to Xpand when making an acquisition decision. (4 marks)**

(Total: 20 marks)

442 PITCARN

The Pitcarn group owns a number of subsidiaries. On 31 March 20X6, the Pitcarn group sold its entire holding in Sitor. The consolidated statement of profit or loss of the Pitcarn group for 20X6 has been produced **without** the results of Sitor due to its disposal. No profit or loss on disposal has been included in the 20X6 consolidated statement of profit or loss.

Extracts from the consolidated statements of profit or loss for the Pitcarn group are below:

Statements of profit or loss (extracts) for the year ended 31 March

	20X6	20X5
	$000	$000
Revenue	86,000	99,000
Cost of sales (note (2))	(63,400)	(67,200)
Gross profit	22,600	31,800
Other income (notes (1) and (3))	3,400	1,500
Operating expenses	(21,300)	(23,200)
Profit from operations	4,700	10,100
Finance costs	(1,500)	(1,900)

The following notes are relevant:

(1) Sitor was based in the Pitcarn head offices, for which it pays annual rent to Pitcarn of $300,000, significantly below the cost of equivalent office space in Sitor's local area. As Sitor is no longer in the group, Pitcarn has included this income within other income. Sitor expenses rent payments in operating expenses.

(2) Sitor sold goods totalling $8 million to Pitcarn (included in Pitcarn's cost of sales above) during the year. Pitcarn held none of these goods in inventory at 31 March 20X6. Sitor made a margin of 40% on all goods sold to Pitcarn.

(3) Pitcarn received a dividend of $1 million from Sitor during the year, as well as recording interest of $500,000 on a loan given to Sitor in 20X3. Both of these amounts are included within Pitcarn's other income.

The following selected ratios for the Pitcarn group have been calculated for the years ended 31 March 20X5 and 31 March 20X6 from the information above.

	20X6	20X5
Gross profit margin	26.3%	32.1%
Operating margin	5.5%	10.2%
Interest cover	3.1 times	5.3 times

(4) Sitor's individual statement of profit or loss for the year ended shows the following:

	$000
Revenue	16,000
Cost of sales	(10,400)
Gross profit	5,600
Operating expenses	(3,200)
Profit from operations	2,400
Finance costs	(900)

Required:

(a) **Calculate the equivalent ratios for the consolidated statement of profit or loss for the year ended 31 March 20X6 if Sitor had been consolidated. (7 marks)**

(b) **Analyse the performance of the Pitcarn group for the year ended 31 March 20X6. This should also include a discussion of Sitor. (8 marks)**

(c) Pitcarn acquired 80% of Sitor's 10 million $1 shares on 1 April 20X1 for $17 million when Sitor had retained earnings of $3 million. Pitcarn uses the fair value method for valuing the non-controlling interest. At acquisition the fair value of the non-controlling interest was $3 million.

On 31 March 20X6, Pitcarn sold its entire shareholding in Sitor for $25 million when Sitor had retained earnings of $7 million. Goodwill had suffered no impairment since acquisition.

Calculate the gain/loss on disposal to be shown in the consolidated statement of profit or loss for the year ended 31 March 20X6. (5 marks)

(Total: 20 marks)

443 GREGORY

Gregory is a listed entity and, until 1 October 20X5, it had no subsidiaries. On that date, it acquired 75% of Tamsin's equity shares by means of a share exchange of two new shares in Gregory for every five acquired shares in Tamsin. These shares were recorded at the market price on the day of the acquisition and were the only shares issued by Gregory during the year ended 31 March 20X6.

The summarised financial statements of Gregory as a group at 31 March 20X6 and as a single entity at 31 March 20X5 are:

	Gregory group	**Gregory single entity**
Statements of profit or loss for the year ended	31 March 20X6	31 March 20X5
	$000	$000
Revenue	46,500	28,000
Cost of sales	(37,200)	(20,800)
Gross profit	9,300	7,200
Operating expenses	(1,800)	(1,200)
Profit before tax (operating profit)	7,500	6,000
Income tax expense	(1,500)	(1,000)
Profit for the year	6,000	5,000
Profit for year attributable to:		
Equity holders of the parent	5,700	
Non-controlling interest	300	
	6,000	

Statements of financial position as at	31 March 20X6	31 March 20X5
Assets	$000	$000
Non-current assets		
Property, plant and equipment	54,600	41,500
Goodwill	3,000	nil
	57,600	41,500
Current assets	44,000	36,000
Total assets	101,600	77,500

	31 March 20X6	**31 March 20X5**
Equity and liabilities	$000	$000
Equity		
Equity shares of $1 each	46,000	40,000
Other component of equity (share premium)	6,000	nil
Retained earnings	18,700	13,000
Equity attributable to owners of the parent	70,700	53,000
Non-controlling interest	3,600	nil
	74,300	53,000
Current liabilities	27,300	24,500
Total equity and liabilities	101,600	77,500

Other information:

(1) Each month since the acquisition, Gregory's sales to Tamsin were consistently $2m. Gregory had chosen to only make a gross profit margin of 10% on these sales as Tamsin is part of the group.

(2) The values of property, plant and equipment held by both entities have been rising for several years.

(3) On reviewing the above financial statements, Gregory's chief executive officer (CEO) made the following observations:

 (i) I see the profit for the year has increased by $1m which is up 20% on last year, but I thought it would be more as Tamsin was supposed to be very profitable.

 (ii) I have calculated the earnings per share (EPS) for 20X6 at 13 cents (6,000/46,000 × 100) and for 20X5 at 12.5 cents (5,000/40,000 × 100) and, although the profit has increased 20%, our EPS has barely changed.

 (iii) I am worried that the low price at which we are selling goods to Tamsin is undermining our group's overall profitability.

 (iv) I note that our share price is now $2.30, how does this compare with our share price immediately before we bought Tamsin?

Required:

(a) Reply to the four observations of the CEO. (8 marks)

(b) Using the above financial statements, calculate the following ratios for Gregory for the years ended 31 March 20X6 and 20X5 and comment on the comparative performance:

(i) Return on capital employed (ROCE)

(ii) Net asset turnover

(iii) Gross profit margin

(iv) Operating profit margin.

Note: Four marks are available for the ratio calculations. **(12 marks)**

Note: Your answers to (a) and (b) should reflect the impact of the consolidation of Tamsin during the year ended 31 March 20X6.

(Total: 20 marks)

444 LANDING

Landing is considering the acquisition of Archway, a retail entity. The summarised financial statements of Archway for the year ended 30 September 20X6 are:

Statement of profit or loss

	$000
Revenue	94,000
Cost of sales	(73,000)
Gross profit	21,000
Distribution costs	(4,000)
Administrative expenses	(6,000)
Finance costs	(400)
Profit before tax	10,600
Income tax expense (at 20%)	(2,120)
Profit for the year	8,480

Statement of financial position

	$000	$000
Non-current assets		
Property, plant and equipment		29,400
Current assets		
Inventory	10,500	
Bank	100	
		10,600
Total assets		40,000

Equity and liabilities		
Equity shares of $1 each		10,000
Retained earnings		8,800
		18,800
Current liabilities		
4% loan notes (redeemable 1 November 20X6)	10,000	
Trade payables	9,200	
Current tax payable	2,000	
		21,200
Total equity and liabilities		40,000

From enquiries made, Landing has obtained the following information:

(1) Archway pays an annual licence fee of $1m to Cardol (included in cost of sales) for the right to package and sell some goods under a well-known brand name owned by Cardol. If Archway is acquired, this arrangement would be discontinued. Landing estimates that this would not affect Archway's volume of sales, but without the use of the brand name packaging, overall sales revenue would be 5% lower than currently.

(2) Archway buys 50% of its purchases for resale from Cardol, one of Landing's rivals, and receives a bulk-buying discount of 10% off normal prices (this discount does not apply to the annual licence fee referred to in note (1) above). This discount would not be available if Archway is acquired by Landing.

(3) The 4% loan notes have been classified as a current liability due to their imminent redemption. As such, they should not be treated as long-term funding. However, they will be replaced immediately after redemption by 8% loan notes with the same nominal value, repayable in ten years' time.

(4) Landing has obtained some of Archway's retail sector average ratios for the year ended 30 September 20X6. It has then calculated the equivalent ratios for Archway as shown below:

	Sector average	**Archway**
Annual sales per square metre of floor space	$8,000	$7,833
Return on capital employed (ROCE)	18.0%	58.5%
Net asset (total assets less current liabilities) turnover	2.7 times	5.0 times
Gross profit margin	22.0%	22.3%
Operating profit (profit before interest and tax) margin	6.7%	11.7%
Gearing (debt/equity)	30.0%	nil

A note accompanying the sector average ratios explains that it is the practice of the sector to carry retail property at market value. The market value of Archway's retail property is $3m more than its carrying amount (ignore the effect of any consequent additional depreciation) and gives 12,000 square metres of floor space.

Required:

(a) After making adjustments to the financial statements of Archway which you think may be appropriate for comparability purposes, restate:

(i) Revenue

(ii) Cost of sales

(iii) Finance costs

(iv) Equity (assume that your adjustments to profit or loss result in retained earnings of $2.3 million at 30 September 20X6) and

(v) Non-current liabilities. (5 marks)

(b) Recalculate comparable sector average ratios for Archway based on your restated figures in (a) above. (6 marks)

(c) Comment on the performance and gearing of Archway compared to the retail sector average as a basis for advising Landing regarding the possible acquisition of Archway. (9 marks)

(Total: 20 marks)

445 FUNJECT CO

Funject Co has identified Aspect Co as a possible acquisition within the same industry. Aspect Co is currently owned by the Gamilton Group and the following are extracts from the financial statements of Aspect Co:

Extract from the statement of profit or loss for the year ended 31 December 20X4

	$000
Revenue	54,200
Cost of sales	(21,500)
Gross profit	32,700
Operating expenses	(11,700)
Operating profit	21,000

Statement of financial position as at 31 December 20X4

	$000	$000
Non-current assets		24,400
Current assets		
Inventory	4,900	
Receivables	5,700	
Cash at bank	2,300	
		12,900
Total assets		37,300

Equity and liabilities		
Equity shares		1,000
Retained earnings		8,000
		9,000
Non-current liabilities: Loan		16,700
Current liabilities		
Trade payables	5,400	
Current tax payable	6,200	
		11,600
Total equity and liabilities		37,300

Additional information:

(1) On 1 April 20X4, Aspect Co decided to focus on its core business, and so disposed of a non-core division. The disposal generated a loss of $1.5m which is included within operating expenses for the year. The following extracts show the results of the non-core division for the period prior to disposal which were included in Aspect Co's results for 20X4:

	$000
Revenue	2,100
Cost of sales	(1,200)
Gross profit	900
Operating expenses	(700)
Operating profit	200

(2) At present Aspect Co pays a management charge of 1% of revenue to the Gamilton Group, which is included in operating expenses. Funject Co imposes a management charge of 10% of gross profit on all of its subsidiaries.

(3) Aspect Co's administration offices are currently located within a building owned by the Gamilton Group. If Aspect Co were acquired, the company would need to seek alternative premises. Aspect Co paid rent of $46,000 in 20X4. Commercial rents for equivalent office space would cost $120,000.

(4) The following is a list of comparable industry average key performance indicators (KPIs) for 20X4:

KPI	
Gross profit margin	45%
Operating profit margin	28%
Receivables collection period	41 days
Current ratio	1.6:1
Acid test (quick) ratio	1.4:1
Gearing (debt/equity)	240%

Required:

(a) **Redraft Aspect Co's statement of profit or loss for 20X4 to adjust for the disposal of the non-core division in note (1) and the management and rent charges which would be imposed per notes (2) and (3) if Aspect Co was acquired by Funject Co. (5 marks)**

(b) **Calculate the 20X4 ratios for Aspect Co equivalent to those shown in note (4) based on the restated financial information calculated in part (a).**

Note: You should assume that any increase or decrease in profit as a result of your adjustments in part (a) will also increase or decrease cash. **(5 marks)**

(c) **Using the ratios calculated in part (b), comment on Aspect Co's 20X4 performance and financial position compared to the industry average KPIs provided in note (4). (10 marks)**

(Total: 20 marks)

446 FLASH CO

Flash Co sells electrical products both directly to the public and also to business trade customers. Flash Co operates from several properties which it owns. During 20X4, one of Flash Co's competitors ceased trading and Flash Co acquired a number of its properties and opened new stores in those properties in February 20X4.

Extracts from the statements of profit or loss for the years ended 31 March 20X3 and 20X4 are shown below, in addition to the statement of cash flows for the year ended 31 March 20X4.

Statement of profit or loss for the years ended 31 March

	20X4	**20X3**
	$000	$000
Revenue	92,600	81,700
Cost of sales	(55,600)	(52,300)
Gross profit	37,000	29,400
Operating expenses	(14,400)	(12,300)
Profit from operations	22,600	17,100
Finance costs	(5,100)	(4,200)
Profit before tax	17,500	12,900

Statement of cash flows for the year ended 31 March 20X4

	$000	$000
Cash flows from operating activities:		
Cash generated from operations (note (1))		29,900
Interest paid		(4,300)
Tax paid		(3,100)
Net cash flows from operating activities		22,500
Cash flows from investing activities:		
Purchase of property, plant and equipment		(31,600)
Cash flows from financing activities:		
8% loan notes issued	10,000	
Dividends paid	(4,000)	
		6,000
Net decrease in cash and cash equivalents		(3,100)
Cash and cash equivalents 31 March 20X3		4,700
Cash and cash equivalents 31 March 20X4		1,600

The following notes are relevant:

(1) Cash generated from operations for the year ended 31 March 20X4 is calculated as follows:

	$000
Profit before tax	17,500
Finance costs	5,100
Depreciation	6,800
Decrease in inventories	3,100
Increase in trade receivables	(6,200)
Increase in trade payables	3,600
Cash generated from operations	29,900

Note: The cash generated from operations for the year ended 31 March 20X3 was $18m.

(2) During the year ended 31 March 20X4, the sale of solar panels was one of Flash Co's key areas of business. During that year, demand has often been greater than supply.

(3) During the year ended 31 March 20X4, Flash Co expanded into new geographical regions in which it was previously unrepresented.

(4) The geographical expansion has allowed Flash Co to negotiate improved terms with some of its major suppliers.

(5) Flash Co's sales director has expressed confusion at the latest financial statements, not understanding the deterioration in cash position despite increased levels of profit.

Required:

(a) Calculate the following ratios for the years ended 31 March 20X3 and 20X4:

- **Gross profit margin %**
- **Operating profit margin %**
- **Interest cover**
- **Cash generated from operations/profit from operations %.** **(4 marks)**

(b) Comment on the performance and cash flows of Flash Co for 20X4.

Note: Your answer should specifically address the sales director's confusion.

(16 marks)

(Total: 20 marks)

447 MOWAIR CO

Mowair Co is an international airline which flies to destinations all over the world. Mowair Co experienced strong initial growth but in recent periods the company has been criticised for under-investing in its non-current assets.

Extracts from Mowair Co's financial statements are provided below.

Statements of financial position as at 30 June:

	20X7	20X6
	$000	$000
Assets		
Non-current assets		
Property, plant and equipment	317,000	174,000
Intangible assets (note ii)	20,000	16,000
	337,000	190,000
Current assets		
Inventories	580	490
Trade and other receivables	6,100	6,300
Cash and cash equivalents	9,300	22,100
Total current assets	15,980	28,890
Total assets	352,980	218,890

Equity and liabilities		
Equity		
Equity shares	3,000	3,000
Retained earnings	44,100	41,800
Revaluation surplus	145,000	Nil
Total equity	192,100	44,800
Liabilities		
Non-current liabilities		
6% loan notes	130,960	150,400
Current liabilities		
Trade and other payables	10,480	4,250
6% loan notes	19,440	19,440
Total current liabilities	29,920	23,690
Total equity and liabilities	352,980	218,890

Other EXTRACTS from Mowair Co's financial statements for the years ended 30 June:

	20X7	**20X6**
	$000	$000
Revenue	154,000	159,000
Profit from operations	12,300	18,600
Finance costs	(9,200)	(10,200)
Cash generated from operations	18,480	24,310

The following information is also relevant:

(1) Mowair Co had exactly the same flight schedule in 20X7 as in 20X6, with the overall number of flights and destinations being the same in both years.

(2) In April 20X7, Mowair Co had to renegotiate its licences with five major airports, which led to an increase in the prices Mowair Co had to pay for the right to operate flights there. The licences with ten more major airports are due to expire in December 20X7, and Mowair Co is currently in negotiation with these airports.

Required:

(a) Calculate the following ratios for the years ended 30 June 20X6 and 20X7:

(1) Operating profit margin

(2) Return on capital employed

(3) Net asset turnover

(4) Current ratio

(5) Interest cover

(6) Gearing (Debt/Equity).

Note: For calculation purposes, all loan notes should be treated as debt. (6 marks)

(b) Comment on the performance and position of Mowair Co for the year ended 30 June 20X7.

Note: Your answer should highlight any issues which Mowair Co should be considering in the near future. **(14 marks)**

(Total: 20 marks)

448 PERKINS

Below are extracts from the statements of profit or loss for the Perkins group and Perkins Co for the years ending 31 December 20X7 and 20X6 respectively.

	20X7	**20X6**
	(Consolidated)	(Perkins Co individual)
	$000	$000
Revenue	46,220	35,714
Cost of sales	(23,980)	(19,714)
Gross profit	22,240	16,000
Operating expenses	(3,300)	(10,000)
Profit from operations	18,940	6,000
Finance costs	(960)	(1,700)
Profit before tax	17,980	4,300

The following information is relevant:

On 1 September 20X7, Perkins Co sold all of its shares in Swanson Co, its only subsidiary, for $28.64m. At this date, Swanson Co had net assets of $26.1m. Perkins Co originally acquired 80% of Swanson Co for $19.2m, when Swanson Co had net assets of $19.8m. Perkins Co uses the fair value method for valuing the non-controlling interest, which was measured at $4.9m at the date of acquisition. Goodwill in Swanson Co has not been impaired since acquisition.

In order to compare Perkin Co's results for the years ended 20X6 and 20X7, the results of Swanson Co need to be eliminated from the above consolidated statements of profit or loss for 20X7. Although Swanson Co was correctly accounted for in the group financial statements for the year ended 31 December 20X7, a gain on disposal of Swanson Co of $9.44m is currently included in operating expenses. This reflects the gain which should have been shown in Perkins Co's individual financial statements.

In the year ended 31 December 20X7, Swanson Co had the following results:

	$m
Revenue	13.50
Cost of sales	6.60
Operating expenses	2.51
Finance costs	1.20

During the period from 1 January 20X7 to 1 September 20X7, Perkins Co sold $1m of goods to Swanson Co at a margin of 30%. Swanson Co had sold all of these goods on to third parties by 1 September 20X7.

Swanson Co previously used space in Perkins Co's properties, which Perkins Co did not charge Swanson Co for. Since the disposal of Swanson Co, Perkins Co has rented that space to a new tenant, recording the rental income in operating expenses.

The following ratios have been correctly calculated based on the above financial statements:

	20X7 (Consolidated)	**20X6** (Perkins Co individual)
Gross profit margin	48.1%	44.8%
Operating margin	41%	16.8%
Interest cover	19.7 times	3.5 times

Required:

(a) **Calculate the gain on disposal which should have been shown in the consolidated statement of profit or loss for the Perkins group for the year ended 31 December 20X7.** **(5 marks)**

(b) **Remove the results of Swanson Co and the gain on disposal of the subsidiary to prepare a revised statement of profit or loss for the year ended 31 December 20X7 for Perkins Co only.** **(4 marks)**

(c) **Calculate the equivalent ratios to those given for Perkins Co for 20X7 based on the revised figures in part (b) of your answer.** **(2 marks)**

(d) **Using the ratios calculated in part (c) and those provided in the question, comment on the performance of Perkins Co for the years ended 31 December 20X6 and 20X7.** **(9 marks)**

(Total: 20 marks)

449 DUKE CO

Duke Co is a retailer with stores in numerous city centres. On 1 January 20X8, Duke Co acquired 80% of the equity share capital of Smooth Co, a service company specialising in training and recruitment. This was the first time Duke Co had acquired a subsidiary.

The consideration for Smooth Co consisted of a cash element and the issue of some shares in Duke Co to the previous owners of Smooth Co.

Duke Co has begun to consolidate Smooth Co into its financial statements, but has yet to calculate the non-controlling interest and retained earnings. Details of the relevant information is provided in notes (1) and (2).

Extracts from the financial statements for the Duke group for the year ended 30 June 20X8 and Duke Co for the year ended 30 June 20X7 are provided below:

	Duke Group	**Duke Co**
	30 June 20X8	30 June 20X7
	$000	$000
Profit from operations	14,500	12,700
Current assets	30,400	28,750
Share capital	11,000	8,000
Share premium	6,000	2,000
Retained earnings	Note (1) and (2)	9,400
Non-controlling interest	Note (1) and (2)	Nil
Long-term loans	11,500	7,000
Current liabilities	21,300	15,600

The following notes are relevant:

(1) The fair value of the non-controlling interest in Smooth Co at 1 January 20X8 was deemed to be $3.4m. The retained earnings of Duke Co in its individual financial statements at 30 June 20X8 are $13.2m.

Smooth Co made a profit for the year ended 30 June 20X8 of $7m. Duke Co incurred professional fees of $0.5m during the acquisition, which have been capitalised as an asset in the consolidated financial statements.

(2) The following issues are also relevant to the calculation of non-controlling interest and retained earnings:

– At acquisition, Smooth Co's net assets were equal to their carrying amount with the exception of a brand name which had a fair value of $3m but was not recognised in Smooth Co's individual financial statements. It is estimated that the brand had a five-year life at 1 January 20X8.

– On 30 June 20X8, Smooth Co sold land to Duke Co for $4m when it had a carrying amount of $2.5m.

(3) Smooth Co is based in the service industry and a significant part of its business comes from three large, profitable contracts with entities which are both well-established and financially stable.

(4) Duke Co did not borrow additional funds during the current year and has never used a bank overdraft facility.

(5) The following ratios have been correctly calculated based on the above financial statements:

	20X8	20X7
Receivables collection period	52 days	34 days
Inventory holding period	41 days	67 days

Other than the recognition of the non-controlling interest and retained earnings, no adjustment is required to any of the other figures in the draft financial statements. All items are deemed to accrue evenly across the year.

Required:

(a) Calculate the non-controlling interest and retained earnings to be included in the consolidated financial statements at 30 June 20X8. (6 marks)

(b) Based on your answer to part (a) and the financial statements provided, calculate the following ratios for the years ending 30 June 20X7 and 30 June 20X8:

Current ratio:

Return on capital employed

Gearing (debt/equity). (4 marks)

(c) Using the information provided and the ratios calculated above, comment on the comparative performance and position for the two years ended 30 June 20X7 and 20X8.

Note: Your answer should specifically comment on the impact of the acquisition of Smooth Co on your analysis. **(10 marks)**

(Total: 20 marks)

450 PIRLO

The consolidated statements of profit or loss for the Pirlo group for the years ended 31 December 20X9 and 20X8 are shown below.

	20X9	20X8
	$000	$000
Revenue	213,480	216,820
Cost of sales	(115,620)	(119,510)
Gross profit	97,860	97,310
Operating expenses	(72,360)	(68,140)
Profit from operations	25,500	29,170
Finance costs	(17,800)	(16,200)
Investment income	2,200	2,450
Profit before tax	9,900	15,420
Share of profit of associate	4,620	3,160
Tax expense	(2,730)	(3,940)
Profit for the year	11,790	14,640
Attributable to:		
Shareholders of Pirlo Co	8,930	12,810
Non-controlling interest	2,860	1,830

The following information is relevant:

(1) On 31 December 20X9, the Pirlo group disposed of its entire 80% holding in Samba Co, a software development company, for $300m. The Samba Co results have been fully consolidated into the consolidated financial statements above. Samba Co does not represent a discontinued operation.

(2) The proceeds from the disposal of Samba Co have been credited to a suspense account and no gain/loss has been recorded in the financial statements above.

(3) Pirlo Co originally acquired the shares in Samba Co for $210m. At this date, goodwill was calculated at $70m. Goodwill has not been impaired since acquisition, and external advisers estimate that the goodwill arising in Samba Co has a value of $110m at 31 December 20X9.

(4) On 31 December 20X9, Samba Co had net assets with a carrying amount of $260m. In addition to this, Samba Co's brand name was valued at $50m at acquisition in the consolidated financial statements. This is not reflected in Samba Co's individual financial statements, and the value is assessed to be the same at 31 December 20X9.

(5) Samba Co is the only subsidiary in which the Pirlo group owned less than 100% of the equity. The Pirlo group uses the fair value method to value the non-controlling interest. At 31 December 20X9, the non-controlling interest in Samba Co is deemed to be $66m.

(6) Until December 20X8, Pirlo Co rented space in its property to a third party. This arrangement ended and, on 1 January 20X9, Samba Co's administrative department moved into Pirlo Co's property. Pirlo Co charged Samba Co a reduced rent. Samba Co's properties were sold in April 20X9 at a profit of $2m which is included in administrative expenses.

(7) On 31 December 20X9, the employment of the two founding directors of Samba Co was transferred to Pirlo Co. From the date of disposal, Pirlo Co will go into direct competition with Samba Co. As part of this move, the directors did not take their annual bonus of $1m each from Samba Co. Instead, they received a similar 'joining fee' from Pirlo Co, which was paid to them on 31 December 20X9. These individuals have excellent relationships with the largest customers of Samba Co, and are central to Pirlo Co's future plans.

(8) Samba Co's revenue remained consistent at $26m in both 20X9 and 20X8 and Samba Co has high levels of debt. Key ratios from the Samba Co financial statements are shown below:

	20X9	**20X8**
Gross profit margin	81%	80%
Operating profit margin	66%	41%
Interest cover	1.2 times	1.1 times

Required:

(a) Calculate the gain/loss on the disposal of Samba Co which will be recorded in:

- **The individual financial statements of Pirlo Co, and**
- **The consolidated financial statements of the Pirlo group. (5 marks)**

(b) Calculate ratios equivalent to those provided in note (8) for the Pirlo group for the years ended 31 December 20X9 and 20X8. No adjustment is required for the gain/loss on disposal from (a). (3 marks)

(c) Comment on the performance and interest cover of the Pirlo group for the years ended 31 December 20X9 and 20X8. Your answer should comment on:

- **The overall performance of the Pirlo group**
- **How, once accounted for, the disposal of Samba Co will impact on your analysis and**
- **The implications of the disposal of Samba Co for the future results of the Pirlo group. (12 marks)**

(Total: 20 marks)

451 BUN CO

Bun Co is a bakery which also owns two shops/cafés. Over the last two years, the company has experienced declining profitability due to increased competition and so the directors wish to investigate if this is a sector-wide problem. Consequently, they have acquired equivalent ratios for the sector, some of which have been reproduced below.

Sector averages for the year ended 30 June 20X7:

Return on capital employed	18.6%
Operating profit margin	8.6%
Net asset turnover	2.01
Inventory holding period	4 days
Debt to equity	80%

The following information has been extracted from the draft financial statements of Bun Co for the year ended 31 December 20X7.

Statement of profit or loss for the year ended 31 December 20X7:

	$000
Revenue	100,800
Cost of sales	(70,000)
Gross profit	30,800
Operating expenses	(17,640)
Profit from operations	13,160

Statement of financial position as at 31 December 20X7:

	$000
Non-current assets	55,000
Inventory	3,960
Equity:	
Equity shares of $1 each	17,000
Revaluation surplus	5,400
Retained earnings	10,480
Total equity	**32,880**
Non-current liabilities: 10% bank loan	14,400

Other information relevant to Bun Co:

(1) In 20X6, Bun Co acquired a popular brand name. At 31 December 20X7, the brand represented 20% of non-current assets. The remaining 80% of non-current assets comprises of the property from which Bun Co operates its bakery and shops. This property is owned by Bun Co and has no directly associated finance. The property was revalued in 20X4.

(2) In the year ended 31 December 20X7, Bun Co began offering discounted meal deals to customers. Bun Co hoped this strategy would help to reduce perishable inventory and reduce inventory holding periods.

(3) In January 20X8, it was decided to discount some slow-moving seasonal inventory which had a selling price of $1.5m. Under normal circumstances, these products have a gross profit margin of 20%. The inventory was sold in February 20X8 for 50% of what it had cost Bun Co to produce. The financial statements for the year ended 31 December 20X7 were authorised for issue on 15 March 20X8.

Required:

(a) Adjust for the information in note (3) and calculate the 20X7 sector average equivalent ratios for Bun Co. (7 marks)

(b) Assess the financial performance and position of Bun Co for the year ended 31 December 20X7 in comparison with the sector average ratios. (10 marks)

(c) Explain three possible limitations of the comparison between Bun Co and the sector average ratios provided. (3 marks)

(Total: 20 marks)

452 PARUL CO

Extracts from the financial statements of the Parul Group and Parul Co for the years ended 31 December 20X8 and 20X7 are shown below.

Statement of profit or loss (extracts):

	Parul Group 20X8	**Parul Co (single entity) 20X7**
	$000	$000
Revenue	267,920	254,680
Cost of sales	(165,840)	(157,360)
Gross profit	102,080	97,320
Net operating expenses	(44,920)	(41,240)
Profit from operations	57,160	56,080

Statement of financial position (extracts):

	Parul Group 20X8	Parul Co (single entity) 20X7
	$000	$000
Inventories	151,920	121,800
Cash and cash equivalents	15,120	19,160
Long-term borrowings	798,400	675,600

On 1 September 20X8, Parul Co acquired a subsidiary, Saachi Co, purchasing 100% of the equity shares. This acquisition has been correctly accounted for. Summary financial information of Saachi Co for the year ended 31 December 20X8 is as follows:

Statement of profit or loss:

	$000
Revenue	87,600
Cost of sales	(30,780)
Gross profit	56,820
Net operating expenses	(8,020)
Operating profit	48,800

Extracts from statement of financial position:

	$000
Inventories	4,240
Cash and cash equivalents	14,680

For several years, Saachi Co has provided a consultancy service to Parul Co, for which it invoices $400,000 per month. Parul Co includes this as an operating expense and pays Saachi as soon as it receives the invoice.

Parul Co is being considered as a possible acquisition target. The following ratios have been calculated based on the 20X8 Parul Co consolidated financial statements:

Gross profit margin	38.1%
Operating profit margin	21.3%
Inventory turnover period	334 days

There is concern that the acquisition of Saachi Co may make it difficult to assess the underlying performance of Parul Co in 20X8 compared to 20X7.

Required

(a) **Restate the following items for the Parul Group for 20X8 as though the acquisition of Saachi Co had not taken place:**

- **the consolidated statement of profit or loss**
- **inventories**
- **cash and cash equivalents** **(6 marks)**

(b) **The scenario provides three ratios calculated for 20X8. Calculate equivalent ratios for Parul Co for 20X7 and, using the adjusted 20X8 figures calculated in part (a), restate the 20X8 ratios.** **(3 marks)**

(c) **Comment on Parul Co's performance and on its liquidity position in respect of inventory and cash.**

Note: Your answer should refer to the impact that the acquisition of Saachi Co might have on your analysis. **(11 marks)**

(Total: 20 marks)

453 FIT CO

Fit Co and Sporty Co both operate in the sportswear sector.

Extracts from the draft financial statements for the companies for the year ended 31 December 20X0 are as follows:

Draft statement of profit or loss for the year ended 31 December 20X0:

	Fit Co	**Sporty Co**
	$000	$000
Revenue	250,000	220,000
Cost of sales	(190,000)	(150,000)
Gross profit	60,000	70,000
Profit on disposal (note (3))	5,000	
Operating expenses	(40,000)	(38,000)
Profit from operations	25,000	32,000
Finance costs	(7,500)	(1,000)
Profit before tax	17,500	31,000

Draft statement of financial position as at 31 December 20X0:

	Fit Co	**Sporty Co**
	$000	$000
Cash	5,000	10,000
Total equity	90,000	60,000
Non-current liabilities	45,000	15,000
Trade payables	35,000	12,000

The following information is also relevant:

(i) Fit Co is a manufacturer and retailer of premium branded sportswear, which it sells online and in its own international chain of branded stores.

(ii) Sporty Co sells mid-market sportswear in department stores and online. It sources its goods directly from the manufacturer and does not make international sales. Sporty Co plans to expand into the international market during the next financial year.

(iii) On 31 December 20X0, Fit Co disposed of its investment in the Active division for consideration of $10m. The cash proceeds have been recorded as a receivable at the date the financial statements were prepared and the gain on disposal is included in the statement of profit or loss above. The Active division had the following ratios for the year ended 31 December 20X0:

Gross profit margin is 40%

Operating profit margin is 5%

(iv) Fit Co also charged $100,000 per month to the Active division for central services, which was deducted from operating expenses in the financial statements.

Required:

(a) Using the financial statement extracts provided, calculate the following ratios for both Fit Co and Sporty Co:

(1) Gross profit margin

(2) Operating profit margin

(3) Trade payables days

(4) Return on capital employed

(5) Gearing (debt/equity) **(6 marks)**

(b) Comment on the performance and position of both companies for the year ended 31 December 20X0. **(14 marks)**

(Total: 20 marks)

454 KARL CO

At 1 January 20X8, the Karl group consisted of the parent, Karl Co, and two wholly-owned subsidiaries. There were no intra-group transactions during the year.

The sale of one of the subsidiaries, Sinker Co, was completed on 31 December 20X8 when Karl Co sold its entire holding for $20m cash. Sinker Co had net assets of $29m at the date of disposal. The sale does not meet the definition of a discontinued operation and has been correctly accounted for in the consolidated financial statements. The gain/loss on disposal of Sinker Co is included in administrative expenses.

Karl Co had originally purchased Sinker Co on 1 January 20X2 for $35m. The fair value and carrying amount of net assets of Sinker Co at the date of acquisition were $28m. Goodwill was considered to be impaired by 70% at 31 December 20X8.

Extracts from the consolidated financial statements for the years ended 31 December 20X8 and 20X7 are shown below:

Extracts from the statements of profit or loss for the year ended 31 December:

	Consolidated	**Consolidated**
	20X8	20X7
	$m	$m
Revenue	289	272
Cost of sales	(165)	(140)
Gross profit	124	132
Administrative expenses	(45)	(23)
Distribution costs	(15)	(13)
Operating profit / (loss)	64	96

Extracts from the statements of financial position as at 31 December:

	Consolidated	**Consolidated**
	20X8	20X7
	$m	$m
Current assets	112	125
Equity	621	578
Non-current liabilities	100	150
Current liabilities	36	161

The following information is also relevant:

(1) The majority of non-current liabilities is comprised of bank loans.

(2) Sales of Sinker Co represented 14% of the total group sales for 20X8, however, in March 20X8, Sinker Co lost a significant customer contract resulting in a number of redundancies. These redundancy costs amounted to $15m and are included in administrative expenses. Overall, Sinker Co made an operating loss of $17m.

(3) The Karl group manufactures food packaging. The inventory included in the above consolidated statements of financial position is:

	Inventory
Group inventory at:	$m
31 December 20X8	65
31 December 20X7	78

(4) At 31 December 20X8, Sinker Co had inventory of $42m.

Required:

(a) **Calculate the gain/loss arising on the disposal of Sinker Co in the consolidated financial statements of the Karl group. (4 marks)**

(b) **Based on the financial statements provided, calculate the following ratios and comment on the financial performance and position of the Karl group for the years ended 31 December 20X8 and 20X7:**

(i) **Gross profit margin**

(ii) **Operating profit margin**

(iii) **Return on capital employed**

(iv) **Current ratio**

(v) **Gearing ratio (debt/(debt+equity))**

Note: a maximum of 5 marks is available for the calculation of ratios **(13 marks)**

(c) **Comment on how the sale of Sinker Co will affect the comparability of the consolidated financial statements for the years ended 31 December 20X7 and 20X8. (3 marks)**

(Total: 20 marks)

455 PASTRY CO

Pastry Co is considering the acquisition of a subsidiary in the catering industry. Two companies have been identified as potential acquisitions and extracts from the financial statements of Cook Co and Dough Co have been reproduced below:

Statements of profit or loss for the year ended 30 September 20X7:

	Cook Co	**Dough Co**
	$000	$000
Revenue	21,500	16,300
Cost of sales	(14,545)	(8,350)
Gross profit	6,955	7,950
Operating expenses	(1,940)	(4,725)
Finance costs	(650)	(200)
Profit before tax	4,365	3,025
Income tax	(1,320)	(780)
Profit for the year	3,045	2,245

Extracts from the statements of financial position as at 30 September 20X7:

	Cook Co	Dough Co
	$000	$000
Non-current assets		
Property	22,250	68,500
Equity		
Equity shares of $1 each	1,000	1,000
Revaluation surplus	–	30,000
Retained earnings	18,310	2,600
Non-current liabilities		
Loan notes	7,300	5,200

Notes:

(1) Both companies are owner-managed. Dough Co operates from expensive city centre premises, selling to local businesses and the public. Cook Co is a large wholesaler, selling to chains of coffee shops. Cook Co operates from a number of low-cost production facilities.

(2) On 1 October 20X6, Dough Co revalued its properties for the first time, resulting in a gain of $30m. The properties had a remaining useful life of 30 years at 1 October 20X6. Dough Co does not make a transfer from the revaluation surplus in respect of excess depreciation. Cook Co uses the cost model to account for its properties. Dough Co and Cook Co charge all depreciation expenses to operating expenses.

(3) Cook Co charges the amortisation of its research and development to cost of sales, whereas Dough Co charges the same costs to operating expenses. These costs amounted to $1.2m for Cook Co and $2.5m for Dough Co.

(4) The notes to the financial statements show that Cook Co paid its directors total salaries of $110,000 whereas Dough Co paid its directors total salaries of $560,000.

(5) The following ratios have been correctly calculated in respect of Cook Co and Dough Co for the year ended 30 September 20X7:

	Cook Co	Dough Co
Gross profit margin	32.3%	48.8%
Operating margin	23.3%	19.8%
Return on capital employed	18.8%	8.3%

Required:

(a) Adjust the relevant extracts from Dough Co's financial statements to apply the same accounting policies as Cook Co and re-calculate Dough Co's ratios provided in note (5). (6 marks)

(b) Based on these adjusted accounting ratios, compare the performance of the two companies. Your answer should comment on the difficulties of making a purchase decision based solely on the extracts of the financial statements and the information provided in notes (1) to (5). (14 marks)

(Total: 20 marks)

456 PINARDI CO 

The Pinardi group operates in the fragrance and cosmetics industry. On 1 January 20X7 Pinardi Co disposed of one of its subsidiaries, Silva Co, for cash of $42m. Silva Co manufactures jewellery and was sold because the Pinardi group wanted to exit this particular sector.

Extracts from the consolidated financial statements of the Pinardi group for the years ended 31 December 20X6 and 20X7 are as follows:

Statement of profit or loss	**20X7**	**20X6**
	$000	$000
Revenue	98,300	122,400
Cost of sales	(47,600)	(71,800)
Gross profit	**50,700**	**50,600**
Operating expenses	(33,700)	(37,400)
Profit from operations	**17,000**	**13,200**
Finance costs	(3,200)	(5,500)
Profit before tax	**13,800**	**7,700**
Statement of financial position		
Inventories	13,300	22,400
Cash	31,400	14,600
Non-current liabilities	42,000	61,000

The following information is relevant:

(1) The accounting assistant has not accounted for Silva Co as a discontinued operation because the disposal occurred on 1 January 20X7. No figures from Silva Co have been included in the 20X7 financial statements extracts above. The proceeds from the disposal have been recorded in cash, with all net assets and goodwill derecognised. The balancing figure was held in a suspense account.

(2) Pinardi Co acquired 100% of Silva Co on 1 January 20X1 and goodwill was calculated as $6m. The goodwill had been impaired by 30% in 20X5. The net assets at 1 January 20X7 were $35m.

(3) As part of the sales agreement, the Pinardi group will receive an annual fee of $2m for the use of the Silva Co brand. The 20X7 annual fee has been included in the Pinardi group revenue for the year ended 31 December 20X7.

(4) Results obtained from Silva Co's individual published financial statements show the following key information:

	20X7	**20X6**
	$000	$000
Revenue	39,000	36,000
Gross profit	18,800	12,600
Profit from operations	8,000	6,000

(5) Prior to the disposal Silva Co used to occupy some property belonging to the Pinardi group. Following the disposal, the Pinardi group moved its cosmetic division into this property.

Previously the cosmetic division had leased external facilities for $2.5m a year. At 1 January 20X7 the lease had ten years remaining. To exit the lease, the Pinardi group made a one-off payment of $3m to the lessor and recorded it as operating expenses.

(6) The Pinardi group acquires raw materials from overseas. In 20X6 the group recorded foreign exchange gains of $3m, and in 20X7 the group made a foreign exchange loss of $1m. Both items were recognised within operating expenses.

Required:

(a) Calculate the gain on disposal of Silva Co that would need to be included in the consolidated statement of profit or loss for the Pinardi group for the year ended 31 December 20X7. (2 marks)

(b) Explain whether or not the disposal of Silva Co is likely to constitute a discontinued operation, and the correct accounting treatment for this. (3 marks)

(c) Calculate the following ratios for the Pinardi group for 20X7 and 20X6:

Gross profit margin

Operating profit margin

Interest cover

Inventory turnover days. (4 marks)

(d) Analyse the performance and position for the Pinardi group for the year ended 31 December 20X7 compared to the year ended 31 December 20X6. (11 marks)

(Total: 20 marks)

457 VENUS CO

Venus Co acquired 70% of the equity share capital of Luto Co, its only subsidiary, on 1 January 20X8.

On reviewing the consolidated financial statements, the managing director of Venus Co was disappointed, commenting that he had expected to see higher gross profit for 20X8 due to the receipt of discounted purchases from Luto Co in the post-acquisition period. He has remarked that the acquisition of Luto Co has not had the positive impact he expected.

Extracts from the draft financial statements of the Venus Group and Venus Co (single entity) for the years ended 30 June 20X7 and 20X8 are:

	Venus Group (consolidated) 30 June 20X8 $'000	**Venus Co (single entity) 30 June 20X7 $'000**
Statement of profit or loss:		
Revenue	39,000	32,000
Cost of sales	(26,500)	(21,000)
Gross profit	12,500	11,000
Net profit for the year	9,800	8,900
Profit attributable to:		
Owners of Venus Co	9,200	
Non-controlling interest	600	
Statement of financial position:		
Equity		
Share capital	30,000	20,000
Other components of equity (share premium)	35,000	5,000
Retained earnings	21,000	17,000
Non-controlling interest (NCI)	1,500	–
	87,500	42,000

The acquisition of Luto Co has been accounted for correctly in the above financial statement extracts and the following notes are relevant:

(1) Luto Co recognised revenue of $5m in the post-acquisition period which resulted in a net profit of $2m.

(2) Since the acquisition, Venus Co is able to acquire goods from Luto Co at a discount. This has resulted in a saving of $500,000 for Venus Co in the post-acquisition period. At 30 June 20X8 Venus Co had no inventory that had been purchased from Luto Co.

(3) The consideration for the acquisition consisted of a share exchange and an additional $5m to be paid on 1 January 20X9. Venus Co has a cost of capital of 8% which is equivalent to a one-year discount factor of 0.926.

(4) The fair values of Luto Co's assets at acquisition were equal to their carrying amounts, except for an item of plant. This plant had a remaining life of three years at the date of acquisition. Its fair value was $900,000 above its carrying amount. Venus Co's assets are held at historical cost.

(5) All revenue and expenses are deemed to accrue evenly throughout the year.

Required:

(a) Based on the extracts provided, calculate the following ratios for the Venus Group and Venus Co for the years ended 30 June 20X8 and 30 June 20X7 respectively: Gross profit %, Net profit %, and Return on equity % (equity should include NCI where applicable). (3 marks)

(b) (i) Calculate Venus Co's consolidated profit for the year ended 30 June 20X8 as if the acquisition of Luto Co had not taken place. Your answer should take account of the information provided in the notes. Your answer should also recalculate the net profit percentage. (5 marks)

(ii) Explain why consolidated financial statements, for example those of the Venus Group, are not comparable to those of a single entity, for example Venus Co. (3 marks)

(c) Based on your answers to parts (a) and (b), comment on the comparative performance of Venus Co for the years ended 30 June 20X7 and 20X8, specifically addressing the managing director's comments. (9 marks)

(Total: 20 marks)

458 TREATS CO

Treats Co manufactures confectionery. The following sector average ratios have been obtained for the year ended 30 September 20X6:

Ratio	Sector average
Return on year-end capital employed (ROCE)	28.8%
Net asset turnover	2.4 times
Gross profit margin	55%
Operating profit margin	12%
Current ratio	1.8:1
Inventory turnover period	25 days
Gearing (debt/equity)	43%
Receivables collection period	15 days

Extracts from the financial statements of Treats Co for the year ended 30 September 20X6 are as follows:

Statement of profit or loss:

	$000
Revenue	214,553
Cost of sales	(108,009)
Gross profit	**106,544**
Operating expenses	(99,078)
Profit from operations	**7,466**
Finance costs	(1,329)
Profit before taxation	**6,137**
Taxation	(1,783)
Profit for the year	**4,354**

Statement of financial position:

	$000	$000
Non-current assets:		
Property, plant and equipment (note (1))		61,984
Current assets:		
Inventories	30,393	
Trade and other receivables	17,603	
		47,996
Total assets		**109,980**
Equity:		
Ordinary shares		7,000
Other components of equity (Share premium)		13,605
Retained earnings (note (2))		5,363
Total equity		25,968
Non-current liabilities:		
Borrowings		33,621
Current liabilities:		
Trade and other payables	25,390	
Overdraft (note (3))	24,090	
Current tax liabilities	911	
		50,391
Total equity and liabilities		**109,980**

The following information is also relevant:

(1) The property, plant and equipment relates to retail stores operated by Treats Co and the manufacturing plant, all of which are depreciated on a straight-line basis over 20 years. The original cost of these assets was $637.84m and the directors are now considering replacing and updating much of the plant and equipment.

(2) Treats Co paid a dividend of $7.14m during the year despite the concern raised by some directors over the existing overdraft.

(3) The overdraft is used for working capital management purposes and does not form part of the long-term financing of Treats Co.

(4) Treats Co sells its products through supermarket chains in addition to its owned retail stores. Most companies in the sector exclusively sell through their own retail stores.

Required:

(a) Calculate for Treats Co the equivalent ratios to those provided for the confectionery manufacturing sector. (5 marks)

(b) Analyse the performance and financial position of Treats Co in comparison to its sector averages. (15 marks)

(Total: 20 marks)

459 SOUTTAR CO

Souttar Co runs a business advice consultancy.

The statements of profit or loss for the years ended 31 December 20X2 and 20X3, and the statement of cash flows for the year ended 31 December 20X3 are shown below.

Statement of profit or loss for the years ended 31 December

	20X3	**20X2**
	$000	$000
Revenue	630	450
Operating costs	(510)	(360)
Profit from operations	120	90
Finance costs	(24)	(9)
Profit before tax	96	81
Income tax expense	(14)	(12)
Profit for the year	82	69

Statement of cash flows for the year ended 31 December 20X3

	$000	$000
Cash flows from operating activities:		
Cash generated from operations (note 1)		108
Interest paid		(19)
Tax paid		(10)
Net cash flows from operating activities		79
Cash flows from investing activities:		
Purchase of property, plant and equipment		(260)
Cash flows from financing activities:		
9% loan notes issued	140	
Dividends paid	(25)	
		115
Net decrease in cash and cash equivalents		(66)
Cash and cash equivalents 31 December 20X2		78
Cash and cash equivalents 31 December 20X3		12

The following notes are relevant:

(1) Cash generated from operations for the year ended 31 December 20X3 is calculated as follows:

	$000
Profit before tax	96
Finance costs	24
Depreciation	75
Increase in trade receivables	(110)
Increase in trade payables	23
Cash generated from operations	108

Note: The cash generated from operations for the year ended 31 December 20X2 was $75,000. The dividend paid by Souttar Co in 20X2 was $20,000.

(2) During the year ended 31 December 20X3, the government launched a range of new-start grants for new businesses, which created significant volumes of work for Souttar Co's consultants, dealing with grant applications for these businesses. In order to avoid any backlog and resultant loss of business and reputation, Souttar Co paid their staff overtime and hired various freelancers to cover any shortfall.

(3) During the year ended 31 December 20X3, Souttar Co opened two new offices to enable them to achieve wider geographical coverage.

(4) This geographical expansion, and the related increase in business volumes, allowed Souttar Co to negotiate improved terms with many of its major suppliers.

(5) The managing director of Souttar Co is pleased with the expansion of the business and increased profit levels, but cannot understand why the levels of cash have fallen during the year. The managing director has expressed concern for the long-term future of Souttar Co and wonders whether they may have expanded too quickly with the opening of the new offices.

Required:

(a) Calculate the following ratios for the years ended 31 December 20X2 and 20X3:

- **Operating profit margin %**
- **Interest cover**
- **Dividend cover**
- **Cash generated from operations/profit from operations %.** **(4 marks)**

(b) Comment on the performance and cash flows of Souttar Co for 20X3. **(16 marks)**

Note: Your answer should include a response to the managing director's concerns.

(Total: 20 marks)

460 MARVELL CO

At 31 December 20X6, Marvell Co owned a number of subsidiaries including 100% of the equity share capital of Bilston Co.

Extracts from the draft summarised consolidated financial statements for the Marvell group are shown below.

Consolidated statement of profit or loss for the year ended 31 December:

	20X7	**20X6**
	$000	$000
Revenue	275,000	375,000
Cost of sales	(215,000)	(295,000)
Gross profit	60,000	80,000
Distribution costs	(12,500)	(15,000)
Administrative expenses	(24,000)	(22,000)
Profit from operations	23,500	43,000
Finance costs	(6,200)	(11,500)
Profit before tax	17,300	31,500
Income tax expense	(8,000)	(15,000)
Profit for the year	9,300	16,500

Extract from the consolidated statement of financial position as at 31 December:

	20X7	20X6
	$000	$000
Assets		
Non-current assets:		
Property, plant and equipment	215,000	250,000
Intangible asset		120,000
Goodwill		8,000
Equity		
Equity shares of $1 each	200,000	200,000
Revaluation surplus	1,500	5,000
Retained earnings	12,000	18,000
	213,500	**223,000**
Non-controlling interest	12,500	15,000
	226,000	**238,000**
Non-current liabilities		
8% loan notes	15,000	140,000

The following additional information is available for the operations of the Marvell group for the year ended 31 December 20X7:

(1) On 30 June 20X7 Marvell Co sold all of its shares in Bilston Co for $22m. Marvell Co had acquired Bilston Co on 1 April 20X1 for $25m. The group gain or loss on disposal has been included in the consolidated administrative expenses.

The net assets of Bilston Co were:

	1 April 20X1	30 June 20X7
	$000	$000
Equity shares of $1 each	20,000	20,000
Revaluation surplus	0	3,200
Retained earnings	3,000	(5,000)

The fair values of the assets and liabilities of Bilston Co at the date of acquisition and disposal were equal to their carrying amounts. Since acquisition the goodwill of Bilston Co has been impaired by 25%.

(2) The group has recently encountered difficulties in trading, which led to the decision to dispose of Bilston Co. The results of Bilston Co were included in the Marvell group's consolidated statement of profit or loss for the six months to 30 June 20X7.

Required:

(a) Calculate the profit or loss on disposal of Bilston Co that will be included in the consolidated statement of profit or loss of the Marvell group for the year ended 31 December 20X7. (4 marks)

(b) Using the financial statements provided, calculate the following ratios for the Marvell group for the years ended 31 December 20X7 and 20X6:

(i) Gross profit margin

(ii) Operating profit margin

(iii) Return on capital employed

(iv) Net asset turnover. (4 marks)

(c) Analyse the performance of the Marvell group for the years ended 31 December 20X7 and 20X6. Your response should include the impact of the disposal of Bilston Co on your analysis. (12 marks)

(Total: 20 marks)

Section 4

ANSWERS TO OBJECTIVE TEST QUESTIONS – SECTION A

CONCEPTUAL FRAMEWORK/INTERNATIONAL FINANCIAL REPORTING STANDARDS

1

	Capitalise	Expense
Clearance of the site prior to commencement of construction	✓	
Professional surveyor fees for managing the construction work	✓	
EW's own staff wages for time spent working on construction	✓	
A proportion of EW's administration costs, based on staff time spent		✓

The allocation of EW's administration costs would not be included as these costs are not directly incurred as a result of carrying out the construction. All of the others are costs which would not have been incurred without the related asset being built.

2 **B**

The cost of the decommissioning is assumed to be an obligation for the entity. An amount should be included in the cost of the asset when it is first recognised (1 July 20X4).

The amount to include in the cost of the asset for decommissioning costs is the present value of the expected future decommissioning costs. The present value is calculated by multiplying the expected future cost by a discount factor, which in this case is the discount factor for Year 5 (20X9) at 12%. $4 million × 0.567 = $2.268 million.

Therefore:

Debit:	Cost of asset	$2.268 million
Credit:	Provision for decommissioning costs	$2.268 million

The asset is depreciated on a straight-line basis over five years.

In addition, the decommissioning cost should be increased to $4 million by the end of Year 5. This is done by charging a finance cost each year. This is charged at the cost of capital (12%) and applied to the balance on the provision account. The finance charge for the year to 30 June 20X5 is 12% × $2.268 million = $272,160.

Debit:	Finance cost	$272,160
Credit:	Provision for decommissioning costs	$272,160

	$
Depreciation charge ($2.268 million/5 years)	453,600
Finance charge	272,160
Total charge	725,760

If you selected A, you have included the depreciation without the finance cost. If you selected C, you have just spread the present value of the dismantling over 5 years. If you selected D, you have expensed the whole asset value.

3 A

	Land	Buildings	Total
	$ million	$ million	$ million
Cost 1 July 20X3	1.00	5.00	6.00
Building depreciation			
= $5 million/50 years = $0.1m per year × 2		(0.2)	(0.2)
Carrying amount 30 June 20X5	1.00	4.80	5.80
Revaluation gain	0.24	0.96	1.20
Revalued amount	1.24	5.76	7.00
Building depreciation			
= $5.76 million/48 years = $0.12m per year × 2		(0.24)	(0.24)
Carrying amount 30 June 20X7	1.24	5.52	6.76
Disposal proceeds			6.80
Gain on disposal			0.04

The gain on disposal is $40,000. The $1.2 million balance on the revaluation reserve is transferred from the revaluation reserve to another reserve account (probably retained earnings) but is not reported through the statement of profit or loss for the year.

If you selected answer B, you have forgotten to record depreciation between 30 June 20X5 and 30 June 20X7. If you selected answer C, you have based the profit on the original depreciation. If you selected D, you have incorrectly transferred the remaining revaluation reserve into the statement of profit or loss.

4 $900,000

The grant should be released over the useful life, not based on the possibility of the item being repaid. Therefore the $1m should be released over 5 years, being a release of $200,000 a year. At 30 June 20X3, 6 months should be released, meaning $100,000 has been released ($^6/_{12}$ × $200,000). This leaves $900,000 in deferred income.

5 B

This is a revenue grant, and would therefore be released to the statement of profit or loss over the 4 year life. By the end of year one, $250,000 would have been credited to the statement of profit or loss, leaving $750,000 held in deferred income. At this point the amount is repaid, meaning that the deferred income is removed, as well as the $250,000 income previously recorded.

If you selected A, you have not removed the income that was released in the prior year. If you selected C, you have missed that $250,000 would have been released in the previous year. If you have chosen D, you have made errors over the deferring of the grant and that the repayment would be treated as an expense.

6 B

Asset A would be classed as a non-current asset held for sale under IFRS 5 *Non-current Assets Held for Sale and Discontinued Operations*. Assets C and D would both be classified as property, plant and equipment per IAS 16 *Property, Plant and Equipment*.

7 $32,000

The weighted average cost of borrowing is 8% (($1m × 6%) + ($2m × 9%))/$3m.

Therefore the amount to be capitalised = 8% × $600,000 × $^8/_{12}$ = $32,000.

8

	Statement 1	Statement 2
True	✓	
False		✓

IAS 16 (para 31) states that when the revaluation model is used, revaluations should be made with sufficient regularity to ensure that the carrying value of the assets remains close to fair value. IAS 16 also states (para 36) that, if one item in a class of assets is revalued, all the assets in that class must be revalued.

9

	Account name	Value
Debit	Other income	$56,000
Credit	Total deferred income	$56,000

The grant of $60,000 represents $1,000 per month ($60,000 / (5 years × 12 months)) =. So Pootle Co should have only recognised $4,000 ($1,000 × 4 months) of income in the statement of profit or loss for the year ended 31 December 20X4, with the remaining $56,000 recognised as deferred income in the statement of financial position. The correcting journal entry required is therefore to debit other income and credit total deferred income with $56,000.

10 A

Six months' depreciation is required on the building structure and air conditioning system.

	$000
Land (not depreciated)	2,000
Building structure (10,000 – (10,000/25 × $^6/_{12}$))	9,800
Air conditioning system (4,000 – (3,500/10 × $^6/_{12}$))	3,825
	15,625

11 $700,000

Six months' depreciation to the date of the revaluation will be $300,000 (12,000/20 years × $^6/_{12}$). Six months' depreciation from the date of revaluation to 31 March 20X5 would be $400,000 (10,800/13.5 years remaining life × $^6/_{12}$). Total depreciation is $700,000.

12 B, C

Item A is incorrect as the deferred income method can be used. Item D is incorrect as any repayment is corrected in the current period, not retrospectively.

13 A

Six months' depreciation should be accounted for up to 30 June 20X5, which is $100,000 expense ($10 million/50 years × $^6/_{12}$).

When the asset is transferred to investment property it should be revalued to the fair value of $11 million. At the date that the asset's use is changed, this gain should be recorded in other comprehensive income and in a revaluation surplus, not in the statement of profit or loss.

From this date, the fair value model is used. No depreciation is accounted for, but the asset will be revalued to fair value with gains or losses going through the statement of profit or loss. As there is a gain of $500,000 from June 20X5 to December 20X5, this would be included in the statement of profit or loss.

Therefore the total net income will be **$400,000**, being the $500,000 fair value gain less the depreciation expense of $100,000 for the first 6 months of the year.

14 $602,500

The interest can only be capitalised during the period of construction, which is from 1 February 20X6. Therefore the interest can be capitalised for 10 months, being from 1 February to 30 November 20X6. This gives $625,000 ($7.5 million × 10% × $^{10}/_{12}$).

Any temporary investment income earned during this period should be netted off the amount capitalised. The amount earned from 1 February to 1 May 20X6 is $22,500 ($2 million × 4.5% × $^3/_{12}$).

Therefore the amount to be capitalised is $625,000 – $22,500 = **$602,500**.

Note that all interest incurred and earned in January 20X6 is before the construction period and therefore is recorded in the statement of profit or loss.

15 $1,000,000

The fair value gain of $1 million ($9m – $8m) should be taken to the statement of profit or loss. Costs to sell are ignored and, since Croft uses the fair value model, no depreciation will be charged on the building.

16 A

The finance was only available after the year end. Therefore the criteria of recognising an asset were not met, as the resources were not available to complete the project.

Even though the brand is internally generated in the subsidiary's accounts, it can be recognised at fair value for the group. Item C can be recognised as a purchased intangible and item D meets the criteria for being capitalised as development costs.

17 D

Item A cannot be capitalised because it does not meet all the criteria as it is not viable.

Item B is research and cannot be capitalised.

Item C cannot be capitalised because it does not meet all the criteria as it is making a loss.

18 B, C

Key staff cannot be capitalised as firstly they are not controlled by an entity. Secondly, the value that one member of key staff contributes to an entity cannot be measured reliably.

19 A

The costs of $750,000 relate to ten months of the year (up to April 20X5). Therefore the costs per month were $75,000. As the project was confirmed as feasible on 1 January 20X5, the costs can be capitalised from this date. So four months of these costs can be capitalised = $75,000 × 4 = $300,000.

The asset should be amortised from when the products go on sale, so one month's amortisation should be charged to 30 June 20X5. Amortisation is ($300,000/5) × $^1/_{12}$ = $5,000. The carrying amount of the asset at 30 June 20X5 is $300,000 – $5,000 = $295,000.

If you chose C you have forgotten to amortise the development costs. If you chose B or D you have either capitalised the full amount or capitalised none of the costs.

20 B

The brand can be measured reliably, so this should be accounted for as a separate intangible asset on consolidation. The customer list cannot be valued reliably, and so will form part of the overall goodwill calculation. It will be subsumed within the goodwill value.

21 D

Write off to 1 January 20X4 to 28 February 20X4 (2 × $40,000)	$80,000
Capitalise March to June = 4 × 40,000 = $160,000	
Amortisation 160,000/5 years × $^3/_{12}$ (July to September)	8,000
	88,000

22

	True	False
All intangible assets must be carried at amortised cost or at an impaired amount, they cannot be revalued upwards.		✓
The development of a new process which is not expected to increase sales revenues may still be recognised as an intangible asset.	✓	

Intangible assets may be revalued upwards using the revaluation model if an active market exists for the asset, although this is unusual.

A new process may produce benefits other than increased revenues (e.g. it may reduce costs) and therefore be recognised as an asset.

23 A

In a cash generating unit, no asset should be impaired below its recoverable amount. The valuation of $2.5 million is an indication that the property is not impaired and should therefore be left at $2.3 million.

$2.5 million cannot be chosen as the entity uses the cost model. If you chose item C or D then you have impaired the asset.

24 $689,000

The cash generating unit is impaired by $1,180,000, being the difference between the recoverable amount of $4 million and the total carrying values of the assets of $5,180,000. In a cash generating unit, no asset should be impaired below its recoverable amount, meaning that the property and other net assets are not impaired. The impairment is allocated to goodwill first, resulting in the entire $700,000 being written off. This leaves a remaining impairment of $480,000 to be allocated across plant and intangible assets.

This should be allocated on a pro-rata basis according to their carrying value. The plant and intangible assets have a total carrying value of $1,750,000 ($950,000 plant and $800,000 intangible assets). Therefore the impairment should be allocated to plant as follows:

$950,000/$1,750,000 × $480,000 = $261,000.

The carrying value of plant is therefore $950,000 – $261,000 = $689,000

25 $6,500

The recoverable amount of an asset is the higher of its value in use (being the present value of future cash flows) and fair value less costs to sell. Therefore the recoverable amount is $6,500.

26 A

Goodwill should be written off in full and the remaining loss is allocated pro rata to property plant and equipment and the product patent.

	Carrying amount	Impairment	Recoverable amount
	$	$	$
Property, plant and equipment	200,000	(45,455)	154,545
Goodwill	50,000	(50,000)	nil
Product patent	20,000	(4,545)	15,455
Net current assets (at NRV)	30,000	nil	30,000
	300,000	(100,000)	200,000

27 D

Although the estimated net realisable value is lower than it was (due to fire damage), the entity will still make a profit on the inventory and thus it is not an indicator of impairment.

28 $17,785

	$
Cost 1 October 20X9	100,000
Depreciation 1 October 20X9 to 30 September 20Y4 (100,000 × $^5/_{10}$)	(50,000)
Carrying amount	50,000

The recoverable amount is the higher of fair value less costs to sell ($30,000) and the value in use ($8,500 × 3.79 = $32,215). Recoverable amount is therefore $32,215.

	$
Carrying amount	50,000
Recoverable amount	(32,215)
Impairment to statement of profit or loss	17,785

29 $214,600

Is the lower of its carrying amount ($217,000) and recoverable amount ($214,600) at 31 March 20X4.

Recoverable amount is the higher of value in use ($214,600) and fair value less costs to ($200,000).

Carrying amount = $217,000 (248,000 – (248,000 × 12.5%))

Value in use is based on present values = $214,600

30 C

Asset held for sale will be measured at lower of carrying amount and fair value less cost to sell. Once reclassified, the asset held for sale is not depreciated.

	$m
Cost	45.0
Depreciation to 30 September 20X3	(6.0)
Depreciation to 1 April 20X4 ($45 \times {}^{1}/_{15} \times {}^{6}/_{12}$)	(1.5)
Carrying amount 1 April 20X4	37.5

Fair value less cost to sell = $36.8 million ((42,000 × 90%) – 1,000).

Therefore the asset is reported at $36.8 million.

31 A

Assets held for sale should be held at the lower of carrying value and fair value less costs to sell. Therefore the asset should be held at $750.

Item B is just the fair value. Item C is the fair value plus the costs to sell, which is incorrect. Item D is the carrying value.

32 C

A sale has to be expected within 12 months, not one month. The others are all criteria which must be met to classify an asset as held for sale.

33

	Shown on the face of the statement of profit or loss	**Not shown**
Revenue		✓
Gross profit		✓
Profit after tax	✓	

One line should be shown regarding profit from discontinued operations. This line is the profit after tax from the discontinued operation, with a full breakdown of the amount in the notes to the accounts.

34

	Discontinued operation Yes/No
Sector X	No
Sector Y	Yes

Although Sector X is the only operation of Rural in Country A, it is not a separate major line of geographical operations, as it only contributes 0.5% of total revenue. Therefore Rural would not report this as a discontinued operation.

Sector Y is a separate major line of business operations, as it contributes a significant amount of Rural revenue, and produces a different item from the other parts of Rural. Therefore Rural would report Sector Y as a discontinued operation.

35 B

Although disclosing discontinued operations separately may help with business valuation, and understanding the business, the primary reason discontinued operations are separately presented is to enhance the predictive nature of the financial statements. Financial statements are historic, and this is a major limitation of them. Separating information about discontinued operations means that the users of the financial statements can use information about just the continuing operations when predicting the future performance of an entity.

36 A

The property would be depreciated by $25,000 (800,000/16 × $^{6}/_{12}$) for six months giving a carrying amount of $775,000 (800,000 – 25,000) before being classified as held-for-sale. This would also be the value at 31 March 20X5 as the property is no longer depreciated and is lower than its fair value less cost to sell.

37 D

The objectives of financial statements are set out in the IASB Framework. Note that the Framework defines users as existing and potential investors, lenders and other creditors.

38 B

	True	**False**
Accounting standards on their own provide a complete regulatory framework.		✓
A regulatory framework is required to ensure that financial reporting meets the needs of primary users.	✓	

In order to fully regulate the preparation of financial statements and the obligations of companies and directors, legal and market regulations are necessary, so accounting standards on their own would not be a complete regulatory framework.

39

	Faithful representation	Relevance
Completeness	✓	
Predictive value		✓
Neutrality	✓	

Information that is relevant has predictive or confirmatory value. For information to have faithful representation, it must be complete, neutral and free from error.

40 B, D

It is important to learn that the two fundamental characteristics are relevance and faithful representation.

41

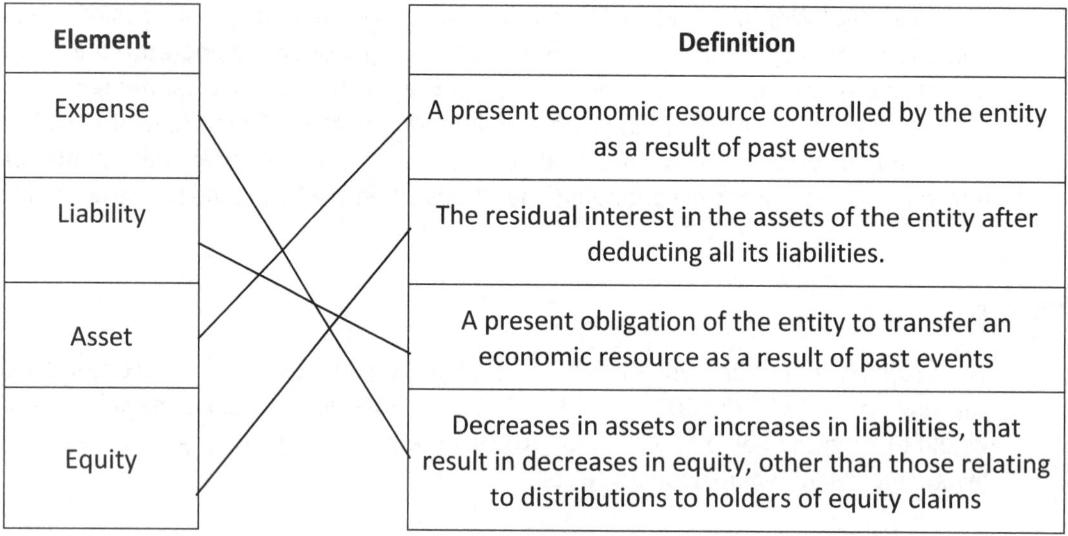

42 C

Relevant information contains information which has both predictive and confirmatory value.

43 D

Faithful representation means presenting transactions according to their economic substance rather than their legal form. Items A to C all represent incorrect accounting treatments, and item D reflects that a sale and repurchase agreement with a bank is likely to represent a secured loan rather than a sale.

44 B

You should learn the structure of the IFRS regulatory framework and the functions of its components.

45 A

Elements are recognised if recognition provides users with useful financial information. In other words recognition must provide relevant information and a faithful representation.

46 D

Information is relevant if it influences the economic decisions of the users. The other definitions describe good treatment but are not explaining the concept of relevance.

47

	True	**False**
It is a principles-based framework	✓	
It is a legal obligation		✓

IFRS Standards are based on a principles-based framework, as they are based on the IASB's Conceptual Framework for Financial Reporting. It does not represent a legal obligation.

48

	Advantage	**Not advantage**
Greater comparability between different firms	✓	
Greater compatibility with legal systems		✓
Easier for large international accounting firms	✓	

Harmonisation would not provide greater compatibility with legal systems, as legal systems differ worldwide. Greater compatibility would arise when a country develops its own accounting standards within the context of their specific legal framework.

49 A, B, C

A principles-based framework recognises that is not possible to draw up a set of rules to cover every eventuality and therefore does not attempt to do so. It is also harder to prove compliance as there are fewer prescriptive rules in place.

50 D

Where there is conflict between the conceptual framework and an IFRS Standard, the IFRS Standard will prevail. An example of this is IAS 20 *Government* grants, where deferred grant income is held as a liability, despite not satisfying the definition of a liability.

51 A

The IFRS Foundation is responsible for funding the other bodies, and attempts to harmonise national and international standards.

The International Accounting Standards Board (the Board) issue new accounting standards, known as IFRS Standards. The IFRS Interpretations Committee gives guidance to the Board where conflicting interpretations of standards exist. The IFRS advisory council provides a forum for the Board to consult interested parties affected by the standard-setting process.

52 D

The substance is that there is no free finance. Its cost is built into the selling price and this will represent a significant financing component.

53 B

By definition irredeemable preference shares do not have a contractual obligation to be repaid and thus do not meet the definition of a liability. They are therefore classed as equity.

54 C

The Conceptual Framework defines an asset as follows: 'An asset is a present economic resource controlled by the entity as a result of past events.' Therefore, the only statement that is NOT included in the definition of an asset is C.

55

Historical cost	✓	Current cost	✓
$300,000		$384,000	✓
$320,000	✓	$600,000	

Historical cost annual depreciation = $90,000 ((500,000 × 90%)/5 years).

After two years carrying amount would be $320,000 (500,000 – (2 × 90,000)).

Current cost annual depreciation = $108,000 ((600,000 × 90%)/5 years).

After two years carrying amount would be $384,000 (600,000 – (2 × 108,000)).

56

	Liability	**Not a liability**
The signing of a non-cancellable contract in September 20X4 to supply goods in the following year on which, due to a pricing error, a loss will be made.	✓	
The cost of a reorganisation which was approved by the board in August 20X4 but has not yet been implemented, communicated to interested parties or announced publicly.		✓
An amount of deferred tax relating to the gain on the revaluation of a property during the current year. Tynan has no intention of selling the property in the foreseeable future.	✓	
The balance on the warranty provision which relates to products for which there are no outstanding claims and whose warranties had expired by 30 September 20X4.		✓

The non-cancellable contract is an onerous contract. The deferred tax provision is required even if there is no intention to sell the property.

57 D

As the receivable is 'sold' with recourse it must remain as an asset on the statement of financial position and is not derecognised.

58 D

As it is a new type of transaction, comparability with existing treatments is not relevant.

59 B

Historical cost is the easiest to verify as the cost can be proved back to the original transaction. Fair value is often more difficult to verify as it may involve elements of estimation.

60 C

The prior period error is corrected by restating the comparative amounts for the previous period at their correct value. A note to the accounts should disclose the nature of the error, together with other details.

61 B

Level 3 inputs do include the best information available, but this is not regarded as the most reliable evidence of fair value, as level 1 inputs are likely to provide the most reliable evidence.

62 B

A change in the method of inventory valuation would be classed as a change in accounting policy under IAS 8. The allowance for receivables, useful life and depreciation method are all accounting estimates.

63 A, D

A change in accounting policy may be made firstly if this is required by an IFRS Standard. If there is no requirement, an entity can choose to change their accounting policy if they believe a new accounting policy would result in a more reliable and relevant presentation of events and transactions.

Entities cannot change their accounting policies simply to make financial reporting easier, or to try and show a more favourable picture of results.

64

	Can be used	**Cannot be used**
Historical cost	✓	
Present value	✓	
Realisable value	✓	

65 A

In times of rising prices, asset values will be understated, as historical cost will not be a true representation of the asset values. Additionally, the real purchase cost of replacement items will not be incorporated, meaning that profits are overstated.

B and D relate to asset values being overstated, which is incorrect. Unrecognised gains is irrelevant.

66 C, D

It is important to learn that the four enhancing characteristics are verifiability, comparability, understandability and timeliness.

67

	Change in accounting policy	**Change in accounting estimate**
Classifying commission earned as revenue in the statement of profit or loss, having previously classified it as other operating income	✓	
Revising the remaining useful life of a depreciable asset		✓

A change of classification in presentation in financial statements is a change of accounting policy under IAS 8.

68 B

Item A is an adjustment when preparing consolidated financial statements. Item C is an accounting estimate, and item D is applying the same policy as previously, with a correction to the figure used.

69 B, E

Inventory should be measured at the lower of cost and net realisable value (NRV). The frames had cost Bouani $20,000 to manufacture. The question does not indicate any selling costs to be incurred so NRV must be the $30,000 agreed selling price. This means that the frames should continue to be carried at $20,000, being the lower of cost and NRV. The fact that the frames could now be manufactured for $15,000 is not relevant.

The cost of the pedals is $60,000 (3,000 pedals × $20). The NRV would be $58,000 ([3,000 pedals x $21] less $5,000 costs to repair). As the pedals are currently being held at a cost of $60,000, the carrying amount should now be reduced to the lower NRV amount.

70 B

The logs will be classed as inventory. The land will be classed as property, plant and equipment. The development costs will be treated as an intangible asset.

71 B, D, E

IAS 2 *Inventories* states that:

(a) selling costs cannot be included in inventory cost, therefore item A cannot be included

(b) general overheads cannot be included (item C)

(c) overhead costs should be added to inventory cost on the basis of '**normal capacity of the production facilities**' (IAS 2, para 13), therefore item F cannot be included in cost

(d) the cost of **factory** management and administration can be included, so that item D can be included in inventory values.

72 $55,800

	Cost	Net Realisable Value (NRV)	Lower of cost and NRV
Item 1	$24,000	(note 1)	$24,000
Item 2	$33,600	$31,800 (note 2)	$31,800
			$55,800

Notes:

(1) The recoverable amount is not known, but it must be above cost because the contract is 'expected to produce a high profit margin'. The subsequent fall in the cost price to $20,000 is irrelevant for the inventory valuation.

(2) The recoverable amount is $36,000 minus 50% of $8,400.

73 B

The costs of inventory should include all costs of bringing inventory to its present location and condition, so Mario should include the raw material cost, import duties, direct labour, subcontracted labour and production overheads in its inventory.

Sales tax would not be included as it is recoverable.

Storage costs are specifically excluded from the value of inventory, as they are incurred once the inventory is ready to be sold.

Abnormal wastage costs are excluded from the valuation of inventory per IAS 2 *Inventories*.

74 $970,000

The normal selling price of the damaged inventory is $300,000 ($210,000/70%). This will now sell for $240,000 ($300,000 × 80%), less commission of $60,000 ($240,000 × 25%) to give a NRV of $180,000. The expected loss on the damaged inventory is $30,000 ($210,000 cost – $180,000 NRV) and therefore the total inventory should be valued at $970,000 ($1,000,000 – $30,000).

75

	Accounted for under IAS 41 Agriculture	Outside the scope of IAS 41 Agriculture
Dairy cattle	✓	
Milk	✓	
Cheese		✓

The cheese will be a product which is the result of processing after harvest, so will be outside the scope of IAS 41 *Agriculture*.

76 D

Biological assets should be revalued to fair value less point of sale costs at the year end, with the gain or loss being taken to the statement of profit or loss.

If you chose A, you have used the cost model. If you chose B or C, you have not deducted the point of sale costs.

77 C

Depreciation of leased plant $68,000 ($340,000/5 years)

Finance cost $25,000 (($340,000 – $90,000) × 10%)

Rental of equipment $13,500 ($18,000 × $^{9}/_{12}$)

Total $106,500.

78 B

	B/f	Interest 7%	Payment	c/f
Year end	$	$	$	$
31 October 20X3	45,000	3,150	(10,975)	37,175
31 October 20X4	37,175	2,602	(10,975)	28,802

The figure to the right of the payment in the next year is the non-current liability. Once 20X4's payment has been made, $28,802 will still be owed, making this the non-current liability. The current liability will be the difference between the total liability of $37,175 and the non-current liability of $28,802, which is $8,373.

If you selected C, you chose the total year-end liability rather than the non-current liability. If you selected A, you deducted the payment of $10,975 from the total. If you selected D you recorded the payment in advance and chose the year end liability rather than the non-current liability.

79 D

Assets permitted to be exempted from recognition are low-value assets and those with a lease term of 12 months or less. The use of the asset is irrelevant, and, although IFRS 16 *Leases* does not define low-value, it is the cost when new that is considered rather than current fair value.

80 A

Initial value of lease liability is the present value of lease payments, $86,240.

	Balance b/f	**Payment**	**Subtotal**	**Interest @ 8%**	**Balance c/f**
20X3	86,240	(20,000)	66,240	5,299	71,539
20X4	71,539	(20,000)	51,539	4,123*	55,662
20X5	55,662	(20,000)*	35,662*		

The non-current liability at 20X4 is the figure to the right of the payment in 20X5, $35,662. The current liability is the total liability of $55,662 less the non-current liability of $35,662, which is $20,000.

The finance cost is the figure in the interest column for 20X4, $4,123.

If you chose B you have done the entries for year one. If you chose C or D, you have recorded the payments in arrears, not in advance.

81 C

The transfer of ownership at the end of the lease indicates that Pigeon will have use of the asset for its entire life, and therefore 7 years is the appropriate depreciation period. Potential transactions at market rate would be ignored as they do not confer any benefit on Pigeon, and Pigeon's depreciation policy for purchased assets is irrelevant.

82 A

Reverse incorrect treatment of rental:

Dr Liability $210,000, Cr Retained Earnings $210,000

Charge asset depreciation ($635,000/5):

Dr Retained earnings $127,000, Cr Property, plant and equipment $127,000

Charge finance cost ($635,000 × 12.2%):

Dr Retained Earnings $77,470, Cr Liability $77,470

This gives a net adjustment of $5,530 to be credited to opening retained earnings.

If you selected B, you have missed the depreciation. If you selected C you have simply reversed the rental payment. If you selected D you assumed that the entries were correct.

83 $58,000

The asset would initially be capitalised at $87,000. This is then depreciated over six years, being the shorter of the useful life and the lease term (including any secondary period).

This would give a depreciation expense of $14,500 a year. After two years, accumulated depreciation would be $29,000 and therefore the carrying amount would be $58,000.

84 A

Sideshow is only leasing the asset for 5 years out of its remaining life of 20 years, so control of the asset has been passed to the purchaser.

The initial liability recognised will be the present value of lease rentals, $599,000, giving a finance cost for the year of $47,920 ($599,000 × 8%).

The proportion of the right-of-use asset retained by Sideshow will be equal to the initial liability as a proportion of the proceeds. So the initial value of the right-of-use asset will be

(599,000/2,000,000) × 1,600,000 = $479,200

Depreciation over 5 years would give an expense of $95,840.

The profit to be recognised on disposal can be calculated in one of two ways.

Create the initial recognition journal and calculate a balancing figure:

	Dr	Cr
	$	$
Bank	2,000,000	
Property, plant & equipment	479,200	
Property plant & equipment		1,600,000
Lease liability		599,000
Profit on disposal (SPL) – balancing figure		280,200

Alternatively the profit to be recognised could be calculated by taking the proportion of the asset not retained by Sideshow (i.e. difference between sale proceeds and lease liability):

$$\frac{(\$2,000,000 - \$599,000)}{\$2,000,000} \times (\$2,000,000 - \$1,600,000) = \$280,200$$

If you chose B you have not capitalised the leased asset. If you chose C you recognised the full profit. If you chose D you capitalised the asset at the present value of the lease payments.

85 B

	b/f	Interest @ 10%	Payment	c/f
Year end	$000	$000	$000	$000
30 September 20X4	23,000	2,300	(6,000)	19,300
30 September 20X5	19,300	1,930	(6,000)	15,230

Current liability at 30 September 20X4 = 19,300,000 – 15,230,000 = $4,070,000

86 D

The value recognised in respect of the lease payments will be the present value of future lease payments rather than the total value.

87 $1,090

As Stark has retained control of the asset, the asset cannot be treated as sold, and will be retained at its carrying amount, depreciated over the remaining life of 10 years. The sale proceeds will effectively be treated as a loan of $7 million, on which interest will be charged at 7%. Therefore the following items will be included in the statement of profit or loss, all figures in $000:

Depreciation: $6,000/10 years = $600

Finance cost: $7,000 × 7% = $490

Total expense = $600 + $490 = $1,090

88 B

The loan notes should initially be recorded at their net proceeds, being the $100,000 raised less the $3,000 issue costs, giving $97,000. This should then be held at amortised cost, taking the effective rate of interest to the statement of profit or loss. The annual payment will be the coupon rate, which will be 5% × $100,000 = $5,000 a year.

Applying this to an amortised cost table gives $7,981, as shown below.

	B/f	Interest 8%	Payment	c/f
	$	$	$	$
20X4	97,000	7,760	(5,000)	99,760
20X5	99,760	**7,981**		

If you chose C, you have done the calculation for 20X4. If you chose D, you have used 8% of the full $100,000 and done the calculation for 20X4. If you chose A, you have used 8% of the full $100,000.

89 B

The amount payable each year is based on the coupon rate of 7%, giving an amount of $210,000 payable each year ($3 million × 7%). This should be discounted at the market rate of interest of 9%, together with the capital repayment to find the value of the liability.

Year 1 ($210,000 × 0.914)	191,940
Year 2 ($210,000 × 0.837)	175,770
Year 3 ($3,210,000 × 0.766)	2,458,860
Total present value of debt	**2,826,570**
Equity element (balance)	**173,430**
Total bond value	3,000,000

If you chose A, you used the incorrect discount rate. If you chose C you forgot to calculate the repayment of $3 million. If you chose D you have not used split accounting.

90 A

The business model test must also be passed, which means that the objective is to hold the instrument to collect the cash flows rather than to sell the asset. The others are irrelevant.

91 $493,000

The investment would initially be recorded at its fair value plus any transaction costs. As the $7m loan note was purchased at a 12% discount and no transaction costs are included in the question, this means that the investment would be recorded on 1 July 20X7 at its fair value of $6,160,000 ($7m × 88%). Interest is charged at the effective rate of 8%.

$000	b/f	Interest @ 8%	Paid ($7m × 5%)	c/f
30 June 20X8	6,160	493	(350)	6,303
30 June 20X9	6,303	504	(350)	6,457

Note that the nominal interest and closing balance at 30 June 20X9 have been included for illustrative purposes only and were not required to reach the answer of $493,000.

92 $9,500

The investment should be classified as fair value through other comprehensive income.

As such, they will initially be valued inclusive of transaction costs.

Therefore, the initial value is 10,000 × $3.50 = $35,000 + $500 = $35,500.

At year-end, these will be revalued to fair value of $4.50 each, therefore 10,000 × $4.50 = $45,000.

The gain is therefore $45,000 – $35,500 = $9,500.

93

Gain
18,750

Where recorded
Statement of profit or loss

Financial assets held for trading will be valued at fair value through profit or loss. These are therefore valued excluding any transaction costs, which will be expensed to profit or loss.

The initial value of the investment is therefore 15,000 × $6.50 = $97,500

The shares will be revalued to fair value as at year-end, and the gain will be taken to profit or loss. The year-end value of the shares is 15,000 × $7.75 = $116,250, giving a gain of $18,750. This is recognised within profit or loss.

94 B

Transaction costs are included when measuring all financial assets and liabilities at amortised cost, and when valuing financial assets valued at fair value through other comprehensive income.

Transaction costs for financial assets valued at fair value through profit or loss are expensed through the statement of profit or loss and not included in the initial value of the asset.

95 $810,000

Year ended 30 September	Cash flow	Discount rate	Discounted cash flows
	$000	at 8%	$000
20X4	500	0.93	465
20X5	500	0.86	430
20X6	10,500	0.79	8,295
Value of debt component			9,190
Equity (balance)			**810**
Proceeds			10,000

96 $1,358,000

The initial liability should be recorded at the net proceeds of $19.4 million. The finance cost should then be accounted for using the effective rate of interest of 7%. Therefore the finance cost for the year is **$1,358,000** ($19.4 million × 7%).

97

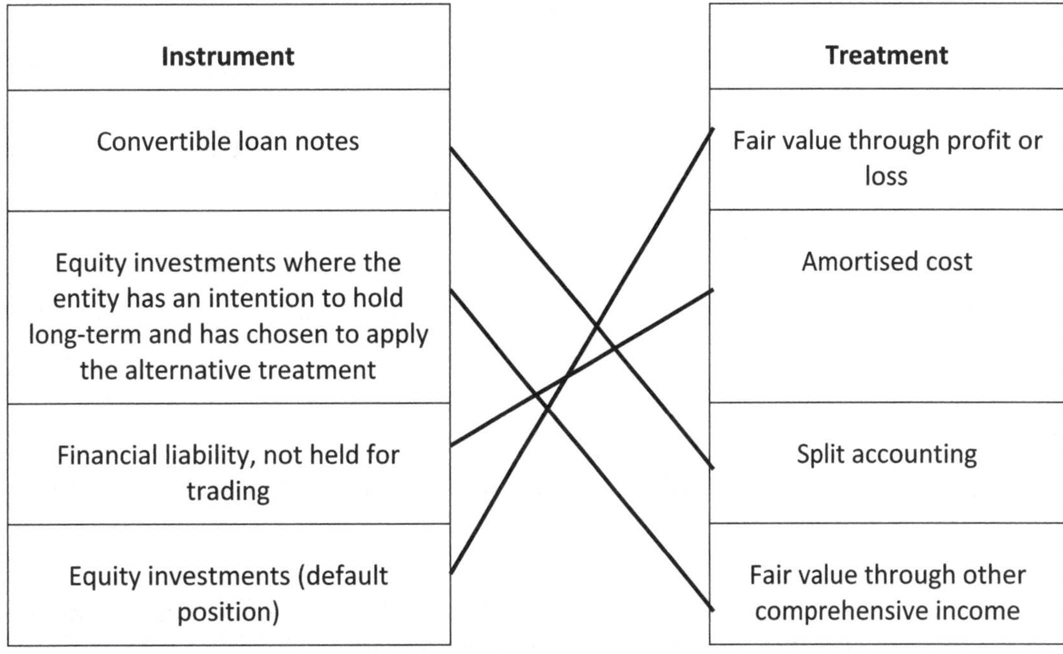

98 D

Functional currency is defined as the currency of the primary economic environment in which an entity operates.

Answer A is the definition of presentation currency. Answer C is one of the primary methods of determining an entity's functional currency.

99 A

Overseas transactions are recorded in the functional currency using the spot rate of exchange. Therefore, the land is initially recorded at $10 million (30m dinars/3). Land is a non-monetary asset and so is not retranslated, meaning that its carrying amount remains at $10 million.

If you selected answer B then you retranslated the land at the closing rate of exchange. If you selected answer C then you translated the land at the average rate of exchange. If you selected answer D then you measured the land at its fair value, despite the fact that it is held using the cost model.

100 B

Statement (i) is false. Exchange gains and losses arising on the retranslation of monetary items are recognised in profit or loss in the period.

101 $207,000

The loan should initially be translated into dollars using the spot rate of 6.0.

The repayment of the loan should be translated using the spot rate of 5.0.

The outstanding loan at the reporting date is a monetary item so is retranslated using the closing rate of 5.6.

The exchange loss is calculated as follows:

	Dinar (000)	**Rate**	$000
1 January 20X1	12,000	6.0	2,000
30 November 20X1	(3,000)	5.0	(600)
Foreign exchange loss	–		207
31 December 20X1	9,000	5.6	1,607

102 C

The machine is recorded in the functional currency using the spot rate, giving an initial value of $10 million (20m dinars/2).

The machine is then depreciated over its useful life. By the reporting date, the carrying amount will be $9.5 million ($10m × 19/20). The machine is a non-monetary item held under a cost model so is not retranslated at the reporting date.

If you selected answer A then you have translated the depreciation at the closing rate of exchange. If you selected answer B then you have translated depreciation at the average rate of exchange. If you selected answer D then you have retranslated the machine at the closing rate of exchange.

103 D

The sale should be treated as a loan secured against the inventory. The inventory would remain with Mango, and a $500,000 loan would be recorded. This loan would incur interest at 10% a year. In year one $50,000 would therefore be recorded as a finance cost.

Answers A and B treat this as a sale, which is incorrect. Deferred income is not taken to the statement of profit or loss, so item C is incorrect.

104 C

Although the invoiced amount is $180,000, $30,000 of this has not yet been earned and must be deferred until the servicing work has been completed.

105 $200,000

Step 1 – Progress

Progress = cost to date / total cost = 1.6 / (1.6 + 2.4) = 40%

Step 2 – Revenue

Revenue to recognise = $5m × 40% = $2m

Step 3 – Statement of financial position	$000
Revenue earned	2,000
Less: Amount billed	(1,800)
Contract asset	200

106

Revenue	Cost of sales
$63 million	$83 million

Step 1 – Overall		$m
Price		90
Total cost	– incurred to date	(77)
	– estimated future	(33)
Overall **loss**		(20)

Step 2 – Progress

Progress = work certified 63/total price 90 = 70%

Step 3 – SPL	$m
Revenue (70% of 90)	63
Cost of sales (balancing figure to recognise full loss)	(83)
FULL loss to be recognised immediately	(20)

107 $90

The discount should be allocated to each part of the bundled sale. Applying the discount across each part gives revenue as follows:

Goods	$50	($75 × $100/$150)
Installation	$20	($30 × $100/$150)
Service	$30	($45 × $100/$150)

The revenue in relation to the goods and installation should be recognised on 1 May 20X1. As 8 months of the service has been performed (from 1 May to 31 December 20X1), then $20 should be recognised ($30 × $^{8}/_{12}$).

This gives a total revenue for the year of 50 + 20 + 20 = $90.

108

Step
Identify the separate performance obligations within a contract
Identify the contract
Determine the transaction price
Recognise revenue when (or as) a performance obligation is satisfied
Allocate the transaction price to the performance obligations in the contract

Correct order
Identify the contract
Identify the separate performance obligations within a contract
Determine the transaction price
Allocate the transaction price to the performance obligations in the contract
Recognise revenue when (or as) a performance obligation is satisfied

109 C

		$m
Price		40
Total cost	– incurred to date	(16)
	– estimated future	(18)
Overall profit		6

The profit calculation is performed as a check to ensure contract is profit-making.

	$m
Revenue (45% of 40)	18
Cost of sales (to date)	(16)
Gross profit	2

Items A and B incorrectly include the full revenue. Item D includes 45% of estimated total costs incorrectly.

110 $30,000

	$
Revenue to date (work certified)	180,000
Costs to date	(135,000)
Profit earned to date	45,000
Recognised in previous year	(15,000)
Current year profit	30,000

111 B

For item B the sale of the goods has fulfilled a contractual obligation so the revenue in relation to this can be recognised. The service will be recognised over time, so the revenue should be deferred and recognised as the obligation is fulfilled.

For item A Hatton acts as an agent, so only the commission should be included in revenue.

For item C any profit or loss on disposal should be taken to the statement of profit or loss. The proceeds should not be included within revenue.

For item D the $1 million should be initially discounted to present value as there is a significant financing component within the transaction. The revenue would initially be recognised at $826,000, with an equivalent receivable. This receivable would then be held at amortised cost with finance income of 10% being earned each year.

112 $500,000

Overall contract	$000
Contract price	8,000
Cost to date	(4,500)
Cost to complete	(5,500)
Estimated loss	(2,000)
Statement of profit or loss	
Revenue recognised (45% × $8m)	3,600
Costs to date	(4,500)
Provision to recognise full loss*	(1,100)
Loss	(2,000)
Contract liability	
Revenue recognised	3,600
Amount received	(3,000)
Provision to recognise loss	(1,100)
Contract liability	(500)

*As the contract is loss-making, Sugar should record the full loss immediately.

113 A

Using the work certified basis, revenue is recognised as the work is certified.

$1,050,000 has been certified as at 30 September 20X5.

As $450,000 was recognised in the prior year, revenue of $600,000 ($1,050,000 – $450,000) should be recognised in the current year statement of profit or loss.

114 A

Contract price	1,000,000
Total contract cost (500,000 + 300,000)	(800,000)
Estimated total profit	200,000
Progress 500,000/800,000 = 62.5%	
Revenue (62.5% × 1,000,000)	625,000
Less: amount billed	(600,000)
Contract asset	25,000

115 D

At 31 March 20X5, the deferred consideration of $12,650 would need to be discounted by 10% for one year to $11,500 (effectively deferring a finance cost of $1,150). The total amount credited to profit or loss would be $24,150 (12,650 + 11,500).

116 D

The tax expense in the statement of profit or loss is made up of the current year estimate, the prior year overprovision and the movement in deferred tax. The prior year overprovision must be deducted from the current year expense, and the movement in deferred tax must be added to the current year expense, as the deferred tax liability has increased.

Tax expense = $60,000 – $4,500 + $600 = $56,100

If you chose A, you have deducted the movement in deferred tax, even though the liability has increased. If you chose C you have added the overprovision. If you chose B you have added the overprovision and the closing deferred tax liability.

117

Statement of profit or loss	Statement of financial position
$88,000	$83,000

The tax expense in the statement of profit or loss is made up of the current year estimate and the prior year underprovision. The year-end liability in the statement of financial position is made up of the current year estimate only.

Tax expense = $83,000 + $5,000 underprovision from previous year = $88,000

Tax liability = $83,000 year end estimate only.

118 C

Deferred tax provision required	9,000 (30,000 × 30%)
Opening balance per trial balance	12,000
Reduction in provision	(3,000)

Tax expense:

Current year estimate	15,000
Prior year overprovision	(4,000)
Deferred tax, as above	(3,000)
Charge for year	8,000

If you chose A, you have added in the full deferred tax liability. If you chose B you have added the full liability and the overprovision. If you chose D, you have not dealt with the overprovision.

119 The amount of the deferred tax liability is: correct

The amount of the revaluation surplus is: correct

The deferred tax provision is calculated as the temporary tax differences multiplied by the tax rate.

	$
Carrying amount of assets ($110,000 + $280,000)	390,000
Tax base of assets ($90,000 + $200,000)	(290,000)
Temporary tax differences	100,000
Deferred tax @ 20%	20,000

The revaluation surplus should be net of deferred tax.

	$
Land at revaluation	280,000
Land at cost	(200,000)
Gain on revaluation	80,000
Less deferred tax @ 20%	(16,000)
Revaluation surplus	64,000

120 A

Deferred taxation increase	7,000	(23,000 – 16,000)
Less tax on revaluation gain	(3,000)	recognised as OCI (10,000 × 30%)
Charge to SPL	4,000	

Tax expense:

Current year estimate	12,000
Prior year overprovision	(7,000)
Deferred tax, as above	4,000
Charge for year	9,000

If you chose B, you have used the full deferred tax increase. If you chose C you have added the overprovision. If you chose D you have deducted the deferred tax movement.

121 89.1¢

EPS = $3,000,000/3,366,667 (W1) = 89.1¢

(W1) Weighted average number of shares

Step 1 – Theoretical ex-rights price (TERP)

2 shares @ $2 =	$4.00
1 share @ $1.40 =	$1.40
3 shares	$5.40

TERP = $5.40/3 = $1.80

Step 2 – Rights fraction = 2/1.8

Step 3 – Weighted average number of shares (WANS)

Date	Number	Fraction of year	Rights fraction	Weighted average
1 January	2,400,000	3/12	2/1.8	666,667
1 April	3,600,000	9/12		2,700,000
				3,366,667

122 A

EPS = $2,000,000/4,250,000 (W1) = 47.1¢

(W1) Weighted average number of shares

Date	**Number**	**Fraction of year**	**Bonus fraction**	**Weighted average**
1 January	3,000,000	5/12	4/3	1,666,667
1 June	4,000,000	4/12		1,333,333
30 September	5,000,000	3/12		1,250,000
				4,250,000

If you chose C or D, you have failed to apply the bonus fraction correctly. If you chose B you have ignored the bonus fraction.

123 75¢

The prior year earnings per share figure must be restated by the inverse of the rights fraction that relates to the current year earnings per share calculation.

The current year rights fraction is calculated below.

Step 1 – Theoretical ex-rights price (TERP)

3 shares @ $2.20 =	$6.60
1 share @ $1.60 =	$1.60
4 shares	$8.20

TERP = $8.20/4 = $2.05

Step 2 – Rights fraction

$$\frac{2.20}{2.05}$$

Therefore the restated earnings per share figure is 81c × 2.05/2.20 = 75¢.

124 D

Diluted EPS is calculated as 10,644,000/7,250,000 = 146.8¢

The earnings adjustment is:	$	
Earnings for basic EPS	10,500,000	
Plus interest saved (2.5m × 8%)	200,000	
Less tax (200,000 × 28%)	(56,000)	
Earnings for Diluted EPS	10,644,000	
Shares for basic EPS	6,000,000	
Shares issued on conversion	1,250,000	(2,500,000/100) × 50
Shares for diluted EPS	7,250,000	

125 C

To calculate diluted earnings per share with an option, you need to work out the number of 'free' shares that will be issued if the options are exercised, and add that to the weighted average number of shares.

If the options are exercised, $3 million will be received ($3 × 1 million options).

At the market value of $5, $3 million would buy 600,000 shares ($3m/$5).

Therefore the cash received is the equivalent of 600,000 shares. As there are 1 million options, this means that 400,000 shares are being issued for free.

Diluted EPS = $2m/(4 million + 400,000) = **45.5¢**

126 $2,250,000

The earnings figure for the EPS calculation is the profit attributable to the parent shareholders.

127 A, E

Redeemable preference dividends will already have been removed from net profit when arriving at this figure in a statement of profit or loss. Therefore this adjustment is not necessary. Dividends are simply the cash paid out of the earnings, and are often compared to the earnings per share. All the other items will need to be removed from the overall net profit figure in the statement of profit or loss.

128

Considered within DEPS	**Considered within Basic EPS**
The issue during the year of a convertible (to equity shares) loan note	A 1 for 5 rights issue of equity shares during the year at $1.20 when the market price of the equity shares was $2.00
The granting during the year of directors' share options exercisable in three years' time	Equity shares issued during the year as the purchase consideration for the acquisition of a new subsidiary

129 B

A and D will give the same impression as overall profit for the year. C is incorrect as diluted EPS is not an indication of future profit.

130 A

(1,550/((2,500 × 2) + 1,200 see below))

2 million shares at $1.20 = $2.4 million which would buy 800,000 shares at full price of $3. Therefore, dilution element (free shares) is 1,200,000 (2,000 – 800).

131

Legal action against AP	Legal action by AP
Provision	Contingent asset

The legal action against AP has a probable outflow, so AP should make a provision. The legal action taken by AP is a contingent asset. As it is probable, it should be disclosed in a note. Assets should only be recognised when there is a virtually certain inflow.

132 C

A provision is only required when there is a present obligation arising as a result of a past event, it is probable that an outflow of resources embodying economic benefits will be required to settle the obligation, and a reliable estimate can be made of the amount. Only answer C meets all these criteria. Answer A is incorrect because the obligation does not exist at the reporting date and also cannot be reliably measured at present. Answer B is an example of an adjusting event after the reporting date as it provides evidence of conditions existing at the reporting. Answer D is a contingent liability. However, as its likelihood is remote no provision is necessary.

133 C

The warehouse fire is an adjusting event as it occurred before the reporting date. Settlement of the insurance claim should therefore be included in the financial statements.

The other events are non-adjusting as they occurred after the reporting date and do not provide evidence of conditions existing at the reporting date. Issue B is a brand new event, and therefore should not be adjusted. As it is clearly material the event should be disclosed in the notes to the accounts.

134 $3,500,000

Per IAS 37 *Provisions, Contingent Liabilities and Contingent Assets*, the amount payable relates to a past event (the sale of faulty products) and the likelihood of payout is probable (i.e. more likely than not). Hence, the full amount of the payout should be provided for.

135 B

The costs associated with ongoing activities (relocation and retraining of employees) should not be provided for.

136 B

Extraction provision at 30 September 20X4 is $2.5 million (250 × 10).

Dismantling provision at 1 October 20X3 is $20.4 million (30,000 × 0.68).

This will increase by an 8% finance cost by 30 September 20X4 = $22,032,000.

Total provision is $24,532,000.

137 B, C

The change in tax rate and the fire will be non-adjusting events as the conditions did not exist at the reporting date.

138

	Adjusting	Non-adjusting
A public announcement in April 20X5 of a formal plan to discontinue an operation which had been approved by the board in February 20X5.		✓
The settlement of an insurance claim for a loss sustained in December 20X4.	✓	

A board decision to discontinue an operation does not create a liability. A provision can only be made on the announcement of a formal plan (as it then raises a valid expectation that the action will be carried out). As this announcement occurs during the year ended 31 March 20X6, this a non-adjusting event for the year ended 31 March 20X5.

The insurance claim was in existence at the year end, so this will be an adjusting event as it provides further evidence of conditions in existence.

139 D

Deferred tax relating to the revaluation of an asset must be provided for even if there is no intention to sell the asset, in accordance with IAS 12 *Income Taxes*.

At 31 March 20X5 there is no present obligation to replace the oven lining, so no provision should be accounted for.

A change in estimated useful life is a change in accounting estimate and should therefore be accounted for prospectively rather than retrospectively.

140

	True	False
IAS 10 *Events After the Reporting Period* covers the period from the reporting date to the annual general meeting		✓
According to IAS 10 *Events After the Reporting Period*, any non-adjusting event should be disclosed as a note in the financial statements		✓

Both are false. IAS 10 *Events After the Reporting Period* covers the period from the reporting date up to the date the financial statements are authorised for issue. Only material non-adjusting events need to be disclosed as notes in the financial statements.

141

There is a present obligation from a past event	No
A reliable estimate can be made	Yes
There is a probable outflow of economic benefits	Yes

Whilst there is an estimate of $500,000 and it is probable that Faubourg will make the changes, there is no present obligation at 31 December 20X4.

If Faubourg changes its mind and sells the building prior to June 20X5, no obligation would arise. Future obligations are not accounted for as provisions.

142 A, D

Changes in provisions are regarded as changes in accounting estimates so should be accounted for prospectively rather than retrospectively.

Provisions should be recorded at the best estimate, reflecting the amount most likely to be paid out, rather than the highest possible liability.

CONSOLIDATED FINANCIAL STATEMENTS

143

	Consolidated	**Not to be consolidated**
Beta is a bank and its activity is so different from the engineering activities of the rest of the group that it would be meaningless to consolidate it.	✓	
Delta is located in a country where local accounting standards are compulsory and these are not compatible with IFRS Standards used by the rest of the group.	✓	
Gamma is located in a country where a military coup has taken place and Petre has lost control of the investment for the foreseeable future.		✓

The investment in Gamma no longer meets the definition of a subsidiary (ability to control) and therefore would not be consolidated.

144 A

Is the correct treatment for a bargain purchase (negative goodwill)?

145 C

While having the majority of shares may be a situation which leads to control, it does not feature in the definition of control per IFRS 10 *Consolidated Financial Statements*.

146 D

At 31 December 20X2 the deferred consideration needs to be discounted to present value by one year.

$200,000/1.1 = $181,818

If you chose C, you have not discounted the consideration. If you chose A, you have not unwound the discount. If you chose B, you have only done the first year calculation.

147 $371,000

To work out the net assets at acquisition, the retained earnings at acquisition must be calculated.

The retained earnings at the end of the year are given as $180,000, and there has been a profit of $36,000 for the year.

As Philip has owned Stanley for 3 months, then 3 months of this profit is regarded as post-acquisition. Therefore $9,000 has been made since acquisition.

Once this has been worked out, the retained earnings at acquisition can be calculated by deducting the post-acquisition retained earnings of $9,000 from the closing retained earnings of $180,000 to give $171,000.

Net assets at acquisition = $200,000 share capital + $171,000 retained earnings = $371,000.

148 $2,780,000

The cost of investment is worked out as follows:

Shares: 800,000 × ¾ × $3.80 = $2,280,000

Deferred cash = $550,000 × $^{1}/_{1.1}$ = $500,000

The professional fees cannot be capitalised as part of the cost of investment. Therefore the total cost of investment is $2,280,000 + $500,000 = **$2,780,000**

149 B

The profit on the $800,000 sale is $160,000 ($800,000 × $^{25}/_{125}$).

As 75% of the goods have been sold on to third parties, 25% remain in inventory at the year end. Unrealised profits only arise on goods remaining in inventory at the year end, so the unrealised profit is $40,000 ($160,000 × 25%).

150 $352,000

The unrealised profit on the non-current asset transfer needs to be removed.

The carrying amount at the year-end after the transfer is $32,000 ($40,000 less 1 year's depreciation).

The carrying amount of the asset if it had not been transferred would have been $24,000 ($30,000 less 1 year's depreciation).

Therefore the unrealised profit on the non-current asset is $8,000 ($32,000 – $24,000)

The total property, plant and equipment is $300,000 + $60,000 – $8,000 = **$352,000.**

151 B, E

The fact that unanimous consent is required would suggest that there is no control over the investee. Preference shares carry no voting rights and therefore are excluded when considering the control held over an investee.

152

	Include in cost of investment	**Do not include in cost of investment**
An agreement to pay a further $30,000 if the subsidiary achieves an operating profit of over $100,000 in the first 3 years after acquisition	✓	
Professional fees of $10,000 in connection with the investment		✓

Any incidental costs associated with the acquisition should be expensed as incurred. Contingent consideration can all be included as part of the cost of an investment in a subsidiary.

153 D

All of Paul's revenue and expenses will be time-apportioned from the date of acquisition to the date of consolidation to reflect the period for which these were controlled by Peter.

154 A

The asset has not been sold outside of the group and therefore there is an unrealised profit to adjust for on consolidation.

155

	True	**False**
Goodwill impairment will always be deducted in full from the parent's retained earnings		✓
Goodwill impairment will be apportioned between the parent and the non-controlling interest (NCI) when the NCI is valued at fair value	✓	

Where the NCI is valued at fair value, the goodwill impairment will be split between the parent and the NCI in accordance with their shareholdings.

156 A

The activities of the subsidiary are irrelevant when making the decision as to whether to produce consolidated financial statements or not.

157 $160m

	$000	
Consideration – shares	100,000	(see below)
Consideration – cash	60,000	

Branch purchased 75% of Leaf's 80 million shares, giving them 60 million shares. Branch issued 2 shares for every 3 purchased, meaning 40 million shares have been issued (60m × 2/3). At a market value of $2.50 each, 40 million shares have a value of $100 million.

158 $108,000

NCI % × S's PAT = 20% × $600k = $120k

NCI% × PUP (S selling to P) = 20% × 60k = ($12k)

Total NCI = $120k – $12k = **$108k**

159 D

Cost of sales = $14.7m + $8.7m ($^9/_{12}$ × $11.6m) – $4.3m (intra-group sale) + $0.2m (PUP) = **$19.3m**

The PUP is $2.2m × $^{10}/_{110}$ = $0.2m.

If you chose B, you have not time-apportioned the results. If you chose A you have deducted the PUP rather than adding it. If you chose C, you have missed the PUP.

160 $970,000

Operating expenses = $600,000 + $350,000 + $20,000 (FV depreciation) = $970,000

The only adjustments to the statement of profit or loss should be the current year income or expenses. Therefore the prior year fair value depreciation and goodwill impairment are ignored.

161 B

The finance costs for the subsidiary must be time apportioned for six months, as A has only owned them for that period of time. Also, the intra-group interest must be split out. The intra-group interest would not have existed in the first half of the year, as the loan was only given to B in July.

The intra-group interest for the second 6 months would have been $20,000 ($500,000 × 8% × $^6/_{12}$). Without this, B's finance costs would have been $50,000 for the year. Splitting this evenly across the year would mean that $25,000 was incurred in each six month period.

Therefore the total finance costs would be $200,000 + $25,000 = **$225,000**.

162 A

	Impacts the NCI share of profit	**Does not impact the NCI share**
Goodwill impairment	✓	
The parent transferring an item of inventory to the subsidiary for $10,000 greater than its carrying amount, all of which remains in the group at the year end		✓
The subsidiary having an item of plant with a fair value of $500,000 above its carrying amount, and a remaining life of 10 years	✓	

The parent transferring inventory at a profit would mean that the parent's profits are overstated. This would have no impact on the non-controlling interest.

163 $6,600,000

Consolidated revenue: AB $5.5m + CD $2.1m – $1m intra-group= $6.6 million

All intra-group sales and cost of sales are removed from the group accounts.

164 B

The dividend would not have been in Allen's statement of profit or loss, so no adjustment to this would be made. The adjustment to remove the dividend would be made in investment income, where Burridge will have recorded the income in its individual financial statements.

The profit needs to be time-apportioned for the six months of ownership, with the $10,000 impairment then deducted.

Share of profit of associate = 30% × $200,000 ($400,000 × 6/12) – $10,000 = **$50,000**

If you chose D, you have not time-apportioned the associate. If you chose C, you have not deducted the impairment. If you chose A, you have only recognised 30% of the impairment.

165 B

Beasant own 30% of Arnie's shares, which is 30,000 shares (30% of Arnie's 100,000 shares).

As Beasant issued 1 share for every 3 purchased, Beasant issued 10,000 shares. These had a market value of $4.50 and were therefore worth $45,000.

In valuing an associate Beasant must include 30% of Arnie's post-acquisition movement in net assets. Arnie has made a post-acquisition loss of $40,000 (net assets at acquisition were $500,000 and net assets at 31 December were $460,000). Therefore Beasant's share of this is a $12,000 loss (30%).

Cost of investment	$45,000
Share of post-acquisition loss	($12,000)
Investment in associate	$33,000

If you chose D, you based the consideration on 30,000 shares rather than 10,000. If you chose C, you have ignored share capital from the net assets movement. If you chose A, you have used the wrong share price for consideration.

166

	Single entity concept	**Going concern concept**
Removing unrealised profits on group sales	✓	
Removing intra-group balances	✓	

167

30% of the share capital of Hansen Co. The other 70% is owned by Lawro, another listed entity, whose directors make up Hansen's board.	→	Investment
80% of the share capital of Kennedy Co, whose activities are significantly different from the rest of the Nicol group.	→	Subsidiary
30% of the share capital of Bruce Co. The Nicol group have appointed 2 of the 5 board members of Bruce Co, with the other board members coming from three other entities.	→	Associate

Normally 30% would suggest that Nicol have significant influence, making Hansen an associate. However, Lawro having 70% and controlling the entire board would mean that it is unlikely that Nicol have influence and therefore treat it as a trade investment.

168 A

	$
Cost of Investment	5,500,000
Badger % of post-acquisition profits	46,875
30% × (625,000 × $^3/_{12}$)	
Total	**5,546,875**

169 $325,000

	$
Share of Net Profit: 30% × 1,500,000	450,000
Share of PUP: 30% × ((2m × 50%) × 30%)	(90,000)
Current year impairment	(35,000)
Total	**325,000**

170 A

IFRS 10 *Consolidated Financial Statements* states that where the reporting date for a parent is different from that of a subsidiary, the subsidiary should prepare additional financial information as of the same date as the financial statements of the parent unless it is impracticable to do so.

If it is impracticable to do so, IFRS 10 allows use of subsidiary financial statements made up to a date of not more than three months earlier or later than the parent's reporting date, with due adjustment for significant transactions or other events between the dates.

The companies do not have to have the same policies in their individual financial statements, but adjustments will be made to prepare the consolidated financial statements using the group policies.

Only the profit relating to goods remaining in the group at year end needs to be adjusted.

171 A, B

Items C and D would signify control.

172 C, D

While the same accounting policies must be used in the consolidated financial statements, the subsidiaries do not have to operate the same policies as the parent. Having different activities is not an acceptable reason for non-consolidation.

173 $127,760

		$
Alpha Co	100% × $80,200	80,200
PUP adjustment	$2,000 × ½	(1,000)
Bravo Co	$51,900 × 4/12 × 80%	13,840
Charlie Co	$86,800 × 40%	34,720
		127,760

Note that only 80% of Bravo Co's post-acquisition profits are included because 20% will be attributable to the non-controlling interests in Bravo Co.

174 $180,000

This question is best resolved by using a balancing figure technique.

	$000	$000
Fair value of consideration transferred:		
Cash consideration (balancing figure)		**180**
Contingent consideration		250
Fair value of NCI at acquisition		100
		530
Less fair value of net assets acquired:		
Share capital	500	
Retained earnings b/f	(300)	
Profit to acquisition 120 × 3/12	30	
		(230)
Goodwill per question		300

175

	True ✓	False ✓
Where a parent company is satisfied that there has been a gain on a bargain purchase (negative goodwill), it should be recognised in the consolidated statement of profit or loss immediately.	✓	
If the liabilities of the acquired entity are overstated, then goodwill will also be overstated.	✓	

A gain on bargain purchase will be credited to the consolidated statement of profit or loss immediately. It is not recognised in the consolidated statement of financial position. If liabilities are overstated, then the net assets would be understated. This would cause any goodwill recognised to be overstated.

176 $63,800,000

	$000
Viagem	51,200
Greca (26,000 × $^{9}/_{12}$)	19,500
Intra-group purchases (800 × 9 months)	(7,200)
URP in inventory (1,500 × $^{25}/_{125}$)	300
	63,800

177 C

Market price of Sact's shares at acquisition was $2.50 ($3 × $^{100}/_{120}$), therefore non-controlling interest (NCI) at acquisition was $50,000 (100,000 × 20% × $2.50). NCI share of the post-acquisition profit is $6,000 (40,000 × $^{9}/_{12}$ × 20%). Therefore non-controlling interest as at 31 March 20X5 is $56,000.

178 C

Germaine only owns 40% of Foll's voting shares so is unlikely to exercise control.

179 $546,000

	$
Wilmslow	450,000
Post-acquisition Zeta ((340 – 200) × 80%)	112,000
Inventory PUP (320,000 × ¼ × $^{25}/_{125}$)	(16,000)
	546,000

180 C, D

The fair value of deferred consideration is its present value. Fair values are applied to the subsidiary's assets, liabilities and contingent liabilities.

While the use of fair value seems to not comply with the historical cost principle, this will effectively form part of the cost of the subsidiary to the parent, so the principle is still applied. Depreciation will not increase if the fair value of assets is lower than the current carrying amount. Patents can be recorded as intangible assets as they are separable.

181

	True	**False**
The profit made by a parent on the sale of goods to a subsidiary is only realised when the subsidiary sells the goods to a third party	✓	
Eliminating intra-group unrealised profits never affects non-controlling interests		✓
The profit element of goods supplied by the parent to an associate and held in year-end inventory must be eliminated in full		✓

182 $1,335,000

	$000	
Investment at cost	1,200	
Share of post-acq profit	150	$(750 \times {}^{8}/_{12} \times 30\%)$
Inventory PUP	(15)	$(300 \times {}^{20}/_{120} \times 30\%)$
	1,335	

183 $98,600,000

The $1 million cash in transit should be treated as if received (Dr Cash $1 million, Cr Receivables $1 million). After this, an intra-group balance of $3 million will remain. This is then removed (Dr Payables $3 million, Cr Receivables $3 million).

Therefore consolidated receivables = 64.6 + 38 – 1.0 – 3.0 = **$98.6m**

184

	True	**False**
If a subsidiary is disposed of on the last day of the reporting period then its assets and liabilities must still be included in the consolidated statement of financial position		✓
The gain or loss arising on the disposal of a subsidiary in the financial statements is recorded in other comprehensive income		✓

185

Cash consideration of $4.8 million
Deferred cash consideration of $8.3 million

The professional fees cannot be capitalised. The deferred cash should be discounted to present value at the date of acquisition, $10 million/$1.1^2$ = $8.3 million.

186 B

The profit or loss on the disposal is calculated as follows:

Proceeds	10m
Goodwill at disposal	(2m)
Net assets at disposal	(9m)
Non-controlling interest at disposal	3m
Profit on disposal	2m

If you selected answer A you have incorrectly identified it as a loss. If you selected answer C you have added the goodwill instead of deducting it. If you selected answer D you have added the non-controlling interest onto the carrying amount of the subsidiary (rather than deducting it) when calculating the profit or loss on disposal.

187 $6,000,000

The profit arising in the individual financial statements of Wind will be the difference between the proceeds received of $10 million and the purchase price of $4 million.

188 $2,500,000

	$m
Proceeds	9.0
Goodwill at disposal	(4.6)
Net assets at disposal	(5.0)
Non-controlling interest at disposal	3.1
Profit on disposal	2.5

189 A

	$m	$m
Proceeds		15
Goodwill at disposal		Nil
Net assets at disposal		(8)
Non-controlling interest:		
At acquisition	2.2	
NCI % of post-acquisition net assets 40% × ($8m – $5m)	1.2	
NCI % of goodwill impairment (40% × $1m)	(0.4)	
Non-controlling interest at disposal		3
Profit on disposal		10

If you selected answer B you have used the non-controlling interest at acquisition when calculating the profit or loss on disposal, instead of the non-controlling interest at disposal. If you selected answer C you have not reduced the non-controlling interest by its share of the goodwill impairment. If you selected answer D you have valued the non-controlling interest at its share of the disposal date net assets.

INTERPRETATION OF FINANCIAL STATEMENTS

190 A

A not-for-profit entity is not likely to have shareholders or 'earnings'.

191 B

A, C and D are all ratios associated with profit. A charity is more likely to be concerned with liquidity rather than the profits made by the entity.

192

	Limitation	**Not a limitation**
Different ways of calculating certain ratios exist	✓	
Accounting policy choices can limit comparability between different companies	✓	

193 35

Inventory turnover is six times, so inventory days must be 365/6 = 61 days.

The cash collection period is inventory days plus receivables days less payables days.

Therefore the trade payables period is 61 + 42 – 68 = 35 days.

194 C, E

A new website selling direct to the public is unlikely to be on credit terms, as payment will be taken on the order.

This should therefore reduce the receivables collection period, as will the new retail units to the public, which will be cash based.

195 C

Return on capital employed is calculated as profit from operations/capital employed. Capital employed consists of debt and equity.

The deferred tax and payables are not included. Therefore the return on capital employed = \$240,000/\$900,000 = **26.7%**.

196 0.87:1

The quick ratio is made up of the current assets excluding inventory divided by the current liabilities = (\$80,000 + \$10,000)/(\$70,000 + \$34,000) = **0.87:1**.

197 A

While the website is new in the year, the additional delivery costs are likely to be incurred every year in the future, meaning it is not a 'one-off' item.

198 C

Delivery costs to customers are not part of cost of sales, so increased prices will have no impact on the gross profit margin.

199

	Available to KRL to use	**Not available to KRL to use**
Details of the overseas country in which the target entity operates	✓	
Recent financial statements of the entity	✓	
Internal business plans of the takeover target		✓

Internal business plans would be internal information for an entity so KRL would not be able to use this information.

200 A

P/E ratio is seen as a marker of risk, and a high P/E ratio is indicative of a lower perceived risk than an entity with a lower P/E ratio. Therefore Marcel is seen as less risky than the sector average.

P/E ratio is also indicative of market confidence, and a high P/E ratio means that high future growth is expected. Therefore, there is more confidence about the future prospects of Marcel than the sector average.

201

	True	False
It acts as a prediction of the future Earnings Per Share figure		✓
It discloses that Earnings Per Share could have been higher		✓

Diluted EPS is not a prediction of the future EPS figure as firstly there is no forecast made of the earnings figure.

Secondly, if there were a range of conversion terms for a convertible, the terms giving the maximum number of issued shares would always be used in the diluted EPS calculation, rather than the most likely conversion terms.

Diluted EPS is a warning to shareholders that the EPS calculation could have been lower if the commitments to issue ordinary shares had been issued as shares in the current period.

202 B

The finance cost in the profit or loss account will be based on the effective interest rate, so the charge will be $2.5m × 8% = $200,000.

If the interest cover to be maintained is 9, then the minimum operating profit to be maintained must be $200 × 9 = $1.8m.

Option A used the coupon rate of 6% to calculate the finance cost, giving $150k.

Option C used the difference between the effective and coupon rate which is $50k.

Option D includes the transaction costs in the initial value of the loan, when calculating effective interest, giving $220k.

203 5.6

Price-earnings (P/E) ratio is current market price per share/earnings per share.

The earnings per share (EPS) for Rogers is net profit/number of ordinary shares in issue. The share capital is $1 million, and as the share capital is divided into 50¢ shares there must be 2 million shares in issue.

Therefore, EPS is 1,250/2,000 = $0.625, or 62.5¢

P/E ratio is therefore 3.50/0.625 = 5.6

204 21.4%

The dividend yield is calculated as the dividend per share/current share price × 100%

Dividend per share is total dividend/total number of shares

Dividend per share is therefore $1.5m/2m = $0.75, or 75¢

The current share price is $3.50

Therefore the dividend yield is 0.75/3.5 × 100% = 21.4%

205 B

ROCE can be sub-divided into net profit × asset turnover.

Alco has a higher net profit, and therefore must be a high end retailer. Its asset turnover is 0.4 times, so it does not use assets intensively to generate a profit.

This would be expected of a high end retailer, as they are not volume driven.

Saleco has a low net profit, and therefore must be a lower end retailer. Its asset turnover is 5 times, so it uses assets intensively to generate a profit.

This would be expected of a lower end retailer, as they are volume driven.

206

	Limitation	**Not a limitation**
Financial statements often use historic cost, meaning that inflation is not taken into account	✓	
Complex items may not fit into any accounting standards and therefore may be omitted from the financial statements		✓

While complex items may exist which don't fit easily into an accounting standard, these cannot simply be omitted from the financial statements. The IFRS Conceptual Framework for Financial Reporting is a principles-based framework, so these would be accounted for using the principles contained within it.

207 A

Lepchem have not yet made any sales, so any ratio involving profit or revenue is irrelevant. The current ratio will be relevant, as Lepchem may have cash flow problems as they spend cash to develop new pharmaceuticals without any cash receipt until they are successful. This could threaten Lepchem's ability to continue as a going concern.

208 C

	Could be used to assess	**Will not be used**
The return given to investors		✓
The success in achieving the organisation's stated aims	✓	
How well costs are being managed	✓	

Not-for-profit entities do not exist to make profits, therefore the return given to investors is irrelevant.

209 D

With a property management business, the value of that business is linked to the properties and the income which they can generate. Therefore the revenue and profits generated will be relevant.

However, there is unlikely to be any inventory so inventory turnover will not be a key measure that is used.

210 B, C

Rising costs are likely to affect the whole industry and would still mean that Quartile could be compared to the sector. As the error has been corrected, there will be no issues over comparability this year.

211 51

Year-end inventory of six times is 61 days (365/6).

Trade payables period is 42 days (230,000 × 365/2,000,000).

Therefore receivables collection period is 51 days (70 – 61 + 42).

212 B, D

Factoring with recourse means Trent still has the risk of an irrecoverable receivable and therefore could not derecognise the receivable. The cash sales are irrelevant as Trent does not include them within the calculation.

213 D

Acquisition of an asset under a lease agreement will increase debt and so increase gearing. The other options either increase equity or have no impact.

214 C

Use of average cost gives a higher cost of sales (and in turn lower operating profit) than FIFO during rising prices.

215 A

The revaluation is at the beginning of the year and will affect the depreciation for the year and therefore reduce operating profit.

The revaluation will increase assets and equity, and therefore also capital employed.

ROCE will decrease due to lower profit and higher assets.

Gearing will decrease due to the increased level of equity with no movement in debt.

Operating profit margin will decrease due to increased depreciation.

Asset turnover will decrease due to increased value of assets.

STATEMENT OF CASH FLOWS

216 A

PPE

b/f	14,400	Disposal (CA)	3,000
Revaluation	2,000	Depreciation	2,500
Provision	4,000		
Additions (balance)	**8,500**	b/f	23,400
	28,900		28,900

217 B

	$
Accrued interest b/f	12,000
Interest per statement of profit or loss	41,000
Less unwinding (this is not cash, $150,000 × 6%)	(9,000)
Accrued interest c/f	(15,000)
Paid	29,000

If you chose A, you have ignored the unwinding of the discount. If you chose C you have made an error between the opening and closing liability. If you chose D you have simply taken the expense for the year.

218 $98,000

Tax liabilities

		b/f (27 + 106)	133
Paid (balance)	**98**	Statement of profit or loss	122
c/f (38 + 119)	157		
	255		255

219 A

Cash paid to employees is shown when using the direct method, not the indirect method.

220 A, C

Purchase of investments and purchase of equipment would both be shown within cash flows from investing activities.

221 D

	$
Profit	37,500
Depreciation	2,500
Increase in receivables	(2,000)
Decrease in inventory	3,600
Increase in payables	700
Cash generated from operations	42,300
Purchase of non-current assets	(16,000)
Net increase in cash and cash equivalents	26,300

If you chose A, you have deducted depreciation. If you chose C you have deducted the payables movement. If you chose B, you have added the movement in receivables.

222 D

	Add to profit before tax	**Deduct from profit before tax**
Decrease in trade receivables	✓	
Increase in inventories		✓
Profit on sale of non-current assets		✓
Depreciation	✓	

Profit on disposal of non-current assets will be deducted from profit, as it relates to non-cash income. Increases in inventories would be deducted as they have a negative impact on cash flow. Decreases in receivables would have a positive impact on cash flow. Depreciation should be added to profit as it relates to a non-cash expense.

223 $10,000

There will be an inflow of $30,000 relating to a share issue (being the total movement in share capital and share premium), and a $20,000 outflow on repayment of the debentures. Therefore the overall movement will be a net $10,000 inflow.

224 A

PPE

b/f	180	Disposal	60
Revaluation	25	Depreciation	20
Paid (balance)	**125**	c/f	250
	330		330

The amounts to be shown in investing activities will be:

Purchase of PPE: ($125,000) (See working above)

Sale of PPE: $50,000 (Given in question)

This gives a **net outflow of $75,000**

If you chose B or D, you have only accounted for one of the cash flows. If you chose C, you have missed the disposal from your PPE working.

225

Amortisation of government grant	**Receipt of grant**
	Cash received from grant $300,000 in investing activities
Decrease of $100,000 to cash generated from operations	

The release of government grant should be deducted within the reconciliation of cash generated from operations, as this represents non-cash income. The grant received of $300,000 can be calculated using a working, as shown below.

Grant liability

		b/f	900,000
Release to SPL	100,000	**Receipt of grant (balance)**	**300,000**
c/f	1,100,000		
	1,200,000		1,200,000

Section 5

ANSWERS TO OBJECTIVE CASE QUESTIONS – SECTION B

CONCEPTUAL FRAMEWORK/INTERNATIONAL FINANCIAL REPORTING STANDARDS

226 $300,000

The engine will be depreciated over the life of 36,000 flight hours. As the aircraft has flown for 1,200 hours in the first 6 months, the depreciation for the engine will be $9 million × 1,200/36,000 = $300,000.

227 D

Replacement components of complex assets can be capitalised. As the new engine has a life of 36,000 hours, the engine will be depreciated over this life rather than the based on the remaining life of the damaged engine.

228

	Capitalise	Expense
$3 million repair of the wing		✓
$2 million repainting of the exterior		✓

Both costs will be regarded as repairs and must be expensed.

229 B

Cabin fittings – at 1 October 20X8 the carrying amount of the cabin fittings is $7.5 million (25,000 – (25,000 × $^{3.5}/_{5}$). The cost of improving the cabin facilities of $4.5 million should be capitalised as it led to enhanced future economic benefits in the form of substantially higher fares.

The cabin fittings would then have a carrying amount of $12 million (7,500 + 4,500) and an unchanged remaining life of 18 months. Thus depreciation for the six months to 31 March 20X9 is $4 million (12,000 × $^{6}/_{18}$), giving a carrying amount of $8 million.

If you selected A, you have depreciated the upgrade over 5 years rather than the remaining life. If you selected C, you have not capitalised the upgrade. If you selected D, you have done a full year's depreciation on the upgrade.

230 Carrying amount

Recoverable amount is calculated by comparing value in use and fair value less costs to sell, so neither of those would be correct, and replacement cost is not relevant to an impairment calculation.

231 A

As Speculate uses the fair value model for investment properties, the asset should be revalued to fair value before being classed as an investment property. The gain on revaluation should be taken to other comprehensive income, as the asset is being revalued while held as property, plant and equipment.

At 1 October, the carrying amount of the asset is $1,950, being $2 million less 6 months' depreciation. As the fair value at 1 October is $2.3 million, this leads to a $350,000 gain which will be recorded in other comprehensive income.

232 B

Investment properties can be accounted for under the cost or fair value model but not the revaluation model, which applies to property, plant and equipment.

233 $190,000

		$000
Gain on investment properties:	A (2,340 – 2,300)	40
	B (1,650 – 1,500)	150

234

Individual	✓	Consolidated	✓
Investment property	✓	Investment property	
Property, plant & equipment		Property, plant & equipment	✓
Within goodwill		Cancelled as an intra-group item	

In the individual financial statements Speculate would treat property B as an investment, but in Speculate's consolidated financial statements property B would be accounted for under IAS 16 *Property, Plant and Equipment* and be classified as owner-occupied. The group is regarded as a single entity, and the group use the building.

235 B

If Speculate uses the cost model, the asset would be transferred to investment properties at its carrying amount and then depreciated over its remaining life. This would mean that the asset would have a year's depreciation applied to it, 6 months while held as property, plant and equipment, 6 months while held as an investment property. Fair values would be irrelevant.

The depreciation would therefore be $2 million/20 years = $100,000, giving a carrying amount of $1.9 million.

If you selected A, you have only accounted for depreciation for 6 months. If you selected C or D, you have applied depreciation to the fair value of the asset.

236 D

The head office and machinery only need an impairment review where there are any indications that these assets might be impaired. The fact that they have previously been impaired does not mean that an annual impairment review is required regardless of whether there are any indicators of impairment.

237 A

At 1 January 20X7, Chestnut Co's factory had a carrying amount of $5m and a useful life of ten years. Therefore, the annual depreciation charge required would be $0.5m ($5m / 10 years) and the carrying amount at 31 December 20X7 would be $4.5m ($5m – $0.5m).

The recoverable amount of the factory was deemed to be $2.5m which means that an impairment loss of $2m is required ($4.5m – $2.5m).

As there is an existing revaluation surplus of $1m relating to this factory, the impairment loss is treated as a revaluation decrease and the impairment loss should first be debited to the revaluation surplus before any remaining loss is debited to the statement of profit or loss.

Therefore, the carrying amount of the factory within non-current assets will reduce by $2.5m in total ($2m impairment and $0.5m depreciation), split between $1m to the revaluation surplus and $1.5m to the statement of profit or loss ($1m impairment and $0.5m depreciation).

238 B

On 31 December 20X4, the carrying amount of the head office would have been $10.8m ($12m × 36/40 years) before the impairment review on that date.

Following the impairment review, the head office would have been impaired to its recoverable amount of $9m with an impairment loss of $1.8m ($10.8m – $9m) being charged to the statement of profit or loss.

The valuation of $11m on 31 December 20X7 means that there is a reversal of this original impairment loss.

In accordance with IAS 36, an increase to the carrying amount of the head office attributable to the reversal of an impairment loss **must not exceed** the carrying amount that would have been determined had no impairment loss been recognised for the asset in prior years.

As the head office is accounted for under the cost model (rather than the revaluation model), the impairment loss can only be reversed to the extent that the asset is carried at the amount that it would have been had no impairment taken place. This would be $9.9m, being $12m less seven years' depreciation (1 January 20X1 to 31 December 20X7) at $0.3m per year ($12m / 40 years).

239 D

Grants related to assets can be accounted for using either the deferred income method or by deducting from the asset's carrying amount, and grants related to assets may similarly either be shown as income or deducted from expenses.

240 B

	$000
Grant received 1 April 20X7	2,600
Recognised in income 20X7 (1/5 × 9/12)	(390)
Total balance at 31 December 20X7	2,210
Less: current liability ($2.6m × 1/5 to be recognised 20X8)	(520)
Non-current liability at 31 December 20X7	**1,690**

241 A and C

Amortisation is the systematic allocation of the depreciable amount of an intangible asset over its useful life. It serves the same function as depreciation for a tangible non-current asset. Where the intangible asset has a finite useful life, it should be amortised.

A variety of amortisation methods can be used (e.g. straight-line or reducing balance method). The method used should be selected on the basis of the expected pattern of consumption of the future economic benefits.

Some intangible assets may have an indefinite useful life (i.e. there is no foreseeable limit to the period over which the asset is expected to generate net cash inflows for the entity) – this includes goodwill. In such cases, these intangible assets are not amortised but are instead tested for impairment annually and whenever there is an indication that the intangible asset may be impaired.

Option B is not correct as this would only apply to intangible assets with an indefinite useful life (such as goodwill). It does not apply to intangible assets as a whole and the question specifically excluded goodwill.

Option D is not correct and would lead to intangible assets being overstated in the accounts.

242 C and D

An entity's accounting policy for intangible assets is separate to its accounting policy for tangible non-current assets. Intangible assets must be measured initially at cost, but subsequently it is possible to measure certain intangible assets under the revaluation model where, after initial recognition, intangible assets will be carried at a revalued amount.

However, it is only possible to hold intangible assets under the revaluation model where an active market exists for such assets. In practice, this means that most intangible assets will not be measured under the revaluation model. IAS 38 states that it is uncommon for an active market to exist for an intangible asset, although it may happen (e.g. for freely transferable intangible assets such as taxi licences, fishing licences or production quotas).

243 A

	$m
Costs between 1 April and 31 December 20X6	15
Costs capitalised (after criteria met) $15m × 6/9	(10)
Costs w/o as research $15m × 3/9	5
Amortisation of development cost $10m × 1/5 × 3/12	0.5
Total charge to profit or loss	5.5

The $15m of project costs incurred cover a nine-month period. As the project did not meet the capitalisation criteria of IAS 38 until 30 June 20X6, this means that any costs related to the first three months of the year (1 April 20X6 – 30 June 20X6) were research expenditure which should be charged to the statement of profit or loss.

As the project was completed and began to generate revenue from 1 January 20X7, the capitalised development expenditure should then be amortised from that date over its useful life of five years. This requires an amortisation expense for three months (1 January 20X7 – 31 March 20X7) which should be charged to the statement of profit or loss.

244

	True ✓	**False** ✓
The cost for project 325 should be expensed in the statement of profit or loss for the year ended 31 March 20X7	✓	
The specialist equipment which was purchased for project 325 should not be depreciated as it has been used in abandoned or research projects		✓
The costs for project 326 should be included as an asset in the statement of financial position as at 31 March 20X7		✓

Statement 1 If the cost were not expensed to the statement of profit or loss it would be capitalised on the statement of financial position as an asset, which would not be appropriate for an abandoned research project.

Statement 2 IAS 16 *Property, Plant and Equipment* would apply to the specialist equipment used in project 325. In accordance with IAS 16, depreciation of the asset would begin when it was available for use. As it was being used for this project, then it should be depreciated and it makes no difference that the project was abandoned.

Statement 3 The requirements for the development phase of an internally generated intangible asset are quite strict and prescriptive, including being able to demonstrate how the intangible asset will generate probable future economic benefits. Since the directors were not confident of the success of the project at the year end, it would not have been possible to recognise this project as an intangible asset and any costs incurred should instead be expensed to the statement of profit or loss.

245 C

An intangible asset can be recognised when it meets the definition of an intangible asset and the recognition criteria.

An intangible asset is an identifiable non-monetary asset without physical substance.

An intangible asset can only be recognised if it is probable that the expected future economic benefits that are attributable to the asset will flow to the entity and the cost of the asset can be measured reliably.

Both the domain name and the patent meet the definition of being intangible assets and the cost of each can clearly be measured reliably. Based on the information available, it appears that economic benefits will flow to the entity through revenue from online sales (domain name) and production cost savings (patent).

Internally generated customer lists are specifically excluded by IAS 38 from being recognised as intangible assets (along with other items such as internally generated brands). This is because any expenditure incurred on such items cannot be distinguished from the cost of developing the business as a whole.

246 D

Loans are regarded as financial liabilities and should be held at amortised cost.

247 A, B

Borrowing costs must be capitalised if they are directly attributable to qualifying assets, which are assets that take a substantial time to complete. Capitalisation should cease once substantially all the activities to prepare the asset are complete. Capitalisation commences when expenditure is incurred on the asset, borrowing costs are being incurred **and** preparation activities have commenced.

248 $125,000

The finance cost of the loan must be calculated using the effective rate of 7.5%, so the total finance cost for the year ended 31 March 20X8 is $750,000 ($10 million × 7.5%). As the loan relates to a qualifying asset, the finance cost (or part of it in this case) can be capitalised in accordance with IAS 23 *Borrowing Costs*.

Capitalisation commences from when expenditure is being incurred (1 May 20X7) and must cease when the asset is ready for its intended use (28 February 20X8), in this case a 10 month period.

The finance cost to be capitalised = $625,000 ($750,000 × $^{10}/_{12}$). The remaining two months finance costs of $125,000 must be expensed.

249 $625,000

The finance cost to be capitalised = $625,000 ($750,000 × $^{10}/_{12}$).

250 B

Temporary investment income earned during the construction period should be netted off the amount capitalised. However, the interest was earned **prior to the period of construction**. Therefore the investment income earned should be taken to the statement of profit or loss as investment income.

251 B

Correct answer includes all costs except training costs.

252 D

Changes in useful lives are changes in accounting estimates. Such changes are always applied prospectively.

253 D

Depreciation to date of revision is $11,250 ((50,000 – 5,000)/8 years × 2 years).

Carrying amount at date of revision is $38,750 (50,000 – 11,250)

Depreciation for year ended 30 June 20X5 is therefore 38,750 – 5,000/5 years = $6,750

254 B

Feasibility studies and market research are research costs which should be written off as incurred.

255 C

The production of a prototype indicates that the development stage has been reached. Development costs must be capitalised if the criteria are satisfied.

256 $320,000

The dismantling costs should be capitalised at the present value of $4 million, with an equivalent liability created. Each year the discount is unwound at 8%, charged to finance cost and increasing the liability.

Finance cost is therefore $4 million × 8% = $320,000

257 A

The $1.2 million government grant should be released over the 5 year life of the asset, meaning that $240,000 will be released to the statement of profit or loss each year. As Shawler only received the grant on 1 October 20X3, only $120,000 ($^{6}/_{12}$) should be released to the statement of profit or loss in the year.

Therefore there is a remaining balance of $1,080,000 at the year-end. Of this, $240,000 will be released in the next year, so $840,000 will be shown as a non-current liability.

If you selected B, you have not split the year-end liability into current and non-current. If you selected C, you have released a full year of the grant and then not split the year-end liability. If you selected D, you have split the year-end liability but have released a full year of the grant rather than 6 months.

258 $3,000,000

The land is initially translated using the spot rate of exchange and so is recognised at $3 million (12m dinar/4).

Land is a non-monetary asset and so is **not** retranslated at the reporting date.

259 B

Training costs cannot be capitalised as it is not possible to restrict the access of others to the economic benefit as staff could leave and take their skills elsewhere.

260 A, B

The deferred income should be removed, with an expense recorded in the statement of profit or loss. No prior year adjustment should be made. The plant cost would only be increased if the grant was accounted for using the netting off method.

261 A

The correct answer is $18.4m. This is calculated as $10m + $0.5m + $1m + $6.6m less unused materials of $0.5m plus borrowing costs of $0.8m.

262 B

The other items are revenue expenses. Only the fixtures and fittings represent an asset to be capitalised.

263 C

Depreciation must be based on the new value in order to reflect the value consumed. As this is a first time revaluation a gain would go to other comprehensive income and a loss to profit or loss. Residual values and remaining useful lives should be reviewed for all tangible assets.

264 D

The impairment loss for the CGU is $2.2m ($11.8m – $9.6m). Current assets are stated at their recoverable amount, so are not impaired. The impairment loss is initially allocated to the goodwill balance of $1.4m. The unallocated impairment loss is $0.8m. This is allocated to the brand and PPE based on their carrying amounts:

Brand	2
PPE	6
Total	8

Impairment of the brand is therefore $0.2m (2/8 × $0.8m) and the brand is impaired to $1.8m ($2m – $0.2m).

265 C

Both statements are true.

266 A, D

Depreciation is usually recognised in the statement of profit or loss but, in circumstances such as an item of plant being used in the construction of an entity's held-for-use property, the depreciation charge for the plant becomes a direct and capitalised cost of the property. A is therefore correct.

The residual value and useful life of non-current assets should, at the very least, be reviewed at year end. D is therefore correct.

If the revaluation model is applied to a classification of property, plant or equipment, then it must be applied to that entire classification. It does not need to be applied across the entirety of property, plant and equipment nor does it need to be applied across all types of assets. B is therefore incorrect.

Any safety measures, equipment or inspections must be capitalised as a direct cost, even though they are unlikely to enhance the economic benefit generated by an asset. C is therefore incorrect.

267 $1,280,000

Aircraft components	**Cost ($'000)**	**Residual value ($'000)**	**Depreciable amount ($'000)**	**Useful life (years)**	**Depreciation charge ($'000)**
Airframe	8,000	500	7,500	20	375
Engines	5,000	600	4,400	8	550
Engine testing costs	600		600	8	75
Interior of aircraft	1,400		1,400	5	280
Total	**15,000**				**1,280**

268 D

Using the year-end exchange rate, the liability will be calculated as $12.5m (10m euros × $1.25).

Although not required, the journal entries (in $'000) for the above information are:

Dr Bank 10,000

Cr Loan liability 10,000

being recognition of loan on 1 January 20X5 at spot rate of 1 euro = $1

Dr Exchange loss 2,500

Cr Loan liability 2,500

being the restatement of the monetary liability (the loan) at the closing rate at 31 December 20X5 of 1 euro = $1.25, with any exchange loss arising recognised in the statement of profit or loss.

269 A, B

At 31 December 20X7, the loan liability is \$5m as the spot rate at that date is 1 euro = \$1 (5m euros × \$1).

As the equivalent loan liability at 31 December 20X6 was \$5.5m (5m euros x \$1.1), there has been an exchange difference of \$0.5m. This represents a gain as there is a decrease in the fair value of the loan liability.

Although not required, the journal entry (in \$'000) for the above information is:

Dr Loan liability 500

Cr Exchange gain 500

being exchange gain on loan payable, recognised in the statement of profit or loss and based on a spot rate at 31 December 20X7 of 1 euro = \$1

270 D

As recoverable amount cannot be estimated reliably for all parts of the aircraft, the aircraft must be considered overall, as a cash-generating unit. Impairment is not simply ignored for one element (A) and, instead, impairment is apportioned based on the carrying amounts of each asset within the aircraft.

Although depreciated replacement cost is a method of valuation, it is not compulsory. Furthermore, as the aircraft is a cash-generating unit, Novair Co wouldn't be calculating the recoverable amount of this component individually for impairment purposes, although it would be relevant when apportioning an impairment loss (B), to ensure that no asset is impaired below its recoverable amount.

The residual value is not necessarily a reliable estimate of recoverable amount and so it cannot be mandatory to use this for valuation (C).

271 B, D

Whilst items A and C are necessary for an item to be capitalised as an asset, they are not linked to the characteristic of them being identifiable.

272

	Capitalise	**Expense**
Training courses for staff		✓
Expenditure on processor chip		✓

Training courses for staff cannot be capitalised as Darby will not be able to restrict the access of others to the economic benefit. The expenditure on the chip would be classed as research expenditure.

273 $320,000

The amounts incurred from 1 February to 30 April should be expensed, meaning that $300,000 (3 × $100,000) should be expensed. Following this, the costs from 1 May to 30 October should be capitalised, meaning that $600,000 should be capitalised.

The development asset should then be amortised over the 5-year remaining life, giving $120,000 amortisation each year. This should be amortised from 1 November, meaning that 2 months' amortisation should be expensed in the year, so $120,000 × $^{2}/_{12}$ = $20,000.

Therefore the total expense = $300,000 + $20,000 = **$320,000**.

274 C

The development costs will not be subject to an annual impairment review, but will be amortised over the 5 year useful life. The development costs will be held at the carrying value, and will not be revalued each year.

Plant used solely on the development project will result in the depreciation being a directly attributable cost of the project. Therefore any depreciation on the asset will be included in the costs to be capitalised and will be taken to the statement of profit or loss as the project is amortised over the 5 year life.

275 D

At the date of the impairment review, the asset had a carrying amount of $450,000 ($^{9}/_{10}$ × $500,000).

The recoverable amount of the asset is the **higher** of the fair value less costs to sell of $380,000 ($400,000 – $20,000) and the value in use of $480,000. The recoverable amount is therefore $480,000.

The carrying amount of the asset is **lower** than the recoverable amount, so no impairment is charged.

276 D

Depreciation 1 January to 30 June 20X4 (80,000/10 × $^{6}/_{12}$) = 4,000

Depreciation 1 July to 31 December 20X4 (81,000/9 × $^{6}/_{12}$) = 4,500

Total depreciation = 8,500

277 A, D

A fall in the cost of capital would increase the value in use of an asset and would therefore not indicate potential impairment.

The entity's market capitalisation would not be reflected within the values on the statement of financial position.

278 B

Value in use of $38,685 is lower than fair value less costs to sell of $43,000, so recoverable amount is $43,000 and impairment is $60,750 – $43,000 = $17,750.

279 D, E

There is no requirement to test cash generating units (CGUs) more often than other assets. A CGU could be a subsidiary, but not necessarily, and the CGU needs to be consistently identified.

280 $262,500

The impairment loss of $220,000 ($1,170 – $950) is allocated: $35,000 to damaged plant and $85,000 to goodwill, the remaining $100,000 allocated proportionally to the building and the undamaged plant. The impairment to be allocated to the plant will be $37,500 ($100,000 × ($^{300}/_{(300+500)}$)), leaving an amended carrying amount of the plant of $262,500 ($300,000 – $37,500).

281 B, D, E

Assets held for sale must be available for immediate sale, being actively marketed under a committed plan which is unlikely to be withdrawn, and expected to sell within 12 months. Whether the asset is in use or not is irrelevant, and it is not necessary for the sale to have been agreed.

282 A

The disposal of outlets in country A represents a separate geographical location and should be treated as a discontinued operation. The change in focus in Country B is not regarded as a separate major line of business, as it is just targeting different customers.

283 D

Depreciation should cease on the date that the asset is classified as held for sale. In this case, this will be 1 January 20X3. Therefore depreciation would be $150,000 ($4 million/ 20 years × $^{9}/_{12}$), giving a carrying amount of $3,850,000.

As the asset is expected to sell for $3.9 million, the asset should be held at $3,850,000 as the asset should be held at the lower of carrying amount and fair value less costs to sell.

284 A

Costs relating to the ongoing activities of the entity cannot be provided for according to IAS 37 *Provisions, Contingent Liabilities and Contingent Assets*. Therefore only the redundancy costs of $300,000 can be provided.

285

	Adjusting event	**Non-adjusting event**
Disposal of plant	✓	
Redundancy settlement	✓	

Both events relate to conditions in existence at the reporting date, so both events should be regarded as adjusting events.

286 B, C

Accounting policies should only be changed if required by a new IFRS Standards or if doing so results in the production of more reliable and relevant information.

287

The change in useful life of the plant will be a change in accounting **estimate** and should be applied **prospectively**.

288 A

A change in accounting policy must be accounted for as if the new policy had always been in place, retrospectively. In this case, for the year ended 30 September 20X9, both the opening and closing inventories would need to be measured at AVCO which would reduce reported profit by the movement in the values of the opening and closing inventories of $400,000 (($20 million – $18 million) – ($15 million – $13.4 million).

The other effect of the change will be on the retained earnings brought forward at 1 October 20X8. These will be restated (reduced) by the effect of the reduced inventory value at 30 September 20X8 i.e. $1.6 million ($15 million – $13.4 million). This adjustment would be shown in the statement of changes in equity.

289 $88,000

The inventories should be valued at the lower of cost and net realisable value (NRV). The items have a cost of $100,000 (20,000 at $5). The NRV is $88,000, being the 20,000 units at their net selling price of $44 ($55 less 20% commission).

290 B

The inventories should be held at the cost of $80,000 as the net realisable value of $150,000 less $20,000 to complete will be higher than the cost. The replacement cost of $50,000 is irrelevant.

291 C

The cattle will be classed as a biological asset and the milk will be classed as agricultural produce. The cheese is produced after processing so will be classed as inventory.

292 $19,000

The sheep will be held at fair value less point of sale costs. Initially the sheep would have been recognised at $95,000, being the $100,000 less 5% selling costs. At 31 March 20X6, they will be valued at $114,000, being $120,000 less 5% selling costs. Therefore a gain of $19,000 will be recorded in the statement of profit or loss.

293 B

Current cost accounting will apply the current cost of the asset less depreciation to date to reflect the age of the asset. As a new asset would cost $300,000, a 4 year old asset under current cost accounting will be valued at $180,000 ($300,000 – ($^4/_{10}$ × $300,000)).

294 B

This will be a level 2 input, as it is using the price of similar assets without adjustment.

295 A, C

The revaluation will increase equity, therefore affecting the gearing and return on capital employed. The depreciation will also increase. As Schrute charges depreciation to operating expenses, this will affect the net profit margin.

296 C

The lease grants the lessee the beneficial rights of asset use, meaning that a right-of-use asset and lease liability are recorded.

A is incorrect as it treats the rental as an expense, which is not permitted under IFRS 16 *Leases*.

B outlines incorrect treatment for interest, which should decrease over the life of the lease as the lease liability decreases.

D is incorrect as the payments reduce the lease liability rather than being treated as prepayments.

297 A

Leased assets are exempt from capitalisation where the lease period is for 12 months or less, or the assets are low-value assets. IFRS 16 *Leases* does not give a value for what is meant by low-value assets, but gives examples, including telephones. In this case the lease rentals would be charged as an expense within the statement of profit or loss.

298 $306,250

The plant would be capitalised at $350,000, equal to the lease liability plus the initial payment. This would then be depreciated over the four year lease term, giving depreciation of $87,500 a year.

As Fino only entered into the lease halfway through the year, this would give depreciation of $43,750. Therefore the carrying amount would be $350,000 less $43,750, which is $306,250.

299 A

	$
Present value of total lease payments	350,000
Less initial lease rental	(100,000)
Initial lease liability	250,000
Interest to 30 September 20X7 (6 months at 10%)	12,500

300

	Increase	**Decrease**
Return on Capital Employed		✓
Gearing	✓	
Interest cover		✓

Recognition of the lease liability would cause debt liabilities and finance costs to increase. This means that the capital employed would be higher, therefore decreasing return on capital employed. Gearing would increase due to the increased debt. Interest cover would decrease due to the higher level of finance costs.

301 $75,780

The initial lease liability will be $1,263,000, on which 12 months interest at 6% would be $75,780.

302 B

	b/f	**Interest @ 6%**	**Payment**	**c/f**
	$000	$000	$000	$000
20X6	1,263	76	(300)	1,039
20X7	1,039	62	(300)	801

At 31 December 20X6 the total lease liability is $1,039,000. This must be split into current and non-current liabilities. The non-current liability is $801,000, being the amount remaining after the payment in 20X7. Therefore the current liability is $238,000, being the difference between $1,039,000 and $801,000.

If you selected A, you have calculated the liability as if payments were made in advance rather than arrears.

If you selected C, you have chosen the total liability.

If you selected D, you have chosen the non-current liability.

303 C

A leased asset would normally be depreciated over the shorter of the lease term and useful life of the asset. However, as ownership transfers to Lotso at the end of the lease term, Lotso will be using the asset for the entire 6 year period. Therefore the asset is depreciated over 6 years, recognising $210,500 ($1,263,000/6) depreciation a year, and leaving a carrying amount as at 31 December 20X6 of $1,052,500.

304 B

This represents a sale and leaseback where the seller-lessee retains the full benefit of the asset over its remaining life. The asset is not derecognised and remains on the statement of financial position at its carrying amount of $10 million, to be depreciated over the remaining 20 years at a rate of $500,000 ($10m/20) per annum. The value after one year is therefore $9.5 million.

The sale proceeds of $11.5 million would be treated as a loan.

305

	True	False
Statement 1		✓
Statement 2		✓

In a sale and leaseback where the seller-lessee does not retain use of the asset over its remaining life then the seller-lessee is deemed to have disposed of part of the asset, and any profit or loss would be recognised on this element of the asset no longer retained.

Sale proceeds in a sale and leaseback transaction would only be treated as a loan where the seller-lessee retains use of the asset over its remaining life.

306 D

Laidlaw should not 'derecognise' the receivables, but instead treat the $1.8 million cash received from Finease as a current liability (a loan or financing arrangement secured on the receivables).

This is a 'with recourse' factoring arrangement, as Finease can return the receivables to Laidlaw, meaning that Laidlaw carries the risk of these.

307 $810,000

The payments should be discounted at the market rate to find the split of the liability and equity, shown in the working below.

Year ended 30 September	**Cash flow**	**Discount rate at**	**Discounted cash flows**
	$000	8%	$000
20X3	500	0.93	465
20X4	500	0.86	430
20X5	10,500	0.79	8,295
Liability component			9,190
Equity (balance)			**810**
Total proceeds			10,000

308 A, D

The substance of this transaction is that the bank has granted a loan of $5 million to Laidlaw. Control of the inventory has not been transferred, so the 'sale' should not be recognised as revenue. Therefore the loan should be recognised, in addition to the interest expense.

309 D

5% will not be charged to the statement of profit or loss, as the liability element will be held at amortised cost with 8% on the outstanding balance being charged to the statement of profit or loss each year.

310 A

Applying split accounting is essential for faithful representation, otherwise the correct accounting treatment is not being applied. While the disclosures may assist relevance, applying the correct accounting treatment is ensuring the fundamental characteristic of faithful representation is met.

311 D

All three items fall under the description of financial instruments. A financial instrument is a contract that gives rise to a financial asset of one entity and a financial liability or equity instrument of another entity. The convertible loan notes will be split between a financial liability and equity. The loan notes will be a financial liability and the investments will be a financial asset.

312 C

The liability should be held at amortised cost using the effective rate of interest at 10%.

	B/f	**Interest 10%**	**Payment**	**c/f**
	$000	$000	$000	$000
20X5	28,508	2,851	(2,400)	28,959

313 $768,000

	$
Nominal value issued	10,000,000
Less: issue costs	(400,000)
Initial value	9,600,000
Interest at effective rate of 8%	$768,000

314 B

Howard should record the dividend income of $100,000 (10 cents × 1 million shares) as well as the gain in value of $1 million.

315

	Capitalised	Not capitalised
Fair value through other comprehensive income investments	✓	
Fair value through profit or loss investments		✓
Amortised cost investments	✓	

Transaction costs relating to fair value through profit or loss investments should be expensed in the statement of profit or loss.

316 B

A is an example of a financial liability, C is an example of a financial asset and D is the definition of a financial instrument.

317 C

Convertible loan notes are a compound instrument and should be accounted for using split accounting

318 B

Cashflow	**Factor**	$	
$2m × 6% = 120,000	× 0.917	110,040	
120,000	× 0.842	101,040	
2,120,000	× 0.772	1,636,640	
		1,847,720	rounded to $1,848,000

319 D

50,000 shares at fair value of $7 each

320 A

Shares held for trading are carried at Fair Value through Profit or Loss, so both revaluation gain and dividends received would be recognised within profit or loss.

321 C

Receivables and loan notes represent contractual rights and obligations, whereas inventory does not.

322 A

The correct answer is $8.95m. This is the $8.6m plus the $0.4m missing items ($0.6m × 100/150) less the write down of $0.05m ($200,000 – $150,000 (normally sold for $300,000 but actually being sold at $150,000)).

323 D

The change represents a change in accounting policy. Such changes are always applied retrospectively.

324 B

Control over the receivables has not passed to Finaid, so the receivables remain in full as an asset. The cash received is recognised as a financial liability.

325 D

The correct answer is \$0.34m. The loan notes should initially be recorded at the net proceeds of \$8.5m. The effective interest rate of 8% would then be applied to this value. As the loan notes were only issued on 1 July 20X8, the expense for the year would be \$0.34m (\$8.5m × 8% × 6/12).

326 C

The payable should initially be translated at the spot rate of Kr10:\$1, giving a payable of \$1,000. As payables are a monetary liability, they should be retranslated at the closing rate of Kr8:\$1. This gives a closing payable of \$1,250. Therefore the foreign exchange loss is \$250, as it will now cost \$250 more to settle the liability. This will be charged to the statement of profit or loss.

327 B

The receivable should initially be translated at the spot rate of Kr10:\$1, giving a receivable of \$6,000. When the cash of Kr 30,000 is received, the foreign currency gain or loss should be recorded.

At the rate of Kr10.5:\$1, this will give a value of \$2,857. As the Kr 30,000 would have originally been included at \$3,000, this gives a loss of \$143.

Finally, the year-end balance must be retranslated at the closing rate of Kr8:\$1. This gives a closing receivable of \$3,750. As this would originally have been included at \$3,000, this gives a gain of \$750. Therefore the net gain is \$750 – \$143 = \$607.

328

	True	**False**
Statement 1		✓
Statement 2		✓

Inventory should not be retranslated as it is not a monetary item. Foreign exchange gains will not be included in revenue.

329 $3,000

The tax expense in the statement of profit or loss consists of the current tax estimate and the movement on deferred tax in the year. The closing deferred tax liability is $90,000, being the temporary differences of $360,000 at the tax rate of 25%. This means that the deferred tax liability has decreased by $40,000 in the year. This decrease should be deducted from the current tax estimate of $43,000 to give a total expense of $3,000.

330 C

A debit balance represents an under-provision of tax from the prior year. This should be added to the current year's tax expense in the statement of profit or loss.

An under- or over-provision only arises when the prior year tax estimate is paid so there is no adjustment required to the current year liability.

331 $8,000,000

Revenue should be recorded by multiplying the contract price by the progress to date. Therefore the revenue to be recorded is $10 million × 80% = $8 million.

332 D

This is a loss making contract. In this situation, the loss should be recorded in full immediately. Revenue should be based on the progress to date.

Overall contract	$000
Price	8,000
Total cost – incurred to date	(4,000)
– estimated future	(6,000)
Overall loss	(2,000)
Statement of profit or loss	
Revenue (60% of 8,000)	4,800
Cost of sales (balancing figure)	**(6,800)**
FULL loss to be recognised immediately	(2,000)

333 C

Overall contract	$000
Contract price	4,000
Total contract cost (500 + 2,000)	(2,500)
Estimated total profit	1,500
Contract asset	
Revenue (25% × 4,000)	1,000
Less: Amount billed	(800)
Contract asset	200

334

	True	False
Statement 1		✓
Statement 2	✓	

There may be a contract asset based on the amount spent to date compared to the amount billed to the customer.

Where the progress and overall profit of a contract are uncertain, revenue is recognised to the level of recoverable costs.

335 As a change in accounting **estimate**, applied **prospectively**.

IFRS 15 *Revenue from Contracts with Customers* explains that a change in the method of measuring progress is a change in accounting estimate. Changes in accounting estimate are always applied prospectively.

336 D

The revenue in relation to the installation and the machine itself can be recognised, with the revenue on the service recognised over time as the service is performed. The service will be recognised over the 2 year period. By 31 December 20X7, 2 months of the service has been performed. Therefore $20,000 can be recognised ($240,000 × $^{2}/_{24}$).

Total revenue is therefore $580,000, being the $800,000 less the $220,000 relating to the service which has not yet been recognised.

337

Sales element	Discount applied	Discount not applied
Machine	✓	
Installation	✓	
Service	✓	

Discounts should be applied evenly across the components of a sale unless any one element is regularly sold separately at a discount. As Creg does not sell the service and installation separately, the discount must be applied evenly to each of the three elements.

338 B

Revenue as an agent is made by earning commission. Therefore the revenue on these sales should only be $600,000 (10% of $6 million). As Creg currently has $6 million in revenue, $5.4 million needs to be removed, with $5.4 million also removed from cost of sales.

339 $9,490,000

The fact that Creg has given the customer a year to pay on such a large amount suggests there is a significant financing component within the sale.

The $990,000 received can be recognised in revenue immediately. The remaining $9.01 million must be discounted to its present value of $8.5 million. This is then unwound over the year, with the interest recognised as finance income.

Therefore total initial revenue = $990,000 + $8,500,000 = $9,490,000.

340 D

This does not represent a real sale as control has not passed to the bank. Creg still maintains responsibility for the upkeep of the goods.

The bank cannot benefit from the price rise as Creg holds the option to repurchase the goods for a price below the expected fair value.

Therefore this will be treated as a $3 million loan. The additional $630,000 represents interest of 10% a year over two years on the $3 million.

341 D

EPS for the year ended 30 September 20X7 ($15 million/43.25 million × 100)	34.7¢

Step 1 – Theoretical ex rights price (TERP)

4 shares at $3.80	15.2	
1 share at $2.80	2.8	
5 shares at **$3.60** (TERP)	18	

Step 2 – Rights fraction

Market value before issue/TERP = $3.80/$3.60

Step 3 – Weighted average number of shares

36 million × $^{3}/_{12}$ × $^{\$3.80}/_{\$3.60}$	9.50	million
45 million × $^{9}/_{12}$	33.75	million
	43.25	million

If you selected A, you have simply divided the profit for the year by the number of shares at the start of the year. If you selected B, you have used the inverse of the rights fraction. If you selected C, you have applied the rights fraction for the whole year rather than for the period up to the rights issue.

342 A

Diluted EPS for the year ended 30 September 2009 ($15.6 million/45.75 million × 100)	34¢	
Adjusted earnings		
15 million + (10 million × 8% × 75%)	$15.6	million
Adjusted number of shares		
43.25 million + (10 million × $^{25}/_{100}$)	45.75	million

If you selected B, you have ignored the additional tax that would be payable on the interest saved. If you selected C, you have ignored the additional shares that would be issued. If you selected D, you have ignored the impact to the profit and simply increased the number of shares.

343 C

EPS for the year ended 30 September 20X7 ($12 million/43.2 million × 100)	28¢	
Weighted average number of shares		
1 Oct 34 million × $^{4}/_{12}$ × $^{6}/_{5}$	13.6	million
1 Feb 37 million × $^{5}/_{12}$ × $^{6}/_{5}$	18.5	million
1 July 44.4 million × $^{3}/_{12}$	11.1	million
	43.2	million

The bonus fraction should be applied from the start of the year up to the date of the bonus issue. If you selected A, you have added the bonus issue in July to the number of shares in addition to the bonus fraction, effectively double counting the bonus issue. If you selected B, you have missed out the bonus fraction completely. If you selected D you have just added the 3 million market issue without considering the bonus issue.

344

Company	Comparative restated	No restatement
Barstead	✓	
Cabott		✓
Dunstan	✓	

Prior year earnings per share figures must be restated when there is a bonus element to a share issue. Rights issues contain a bonus element so Barstead must restate the prior year figure. Dunstan performed a bonus issue so must restate the prior year figure.

345

	Correct	Incorrect
Statement 1		✓
Statement 2	✓	

Diluted EPS uses the current year's profit, adjusted for items currently in existence such as options or convertibles. It is not a predictor of future earnings.

346 C

To recognise a provision, it must be **probable** that an outflow of resources will be required.

347 C

A provision is recognised at the best estimate of the expenditure required. For a single obligation, this should be the most likely outcome.

If you selected answer B you have calculated an expected value. This is used when the provision being measured involves a large population of items.

348 $840,000

The provision being measured involves a large population of items, so an expected value must be calculated:

(100,000 × 6% × $100) + (100,000 × 8% × $30) = $840,000

349 A

The employees affected have been told about the restructuring and therefore a constructive obligation exists. The provision must not include any costs related to the ongoing activities of the entity. This means that only the redundancy payments should be provided for.

350

	Provision	**No provision**
Situation 1		✓
Situation 2		✓

A provision should not be recognised for situation 1 because it does not give rise to an obligation. Hermione could change its operations in order to avoid the legal requirement to fit smoke filters.

A provision should not be recognised for situation 2. Future operating losses can be avoided, meaning that no obligation exists.

351 B

Provisions must be made if a legal or constructive obligation exists. The provision will be made at present value and added to the cost of the asset. Over the 10 year period, the asset will be depreciated and the discount on the provision will be unwound.

352 $7,452,000

The provision should be recorded at the present value of $6.9 million initially ($15 million × 0.46). After this, the discount on the provision must be unwound, meaning the provision will increase by 8% a year. Therefore the year-end provision is $6.9 million × 1.08 = $7,452,000.

353

	Adjusting	**Non-adjusting**
Fire in the warehouse		✓
Sale of inventory	✓	

The fire will be a non-adjusting event as the condition did not exist at the year end. The sale of inventory will be an adjusting event, as this shows that the net realisable value of the inventory is lower than its cost, meaning that inventory was incorrectly valued at the year end.

354 C

The date of the government announcement of the tax change is beyond the period of consideration in IAS 10 *Events After the Reporting Period*. Thus this would be neither an adjusting nor a non-adjusting event. The increase in the deferred tax liability will be provided for in the year to 30 September 20X9. Had the announcement been before 6 November 20X8, it would have been treated as a non-adjusting event requiring disclosure of the nature of the event and an estimate of its financial effect in the notes to the financial statements.

355 A

From Promoil's perspective, as a separate entity, the guarantee for Hamlet's loan is a contingent liability of $10 million. As Hamlet is a separate entity, Promoil has no liability for the secured amount of $15 million, not even for the potential shortfall for the security of $3 million. The $10 million contingent liability would be disclosed in the notes to Promoil's financial statements.

In Promoil's consolidated financial statements, the full liability of $25 million would be included in the statement of financial position as part of the group's non-current liabilities – there would be no contingent liability disclosed.

356 B

Both statements are true.

357 B

The acquisition of a subsidiary after the accounting period does not provide evidence of a situation or condition existing at the year-end.

358 B

Property is depreciated by $130,000 ($2,600,000/20) giving a carrying amount of $2,470,000. When classed as held for sale, property is revalued to its fair value of $2,500,000 (as it is carried under the revaluation model, $30,000 would go to revaluation surplus). Held for sale assets are measured at the lower of carrying amount (now $2,500,000) and fair value less costs to sell ($2,500,000 – $50,000 = $2,450,000), giving an impairment of $50,000. Total charge to profit or loss is $130,000 + $50,000 = $180,000.

359 C

Carrying amount at 1 April 20X3 is $455,000 (490 – (490/7 × 6/12)). This is below the fair value less costs to sell, and is therefore the value shown in the statement of financial position.

360 C

An asset held for sale needs to be available for immediate sale in its present condition, so the land does not satisfy this criterion. The sale needs to be highly probable, which discounts both the brand and the overpriced plant.

361 D

'Events after the reporting period' are deemed to be all events from the reporting date until the financial statements are authorised for issue. Non-adjusting events should be disclosed in the notes to an entity's financial statements.

362 A

The acquisition of a subsidiary is a non-adjusting event.

363 C

The provision should be recorded at the most likely outcome. This will be $5.2m discounted at 10% for one year which is $4.7m.

364 A

Nothing is recognised or disclosed in the financial statements as the claim is unlikely to be successful.

365 B

As Jeffers believes it is unable to continue trading the financial statements can no longer be prepared on a going concern basis.

CONSOLIDATED FINANCIAL STATEMENTS

366 B

Share for share exchange: 15m × 80% = 12m shares acquired × $^2/_5$ = 4.8m Penfold shares issued @ $5.30 = $25,440,000 consideration given for Superted.

Penfold have issued 4.8m shares so 4.8m will be added to share capital with the remaining $20.64m added to other components of equity. As Penfold currently has $6m other components of equity, the total will be $26,640,000.

If you selected C, you have added Superted's other components of equity, and the subsidiary's equity is not included in the consolidated equity.

If you selected A, you have added the entire share consideration, and if you selected D, you have added the entire share consideration and Superted's other components of equity.

367 $62,400,000

The cash-in-transit must be treated as if received. To do this, $2 million will be added to cash and deducted from receivables. This will leave a $6 million intra-group receivable balance, which will then be removed along with the $6 million intra-group payable balance.

Total receivables = 32,400 + 38,000 – 2,000 – 6,000 = $62,400,000.

368 A

The non-controlling interest **at acquisition** will be $7.2 million.

Penfold has owned Superted for 6 months so 6 months' profit should be included in the consolidated financial statements for the year. Therefore the NCI's share of this will be $2.4 million ($24 million × $^{6}/_{12}$ × 20%).

The sale of plant from Penfold to Superted requires an adjustment to the depreciation charge recorded within the accounts of Superted. The increase in value of $5 million will result in an additional depreciation charge of $0.5 million ($5m × $^{1}/_{5}$ × $^{6}/_{12}$) to be reversed as part of the PUP adjustment. The NCI's share of this is $0.5m × 20% = $0.1 million.

Therefore NCI = $7.2 million + $2.4 million + $0.1 million = $9.7 million.

If you selected B, you deducted the PUP adjustment.

If you selected C, you have taken the NCI at acquisition.

If you selected D, you have ignored the PUP adjustment.

369 $481,500,000

The unrealised profit on the non-current asset transfer needs to be removed.

The carrying amount at the year-end after the transfer is $22.5 million ($25 million less 6 months depreciation).

The carrying amount of the asset if it had never been transferred would have been $18 million ($20 million less 6 months depreciation).

Therefore the unrealised profit on the non-current asset is $4.5 million.

The total PPE is therefore $345 million + $141 million – $4.5 million = $481.5 million.

370 C

There is no control or significant influence as Arnold is controlled by the other investor. Therefore the investment in Arnold will be held as an equity investment, which is a financial instrument.

371 $5,350,000

The deferred consideration should be discounted to the present value at acquisition. $6 million/1.08^2 = $5.144 million.

At 31 March 20X5, 6 months have elapsed, so the discount needs to be unwound for 6 months. $5.144 million × 8% × $^{6}/_{12}$ = $206,000. Therefore the liability at 31 March 20X5 = $5,144,000 + $206,000 = $5,350,000.

372 B

(Workings in $000)

Cost of sales = 319,200 + (176,400 × $^6/_{12}$) – 6,000 (intra-group) + 360 (PUP) = 401,760

PUP = $6,000 × 20% margin × 30% remaining = $360

If you selected A, you have adjusted for all the profit, rather than the 30% remaining in the group at the year-end. If you selected C you have taken out a full year's sales rather than 6 months. If you selected D you have taken out a full year's sales and adjusted for all the profit rather than the amount remaining in the group.

373 D

Operating expenses = 50,610 + (33,120 × $^6/_{12}$) + 100 FV depreciation* + 600 impairment = 67,870.

*Fair value depreciation = $4 million/20 years = $200,000 a year × $^6/_{12}$ = $100,000.

If you selected A, you have added a full year's fair value depreciation. If you selected B, you have deducted the fair value depreciation. If you selected C, you have either time apportioned the impairment or deducted a full year's fair value depreciation.

374 C

Unrealised profits from note (i) would only affect the non-controlling interest if the subsidiary sold goods to the parent, which is not the case. Fair value depreciation (note (ii)) always affects the NCI. Goodwill impairment (note (iii)) will affect the NCI if the NCI is measured at fair value, which it is here.

375

	Correct	**Incorrect**
Statement 1	✓	
Statement 2		✓

A subsidiary's assets, liabilities and contingent liabilities must be included at fair value in the consolidated financial statements. Professional fees associated with the acquisition of a subsidiary cannot be capitalised, regardless of which method is used to measure the non-controlling interest.

376 D

Consolidated retained earnings will consist of 100% of Prunier's retained earnings plus 80% of Sheringham's post acquisition loss ($3.5m – $4m), including the fair value depreciation on Sheringham's assets ($800 × $^1/_{20}$).

	$000
Prunier	11,000
Sheringham (500 + 40) × 80%	(432)
	10,568

377 $2,400,000

The other comprehensive income attributable to the parent will be 100% of Prunier's revaluation gain in the year and 80% of Sheringham's post acquisition revaluation gain. Prunier has made a gain of $2 million in the year and Sheringham has made $500,000. Therefore the other comprehensive income attributable to the parent is $2 million plus 80% × $500,000 = $2,400,000.

378

	Recognise	**Not to be recognised**
Sheringham's brand name, which was internally generated so not shown in Sheringham's financial statements but has a fair value of $3 million	✓	
A research project in progress, which was one of the main reasons Prunier purchased Sheringham and has a fair value of $2 million	✓	
An intangible asset related to an encryption process which has now been deemed illegal. This is included within intangibles at $1.5 million		✓

Internally generated assets and research projects can be recognised within consolidated financial statements if a fair value can be attached to them. The encryption process is now illegal so cannot be recognised as an asset.

379 B

Profit on all sales = 3,000 × 20/120 = $500,000. Anderson has a quarter left, so this is $125,000. As Anderson is an associate, only 30% of this needs to be removed, which is $37,500. If you selected A, you have used margin and not mark-up, and not adjusted for the associate. If you selected C, you have taken all of the unrealised profit, rather than 30%. If you selected D, you have used margin and not mark-up.

380 A

The profit or loss on the disposal is calculated as follows:

	$000
Proceeds	9,000
Goodwill at disposal	(1,000)
Net assets at disposal	(10,600)
Non-controlling interest at disposal	2,500
Loss on disposal	(100)

If you selected B, you have added the goodwill instead of deducting it. If you selected C, you have deducted the non-controlling interest at disposal. If you selected D, you have deducted 80% of the net assets, rather than all of them.

INTERPRETATION OF FINANCIAL STATEMENTS

381 B

B is correct, as follows:

	A		B
	$m		$m
Gross profit = 26% × $160m	41.6	Gross profit = 17% × $300m	51
Operating profit = 9% × $160m	14.4	Operating profit = 11% × $300m	33
Operating expenses	27.2		18

A is incorrect. A's revenue is significantly lower than B's and therefore B is more likely to be benefiting from economies of scale.

C is incorrect. A has higher gearing than B and would therefore be considered a higher risk by lenders. (The low interest rate may however explain why A are using debt finance in the first place.)

D is incorrect. LOP's gross profit margin is higher than both A's and B's and therefore acquisition of either entity is likely to reduce the overall margin of the combined business (unless cost savings can be achieved as a result of the acquisition).

382 A, D

B is incorrect. A has higher gearing than B and therefore reduced capacity for additional borrowings.

C is incorrect. LOP's P/E ratio is higher than B's suggesting that the market is more confident about the future performance of LOP.

E is incorrect. The share price may react positively or negatively, depending on the investor's view of the impact the acquisition will have on LOP.

383 B

A and B may target different customers, but that would not mean that their financial statements are incomparable. It may lead to different margins earned, but comparison could still be made, and would help LOP to assess which type of customer and market they made wish to target.

384 24.5%

	LOP		B
	$m		$m
Gross profit = 28% × $500m	140	Gross profit = 17% × $300m	51

Without the cost savings, LOP and B are making a gross profit of $191 million on revenue of $800 million. If the cost savings of $5 million are taken into account, the gross profit will increase to $196 million. This will give a gross profit margin of **24.5%** (196/800).

385

	Correct	Incorrect
Statement 1		✓
Statement 2	✓	

If B has treated the leases incorrectly, then B's liabilities will be understated, meaning that gearing would be understated. B would also not have included any finance costs in the statement of profit or loss, meaning the average interest rate expensed will not have included the interest on the lease.

386 7.5%

1,500/(15,000 + 3,000 + 2,000) = 1,500/20,000 = 7.5%

387 D

Combined profit from operations = \$1,5m – \$0.6m = \$900,000.

Combined revenue = \$9.4m + \$1.2m = \$10,600,000.

Operating margin = 900/10,600 = 8.5%.

If you selected C, you have just used Franck's profit. If you selected B, you have added the loss of 600 rather than deducting it. If you selected A, you have just used Franck's revenue rather than the combined revenue.

388

	Correct	Incorrect
Statement 1	✓	
Statement 2	✓	

Return on capital employed will clearly decrease, as Franck has made a loss. The capital employed will increase, but overall profit will decrease. Duik has a higher level of gearing (4,000/22,800 = 17.5%) compared to Franck (2,000/18,000 = 11%), which means gearing will increase when the two companies are combined.

389 C

Individual entity financial statements should not contain errors, and if they do, this is not a problem specific to being a subsidiary of another entity.

390 C

The upcoming projects are unlikely to be publicly available information, whereas A, B and D can all be assessed from looking at Duik's financial statements for the current or previous periods.

STATEMENT OF CASH FLOWS

391 C

Cooper has used the indirect method. The direct method is an alternative method of calculating cash generated from operations.

Classification by function and nature relate to the way that items are presented in the statement of profit or loss.

392

	$000
Profit from operations	3,500
Depreciation	4,600
Release of government grant	1,400
Profit on disposal of property	(3,700)
Increase in inventories	(400)
Decrease in trade and other receivables	(300)
Increase in trade and other payables	900

The release of government grant is non-cash income, so should be deducted from profit from operations.

The decrease in trade receivables is good for cash so would be added to profit rather than being deducted.

393 A

Property

b/f	39,500	Depreciation	4,600
		Disposal (balance)	**5,900**
		c/f	29,000
	39,500		39,500

The carrying amount of the property disposed was $5.9 million. As Cooper made a profit of $3.7 million on disposal, the sale proceeds must have been **$9.6 million**.

If you selected B, you have deducted the profit on disposal rather than adding it.

If you selected C, you have used the profit on disposal.

If you selected D, you have selected the carrying amount disposed rather than the sale proceeds.

394 $3,400,000

Grant deferred income

		b/f	6,000
Released in year	1,400	**Received (balance)**	**3,400**
c/f	8,000		
	9,400		9,400

395 B

A rights issue will mean that cash has been raised, increasing the cash from financing activities. Intangible assets can affect the statement of cash flow if they are purchased as this will lead to an outflow of cash.

396 A

Retained earnings

		b/f	940
Dividend paid (balance)	**145**	Revaluation surplus	20
c/f	900	Profit for the year	85
	1,045		1,045

When the land is disposed, the remaining revaluation surplus will be taken to retained earnings. If you selected B, you have deducted the revaluation surplus. If you selected C, you have taken the movement in retained earnings. If you selected D, you have missed out the revaluation surplus transfer into retained earnings.

397 C

The loan notes should be held at amortised cost, with the effective rate of interest being taken to the statement of profit or loss. As these have an effective rate of 8%, $40,000 has been taken to the statement of profit or loss. However, it is only the coupon rate of 5% which has been paid in the year, so $500,000 × 5% = $25,000.

In addition Depay has paid interest on the lease. The total interest charge for the year is $60,000, comprising loan note and lease interest. The loan note interest charged is $40,000, which means that the lease interest, paid as part of the lease payment on 30 September 20X2, must be the balance, $20,000.

So the total interest paid in the year is $45,000.

398 $42,000

Tax liabilities ($000)

		b/f (40 + 125)	165
Tax paid (balance)	**42**	Tax expense	57
c/f (30 + 150)	180		
	222		222

399 B

Dividends received are shown within cash flows from investing activities.

400 $80,000

Lease liabilities ($000)

		b/f	310
Paid (balance)	**80**	New asset additions	70
c/f	300		
	380		380

As the interest has been both charged and paid during the year we may ignore it in our T-account calculation. The resulting calculation above uses the capital balances to identify the capital repaid.

Section 6

ANSWERS TO CONSTRUCTED RESPONSE QUESTIONS – SECTION C

PREPARATION OF SINGLE ENTITY FINANCIAL STATEMENTS

401 PRICEWELL

(a) Pricewell – Statement of profit or loss for the year ended 31 March 20X9

	$000
Revenue (310,000 + 22,000 (W1) – 6,400 (W2))	325,600
Cost of sales (W3)	(255,900)
Gross profit	69,700
Distribution costs	(19,500)
Administrative expenses	(27,500)
Finance costs (W5)	(1,248)
Profit before tax	21,452
Income tax expense (700 + 4,500 – 2,800 (W7))	(2,400)
Profit for the year	19,052

(b) Pricewell – Statement of financial position as at 31 March 20X9

Assets	$000	$000
Non-current assets		
Property, plant and equipment (W4)		66,400
Current assets		
Inventory	28,200	
Trade receivables	33,100	
Contract asset (W1)	16,300	
Bank	5,500	
		83,100
Total assets		149,500

Equity and liabilities		
Equity shares of 50 cents each		40,000
Retained earnings (W6)		55,152
		95,152
Non-current liabilities		
Deferred tax (W7)	5,600	
Lease liability (W5)	5,716	
		11,316
Current liabilities		
Trade payables	33,400	
Lease liability (W5)	5,132	
Current tax payable	4,500	43,032
Total equity and liabilities		149,500

Workings

(W1) Contract with customer:

(i) Overall

	$000
Selling price	50,000
Costs to date	(12,000)
Costs to complete	(10,000)
Plant	(8,000)
Estimated profit	20,000

(ii) Progress

Work completed to date has been agreed at $22 million so the contract is 44% complete ($22m/$50m).

(iii) Statement of profit or loss

Revenue (44% × $50m)		22,000
Cost of sales: per TB	12,000	
Plant depreciation (W4)	2,000	
		(14,000)
Profit to date		8,000

(iv) Statement of financial position

Revenue to date	22,000
Payment from customer	(5,700)
Contract asset	16,300

(W2) Pricewell is acting as an agent (not the principal) for the sales on behalf of Trilby. Therefore the statement of comprehensive income should only include $1.6 million (20% of the sales of $8 million). Therefore $6.4 million ($8m – $1.6m) should be deducted from revenue and cost of sales. It would also be acceptable to show agency sales (of $1.6 million) separately as other income.

(W3) Cost of sales

		$000
Per question		234,500
Contract (W1)		14,000
Agency cost of sales (W2)		(6,400)
Depreciation (W4)	– leasehold property	1,800
	– owned plant	8,500
	– right-of-use asset (20,000 × 25%)	5,000
Surplus on revaluation of leasehold property (W4)		(1,500)
		255,900

(W4) Non-current assets

Property, plant and equipment

	Leasehold property	**Owned plant & equipment**	**Right-of-use plant**	**Specialist plant for contract**	**Total**
	$000	$000	$000	$000	$000
Valuation/cost 1 April 20X8	25,200	46,800	20,000		
Depreciation 1 April 20X8		(12,800)	(5,000)		
		34,000			
Acquisition				8,000	
Depreciation charge					
$25,200 × $^{1}/_{14}$	(1,800)				
$34,000 × 25%		(8,500)			
$8,000 × ½ × $^{6}/_{12}$				(2,000)	
$20,000 × 25%			(5,000)		
	23,400				
Revaluation surplus	1,500				
Revaluation/carrying amount 31 March 20X9	24,900	25,500	10,000	6,000	66,400

The leasehold property has 14 years useful life remaining at the beginning of the year. The specialist plan was acquired on 1 October 20X8 and is therefore only depreciated for 6 months.

The $1.5 million revaluation surplus is credited to cost of sales (W3) in the statement of profit or loss because this represents the partial reversal of the $2.8 million impairment loss recognised in the statement of profit or loss in the previous year ended 31 March 20X8.

(W5) Lease liability ($000)

	Balance b/f	Interest 8%	Payment	Balance c/f
Year to 31 March 20X9	15,600	1,248	(6,000)	10,848
Year to 31 March 20Y0	10,848	868	(6,000)	5,716

Finance cost to profit or loss	1,248
Non-current liability	5,716
Current liability (10,848 – 5,716)	5,132

(W6) Retained earnings

	$000
Balance at 1 April 20X8	44,100
Profit for year per part (a)	19,052
Equity dividend paid per trial balance	(8,000)
Balance at 31 March 20X9	55,152

(W7) Deferred taxation

	$000
Provision required at 31 March 20X9	5,600
Balance b/f per trial balance	(8,400)
Credit to tax expense	(2,800)

	ACCA marking guide		
			Marks
(a)	Statement of profit or loss		
	Revenue		2
	Cost of sales		4½
	Distribution costs		½
	Administrative expenses		½
	Finance costs		1
	Income tax expense		1½
		Maximum	**10**
(b)	Statement of financial position		
	Property, plant and equipment		1½
	Right-of-use asset		½
	Inventory		½
	Due on construction contract		2
	Trade receivables and bank		½
	Equity shares		½
	Retained earnings		1
	Deferred tax		1
	Lease – non-current liability		½
	Trade payables		½
	Lease – current liability		1
	Current tax payable		½
		Maximum	**10**
Total			**20**

402 KEYSTONE

(a) Keystone – Statement of profit or loss and other comprehensive income for the year ended 30 September 20X1

	$000	$000
Revenue		377,600
Cost of sales (W1)		(258,100)
Gross profit		119,500
Distribution costs		(14,200)
Administrative expenses		
(46,400 – 24,000 dividend (50,000 × 5 × $2.40 × 4%))		(22,400)
Profit from operations		82,900
Investment income		800
Finance costs		(350)
Profit before tax		83,350
Income tax expense (24,300 + 1,800 (W3))		(26,100)
Profit for the year		57,250
Other comprehensive income		
Revaluation of leased property	8,000	
Transfer to deferred tax (W3)	(2,400)	
		5,600
Total comprehensive income for the year		62,850

(b) Keystone – Statement of financial position as at 30 September 20X1

	$000	$000
Assets		
Non-current assets		
Property, plant and equipment (W2)		78,000
Current assets		
Inventory	56,600	
Trade receivables	31,150	
		87,750
Total assets		165,750
Equity and liabilities		
Equity shares of 20 cents each		50,000
Revaluation surplus (W2)	5,600	
Retained earnings (15,600 + 57,250 – 24,000 dividend paid)	48,850	
		54,450
		104,450
Non-current liabilities		
Deferred tax (W3)		6,900
Current liabilities		
Trade payables	27,800	
Bank overdraft	2,300	
Current tax payable	24,300	
		54,400
Total equity and liabilities		165,750

Workings (figures in brackets in $000)

(W1) Cost of sales

	$000
Opening inventory	46,700
Materials (64,000 – 3,000)	61,000
Production labour (124,000 – 4,000)	120,000
Factory overheads (80,000 – (4,000 × 75%))	77,000
Amortisation of leased property (W2)	3,000
Depreciation of plant (1,000 + 6,000 (W2))	7,000
Closing inventory	(56,600)
	258,100

The cost of the self-constructed plant is $10 million (3,000 + 4,000 + 3,000 for materials, labour and overheads respectively that have also been deducted from the above items in cost of sales). It is not permissible to add a profit margin to self-constructed assets.

(W2) Non-current assets

The leased property has been amortised at $2.5 million per annum (50,000/ 20 years). The accumulated amortisation of $10 million therefore represents four years, so the remaining life at the date of revaluation is 16 years.

	$000
Carrying amount at date of revaluation (50,000 – 10,000)	40,000
Revalued amount	48,000
Gross gain on revaluation	8,000
Transfer to deferred tax at 30%	(2,400)
Net gain to revaluation surplus	5,600

The revalued amount of $48 million will be amortised over its remaining life of 16 years at $3 million per annum.

The self-constructed plant will be depreciated for six months by $1 million ($10m × 20% × 6/12) and have a carrying amount at 30 September 20X1 of $9 million. The plant in the trial balance will be depreciated by $6 million ((44.5m – 14.5m) × 20%) for the year and have a carrying amount at 30 September 20X1 of $24 million.

In summary:

	$000
Leased property (48,000 – 3,000)	45,000
Plant (9,000 + 24,000)	33,000
Property, plant and equipment	78,000

(W3) Deferred tax

Provision required at 30 September 20X1 ((15,000 + 8,000) × 30%)	6,900
Provision at 1 October 20X0	(2,700)
Increase required	4,200
Transferred from revaluation surplus (W2)	(2,400)
Charge to statement of profit or loss	1,800

ACCA marking guide			
			Marks
(a)	Statement of profit or loss		
	Revenue		½
	Cost of sales		5½
	Distribution costs		½
	Administrative expenses		1½
	Investment income		1
	Finance costs		½
	Income tax expense		1½
	Other comprehensive income		1
		Maximum	**12**
(b)	Statement of financial position		
	Property, plant and equipment		1
	Inventory		½
	Trade receivables		½
	Equity shares		½
	Revaluation surplus		1½
	Retained earnings		1½
	Deferred tax		1
	Trade payables & overdraft		1
	Current tax payable		½
		Maximum	**8**
Total			**20**

403 FRESCO

(a) Fresco – Statement of profit or loss and other comprehensive income for the year ended 31 March 20X2

	$000
Revenue	350,000
Cost of sales (W1)	(311,000)
Gross profit	39,000
Distribution costs	(16,100)
Administrative expenses (26,900 + 3,000 re fraud)	(29,900)
Gain on investments (7,200 – 6,000)	1,200
Finance costs (300 + 2,300 (W3))	(2,600)
Loss before tax	(8,400)
Income tax relief (2,400 + 200 (W4) – 800)	1,800
Loss for the year	(6,600)
Other comprehensive income	
Revaluation of leased property (W2)	4,000
Total comprehensive losses	(2,600)

(b) Fresco – Statement of changes in equity for the year ended 31 March 20X2

	Share capital	Share premium	Revaluation surplus	Retained earnings	Total equity
	$000	$000	$000	$000	$000
Balances at 1 April 20X1	45,000	5,000	nil	5,100	55,100
Prior period adjustment (re fraud)				(1,000)	(1,000)
Restated balance				4,100	
Rights share issue (see below)	9,000	4,500			13,500
Total comprehensive losses (see (i) above)			4,000	(6,600)	(2,600)
Transfer to retained earnings (W2)			(500)	500	
Balances at 31 March 20X2	54,000	9,500	3,500	(2,000)	65,000

The rights issue was 18 million shares (45,000/50 cents each × $^1/_5$) at 75 cents = $13.5 million. This equates to the balance on the suspense account. This should be recorded as $9 million equity shares (18,000 × 50 cents) and $4.5 million share premium (18,000 × (75 cents – 50 cents)).

The discovery of the fraud represents an error part of which is a prior period adjustment ($1 million) in accordance with IAS 8 *Accounting Policies, Changes in Accounting Estimates and Errors*. The balance of $3m is charged to administrative expenses.

Workings (figures in brackets are in $000)

(W1) Cost of sales

	$000
Per question	298,700
Amortisation of leased property (W2)	4,500
Depreciation of right-of-use asset (W2)	5,000
Depreciation of other plant and equipment (W2)	2,800
	311,000

(W2) Property, plant and equipment

	Leasehold property	Plant & Equipment	Right-of-use plant	Total
	$000	$000	$000	$000
1 April 20X1 Cost b/f	48,000	47,500		
Depreciation b/f	(16,000)	(33,500)		
Addition (23,000 + 2,000 deposit)			25,000	
	32,000	14,000		
Revaluation gain *	4,000			
Revaluation	36,000			
Amortisation/depreciation				
36,000 × $^1/_8$	(4,500)			
14,000 × 20%		(2,800)		
25,000 × $^1/_5$			(5,000)	
	31,500	11,200	20,000	62,700

* $500,000 (4,000/8 years) of the revaluation surplus will be transferred to retained earnings (reported in the statement of changes in equity).

(W3) Lease liability

	Balance b/f	Interest @ 10%	Payment	Balance c/f
Year to 31 March 20X2	23,000	2,300	(6,000)	19,300
Finance cost:		$2,300		

(W4) Deferred tax

Provision required at 31 March 20X2 (12,000 × 25%)	3,000
Provision at 1 April 20X1	(3,200)
Credit (reduction in provision) to statement of profit or loss	(200)

ACCA marking guide		
		Marks
(a)	Statement of profit or loss and other comprehensive income	
	Revenue	½
	Cost of sales	4
	Distribution costs	1
	Administrative expenses	1½
	Gain on investment	1
	Finance costs	2
	Income tax expense	2
	Other comprehensive income	1
	Maximum	**13**
(b)	Statement of changes in equity	
	Balances brought forward ½ each	1½
	Prior period adjustment	1
	Rights issue	2
	Total comprehensive income	1
	Retained earnings transfer	1½
	Maximum	**7**
Total		**20**

404 QUINCY

(a) Quincy – Statement of profit or loss and other comprehensive income for the year ended 30 September 20X2

	$000
Revenue (213,500 – 1,600 (W1))	211,900
Cost of sales (W2)	(144,300)
Gross profit	67,600
Distribution costs	(12,500)
Administrative expenses (19,000 – 1,000 loan issue costs (W4))	(18,000)
Loss on fair value of equity investments (17,000 – 15,700)	(1,300)
Investment income	400
Finance costs (W4)	(1,920)
Profit before tax	34,280
Income tax expense (1,100 + 7,400 – 200 (W5))	(8,300)
Profit for the year	25,980

(b) Quincy – Statement of financial position as at 30 September 20X2

Assets	$000	$000
Non-current assets		
Property, plant and equipment (W3)		42,500
Equity financial asset investments		15,700
		58,200
Current assets		
Inventory	24,800	
Trade receivables	28,500	
Bank	2,900	
		56,200
Total assets		114,400
Equity and liabilities		
Equity shares of 25 cents each		60,000
Retained earnings (6,500 + 25,980 – 19,200)		13,280
		73,280
Non-current liabilities		
Deferred tax (W5)	1,000	
Deferred revenue (W1)	800	
6% loan note (W4)	24,420	
		26,220
Current liabilities		
Trade payables	6,700	
Deferred revenue (W1)	800	
Current tax payable	7,400	
		14,900
Total equity and liabilities		114,400

Workings (figures in brackets in $000)

(W1) The revenue for the service must be deferred. The deferred revenue must include the normal profit margin (25%) for the deferred work. At 30 September 20X2, there are two more years of servicing work, thus $1.6 million ((600 × 2) × $^{100}/_{75}$) must be deferred, split equally between current and non-current liabilities.

(W2) Cost of sales

	$000
Per trial balance	136,800
Depreciation of plant (W3)	7,500
	144,300

(W3) Plant and equipment:

	$000
Carrying amount as at 1 October 20X1 (83,700 – 33,700)	50,000
Depreciation at 15% per annum	(7,500)
Carrying amount as at 30 September 20X2	42,500

(W4) Loan note

The finance cost of the loan note is charged at the effective rate of 8% applied to the carrying amount of the loan. The issue costs of the loan ($1 million) should be deducted from the proceeds of the loan ($25 million) and not treated as an administrative expense, to give an initial carrying amount of $24 million and a finance cost of $1,920,000 (24,000 × 8%). The interest actually paid is $1.5 million (25,000 × 6%) and the difference between these amounts, of $420,000 (1,920 – 1,500), is accrued and added to the carrying amount of the loan note. This gives $24.42 million (24,000 + 420) for inclusion as a non-current liability in the statement of financial position.

(W5) Deferred tax

	$000
Provision required as at 30 September 20X2 (5,000 × 20%)	1,000
Less provision b/f	(1,200)
Credit to statement of profit or loss	(200)

ACCA marking guide		
		Marks
(a)	Statement of profit or loss	
	Revenue	1½
	Cost of sales	1½
	Distribution costs	½
	Administrative expenses	1½
	Loss on investments	1
	Investment income	½
	Finance costs	1½
	Income tax expense	2
	Maximum	**10**
(b)	Statement of financial position	
	Property, plant and equipment	1
	Equity investments	1
	Inventory	½
	Trade receivables	½
	Bank	½
	Share capital	½
	Retained earnings	1½
	Deferred tax	1
	Deferred revenue	1
	6% loan note	1½
	Trade payables	½
	Current tax payable	½
	Maximum	**10**
Total		**20**

405 ATLAS

(i) Atlas – Statement of profit or loss and other comprehensive income for the year ended 31 March 20X3

Monetary figures in brackets are in $000

	$000
Revenue (550,000 – 10,000 in substance loan (W3))	540,000
Cost of sales (W1)	(420,600)
Gross profit	119,400
Distribution costs	(21,500)
Administrative expenses (30,900 + 5,400 re directors' bonus of 1% of sales made)	(36,300)
Finance costs (700 + 500 (10,000 × 10% × $^6/_{12}$ re in substance loan))	(1,200)
Profit before tax	60,400
Income tax expense (27,200 – 1,200 + (9,400 – 6,200) deferred tax)	(29,200)
Profit for the year	31,200
Other comprehensive income	
Revaluation gain on land and buildings (W2)	7,000
Total comprehensive income for the year	38,200

(ii) Atlas – Statement of financial position as at 31 March 20X3

Assets	$000	$000
Non-current assets		
Property, plant and equipment (44,500 + 52,800 (W2))		97,300
Current assets		
Inventory (43,700 + 7,000 re in substance loan (W3))	50,700	
Trade receivables	42,200	
	———	92,900
Plant held for sale (W2)		3,600
		———
Total assets		193,800
		———
Equity and liabilities		
Equity		
Equity shares of 50 cents each		50,000
Revaluation surplus		7,000
Retained earnings (11,200 + 31,200)		42,400
		———
		99,400
Non-current liabilities		
In-substance loan from Xpede		
(10,000 + 500 accrued interest (W3))	10,500	
Deferred tax	9,400	
	———	19,900
Current liabilities		
Trade payables	35,100	
Income tax	27,200	
Accrued directors' bonus	5,400	
Bank overdraft	6,800	
	———	74,500
		———
Total equity and liabilities		193,800
		———

Workings (figures in brackets are in $000)

(W1) Cost of sales

	$000
Per question	411,500
Closing inventory re in substance loan (W3)	(7,000)
Depreciation of buildings (W2)	2,500
Depreciation of plant and equipment (W2)	13,600
	———
	420,600
	———

(W2) Non-current assets

Land and buildings

The gain on revaluation and carrying amount of the land and buildings will be:

	$000
Carrying amount at 1 April 20X2 (60,000 – 20,000)	40,000
Revaluation at that date (12,000 + 35,000)	47,000
Gain on revaluation	7,000
Buildings depreciation (35,000/14 years)	(2,500)
Carrying amount of land and buildings at 31 March 20X3 (47,000 – 2,500)	44,500

Plant

The plant held for sale should be shown separately and not be depreciated after 1 October 20X2.

Other plant	
Carrying amount at 1 April 20X2 (94,500 – 24,500)	70,000
Plant held for sale (9,000 – 5,000)	(4,000)
	66,000
Depreciation for year ended 31 March 20X3 (20% reducing balance)	(13,200)
Carrying amount at 31 March 20X3	52,800
Plant held for sale:	
At 1 April 20X2 (from above)	4,000
Depreciation to date of reclassification (4,000 × 20% × $^6/_{12}$)	(400)
Carrying amount at 1 October 20X2	3,600
Total depreciation of plant for year ended 31 March 20X3 (13,200 + 400)	13,600

As the fair value of the plant held for sale at 1 October 20X2 is $4.2 million, it should continue to be carried at its (lower) carrying amount, and no longer depreciated.

(W3) The transaction with Xpede will not be recognised as a sale. The presence of the option suggests that control of the goods has not passed to Xpede. Therefore this transaction will be recognised as a financial liability, with interest of 10% accruing each year.

As the transaction occurred partway through the year, 6 months interest ($500k) should be included within finance costs and added to the liability.

As this is not a sale, the goods should be transferred back into inventory at the cost of $7 million. This amount should also be deducted from cost of sales.

ACCA marking guide			
			Marks
(i)	Statement of profit or loss and other comprehensive income		
	Revenue		1
	Cost of sales		3
	Distribution costs		½
	Administrative expenses		1
	Finance costs		1
	Income tax		1½
	Other comprehensive income		1
		Maximum	**9**
(ii)	Statement of financial position		
	Property, plant and equipment		2½
	Inventory		1
	Trade receivables		½
	Plant held for sale (at 3,600)		1
	Retained earnings		1
	Revaluation surplus		1
	In substance loan		1
	Deferred tax		1
	Trade payables		½
	Current tax		½
	Directors' bonus		½
	Bank overdraft		½
		Maximum	**11**
Total			**20**

406 MOBY

(a) Moby – Statement of adjustments to retained earnings as at 30 September 20X3

	$000
Retained earnings balance per trial balance	53,250
Contract with customer (W1)	2,000
Depreciation: building (W2)	(2,400)
Depreciation: right-of-use asset (W2)	(7,000)
Lease interest (W3)	(2,930)
Current year taxation provision (note (iv))	(3,400)
Deferred tax reduction (W4)	2,000
Removal of provision (W5)	150
Loan note interest ($40m × 10% (note (v)))	(4,000)
Restated retained earnings per statement of financial position	37,670

(b) Moby – Statement of financial position as at 30 September 20X3

Assets	$000	$000
Non-current assets		
Property, plant and equipment (W2)		73,000
Current assets		
Inventory	56,600	
Trade receivables	38,500	
Contract asset (W1)	3,000	
	———	98,100
		———
Total assets		171,100
		———
Equity and liabilities		
Equity shares of $1 each		27,000
Revaluation surplus (4,400 (W2) – 1,100 (W4))	3,300	
Retained earnings (per (a))	37,670	
	———	40,970
		———
		67,970
Non-current liabilities		
Lease liability (W3)	16,133	
Deferred tax (W4)	7,100	
Loan note (40,000 + 4,000 interest)	44,000	
	———	67,233
Current liabilities		
Lease liability (W3)	6,897	
Trade payables	18,300	
Bank overdraft	7,300	
Current tax payable	3,400	
	———	35,897
		———
Total equity and liabilities		171,100
		———

Workings (monetary figures in brackets in $000)

(W1) Contract with customer

Step 1 – Overall

	$000	$000
Total contract revenue		25,000
Costs incurred to date	8,000	
Estimated costs to complete	12,000	
		(20,000)
Total contract profit		5,000

Step 2 – Progress

Percentage of completion is 40% (10,000/25,000)

Step 3 – Statement of profit or loss

Revenue (40% × 25,000)	10,000
Cost of sales (to date)	(8,000)
Profit for year	2,000

Step 4 – Statement of financial position

Revenue to date	10,000
Billed to date	(7,000)
Contract asset	3,000

(W2) Property, plant & equipment

	Land	Building	Right-of-use plant	Total
	$000	$000	$000	$000
1 October 20X2 Cost	12,000	48,000	35,000	
Accumulated depreciation		(10,000)	(7,000)	
	12,000	38,000	28,000	
Revaluation gain	4,000	400		
Revalued amount	16,000	38,400		
Depreciation charge				
38,400 × $^1/_{16}$		(2,400)		
35,000 × $^1/_5$			(7,000)	
	16,000	36,000	21,000	73,000

(W3) Lease liability

	Balance b/f	**Interest @ 10%**	**Payment**	**Balance c/f**
Year to 30 September 20X3	29,300	2,930	(9,200)	23,030
Year to 30 September 20X4	23,030	2,303	(9,200)	16,133

Finance cost: $2,930

Non-current liability: $16,133

Current liability: (23,030 – 16,133) $6,897

(W4) Deferred tax

	$000	$000
Provision b/f at 1 October 20X2		(8,000)
Provision c/f required at 30 September 20X3		
Temporary differences per question	24,000	
Revaluation of land and buildings (W2)	4,400	
	28,400	
	× 25%	7,100
Net reduction in provision		(900)
Charged to other comprehensive income on revaluation gain (4,400 × 25%)		(1,100)
Credit to profit or loss		2,000

(W5) Insurance provision

The remaining provision balance of $150,000 does not meet the criteria to be recognised as a provision as there is no present obligation. The balance is therefore reversed, removing the provision and increasing the retained earnings.

ACCA marking guide			
			Marks
(a)	Statement of adjustments to retained earnings		
	Retained earnings balance		½
	Contract with customer		1
	Depreciation: building		1
	Depreciation: right-of-use asset		1
	Lease interest		1
	Current year tax		½
	Deferred tax		1
	Removal of provision		1
	Loan note interest		1
		Maximum	**8**
(b)	Statement of financial position		
	Property, plant and equipment		2
	Inventory		½
	Contract asset		1
	Trade receivables		½
	Equity shares		½
	Revaluation surplus		2
	Retained earnings		½
	Non-current lease obligation		1
	Deferred tax		1
	Loan note		1
	Current lease obligation		½
	Bank overdraft		½
	Trade payables		½
	Current tax payable		½
		Maximum	**12**
Total			**20**

407 XTOL

(a) Xtol – Statement of profit or loss for the year ended 31 March 20X4

	$000
Revenue	490,000
Cost of sales (W1)	(304,600)
Gross profit	185,400
Operating costs	(70,300)
Finance costs (900 bank + 3,676 (W2))	(4,576)
Profit before tax	110,524
Income tax expense (3,200 + 28,000 + 3,700 (W3))	(34,900)
Profit for the year	75,624

(b) Xtol – Statement of financial position as at 31 March 20X4

	$000	$000
Non-current assets		
Property, plant and equipment		98,000
(155,500 – 43,500 – 14,000 (W1))		
Current assets		
Inventory	96,000	
Trade receivables	103,000	
		199,000
Total assets		297,000
Equity and liabilities		
Equity shares of $1 each		66,000
Share premium		15,000
Other component of equity – equity option (W2)		4,050
Retained earnings (15,200 + 75,624 profit for year)		90,824
		175,874
Non-current liabilities		
Deferred tax	8,300	
5% convertible loan note (W2)	47,126	
		55,426
Current liabilities		
Trade payables	32,200	
Bank overdraft	5,500	
Current tax payable	28,000	
		65,700
Total equity and liabilities		297,000

(c) Basic earnings per share for the year ended 31 March 20X4

Profit per statement of profit or loss	$75.624 million
Weighted average number of shares (W4)	62.255 million
Earnings per share (75.624/62.255)	121.5¢

Workings (figures in brackets in $000)

(W1) Cost of sales

	$000
Cost of sales per question	290,600
Depreciation of plant and equipment ((155,500 – 43,500) × 12½%)	14,000
	304,600

(W2) 5% convertible loan note

The convertible loan note is a compound financial instrument having a debt and an equity component which must be accounted for separately:

Year ended 31 March	Outflow	8%	Present value
	$000		$000
20X4	2,500	0.93	2,325
20X5	2,500	0.86	2,150
20X6	52,500	0.79	41,475
Debt component			45,950
Equity component (= balance)			4,050
Proceeds of issue			50,000

The finance cost for the year will be $3,676,000 (45,950 × 8%) and the carrying amount of the loan as at 31 March 20X4 will be $47,126,000 (45,950 + 3,676 interest – 2,500 paid).

(W3) Deferred tax

	$000
Provision at 31 March 20X4	8,300
Balance at 1 April 20X3	(4,600)
Charge to statement of profit or loss	3,700

(W4) Earnings per share

Step 1 – Theoretical ex-rights price (TERP)

5 shares @ $2.50 =	$12.50
1 share @ $1.60 =	$1.60
6 shares	$14.10

TERP = $14.10/6 = $2.35

Step 2 – Rights fraction = $^{2.50}/_{2.35}$

Step 3 – Weighted average number of shares

Date	Number	Fraction of year	Rights fraction	Weighted average
1 April	55,000,000	$^{6}/_{12}$	$^{2.50}/_{2.35}$	29,255,319
1:5 rights	11,000,000			
1 October	66,000,000	$^{6}/_{12}$		33,000,000
				62,255,319

There are 66 million shares at 31 March 20X4, after the 1 for 5 rights issue. Therefore anyone who held 5 shares at the start of the year now has 6 shares, and the opening number of shares would be 55 million (66 million × $^5/_6$).

ACCA marking guide		
		Marks
(a)	Statement of profit or loss	
	Revenue	½
	Cost of sales	1½
	Operating costs	½
	Finance costs	1½
	Income tax expense	2
(b)	Statement of financial position	
	Property, plant and equipment	1
	Inventory	½
	Trade receivables	½
	Share capital	½
	Share premium	½
	Convertible option – Equity component	1
	Retained earnings	1
	5% loan note	1½
	Deferred tax	1
	Trade payables	½
	Bank overdraft	½
	Current tax	½
(c)	Calculation of opening shares	1
	Calculation of TERP	1
	Application of fraction to first 6 months only	1
	Time apportionment	1
	Use of own profit from SPL	1
Total		**20**

408 DUNE

Key answer tips

This question contained many of the usual adjustments that you would expect with a published accounts question such as depreciation and tax adjustments. You were also expected to demonstrate your knowledge of accounting for held for sale assets and financial assets and liabilities in this time-consuming question.

(a) Dune – Statement of profit or loss for the year ended 31 March 20X4

	$000
Revenue (400,000	400,000
Cost of sales (W1)	(306,100)
Gross profit	93,900
Distribution costs	(26,400)
Administrative expenses (34,200 – 500 loan note issue costs)	(33,700)
Investment income	1,200
Gain on investments at fair value through profit or loss (28,000 – 26,500)	1,500
Finance costs (200 + 1,950 (W3)	(2,150)
Profit before tax	34,350
Income tax expense (12,000 – 1,400 – 1,800 (W4))	(8,800)
Profit for the year	25,550

Dune – Statement of financial position as at 31 March 20X4

	$000	$000
Assets		
Non-current assets		
Property, plant and equipment (W5)		37,400
Investments at fair value through profit or loss		28,000
		65,400
Current assets		
Inventory	48,000	
Trade receivables	40,700	
Bank	15,500	
		104,200
Non-current assets held for sale (W2)		33,500
Total assets		203,100
Equity and liabilities		
Equity		
Equity shares of $1 each		40,000
Other components of equity		20,000
Retained earnings (38,400 + 25,550 – 10,000 dividend)		53,950
		113,950

Non-current liabilities		
Deferred tax (W4)	4,200	
5% loan notes (W3)	20,450	
		24,650
Current liabilities		
Trade payables	52,000	
Accrued loan note interest (W3)	500	
Current tax payable	12,000	
		64,500
Total equity and liabilities		203,100

(b) Earnings per share:

EPS = $25,550,000/36,594,595 (W6)) = $0.70

Re-stated 20X3 EPS = 68c × ($^{0.74}/_{0.82}$) = $0.61

Workings (figures in brackets in $000)

(W1) Cost of sales

	$000
Per question	294,000
Depreciation of leasehold property (see below)	1,500
Impairment of leasehold property (see below)	4,000
Depreciation of plant and equipment ((67,500 – 23,500) × 15%)	6,600
	306,100

(W2) The leasehold property must be classed as a non-current asset held for sale from 1 October 20X3 at its fair value less costs to sell. It must be depreciated for six months up to this date (after which depreciation ceases). This is calculated at $1.5 million (45,000/15 years × $^{6}/_{12}$). Its carrying amount at 1 October 20X3 is therefore $37.5 million (45,000 – (6,000 + 1,500)).

Its fair value less cost to sell at this date is $33.5 million ((40,000 × 85%) – 500). It is therefore impaired by $4 million (37,500 – 33,500).

(W3) The finance cost of the loan note, at the effective rate of 10% applied to the correct carrying amount of the loan note of $19.5 million, is $1.95 million. The issue costs must be deducted from the proceeds of the loan note as they are not an administrative expense. The interest actually paid is $500,000 (20,000 × 5% × $^{6}/_{12}$) but a further $500,000 needs to be accrued as a current liability (as it will be paid soon). The difference between the total finance cost of $1.95 million and the $1 million interest payable is added to the carrying amount of the loan note to give $20.45 million (19,500 + 950) for inclusion as a non-current liability in the statement of financial position.

(W4) Deferred tax

Provision required at 31 March 20X4 (14,000 × 30%)	4,200
Less provision at 1 April 20X3	(6,000)
Credit (reduction in provision) to statement of profit or loss	(1,800)

(W5) Property, plant and equipment

Property, plant and equipment (67,500 – 23,500 – 6,600)	37,400

(W6) Weighted average number of shares

Step 1 – Theoretical ex-rights price (TERP)

4 shares @ \$0.82 =	\$3.28
1 share @ \$0.42 =	\$0.42
5 shares	\$3.70

TERP = \$3.70/5 = \$0.74

Step 2 – Rights fraction = $^{0.82}/_{0.74}$

Step 3 – Weighted average number of shares

Date	Number of shares	Fraction of year	Rights fraction	Weighted average
1 April	32,000,000	$^{9}/_{12}$	$^{0.82}/_{0.74}$	26,594,595
1 January	40,000,000	$^{3}/_{12}$		10,000,000
				36,594,595

Based on 40 million shares in issue at 31 March 20X4, a rights issue of 1 for 4 on 1 January 20X4 would have resulted in the issue of 8 million new shares (40 million × $^{1}/_{5}$). Therefore there would have been 32 million shares at the start of the year.

ACCA marking guide		
		Marks
(a)	**Statement of profit or loss**	
	Revenue	½
	Cost of sales	2
	Distribution costs	½
	Administrative expenses	1
	Investment income	½
	Gain on investments	½
	Finance costs	1½
	Income tax expense	2
	Maximum	**7½**
	Statement of financial position	
	Property, plant and equipment	½
	Investments	½
	Inventory	½
	Trade receivables	½
	Bank	½
	Non-current asset held for sale	1
	Equity shares	½
	Retained earnings (1 for dividend)	1
	Deferred tax	1
	5% loan note	1
	Trade payables	½
	Accrued loan note interest	½
	Current tax payable	½
	Maximum	**7½**
(b)	Number of shares at start of year	1
	TERP	1
	Application of rights fraction and time apportionment	1
	Use of own profit	1
	Restatement of prior year	1
Total		**20**

Examiners' report

This was a question of preparing financial statements from a trial balance with various adjustments required. These involved the dealing with the use of the effective interest rate for a loan, a fair value investment, an impairment of a leasehold property (including presenting it as 'held for sale'), and accounting for taxation. The most common errors were:

The issue costs of the loan were often ignored and calculating the finance charge at the nominal rate of 5% instead of the **effective rate of 10%**. Omission of accrued interest from current liabilities or including it at the incorrect amount.

A failure to depreciate leasehold property up to the date it became 'held for sale', not calculating the subsequent impairment loss, and most candidates continuing to **show it as a non-current, rather than a current, asset**.

There were **many errors in the treatment of the taxation**, including debiting the over provision of the previous year's tax instead of crediting, treating the closing provision of deferred tax as the charge in the statement of profit or loss and confusion over SFP entries.

409 KANDY

(a) Kandy – Schedule of retained earnings of Kandy as at 30 September 20X4

		$000
Retained earnings per trial balance		19,500
Adjustments re:		
Note (i)	Add back issue costs of loan note (W1)	1,000
	Loan finance costs (W1)	(2,610)
Note (ii)	Depreciation of buildings (W2)	(2,600)
	Depreciation of plant and equipment (W2)	(3,000)
Note (iii)	Income tax expense (W3)	(800)
Note (iv)	Gain on investments at fair value through profit or loss ($2.6m – $2m)	600
	Adjusted retained earnings	12,090

(b) Kandy – Statement of financial position as at 30 September 20X4

Assets	$000	$000
Non-current assets		
Property, plant and equipment (W2)		65,400
Investments at fair value through profit or loss (per note (iv))		2,600
Current assets (per trial balance)		68,700
Total assets		136,700
Equity and liabilities		
Equity		
Equity shares of $1 each		40,000
Revaluation surplus (12,000 – 2,400 (W2 and W3))	9,600	
Retained earnings (from (a))	12,090	
		21,690
		61,690
Non-current liabilities		
Deferred tax (W3)	4,400	
6% loan note (W1)	29,810	
		34,210
Current liabilities (per trial balance)	38,400	
Current tax payable	2,400	
		40,800
Total equity and liabilities		136,700

Workings

(W1) Loan note

	$000
Proceeds	30,000
Less issue costs incorrectly charged as expense	(1,000)
Initial liability	29,000
Interest at 9% effective rate	2,610
Less interest paid per trial balance	(1,800)
	29,810

The loan note is carried at amortised cost, calculated as above. The initial value is calculated by deducting the issue costs from the proceeds of the loan note. Interest is always calculated using the effective rate.

(W2) Non-current assets

	Land	**Buildings**	**Plant & equipment**	**Total**
	$000	$000	$000	$000
Cost b/f	5,000	50,000	58,500	
Depreciation b/f	–	(20,000)	(34,500)	
	5,000	30,000	24,000	
Gain on revaluation	3,000	9,000		
Revaluation	8,000	39,000		
Depreciation charge				
39,000 × $^1/_{15}$		(2,600)		
24,000 × $12^1/_2$%			(3,000)	
	8,000	36,400	21,000	65,400

Total revaluation gain is $12 million ($3m + $9m).

(W3) Taxation

Income tax expense	$000
Provision for year ended 30 September 20X4	2,400
Less over-provision in previous year	(1,100)
Deferred tax (see below)	(500)
	800

Deferred tax	$000
Provision required at 30 September 20X4 (($10m temporary differences + $12m revaluation) × 20%)	4,400
Provision b/f at 1 October 20X3	(2,500)
Movement in provision	1,900
Charge to revaluation of land and buildings ($12m × 20%)	(2,400)
Balance – credit to profit or loss above	(500)

ACCA marking guide

		Marks
(a)	Schedule of retained earnings as at 30 September 20X4	
	Retained earnings per trial balance	1
	Issue costs	1
	Loan finance costs	2
	Depreciation charges	2
	Income tax expense	2
	Investments	1
	Maximum	**9**
(b)	Statement of financial position	
	Property, plant and equipment	2
	Investments	1
	Current assets	1½
	Equity shares	½
	Revaluation surplus	2
	Deferred tax	1
	6% loan note	1½
	Current liabilities (per trial balance)	½
	Current tax payable	1
	Maximum	**11**
Total		**20**

410 CLARION

(a) Clarion – Statement of financial position as at 31 March 20X5

Assets	$000	$000
Property, plant and equipment		49,000
(77,000 + 8,000 – 19,000 – 17,000 (W1))		
Investments through profit or loss		6,500
		55,500
Current assets		
Inventory	11,700	
Trade receivables	20,500	
		32,200
Total assets		87,700
Equity		
Equity shares of $1 each		35,000
Retained earnings (W1)		10,810
		45,810
Non-current liabilities		
8% loan notes (20,000 – 5,000 redeemed)	15,000	
Deferred tax (W3)	3,000	
Environmental provision (4,000 + 320 (W1))	4,320	
Lease liability (W4)	3,747	
		26,067
Current liabilities		
Trade payables	9,400	
Lease liability (W4)	1,023	
Bank overdraft	1,900	
Current tax payable	3,500	
		15,823
Total equity and liabilities		87,700

(b) Clarion – Extracts from the statement of cash flows for the year ended 31 March 20X5

	$000
Cash flows from investing activities	
Purchase of plant and equipment (note (ii))	(14,000)
Dividends received (W2)	300
Sale of investments (note (iv))	1,600
Cash flows from financing activities	
Redemption of loan notes (W5)	(5,000)
Repayment of lease liability (2,300 + (1,500 – 570)) (W5)	(3,230)

Workings (figures in brackets in $000)

(W1) Retained earnings

	$000
Per trial balance	33,100
Depreciation of plant and equipment ((77,000 + 8,000) × 20%)	(17,000)
Finance costs: 8% loan notes (800 TB + 800 suspense (W5))	(1,600)
Lease interest (W4)	(570)
Environmental provision (4,000 × 8%)	(320)
Investment income (W2)	1,000
Tax: current year	(3,500)
Deferred tax (W3)	(300)
	10,810

(W2) Investment income

Dividends received and profit on sale per TB *	500
Gains on fair value (6,500 – 6,000)	500
	1,000

*Profit on sale = 200 (1,600 – 1,400), dividends received = 300 (500 – 200)

(W3) Deferred tax

Provision required as at 31 March 20X5 (12,000 × 25%)	3,000
Balance at 1 April 20X4	(2,700)
Charge to retained earnings	300

(W4) Lease liability

	Balance b/f	Interest at 10%	Paid	Balance c/f
	$000	$000	$000	$000
Year to 31 March 20X5	5,700	570	(1,500)	4,770
Year to 31 March 20X6	4,770	477	(1,500)	3,747

Interest charge		$570
Non-current liability		$3,747
Current liability	(4,770 – 3747)	$1,023

(W5) Elimination of suspense account

	$000
Cash cost of loan note redemption (20,000 × 25%)	5,000
Six months' interest on loan note (20,000 × 8% × $^{6}/_{12}$)	800
	5,800

ACCA marking guide		
		Marks
(a)	Statement of financial position	
	Property, plant and equipment	1½
	Investments through profit or loss	½
	Inventory	½
	Receivables	½
	Share capital	½
	Retained earnings	5½
	8% loan notes	1
	Deferred tax	1
	Environmental provision	1
	Non-current lease obligation	1
	Trade payables	½
	Bank overdraft	½
	Current lease obligation	½
	Current tax payable	½
		15
(b)	Extract from statement of cash flows	
	Purchase of property, plant and equipment	½
	Sale of investments	½
	Dividends received	1
	Redemption of loan notes	1
	Payment of lease liability	2
		5
Total		**20**

411 MOSTON  Walk in the footsteps of a top tutor

(a) Moston – Statement of profit or loss and other comprehensive income for the year ended 30 June 20X5

	$000
Revenue	113,500
Cost of sales (W1)	(97,700)
Gross profit	15,800
Distribution costs	(2,800)
Administrative expenses (6,800 – 500 loan note issue costs)	(6,300)
Investment income	300
Finance costs (W2)	(1,560)
Profit before tax	5,440
Income tax expense (1,200 + 800)	(2,000)
Profit for the year	3,440
Other comprehensive income	
Items that will not be reclassified to profit or loss	
Gain on revaluation of property (29,000 – (28,500 – 1,900) (W1))	2,400
Total comprehensive income for the year	5,840

(b) Moston – Statement of changes in equity for the year ended 30 June 20X5

	Share capital	Other components of equity	Revaluation surplus	Retained earnings	Total equity
	$000	$000	$000	$000	$000
Balance at 1 July 20X4	20,000	2,300	3,000	6,200	31,500
Share issue (W3)	10,000	7,000			17,000
Total comprehensive income for the year			2,400	3,440	5,840
Dividends paid (W3)				(4,000)	(4,000)
Balance at 30 June 20X5	30,000	9,300	5,400	5,640	50,340

(c) Moston – Statement of cash flows for the year ended 30 June 20X5

	$000
Cash flows from investing activities	
Capitalised development costs	(3,200)
Investment income	300
Cash flows from financing activities	
Shares issued	17,000
Dividends paid	(4,000)
Loan notes issued	19,500

Tutorial note

It is crucial that you know what each section of the statement of cash flows contains so that you are able to produce extracts if required. This is likely to contain a number of figures given to you in the question, such as the loan notes and shares issued so there is scope to pick up some simpler marks here.

Workings (monetary figures in brackets in $000)

(W1) Cost of sales

	$000
Per trial balance	88,500
Depreciation of property (28,500/15 years)	1,900
Depreciation of plant and equipment ((27,100 – 9,100) × 15%)	2,700
Research and development expenses (see below)	4,600
	97,700

Tutorial note

Development costs can only be capitalised from the date the directors became confident that the new product would be commercially successful, which is 1 May. Research of $3 million (3 months at $1 million per month) from January to March and April's costs of $1.6 million should be expensed, a total of $4.6m. This leaves $3.2 million (2 months at $1.6 million per month) to be capitalised at the year end.

(W2) Loan interest

	$000
5% loan note ((20,000 – 500) × 8% see below)	1,560

The 5% loan note issue costs should not be charged to administrative expenses, but deducted from the proceeds of the loan, leaving an initial value of $19.5m.

(W3) Dividend paid and share issue

Note that the dividend was paid prior to the share issue and is therefore calculated based on 20 million shares (30 million – 10 million).

	$000
Dividend paid 20 million × 20¢	4,000

Share issue: 10 million × $1.70 = $17m, split $10m capital, $7m premium.

ACCA marking guide

		Marks
(a)	Statement of profit or loss and other comprehensive income	
	Revenue	½
	Cost of sales	3½
	Distribution	½
	Administration	1½
	Investment income	½
	Finance costs	1½
	Income tax expense	1
	Gain on property	1
		10
(b)	Statement of changes in equity	
	Balances brought forward	1
	Share issue	2
	Comprehensive income	1
	Dividend	1
		5

(c)	Extract from statement of cash flows	
	Capitalised development costs	1
	Investment income	½
	Shares issued	1
	Dividends paid	1
	Loan notes issued	1½
		5
Total		**20**

412 TRIAGE

(a) Triage – schedule of adjustments to profit for the year ended 31 March 20X6

	$000
Draft profit before interest and tax per trial balance	30,000
Adjustments re:	
Note (i)	
Convertible loan note finance costs (W1)	(3,023)
Note (ii)	
Depreciation of property (1,500 + 1,700 (W2)	(3,200)
Depreciation of plant and equipment (W2)	(6,600)
Note (iii)	
Current year loss on fraud (700 – 450 see below)	(250)
Note (iv)	
Income tax expense (2,700 + 700 – 800 (W3))	(2,600)
Profit for the year	14,327

(b) Triage– Statement of financial position as at 31 March 20X6

	$000	$000
Assets		
Non-current assets		
Property, plant and equipment (64,600 + 37,400 (W2))		102,000
Current assets		
Trade receivables (28,000 – 700 fraud)	27,300	
Other current assets per trial balance	9,300	
		36,600
Total assets		138,600
Equity and liabilities		
Equity		
Equity shares of $1 each		50,000
Other component of equity (W1)	2,208	
Revaluation surplus (7,800 – 1,560 (W2))	6,240	
Retained earnings (W4)	17,377	
		25,825
		75,825

Non-current liabilities		
Deferred tax (W3)	3,960	
6% convertible loan notes (W1)	38,415	
		42,375
Current liabilities		
Per trial balance	17,700	
Current tax payable	2,700	
		20,400
Total equity and liabilities		138,600

(c) Diluted earnings per share (W5) 28.9 cents

Workings (monetary figures in brackets in $000)

Note:

The $450,000 fraud loss in the previous year is a prior period adjustment (reported in the statement of changes in equity). The possible insurance claim is a contingent asset and should be ignored.

(W1) 6% convertible loan notes

The convertible loan notes are a compound financial instrument having a debt and an equity component which must both be quantified and accounted for separately:

Year ended 31 March	Outflow	8% factor	Present value
	$000		$000
20X6 Interest – $4m × 6%	2,400	0.93	2,232
20X7 Interest	2,400	0.86	2,064
20X8 Capital + interest	42,400	0.79	33,496
Debt component			37,792
Equity component (= balance)			2,208
Proceeds of issue			40,000

The finance cost will be $3,023,000 (37,792 × 8%) and the carrying amount of the loan notes at 31 March 20X6 will be $38,415,000 (37,792 + 3,023 – 2,400).

(W2) Non-current assets

	$000
Property carrying amount at 1 April 20X5 (75,000 – 15,000)	60,000
Depreciation to date of revaluation (1 October 20X5) (75,000 × $^6/_{12}$)	(1,500)
Carrying amount at revaluation	58,500
Gain on revaluation = balance	7,800
Revaluation at 1 October 20X5	66,300
Depreciation to year ended 31 March 20X6 (66,300/19.5 years × $^6/_{12}$)	(1,700)
Carrying amount at 31 March 20X6	64,600

Prior to the revaluation annual depreciation is $3m (75,000/25 years). Therefore the accumulated depreciation at 1 April 20X5 of $15m represents five years' depreciation. At the date of revaluation (1 October 20X5), there will be a remaining life of 19.5 years.

Of the revaluation gain, $6.24m (80%) is credited to the revaluation surplus and $1.56m (20%) is credited to deferred tax.

Plant and equipment

	$000
Carrying amount at 1 April 20X5 (72,100 – 28,100)	44,000
Depreciation for year ended 31 March 20X6 (15% reducing balance)	(6,600)
Carrying amount at 31 March 20X6	37,400

(W3) Deferred tax

Provision required at 31 March 20X6:	
Revalued property and other assets (7,800 + 12,000) × 20%)	3,960
Provision at 1 April 20X5	(3,200)
Increase in provision	760
Revaluation of land and buildings (7,800 × 20%)	(1,560)
Balance credited to profit or loss	800

(W4) Retained earnings

Balance at 1 April 20X5	3,500
Prior period adjustment (fraud)	(450)
Adjusted profit for year (from (a))	14,327
Balance at 31 March 20X6	17,377

(W5) The maximum additional shares on conversion is 8 million (40,000 × $^{20}/_{100}$), giving total shares of 58 million. The notional saving in loan interest is $2.418m (3,023 (from (W1) above × 80% (i.e. after tax)), giving adjusted earnings of $16.745m (14,327 + 2,418).

Therefore diluted EPS is $16,745,000/58,000,000 = 28.9 cents

ACCA marking guide

		Marks
(a)	Schedule of adjustments to profit for year ended 31 March 20X6	
	Profit before interest and tax b/f	½
	Loan finance costs	1
	Depreciation charges	1½
	Fraud loss	½
	Income tax expense	1½
		5
(b)	Statement of financial position	
	Property, plant and equipment	2½
	Trade receivables	1
	Other current assets (per trial balance)	½
	Equity shares	½
	Equity option	1
	Revaluation surplus	1
	Retained earnings	1½
	Deferred tax	1
	6% loan note	1½
	Current liabilities (per trial balance)	½
	Current tax payable	1
		12
(c)	Diluted earnings per share	**3**
Total		**20**

Examiners' report

The question was reasonably well answered with many candidates scoring at least half marks.

In part (a) a significant number of candidates prepared a series of workings but did **not attempt to either summarise these or state their effect on the statement of profit or loss,** which restricted the number of marks that could be awarded. The requirement for a schedule is an alternative approach to the preparation of a full statement of profit or loss, whilst still testing key principles of profit measurement. Future candidates should ensure that they avoid the common errors noted in this session:

Some candidates did **not attempt to calculate the debt component** of the convertible loan note and a few calculated interest paid at the underlying rate rather than the "coupon" rate.

A number of candidates did not correctly **split the amortisation of the leased property between the two halves of the year** and often used an incorrect remaining useful life to determine the amortisation charge for the second half of the year.

Many candidates did not correctly **split the fraud** between the amount related to the current year and the remainder which related to the previous year and therefore was not relevant to profit or loss.

Some candidates included the estimated amount the directors hoped could be recovered from insurers. This was a contingent asset and, as many candidates correctly noted, should be ignored.

Candidates' **understanding of current and deferred tax issues seems to have been a particular problem**.

Part (b) required the preparation of the statement of financial position incorporating figures in the given trial balance and the adjustments from part (a). Common errors noted were:

Some candidates **did not include the equity component** of the convertible loan note as an "other component of equity" and sometimes included it as a liability rather than equity.

A number of candidates **did not reduce the revaluation surplus by the deferred tax** element or did not report the revaluation surplus at all.

Candidates also incorrectly showed an **incomplete (or omitted to show) deferred tax provision**.

Some candidates omitted the current tax liability or incorrectly adjusted it by the underprovision for the previous year.

Part (c) required a calculation of Triage's potential diluted earnings per share for the year. Many candidates either did not attempt this part of the question or made no adjustment for dilution. As the question did not ask for the basic earnings per share no marks were awarded for calculating it – the **marks were specifically for the diluting adjustments**.

413 HAVERFORD CO

(a) Adjustments to Haverford Co's profit for the year ended 31 December 20X7

	$000
Draft profit	2,250
Convertible loan notes (W1)	(135)
Contract revenue (W2)	5,600
Contract cost of sales (W2)	(3,600)
Depreciation (W4)	(720)
Property impairment (W4)	(480)
Closing inventories (W5)	390
Revised profit	3,305

(b) Statement of changes in equity for the year ended 31 December 20X7

	Share capital	OCE	Retained earnings	Reval'n surplus	Option
Balance 1 January 20X7	20,000	3,000	6,270	800	–
Profit – from (a)			3,305		
Revaluation loss (W4)				(800)	
Bonus issue (W3)	4,000	(3,000)	(1,000)		
Convertible loan notes issued (W1)					424
Dividend paid			(3,620)		
Balance 31 December 20X7	24,000	–	4,955	–	424

(c) Statement of financial position for Haverford Co as at 31 December 20X7

	$000
Assets	
Non-current assets:	
Property (W3)	16,000
Current assets:	
Inventory (W5)	4,700
Trade receivables	5,510
Contract asset (W2)	2,500
Cash	10,320
Total assets	39,030

Equity and liabilities	
Equity:	
Share capital	24,000
Retained earnings	4,955
Convertible option	424
Total equity	29,379
Non-current liabilities:	
Convertible loan notes (W1)	7,711
Current liabilities:	1,940
Total equity and liabilities	39,030

Working 1 – Convertible loan notes

	Payment	**Discount factor**	**Present value**
	$000	$000	$000
20X7	320	0.943	302
20X8	320	0.890	285
20X9	8,320	0.840	6,989
			7,576

As the full amount of $8m has been taken to liabilities, adjustment required is:

Dr Liability $424,000
Cr Equity $424,000

The liability is then carried at amortised cost, using the effective interest rate.

Balance b/f	**Interest** 6%	**Payment**	**Balance** c/f
$000	$000	$000	$000
7,576	455	(320)	7,711

As only $320k has been recorded in finance costs:

Dr Finance costs $135k
Cr Liability $135k

Working 2 – Contract with customer

Overall contract:

	$000
Price	14,000
Costs to date	(3,600)
Costs to complete	(5,400)
	5,000

Progress: 40%

Statement of profit or loss:

	$000
Revenue ($14,000 × 40%)	5,600
Cost of sales (to date)	(3,600)
	2,000

Statement of financial position:

	$000
Revenue recognised	5,600
Amount billed to date	(3,100)
	2,500

$5.6m should be recorded in revenue, and $3.6m in cost of sales, giving an overall increase to the draft profit of $2m. $2.5m should then be recorded in the statement of financial position as a current asset.

Working 3 – Bonus issue

The 1 for 5 bonus issue will lead to an increase in share capital of $4m ($20m × 1/5). Of this, $3m will be debited to other components of equity to take it to zero. The remaining $1m will be deducted from retained earnings.

Adjustment:

Dr Share premium	$3m
Dr Retained earnings	$1m
Cr Share capital	$4m

Working 4 – Property

The asset should first be depreciated. $18m/25 = $720k. This should be deducted from the draft profit and the asset, giving a carrying amount of $17,280k.

Dr Draft profit	$720k
Cr Property	$720k

Then the asset should be revalued from $17,280k to $16,000k, giving a revaluation loss of $1,280k. As the revaluation surplus is only $800k, only $800k can be debited to this, with the remaining $480k being debited from the draft profit for the year.

Dr Revaluation surplus	$800k
Dr Draft profit	$480k
Cr Property	$1,280k

Working 5 – Inventories

Closing inventories should be adjusted from $4,310k to $4,700k.

Dr Inventories	$390k
Cr Draft profit	$390k

ACCA marking guide		
		Marks
(a)	Convertible loan notes	1
	Contract	2
	Depreciation/impairment	2
	Inventory	1
		6
(b)	Opening balances	1
	Convertible loan notes	1
	Bonus issue	2
	Profit/dividend/revaluation	2
		6
(c)	PPE	1
	Contract	2
	Other current assets	2
	Equity	½
	Convertible loan notes	2
	Current liabilities	½
		8
Total		**20**

414 DUGGAN CO

(a) Duggan Co statement of profit or loss for the year ended 30 June 20X8

	$000
Revenue (43,200 + 2,700 (W1))	45,900
Cost of sales (21,700 + 1,500 (W1))	(23,200)
Gross profit	22,700
Operating expenses (13,520 + 120 (W2) – 8 (W5) + 900 (W6))	(14,532)
Profit from operations	8,168
Finance costs (1,240 + 46 (W2) + 86 (W4) + 640 (W5))	(2,012)
Investment income	120
Profit before tax	6,276
Income tax expense (2,100 – 500 – 130 (W3))	(1,470)
Profit for the year	4,806

(b) Statement of changes in equity for the year ended 30 June 20X8

	Share capital	Share premium	Retained earnings	Convertible option
	$000	$000	$000	$000
Balance at 1 July 20X7	12,200		35,400	
Prior year error			(1,600)	
Restated balance			33,800	
Share issue	1,500	1,800		
Profit (from (a))			4,806	
Convertible issue				180
Balance at 30 June 20X8	13,700	1,800	38,606	180

(c) Basic earnings per share:

4,806	Profit from (a)
13,200	(W7)

= $0.36 per share

Working 1 – Contract

	$000
Revenue	2,700 (80% × $9m = $7.2m. As $4.5m (50%) in X7, X8 = $2.7m)
COS	1,500 (80% × $5m = $4m. As $2.5m (50%) in X7, X8 = $1.5m)

Working 2 – Court case

As the most likely outcome is that $1.012m will be paid, this must be included in full. This is discounted to present value as the payment was not expected for 12 months. The initial entry on 1 January 20X8 in operating expenses should be $920,000 (rounded), being $1.012m × 1/1.1 (or $1.012m × 0.9091). As $800,000 has been included, an adjustment of $120,000 is required.

This discount should then be unwound for six months, resulting in an increase in finance costs of $46,000.

Working 3 – Tax

	$000	
Current estimate	2,100	Add to expense and current liabilities
Decrease in deferred tax	(500)	$2m decrease in temporary differences × 25%
Prior year overprovision	(130)	Credit balance in trial balance
	1,470	

Working 4 – Convertible

	Payment $000	Discount factor	Present value
Year ended 30 June 20X8	300	0.926	278
Year ended 30 June 20X9	5,300	0.857	4,542
Liability element			4,820

The equity element is therefore $180,000, to be shown in the statement of changes in equity.

Interest needs to be applied to the liability element. $4,820 × 8% = $386,000. As $300,000 has been recorded, an adjustment of $86,000 is required.

Working 5 – Capitalised interest

Of the $2.56m capitalised, 3/12 of this was after the construction was complete and so should be expensed. This will lead to an increase in finance costs of $640,000.

An adjustment must also be made to the depreciation, being $640,000/20 × 3/12 = $8,000 reduction in the depreciation charge for the year.

Working 6 – Fraud

The $1.6m must be taken to retained earnings as a prior year error. The remaining $0.9m will be taken to operating expenses.

Working 7 – Weighted average number of shares

Date	No. of shares	Fraction of year	Weighted average number of shares
	000		000
1 July 20X7	12,200	4/12	4,067
1 November 20X7	13,700	8/12	9,133
			13,200

ACCA marking guide

		Marks
(a)	Revenue and COS	2½
	Operating costs	3½
	Finance costs	3½
	Investment income and tax	2½
		12
(b)	Opening balances (including error)	2
	Share issue, profit, loan notes	3
		5
(c)	EPS calculation	**3**
Total		**20**

Examiners' report

Overall the performance on this question was reasonably good. There were, however, some common errors and weaknesses:

A contract, where the performance obligation was satisfied over the time, was well attempted by most candidates. However, several candidates **recorded the profit for the year as revenue** instead of recognising the revenue and costs separately. Some candidates also failed to spot that this **contract was in the second year** and recorded the total revenue and costs to date.

There were several variations being noted by the marking team on the accounting for the unfair dismissal. Many candidates attempted to discount the $800,000 or to include the full $1.021 million. The question had included a provision of $800,000 to date, being 80% of the future expected payment. However, this treatment is incorrect. In accordance with IAS 37, the **future liability should be recognised in full**, but at present value (to take into account the liability being paid 12 months after recognition). Many candidates attempted discounting, but then failed to unwind the discount and recognise the subsequent finance cost.

Generally, the convertible loan was dealt with well. The most common mistake was where the market rate of interest was taken to finance costs in full and candidates did not deduct the interest already paid. Some candidates incorrectly split the convertible loan between the debt and equity components using the coupon rate of interest at 6%, this was then generally accounted for correctly thereafter earning 'own figure' marks. For those candidates who dealt with the convertible loan correctly, **only a minority transferred the equity component into the statement of changes in equity**. Many candidates failed to discount the liability to present value at all and made **no attempt to split it**. This is surprising as convertible loans have been tested on numerous occasions. Candidates are therefore encouraged to revise this topic area.

The borrowing cost treatment varied considerably with many candidates **making no adjustment for borrowing costs at all**. The interest on borrowing costs must be capitalised on a qualifying asset, but only for the period up to the date that the asset is complete. For Duggan, interest should have been capitalised between 1 July 20X7 and 31 March 20X8 (9 months). A full 12 months' interest had been capitalised and therefore **three months' interest needed to be removed** from property, plant and equipment and allocated to finance costs. This then had a knock-on-effect in the depreciation calculation which had been overstated by Duggan. A further adjustment was then required to **eliminate this excess depreciation** for the three-month period from the date the asset was completed.

The share issue was also well done by the majority of candidates and recorded in the statement of changes in equity. Most candidates, however, did not deal with the share issue correctly in part (c) when asked to calculate the earnings per share for Duggan. The **market issue of shares would require a weighted average** of the share capital to be performed when calculating EPS and only a small minority of candidates remembered to do this.

Candidates should know that all of these issues have been assessed previously by the FR examiner and so they should **attempt as many past exam questions as possible** for practice and exposure to all possible learning outcomes.

415 VERNON CO

(a) Statement of profit or loss and other comprehensive income

		£000
Revenue	75,350 + 3,407 (W1) + 1,875 (W2)	80,632
Cost of sales		(46,410)
Gross profit		34,222
Operating expenses	20,640 – 125 (W2) – 400 (W3)	(20,115)
Profit from operations		14,107
Finance costs		(4,050)
Investment income	1,520 + 296 (W1) + 302 (W3) + 4,000 (W4)	6,118
Profit before tax		16,175
Tax expense	130 + 3,200 (W5)	(3,330)
Profit for the year		12,845
Other comprehensive income		
Gain on revaluation	12,000 – 3,000 (W4)	9,000
Total comprehensive income		21,845

Workings:

(W1) Sale with significant financing component

As the sale has a significant financing component, the initial revenue should be recorded at present value, with the discount unwound and recorded as finance income.

Therefore, the initial revenue should be $7.407m ($8m/1.08), which is taken to revenue and receivables. As $4m has been already taken, a further $3.407m must be added to revenue and receivables.

The receivable of $7.407m is then increased by 8% over the year to get to the $8m in June 20X9. As Vernon Co has a reporting date of 31 December 20X8, six months' interest should be added.

$7.407m × 8% × 6/12 = $296k, which is added to receivables and finance income.

(W2) Overseas sale

The sale should initially be recorded at the historic rate at the date of the transaction, which is $1.875m (12m Kr/6.4). This should be recorded in revenue and receivables.

At 31 December 20X8, the unsettled receivable must be retranslated at the closing rate.

12m Kr/6 = $2m. Therefore the receivable must be increased by $125k, with the increase going through the profit or loss (although not through revenue).

(W3) Bonds

The professional fees on the bonds must be added to the bond asset, and not expensed, resulting in a $0.4m decrease to operating expenses.

If the bonds are held at amortised cost, the following calculation will take place:

b/f	Interest 8%	Payment	c/f
$000	$000	$000	$000
9,400	752	(450)	10,602

Vernon Co should record $752k in investment income. As only $450k has been recorded, a further $302k must be added into investment income.

(W4) Revaluations

The $12m gain on the property used by Vernon Co must be shown in other comprehensive income, net of the $3m deferred tax liability applicable to it.

The $4m gain on investment properties must go through the statement of profit or loss, not other comprehensive income.

(W5) Tax

The tax of $130k in the trial balance will represent an under-provision, as it is a debit balance. The $3.2m tax estimate for the year should be added to this in order to calculate the tax expense for the year.

(b) Earnings per share

12,845,000/41,870,689 (W1) = $0.307, or 30.7c

(W1) Weighted average number of shares

Date	Number	Rights fraction	Period	Weighted average
1 January	30,000,000	3.10/2.9 (W2)	3/12	8,017,241
1 April	35,000,000	3.10/2.9 (W2)	3/12	9,353,448
1 July	49,000,000	–	6/12	24,500,000
				41,870,689

(W2) Theoretical ex-rights price

No	Price $	Value $
5	3.10	15.50
2	2.40	4.80
7		20.30

TERP = $20.30/7 = $2.90

The rights fraction is market value before issue/TERP (3.10/2.90) and should be applied to all periods up to the date of the rights issue.

ACCA marking guide		
		Marks
(a)	Revenue/cost of sales	3½
	Operating expenses	3
	Finance cost/investment income	5
	Tax/other comprehensive income	3½
		15
(b)	Earnings per share	**5**
Total		**20**

Examiners' report

Note (i) to the question indicated that Vernon Co had incorrectly accounted for a sale with a significant financing component. Candidates were expected to record the full $8 million but take into account the time value of money. Candidates were required to **adjust for the difference between the discounted total revenue and the amount already recorded**.

Several variations were noted by the marking team including adjustments which **ignored discounting all together**. For those candidates who attempted to discount the revenue to present value, only a few then proceeded to unwind the discount for the first 12 months. Many who did attempt to unwind incorrectly recorded the unwinding within finance costs rather than in finance income.

The initial adjustment to record goods sold to an overseas customer was well attempted with many candidates completing this adjustment correctly. Some candidates made errors by recording the sale either in the foreign currency, or by **using an incorrect exchange rate**.

Many candidates failed to recognise the receivable as a monetary item and retranslate it at the closing rate with any gain or loss being recognised immediately in profit or loss.

A significant number of candidates recorded the adjustment to bonds as **financial liabilities rather than financial assets**. Many candidates correctly removed the initial direct cost of acquiring the bonds from administrative expenses but did not then capitalise it as part of the initial value of the bond. Another common error for this adjustment arose when candidates adjusted the full 8% interest in the statement of profit or loss rather than recognising the difference between this amount and the cash received so far to date.

The revaluation, which has been **examined many times before**, was dealt with well by the majority of candidates with the gain often being recorded correctly within other comprehensive income. In addition to this, compared to previous examination diets, more candidates were able to correctly deal with the deferred tax implication.

A significant number of candidates were **not able to deal with the deferred tax on a revaluation**, with many including it within the profit or loss tax expense. This adjustment has been dealt with many times before and candidates are advised to revise it.

On the whole investment properties were dealt with well but a minority of candidates failed to deal with this adjustment at all which was surprising as it is a relatively straightforward adjustment. Many candidates **recorded the gain incorrectly within other comprehensive income** which was disappointing to see.

> Part (b) to this question required candidates to calculate the earnings per share following a rights issue of shares made during the year. **Some candidates made basic mistakes** by not using profit after tax in their calculation or by time-apportioning the shares incorrectly.
>
> **Some candidates made more significant errors** such as not being able to deal correctly with the weighted average of shares following a rights issue and omitted the rights issue bonus fraction altogether. Others incorrectly calculated the theoretical ex-rights price by using the nominal value of the share capital rather than the market value and issue price.

416 LOUDON CO

(a) Schedule of adjusted retained earnings of Loudon as at 30 September 20X8

	$000
Retained earnings per trial balance	4,122
Add back issue costs of loan	125
Loan finance costs **(W1)**	(390)
Building depreciation (400 + 500) **(W2)**	(900)
Impairment **(W2)**	(3,600)
Factory depreciation **(W2)**	(3,885)
Disposal gain on factory **(W2)**	500
Unwinding of discount on environmental provision (1,228 × 5%)	(61)
Deferred tax adjustment **(W3)**	(203)
Adjusted retained earnings	(4,292)

(b) Statement of financial position as at 30 September 20X8

	$000	$000
Non-current assets		
Property, plant and equipment (11,500 + 22,015) **(W2)**		33,515
Current assets (per TB)		14,700
Total assets		48,215
Equity		
Equity shares $1 each (per TB)		10,000
Retained earnings (part (a))		(4,292)
		5,708
Non-current liabilities		
5% loan note **(W1)**	5,015	
Environmental provision (1,228 + 61 (part(a))	1,289	
Deferred Taxation **(W3)**	1,703	
		8,007
Current liabilities (per TB)		34,500
Total equity and liabilities		48,215

Workings

(W1) Loan note

The issue costs should be deducted from the proceeds of the loan note and not charged as an expense. This gives the loan note an opening carrying amount of \$4,875,000 (\$5,000,000 – \$125,000). The finance cost of the loan note, at the effective interest rate of 8% applied to the carrying amount of the loan, is \$390,000. The actual interest paid is \$250,000 (see TB) which leaves a closing carrying amount of \$5,015,000 for inclusion as a non-current liability in the statement of financial position.

Opening balance 1 October 20X7	**Finance costs 8% × opening balance**	**Interest paid 5% × principal**	**Closing balance 30 September 20X8**
\$000	\$000	\$000	\$000
4,875	390	(250)	5,015

(W2) Non-current assets

Office Building	\$000
Carrying amount at 1 September 20X7 (\$20,000 – \$4,000)	16,000
Depreciation to 1 April 20X8 (\$20,000/25 years × $^6/_{12}$)	(400)
Carrying amount at 1 April 20X8	15,600
Impairment	(3,600)
Fair value at 1 April 20X8	12,000
Depreciation to 30 September 20X8 (\$12,000/12 years × $^6/_{12}$)	(500)
	11,500

Factories	
Carrying amount at 1 September 20X7 (\$40,000 – \$11,100)	28,900
Disposal at carrying amount	(3,000)
Carrying amount at 1 September 20X8	25,900
Depreciation for the year to 30 September 20X8 (\$25,900 × 15%)	(3,885)
	22,015

Disposal of factory	
Proceeds	3,500
Carrying amount	(3,000)
Gain on disposal	500

(W3) Deferred Tax

	$000
Carrying amount of assets at 30 September 20X8 per SFP	33,515
Tax written down value of assets at 30 September 20X8	(25,000)
	8,515
Deferred tax provision required at 30 September 20X8 (8,515 × 20%)	1,703
Deferred tax provision at 30 September 20X7 (per TB)	(1,500)
Deferred tax charge for year ended 30 September 20X8	203

ACCA marking guide		
		Marks
(a)	Adjust profit	8
(b)	Statement of financial position	12
Total		**20**

417 MIMS CO

Key answer tips

When creating the proforma for your answer, include the cash flow section for part (c). Then enter the cash flow items into (c) as you work through parts (a) and (b).

(a) Statement of profit or loss for the year ended 31 December 20X5

	$000
Revenue	24,300
Cost of sales (11,600 – 700 (W2))	(10,900)
Gross profit	**13,400**
Administrative expenses (W1)	(9,700)
Distribution costs	(7,300)
Loss from operations	**(3,600)**
Finance costs	(1,400)
Investment income (500 + 2,000 (W6))	2,500
Loss before taxation	**(2,500)**
Taxation (W4)	560
Loss for the year	**(1,940)**

(b) Statement of changes in equity for the year ended 31 December 20X5

	Share capital	Share premium	Retained earnings
	$000	$000	$000
Balance at 1 January 20X5	60,000	–	43,200
Prior period error (W2)			(700)
Restated balance 1 January 20X5	60,000	–	42,500
Share issue (W5)	15,000	37,500	
Loss for the year			(1,940)
Dividends paid (W8)			(3,000)
Balance 31 December 20X5	75,000	37,500	37,560

(c) Extract from statement of cash flows for the year ended 31 December 20X5

	$000
Cash flows from investing activities	
Purchase of brand (W7)	(2,000)
Purchase of investment property (W6)	(20,000)
Investment income per TB	500
Net cash used in investing activities	(21,500)
Cash flows from financing activities	
Proceeds from issue of share capital (W5)	52,500
Dividends paid (W8)	(3,000)
Net cash from financing activities	49,500

Tutorial note

The workings below provide more detailed guidance to the answers shown above which were published by the ACCA in summary form, with more detail provided within the Examiners' Report.

Remember that you should always provide workings for any figures not provided within the question.

(W1) Administrative expenses

	$000
Per trial balance	10,900
Balance on provision (W3)	1,400
Investment property depreciation (W5)	(1,000)
Brand promotion (W7)	1,300
Brand amortisation (W7)	100
Dividend removed (W8)	(3,000)
	9,700

(W2) Inventory count

A restatement of the value of inventory at 31 December 20X4 would result in the following adjustment to the results for the year ended 31 December 20X5:

Dr Retained earnings (on SOCIE)	700
Cr Cost of sales	700

(W3) Provision

The provision has now been settled so should be removed, as should the $6 million in suspense, with the balance being written off to administrative expenses.

Dr Provision	4,600
Dr Administrative expenses	1,400
Cr Suspense	6,000

(W4) Tax expense

The tax expense comprises:

	$000
Underprovision from 20X4	140
Current year estimate	(1,200)
Increase in deferred tax liability (8,200 – 7,700)	500
Net tax credit to SPL	(560)

(W5) Rights issue

	$000
Number of shares issued: 60,000 × ¼ = 15,000 shares	
Issue proceeds 15,000 × $3.50 =	52,500
Comprising: Share capital 15,000 × $1	15,000
Share premium 15,000 × $2.50	37,500

(W6) Investment property

Mims Co has chosen to use the fair value model to account for its investment property, which means that the gain or loss on the property each year should be recognised in profit or loss, and the property should not be depreciated.

Depreciation incorrectly charged on the property is $20m × 1/20 = $1 million. This should be removed from administrative expenses and added back to the investment property.

The gain on the property to be recognised is $22m – $20m = $2 million.

(W7) Brands

The cost of promoting one of Mim Co's own brands would represent an internally generated intangible and so should not be capitalised. The cost of $1.3 million should therefore be written off to administrative expenses.

The brand acquired on 1 October 20X5 for $2 million should be amortised over its expected life of five years. Amortisation to be charged to administrative expenses is $2m × 1/5 × 3/12 = $100,000.

(W8) Dividend

The dividend was paid on 31 December 20X5 and would therefore have included the shares from the rights issue.

The dividend paid was (60,000 + 15,000) × $0.04 = $3 million. This should be removed from administrative expenses and deducted from retained earnings on the SOCIE.

ACCA marking guide		
		Marks
(a)	Statement of profit or loss	12
	Statement of changes in equity	5
	Extracts from statement of cash flows	3
Total		**20**

Extract from examiners' report (for detailed report see ACCA website)

Mims Co is a typical example of a single entity accounts preparation question from section C of the exam. In this type of question, you will be provided with a trial balance (or an extract from a trial balance) and some additional information that will require adjustments in accordance with relevant IFRS Standards and accounting principles.

Question requirements will vary, but you can expect to be asked to prepare a mixture of a statement of profit or loss and other comprehensive income, a schedule of adjustments to profit, a statement of changes in equity, a statement of financial position, or a specific extract from the financial statements such as, 'financing activities' from the statement of cash flows.

Before you attempt this question, make sure you are clear on what the requirement is asking for. There is no point in, for example, preparing a statement of financial position when the requirement has not asked for this. Providing additional statements that are not required wastes valuable time and will not attract any marks.

From an exam technique perspective, it is advised that you set up the answer/layout for the requirements first. For example, for Mims Co, lay out the working for the statement of profit or loss, the statement of changes in equity and the statement of cash flow extracts within the spreadsheet. Leave a couple of rows between each statement so that it is easy for the marker to distinguish between where one statement ends, and another begins.

As a general comment, you must ensure that all trial balance items are included either in the relevant working or within the financial statements themselves. It is often noted by the marking team that some balances are not transferred from the trial balance into the answer and therefore, what are considered to be easy marks, are lost. In this question, revenue, distribution costs and finance costs did not require adjustment as a result of the additional information and could be transferred directly to the statement of profit or loss. Including these balances in this statement attracted marks from the marking scheme. Similarly, the share capital and retained earnings in the trial balance at 1 January 20X5 could have been included in the opening balances on the statement of changes in equity.

It is important to note that you do not have to deal with the adjustments in the order presented in the question, although this is a logical approach and will ensure you do not miss out any required adjustments. However, in this question you may, for example, be most confident in adjusting for income tax and deferred tax at note (3) and be less confident with intangible assets in note (6). Dealing with the adjustments that you are most familiar with first may ease you into the question and help to stop panic setting in.

Inventory

Many candidates recognised that an adjustment was required to cost of sales, but some added the adjustment on in error. This was generally due to candidates misreading the scenario and thinking that the error related to the 20X5 closing balances, as most candidates that did this failed to go on and adjust opening retained earnings in the statement of changes in equity.

Investment property

Many candidates failed to reverse the incorrect depreciation and simply recorded a gain of $3m, being the difference between the fair value of $22m and the incorrect carrying amount on the trial balance of $19m.

It is important to note that gains (or losses) on investment property must be recorded in profit or loss and not in other comprehensive income. Many candidates did this and were not able to score full marks as a result.

Brand names

Many candidates who recognised the need for amortisation often calculated a full year. Some merit was awarded for this, but for full marks the expense had to be time apportioned.

Dividend

Many candidates unfortunately calculated the dividend based on the opening share capital, which was incorrect. Some merit was awarded where the correct adjustment took place.

Overall, the preparation of financial statements is an integral part of the FR syllabus and is something that should be practised. Please ensure that you attempt to use the ACCA Practice Platform on the ACCA website so that you get used to completing your answer on a spreadsheet. It is vital that you show all workings. If you use the functionality of the spreadsheet, markers will be able to view your workings within the cell. If you do not use the spreadsheet to calculate your figures, you must ensure that you set out all workings and calculations so that the marker is able to follow through what you have done and award marks accordingly.

On a final note, when completing this question, don't forget to make sure that all trial balance items have been used or transferred into the relevant statements, and when asked to prepare a statement of changes in equity, ensure that you transfer the profit for the year into retained earnings.

418 PRINT CO

All figures are in $000 unless stated otherwise.

(a) Statement of profit or loss for the year ended 30 June 20X2

		$000
Revenue		97,400
Cost of sales	(W1)	(63,910)
Gross profit		**33,490**
Distribution costs		(7,200)
Administrative expenses	(29,570 + 3,375 (W5))	(32,945)
Profit from operations		**(6,655)**
Finance costs	(750 – 350 (W4))	(400)
Loss before tax		**(7,055)**
Income tax refund		2,530
Net loss for the period		**(4,525)**

(b) Statement of financial position as at 30 June 20X2

		$000	$000
Assets			
Non-current assets			
Property, plant and equipment	(W2)		50,340
Current assets			
Inventories	(W6)	5,560	
Trade and other receivables		25,010	
Taxation		2,530	
Bank		4,700	
		37,800	
Non-current assets held for sale	(W3)	1,100	
			38,900
Total assets			89,240

Equity and liabilities			
Equity			
Ordinary share capital	(29,600 + 7,000 (W7))	36,600	
Other components of equity	(15,500 + 7,000 (W7))	22,500	
Retained earnings	(11,470 – 4,525)	6,945	
			66,045
Non-current liabilities			
Bank loan	(30,000 – 14,000 (W7))	16,000	
Provisions	(W5)	2,250	
			18,250
Current liabilities			
Trade and other payables	(4,170 – 350 (W4))	3,820	
Provisions	(W5)	1,125	
			4,945
Total equity and liabilities			**89,240**

(W1) Cost of sales

		$000
Opening inventory		6,850
Production costs		60,150
Less closing inventory	(W6)	(5,560)
Depreciation charge	(W2)	2,070
Held for sale asset impairment	(W3)	400
		63,910

(W2) Property, plant and equipment

	Land $000	**Plant and machinery** $000	**Total** $000
Cost			
Brought forward	45,000	16,200	61,200
HFS asset	–	(2,400)	(2,400)
	45,000	13,800	58,800
Accumulated depreciation			
Brought forward	–	(7,290)	(7,290)
Charge for the year (13,800 × 15%)	–	(2,070)	(2,070)
HFS asset accumulated depreciation (2,400 – 1,500)	–	900	900
	–	(8,460)	(8,460)
Carrying amount	45,000	5,340	50,340

(W3) Held for sale asset

	$000
Carrying amount at 1 July 20X1	1,500
Fair value less costs to sell at 30 June 20X2	(1,100)
Impairment loss to be recognised in the year ended 30 June 20X2	400

Tutorial note

A non-current asset classified as held for sale (i.e. a held for sale asset) should be measured at the lower of its carrying amount and fair value less costs to sell. The fair value less costs to sell at 30 June 20X2 will be the same as the net sales proceeds received on 1 July 20X2. The above working simplifies this to a single adjustment since no accounting has been done to date, but it could also be shown as:

	$000	$000
Carrying amount at 1 July 20X1	1,500	
Impairment	(360)	360
Fair value less costs to sell at 1 July 20X1	1,140	
Further impairment required	(40)	40
Fair value less costs to sell at 30 June 20X2 (using net proceeds received on 1 July 20X2)	1,100	
Total impairment for year ended 30 June 20X2		400

(W4) Finance costs

		$000
Included in TB	(30,000 × 5% × 6/12)	750
Correction of error	(14,000 × 5% × 6/12)	(350)
		400

(W5) Onerous contract

		$000
Price per unit		450
Costs of conversion		600
Total cost		1,050
Net realisable value		900
Loss per unit		(150)
		$000
Loss on fulfilling contract	($150 × 22,500 units)	3,375
Loss expected in the next 12 months (current)	(3,375 × 1/3 years)	1,125
Loss expected beyond 12 months (non-current)	(3,375 – 1,125)	2,250
		3,375

Tutorial note

As the loss on fulfilling the contract ($3.375m) is lower than the cost of cancelling the contract ($4m), a loss of $3.375m should be provided for.

(W6) Inventory

		$000
Cost of units requiring modification	$1,400 × 700 units	980
Net realisable value of units requiring additional modification	($1,600 – $400) × 700 units	(840)
Inventory write down required		140
Closing inventory (note 2)		5,700
Inventory write down		(140)
Adjusted closing inventory		5,560

(W7) Correction of share issue and bank loan

		$000
Share capital	7,000 share × $1	7,000
Share premium (other components of equity)	14,000 proceeds – 7,000 share capital	7,000
Proceeds received incorrectly included as part of the bank loan		14,000

ACCA marking guide		
		Marks
Print Co		
(a)	Statement of profit or loss	8
(b)	Assets	6
	Equity and liabilities	6
		12
Total		**20**

Extract from examiners' report (for detailed report see ACCA website)

Print Co is a typical example of a single entity accounts preparation question from section C of the exam. In this type of question, candidates are provided with a trial balance (or an extract from a trial balance) and some additional information that will require adjustments to be made in accordance with relevant IFRS Standards and accounting principles.

From an exam technique perspective, it is advised that you **set up the answer/layout for the requirements first**. For example, for Print Co, lay out the working for the statement of profit or loss and the statement of financial position within the response area. Leave a space between each statement so that it is easy for the marker to distinguish between where one statement ends and another begins.

As a general comment, you must **ensure that all trial balance items are included** either in the relevant working or within the financial statements themselves. It is often noted by the marking team that some balances are not transferred from the trial balance into the answer and therefore, what are considered to be easy marks, are lost.

It is important to note that **you do not have to deal with the adjustments in the order presented** in the question, although this is a logical approach and will ensure you do not miss out any required adjustments. For example, in this question you may be most confident in adjusting for depreciation in note (v) and be less confident with the bank loan/share issue in note (i). Dealing with the adjustments that you are most familiar with first could help to ease you into the question and stop panic setting in.

(i) Bank loan/Share issue

Most candidates were able to recognise that the bank loan in the trial balance was overstated and needed to be reduced by $14m. The correcting entry for the share issue was sometimes confused and many candidates simply added $14m on to share capital. Whilst this did attract some credit, the correct adjustment needed to be split between share capital and share premium.

Having corrected the original error, candidates then needed to recognise that an error had also been made when recording the loan interest accrual as this had incorrectly been based on the full $30m.

(ii) Inventories

Many candidates incorrectly recorded closing inventory at $5.7m. This note states that included within this amount are 700 units recorded at a cost of $1,400 per unit. However, before the goods can be sold, an additional $400 per unit will be incurred. Candidates are advised to calculate cost and compare to the NRV before recording closing inventory.

Cost $1,400

NRV ($1,600 – $400) $1,200

NRV is lower and therefore the original estimate of $5.7m included 700 units that are overstated by $200 per unit ($1,400 – $1,200) and therefore an inventory write-down of $140,000 is required (700 units × $200). Candidates can then adjust the cost of sales and closing inventory to record $5.56m of closing inventories ($5.7m – $140,000).

(iii) Contract to purchase electrical components

This is an example of an onerous contract, where the unavoidable costs of fulfilling the contract exceed any revenues expected to be received from the sale of the goods. Per IAS 37 Provisions, Contingent Liabilities and Contingent Assets, if an entity has a contract that is onerous, the present obligation under the contract should be recognised as a provision.

Many candidates incorrectly recognised a provision for the penalty costs of $4m. Whilst some credit was awarded for this, the provision should be recorded at the lower of the costs of fulfilling the contract or penalties from failure to fulfil the contract.

The provision created relates to the next three years and should therefore be split between its non-current and current liability.

(iv) Held for sale machinery

In accordance with IFRS 5 Non-current Assets Held for Sale and Discontinued Operations, the machine should be removed from property, plant and equipment and recorded as a separate class of assets at the lower of carrying amount or fair value.

In this question, there was an added complication that candidates were told the fair value of the machine on 1 July 20X1 (the date that the held for sale criteria were met) and the actual selling price on 1 July 20X2. Some candidates incorrectly used the fair value at 1 July 20X1, but own figure marks were awarded thereafter.

To correctly adjust for the held for sale machinery, candidates should remove the carrying amount from property, plant and equipment and then compare carrying amount and fair value to determine the appropriate amount to recognise as a held for sale asset:

(v) Depreciation

The depreciation calculation was relatively straightforward and was correctly calculated by many candidates. However, to correctly calculate the depreciation expense for the year, candidates needed to remove the held for sale asset from the plant and machinery cost in the trial balance. Some candidates overlooked this part of the calculation but were able to correctly adjust the financial statements thereafter using their own figure.

A number of candidates incorrectly calculated depreciation on a reducing balance basis. In this instance, candidates would not have been awarded any related marks within cost of sales but own figure marks applied within the statement of financial position.

(vi) Income tax refund

The question specifically stated that income tax for the year was estimated at $2.53m and that this is a tax **refund**. Despite this, many candidates incorrectly treated this as an expense in the statement of profit or loss and a liability in the statement of financial position. Unfortunately, these candidates were not awarded the marks for a relatively straight forward adjustment.

Where you are provided with a spreadsheet response option, if you use the functionality of the spreadsheet, markers will be able to view your workings within the cell. If you do not use the spreadsheet to calculate your figures, you must **ensure that you set out all workings and calculations** so that the marker is able to follow through what you have done and award marks accordingly.

BUSINESS COMBINATIONS

419 PREMIER  Walk in the footsteps of a top tutor

Consolidated statement of financial position as at 30 September 20X0

		$000
Non-current assets		
Property, plant and equipment		38,250
(25,500 + 13,900 – 1,200 (FV adj) + 50 (FV adj))		
Goodwill (W3)		7,800
Investments (1,800 – 800 (consideration) + 300 (gain on FVOCI))		1,300
		47,350
Current assets		
Inventory (5,300 + 500 – 400 (W2))	5,400	
Receivables	4,820	
(4,200 + 1,100 – 130 (cash in transit) – 350 (intra-group))		
Bank (3,000 + 800 + 130 (cash in transit))	3,930	
		14,150
		61,500
Equity		
Equity shares of $1 each ((12,000 + 2,400 (W3))		14,400
Share premium (W3)		9,600
Other equity reserve (500 + 300 (gain on FVOCI))		800
Retained earnings (W5)		11,860
		36,660
Non-controlling interest (W4)		3,390
		40,050
Current liabilities		21,450
(15,000 + 6,800 – 350 intra group balance)		
		61,500

Workings in $000

(W1) Group structure

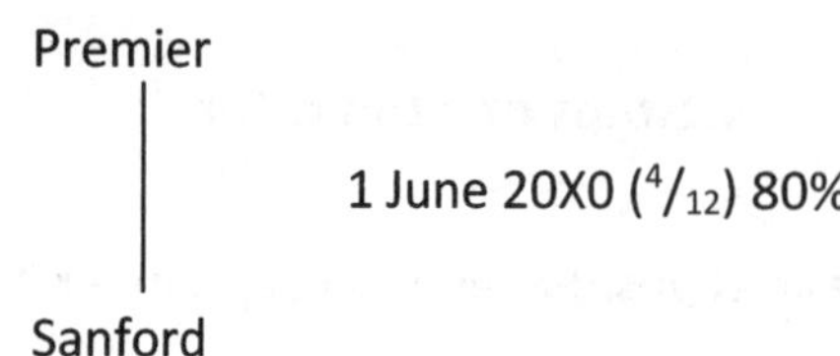

(W2) Net assets

	At acquisition	At reporting date	Post-acquisition
Share capital	5,000	5,000	–
Retained earnings (4,500 – (3900 × $^{4}/_{12}$))	3,200	4,500	1,300
Property fair value	(1,200)	(1,200)	–
Depreciation reduction (below)		50	50
PUP (below)		(400)	(400)
	7,000	7,950	950
	W3		W4/W5

The depreciation reduction is calculated as $1,200/8 years × $^{4}/_{12}$ = $50,000.

The unrealised profit in inventory is calculated as $2m × $^{25}/_{125}$ = $400,000.

Tutorial note

The fair value adjustment for property is a downwards fair value adjustment and therefore should be deducted from W2 and non-current assets. The reduction in depreciation should be added back in W2 and added back to non-current assets.

(W3) Goodwill

Parent holding (investment) at fair value:	
Shares ((5,000 × 80%) × $^{3}/_{5}$ × $5)	12,000
Cash	800
NCI value at acquisition	3,500
	16,300
Less: Fair value of net assets at acquisition (W2)	(7,000)
Goodwill on acquisition	9,300
Impairment	(1,500)
	7,800

Tutorial note

The 2.4 million shares (5,000 × 80% × $^3/_5$) issued by Premier at $5 each would be recorded as share capital of $2.4 million and share premium of $9.6 million.

(W4) Non-controlling interest (SFP)

NCI value at acquisition	3,500
NCI share of post-acquisition reserves (W2) (950 × 20%)	190
NCI share of impairment (W3) (1,500 × 20%)	(300)
	3,390

(W5) Consolidated retained earnings

Premier	12,300
Share of Sanford post-acquisition reserves (W2) (950 × 80%)	760
Share of impairment (W3) (1,500 × 80%)	(1,200)
	11,860

ACCA marking guide

	Marks
Property, plant and equipment	2
Goodwill	4
Investments	1
Inventory	1½
Receivables	1½
Bank	1
Equity shares	1½
Share premium	1
Other equity reserve	1
Retained earnings	2½
Non-controlling interest	2
Current liabilities	1
Total	**20**

420 PANDAR  Walk in the footsteps of a top tutor

(a) Carrying amount of investment in Ambra at 30 September 20X9

	$000
Cost (40 million × 40% × $2)	32,000
Share of post-acquisition losses (5,000 × 40% × $^6/_{12}$)	(1,000)
Impairment charge	(3,000)
Unrealised profit (6,000 × 20% × ½ × 40%)	(240)
	27,760

(b) Pandar Group

Consolidated statement of profit or loss for the year ended 30 September 20X9

	$000	$000
Revenue (210,000 + (150,000 × $^6/_{12}$) – 15,000 intra-group sales)		270,000
Cost of sales (W1)		(162,740)
Gross profit		107,260
Distribution costs (11,200 + (7,000 × $^6/_{12}$))		(14,700)
Administrative expenses (18,300 + (9,000 × $^6/_{12}$) + 2,000 impairment)		(24,800)
Investment income (W2)		1,100
Finance costs (W3)		(2,300)
Share of loss from associate (5,000 × 40% × $^6/_{12}$)	(1,000)	
Impairment of investment in associate	(3,000)	
		(4,000)
Profit before tax		62,560
Income tax expense (15,000 + (10,000 × $^6/_{12}$))		(20,000)
Profit for the year		42,560
Attributable to:		
Owners of the parent		41,160
Non-controlling interest (W4)		1,400
		42,560

Workings (figures in brackets in $000)

(W1) Cost of sales

	$000
Pandar	126,000
Salva (100,000 × $^6/_{12}$)	50,000
Intra-group purchases	(15,000)
Additional depreciation: plant (5,000/5 years × $^6/_{12}$)	500
Unrealised profit in inventories (15,000/3 × 20%)	1,000
Unrealised profit (Ambra) (6,000 × 20% × ½ × 40%)	240
	162,740

(W2) Investment income

	$000
Per statement of comprehensive income	9,500
Intra-group interest (50,000 × 8% × $^6/_{12}$)	(2,000)
Intra-group dividend (8,000 × 80%)	(6,400)
	1,100

(W3) Finance costs

	$000
Pandar	1,800
Salva post-acquisition (((3,000 – 2,000) × $^6/_{12}$) + 2,000)	2,500
Intra-group interest (W2)	(2,000)
	2,300

Tutorial note

The interest on the loan note is $2 million ($50 million × 8% × $^6/_{12}$). This is in Salva's profit in the post-acquisition period. Thus Salva's profit of $21 million has a split of $11.5 million pre-acquisition ((21 million + 2 million interest) × $^6/_{12}$) and $9.5 million post-acquisition.

(W4) Non-controlling interest

Salva's post-acquisition profit (see tutorial note above)	9,500
Fair value depreciation (W1)	(500)
Impairment (W1)	(2,000)
	7,000
Non-controlling interest share at 20%	1,400

ACCA marking guide			
			Marks
(a)	Carrying amount of Ambra		
	Cost		1
	Share of post-acquisition losses		1
	Impairment charge		1
	PUP adjustment		1
		Maximum	**4**
(b)	Statement of comprehensive income:		
	Revenue		1½
	Cost of sales		3
	Distribution costs and administrative expenses		½
	Administrative expenses		1½
	Investment income		2½
	Finance costs		1½
	Share of associate's losses and impairment charge		1½
	Income tax		1
	Non-controlling interests		3
		Maximum	**16**
Total			**20**

Examiners' report

The calculation of the carrying amount of the associate was very good, often gaining full marks. The main problems were not apportioning (by $^6/_{12}$) the losses in the year of acquisition and not applying the 40% group holding percentage. Some treated the losses as profits.

The main errors in the consolidated statement of profit or loss were with the more complex adjustments:

A **full year's additional depreciation of the plant was charged**, but it should have been only for the post-acquisition period of six months.

Many candidates **incorrectly amortised the domain name**. Its registration was renewable indefinitely at negligible cost so it should not have been amortised.

Surprisingly a number of candidates incorrectly calculated the PUP on inventory by treating the gross profit of 20% as if it were a mark-up on cost of 20%

The elimination of **intra-group dividend was often ignored** or the full $8 million was eliminated instead.

Often the **trading and impairment losses of the associate were ignored** in preparing the statement of comprehensive income

The **non-controlling interest was frequently ignored** and where it was calculated, many forgot to adjust for the additional depreciation on the fair value of the plant.

Despite the above, this was the **best answered question** and many candidates gained good marks.

421 PRODIGAL

(a) Prodigal – Consolidated statement of profit or loss and other comprehensive income for the year ended 31 March 20X1

	$000
Revenue (450,000 + (240,000 × $^6/_{12}$) – 40,000 intra-group sales)	530,000
Cost of sales (W1)	(278,800)
Gross profit	251,200
Distribution costs (23,600 + (12,000 × $^6/_{12}$))	(29,600)
Administrative expenses (27,000 + (23,000 × $^6/_{12}$))	(38,500)
Finance costs (1,500 + (1,200 × $^6/_{12}$))	(2,100)
Profit before tax	181,000
Income tax expense (48,000 + (27,800 × $^6/_{12}$))	(61,900)
Profit for the year	119,100
Other comprehensive income	
Gain on revaluation of land (2,500 + 1,000)	3,500
Total comprehensive income	122,600
Profit attributable to:	
Owners of the parent (balance)	111,550
Non-controlling interest (W2)	7,550
	119,100
Total comprehensive income attributable to:	
Owners of the parent (balance)	114,800
Non-controlling interest (W2)	7,800
	122,600

(b) Prodigal – Equity section of the consolidated statement of financial position as at 31 March 20X1

	$000
Equity attributable to owners of the parent	
Revaluation surplus (land) (W6)	11,650
Retained earnings (W5)	201,550
	213,200
Non-controlling interest (W4)	107,800
Total equity	321,000

Workings

(W1) Cost of sales

	$000
Prodigal	260,000
Sentinel (110,000 × $^{6}/_{12}$)	55,000
Intra-group purchases	(40,000)
Unrealised profit on sale of plant	1,000
Depreciation adjustment on sale of plant (1,000/2½ years × $^{6}/_{12}$)	(200)
Unrealised profit in inventory (12,000 × 10,000/40,000)	3,000
	278,800

(W2) NCI (SPL)

	$000
Sentinel's post-acquisition profit (66,000 × $^{6}/_{12}$)	33,000
PUP – inventory (W1)	(3,000)
PUP – plant depreciation (W1)	200
Sentinel's adjusted profit	30,200
Non-controlling interest at 25%	7,550
NCI (Total comprehensive income)	
As above	7,550
Other comprehensive income (1,000 × 25%)	250
	7,800

(W3) Net assets

	Acquisition	Reporting date	Post-acquisition
	$000	$000	$000
Retained earnings	158,000	191,000	33,000
Revaluation surplus (W6)	–	1,000	1,000
PUP – inventory	–	(3,000)	(3,000)
PUP – plant depreciation	–	200	200
	158,000	189,200	31,200

Note: Only the post-acquisition impact on retained earnings should go to the group retained earnings. This will be the 33,000 post acquisition profits less the 3,000 PUP on inventory plus the PUP on plant depreciation. Therefore Prodigal's share of Sentinel's post-acquisition retained earnings = 75% × 30,200 = 22,650.

(W4) Non-controlling interest

	$000
NCI value at acquisition (note (iv))	100,000
NCI share of post-acquisition reserves (31,200 × 25% (W3))	7,800
	107,800

(W5) Group retained earnings

	$000
Prodigal's retained earnings (90,000 b/f + 89,900 profit for year)	179,900
Sentinel's post-acquisition profits (30,200 (W3) × 75%)	22,650
NCA PUP	(1,000)
	201,550

(W6) Revaluation surplus

	$000
Prodigal's revaluation surplus (8,400 + 2,500 gain in year)	10,900
Sentinel's post-acquisition surplus (1,000 (W3) × 75%)	750
	11,650

Alternative workings for the equity section:

Prodigal – Equity section

Equity attributable to owners of the parent	$000
Revaluation surplus (land) (8,400 + 2,500 + (1,000 × 75%))	11,650
Retained earnings (see below)	201,550
	213,200
Non-controlling interest (see below)	107,800
Total equity	321,000

Retained earnings

Prodigal at 1 April 20X0	90,000
Per statement of profit or loss	111,550
	201,550

NCI

At acquisition	100,000
Per statement of profit or loss	7,800
	107,800

ACCA marking guide

		Marks
(a)	Statement of profit or loss and other comprehensive income	
	Revenue	2
	Cost of sales	5
	Distribution costs and administrative expenses	1
	Finance costs	1
	Income tax expense	1
	Non-controlling interest in profit for year	2
	Other comprehensive income	1
	Non-controlling interest in other comprehensive income	2
	Maximum	**15**
(b)	Consolidated equity	
	Revaluation surplus	1½
	Retained earnings	2
	Non-controlling interest	1½
	Maximum	**5**
Total		**20**

422 PALADIN

Consolidated statement of financial position of Paladin as at 30 September 20X1

	$000
Assets	
Non-current assets:	
Property, plant and equipment	
(40,000 + 31,000 + 4,000 FV – 1,000 FV depreciation)	74,000
Intangible assets	
– goodwill (W3)	15,000
– other intangibles (7,500 + 3,000 FV – 500 FV amortisation)	10,000
Investment in associate (W6)	7,700
	106,700
Current assets (22,000 + 13,700 – 600 PUP (W7))	35,100
Total assets	141,800
Equity and liabilities	
Equity attributable to owners of the parent	
Equity shares of $1 each	50,000
Retained earnings (W5)	35,200
	85,200
Non-controlling interest (W4)	7,900
Total equity	93,100
Non-current liabilities	
Deferred tax (15,000 + 8,000)	23,000
Current liabilities (11,600 + 8,700 + 5,400 deferred consideration)	25,700
Total equity and liabilities	141,800

Workings

(W1) Group structure

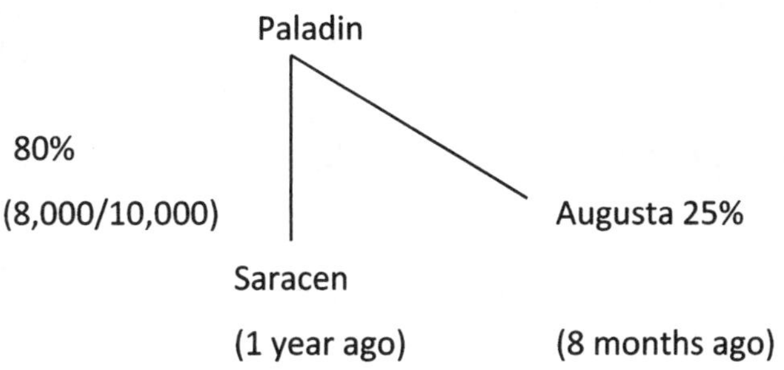

(W2) Net assets

	Acquisition	Reporting date	Post-acquisition
	$000	$000	$000
Share capital	10,000	10,000	–
Retained earnings	12,000	18,000	6,000
Fair value adjustment to plant	4,000	4,000	–
Fair value depreciation (4,000/4 years)		(1,000)	(1,000)
Fair value adjustment to intangible	3,000	3,000	–
Fair value amortisation (3,000/6 years)		(500)	(500)
	29,000	33,500	4,500
	W3		W4/W5

(W3) Goodwill

	$000
Cash on acquisition	32,000
Deferred consideration (5,400 × $^{100}/_{108}$)	5,000
NCI at acquisition (2,000 shares owned × $3.50)	7,000
Less: Fair value of net assets at acquisition (W2)	(29,000)
Goodwill on acquisition	15,000

(W4) Non-controlling interest

	$000
Fair value on acquisition (W3)	7,000
Post-acquisition profits (4,500 (W2) × 20%)	900
	7,900

(W5) Group retained earnings

	$000
Paladin's retained earnings (25,700 + 9,200)	34,900
Saracen's post-acquisition profits (4,500 (W2) × 80%)	3,600
Augusta's post-acquisition profits (W6)	200
Augusta's impairment loss	(2,500)
PUP (W7)	(600)
Finance cost of deferred consideration (5,000 × 8%)	(400)
	35,200

(W6) Investment in associate

	$000
Cash consideration	10,000
Share of post-acquisition profits (1,200 × $^{8}/_{12}$ × 25%)	200
Impairment loss	(2,500)
	7,700

(W7) PUP

The PUP in Saracen's inventory is $600,000 (2,600 × $^{30}/_{130}$).

ACCA marking guide	
	Marks
Property, plant and equipment	2
Goodwill	5
Other intangibles	1½
Investment in associate	1½
Current assets	1½
Equity shares	½
Retained earnings	5
Non-controlling interest	1
Deferred tax	½
Current liabilities	1½
Total	**20**

423 PYRAMID

Pyramid – Consolidated statement of financial position as at 31 March 20X2

	$000	$000
Assets		
Non-current assets:		
Property, plant and equipment (38,100 + 28,500 + 3,000 fair value – 600 depreciation)		69,000
Goodwill (W3)		7,400
– fair value equity investments		2,800
		79,200
Current assets		
Inventory (13,900 + 10,400 + 1,500 GIT (W6) – 500 PUP (W5))	25,300	
Trade receivables (11,400 + 5,500 – 1,200 CIT – 3,200 intra group (W6))	12,500	
Bank (9,400 + 600 + 1,200 CIT (W6))	11,200	
		49,000
Total assets		128,200
Equity and liabilities		
Equity attributable to owners of the parent		
Equity shares of $1 each		25,000
Reserves:		
Share premium	17,600	
Retained earnings (W5)	35,780	
		53,380
		78,380
Non-controlling interest (W4)		8,480
Total equity		86,860
Non-current liabilities (16,500 + 4,000 + 1,000 deferred tax)		21,500
Current liabilities		
Deferred consideration (6,400 + 640 unwinding of discount (W5))	7,040	
Other current liabilities (9,500 + 5,000 + 1,500 GIT – 3,200 intra group (W6)	12,800	
		19,840
Total equity and liabilities		128,200

Workings

(W1) Group structure

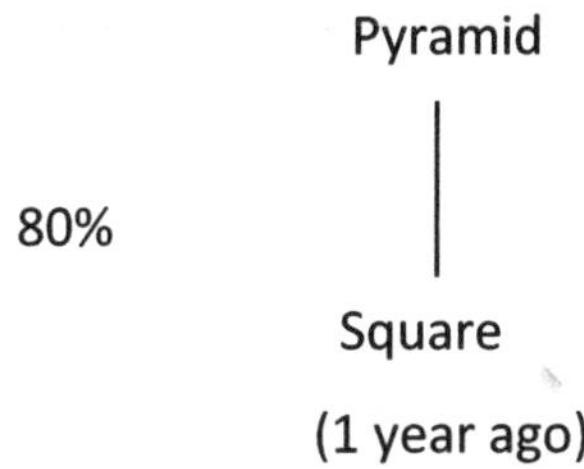

(W2) Net assets

	Acquisition	Reporting date	Post-acquisition
	$000	$000	$000
Share capital	10,000	10,000	–
Retained earnings	18,000	26,000	8,000
Fair value: plant	3,000	3,000	–
Fair value plant depreciation		(600)	(600)
Fair value: deferred tax	(1,000)	(1,000)	–
	30,000	37,400	7,400
	W3		W4/W5

(W3) Goodwill

	$000
Shares	24,000
Deferred consideration (8,000 × 88c × $^{1}/_{1.1}$)	6,400
	30,400
NCI at acquisition (2,000 shares owned × $3.50)	7,000
	37,400
Less:	
Fair value of net assets at acquisition (W2)	(30,000)
Goodwill on acquisition	7,400

(W4) Non-controlling interest

	$000
Fair value on acquisition (W3)	7,000
Post-acquisition profits (7,400 (W2) × 20%)	1,480
	8,480

(W5) Group retained earnings

	$000
Pyramid's retained earnings (16,200 + 14,000)	30,200
Square's post-acquisition profits (7,400 (W2) × 80%)	5,920
Gain on equity investments (2,800 – 2,000)	800
PUP ($1.5m × $^{50}/_{150}$)	(500)
Finance cost of deferred consideration (6,400 × 10%)	(640)
	35,780

(W6) Intra-group current accounts

The goods-in-transit and cash-in-transit need to be dealt with first.

Goods in transit: Dr Inventory 1,500, Cr Payables 1,500

Cash in transit: Dr Cash 1,200, Cr Receivables 1,200

This leaves $3,200 in receivables/payables, which can now be cancelled out.

ACCA marking guide	
	Marks
Statement of financial position:	
Property, plant and equipment	2
Goodwill	4½
Other equity investments	1
Inventory	1½
Receivables	1½
Bank	1
Share capital and share premium	½
Retained earnings	3½
Non-controlling interest	1
Non-current liabilities	1
Deferred consideration	1
Other current liabilities	1½
Total	**20**

424 VIAGEM

(a) Viagem consolidated goodwill on acquisition of Greca as at 1 January 20X2

	$000	$000
Investment at cost		
Shares (10,000 × 90% × $^2/_3$ × $6.50)		39,000
Deferred consideration (9,000 × $1.76/1.1)		14,400
Non-controlling interest (10,000 × 10% × $2.50)		2,500
		55,900
Net assets (based on equity) of Greca as at 1 January 20X2		
Equity shares	10,000	
Retained earnings b/f at 1 October 20X1	35,000	
Earnings 1 October 20X1 to acquisition (6,200 × $^3/_{12}$)	1,550	
Fair value adjustments: plant	1,800	
contingent liability recognised	(450)	
Net assets at date of acquisition		(47,900)
Consolidated goodwill		8,000

(b) Viagem Consolidated statement of profit or loss for year ended 30 September 20X2

	$000
Revenue (64,600 + (38,000 × $^9/_{12}$) – 7,200 intra-group sales)	85,900
Cost of sales (W1)	(64,250)
Gross profit	21,650
Distribution costs (1,600 + (1,800 × $^9/_{12}$))	(2,950)
Administrative expenses (3,800 + (2,400 × $^9/_{12}$) + 2,000 goodwill impairment)	(7,600)
Income from associate (2,000 × 40% based on underlying earnings)	800
Finance costs (420 + (14,400 × 10% × $^9/_{12}$ re deferred consideration))	(1,500)
Profit before tax	10,400
Income tax expense (2,800 + (1,600 × $^9/_{12}$))	(4,000)
Profit for the year	6,400
Profit for year attributable to:	
Equity holders of the parent (balance)	6,180
Non-controlling interest (W2)	220
	6,400

Workings

(W1) Cost of sales

	$000
Viagem	51,200
Greca (26,000 × $^{9}/_{12}$)	19,500
Intra-group purchases (800 × 9 months)	(7,200)
PUP in inventory (1,500 × $^{25}/_{125}$)	300
Additional depreciation (1,800/3 years × $^{9}/_{12}$)	450
	64,250

(W2) NCI

	$000
Greca post-acquisition profit (6,200 × $^{9}/_{12}$)	4,650
Fair value depreciation	(450)
Impairment	(2,000)
Greca adjusted profit	2,200
Non-controlling interest at 10%	220

ACCA marking guide

			Marks
(a)	Consolidated goodwill:		
	Consideration – share exchange		1½
	– deferred		1½
	– NCI		1
	Net assets – equity		½
	– retained at acquisition		1
	– fair value adjustments		1½
		Maximum	**7**
(b)	Consolidated statement of profit or loss		
	Revenue		1½
	Cost of sales		3½
	Distribution costs		½
	Administrative expenses		1½
	Income from associate		1½
	Finance costs		2
	Income tax		½
	NCI		2
		Maximum	**13**
Total			**20**

425 PARADIGM

(a) Paradigm – Consolidated statement of financial position as at 31 March 20X3

	$000	$000
Assets		
Non-current assets:		
Property, plant and equipment		
(47,400 + 25,500 – 3,000 fair value + 500 depreciation)		70,400
Goodwill (W3)		8,500
Financial asset: equity investments (7,100 + 3,900)		11,000
		89,900
Current assets		
Inventory (20,400 + 8,400 – 600 PUP (W6))	28,200	
Trade receivables (14,800 + 9,000)	23,800	
Bank	2,100	
		54,100
Total assets		144,000
Equity and liabilities		
Equity attributable to owners of the parent		
Equity shares of $1 each (40,000 + 6,000 (W3))		46,000
Share premium (W3)		6,000
Retained earnings (W5)		33,925
Non-controlling interest (W4)		8,800
Total equity		94,725
10% loan notes (8,000 + 1,500 (W3))		9,500
Current liabilities		
Trade payables (17,600 + 13,000 + 75 interest (W7))	30,675	
Bank overdraft	9,100	
		39,775
Total equity and liabilities		144,000

Workings

(W1) Group structure

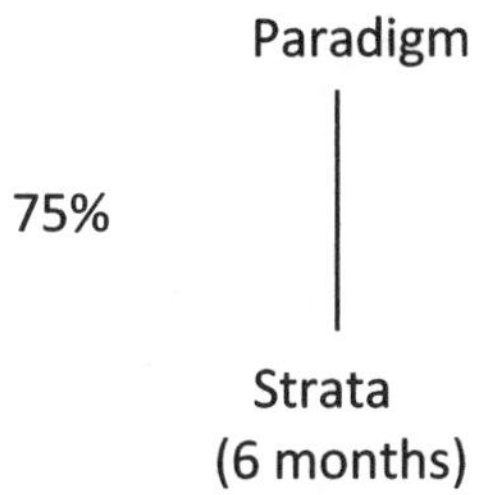

(W2) Net assets

	At acquisition	At reporting date	Post-acquisition
	\$000	\$000	\$000
Share capital	20,000	20,000	–
Retained earnings	(6,000)	4,000	10,000
Fair value adjustment	(3,000)	(3,000)	–
Fair value depreciation (3,000 × $^6/_{36}$)		500	500
Gain on equity investment		700	700
	11,000	22,200	11,200

(W3) Goodwill

	\$000
Share exchange ((20,000 × 75%) × $^2/_5$ × \$2)	12,000
10% loan notes (15,000 × $^{\$100}/_{1,000}$)	1,500
Non-controlling interest (20,000 × 25% × \$1.20)	6,000
Less: Fair value of net assets at acquisition (W2)	(11,000)
Goodwill on acquisition	8,500

The market value of the shares issued of \$12 million would be recorded as \$6 million share capital and \$6 million share premium as the shares have a nominal value of \$1 each and an issue value of \$2 each.

(W4) Non-controlling interest

	\$000
Fair value on acquisition (W3)	6,000
Post-acquisition profits (11,200 (W2) × 25%)	2,800
	8,800

(W5) Group retained earnings

	\$000
Paradigm's retained earnings (19,200 + 7,400)	26,600
Strata's post-acquisition profit (11,200 (W2) × 75%)	8,400
PUP in inventory (4,600 × $^{15}/_{115}$)	(600)
Loss on equity investments (7,500 – 7,100)	(400)
Additional loan note interest (1,500 × 10% × $^6/_{12}$)	(75)
	33,925

(b) IFRS 3 *Business Combinations* requires the purchase consideration for an acquired entity to be allocated to the fair value of the assets, liabilities and contingent liabilities acquired (henceforth referred to as net assets) with any residue being allocated to goodwill. This also means that those net assets will be recorded at fair value in the consolidated statement of financial position. This is entirely consistent with the way other net assets are recorded when first transacted (i.e. the initial cost of an asset is normally its fair value). This ensures that individual assets and liabilities are correctly valued in the consolidated statement of financial position. Whilst this may sound obvious, consider what would happen if say a property had a carrying amount of $5 million, but a fair value of $7 million at the date it was acquired. If the carrying amount rather than the fair value was used in the consolidation it would mean that tangible assets (property, plant and equipment) would be understated by $2 million and intangible assets (goodwill) would be overstated by the same amount.

There could also be a 'knock-on' effect with incorrect depreciation charges in the years following an acquisition and incorrect calculation of any goodwill impairment. Thus the use of carrying amounts rather than fair values would not give a 'faithful representation' as required by the Framework.

The assistant's comment regarding the inconsistency of value models in the consolidated statement of financial position is a fair point, but it is really a deficiency of the historical cost concept rather than a flawed consolidation technique. Indeed the fair value of the subsidiary's net assets represents the historical cost to the parent. To overcome much of the inconsistency, there would be nothing to prevent the parent from applying the revaluation model to its property, plant and equipment.

ACCA marking guide		
		Marks
(a)	Property, plant and equipment	1½
	Goodwill	3½
	Equity investments	1
	Inventory	½
	Receivables	½
	Bank	½
	Equity shares	1
	Share premium	½
	Retained earnings	2½
	Non-controlling interest	1½
	10% loan notes	1
	Trade payables	½
	Bank overdraft	½
(b)	One mark per point made	5
Total		**20**

426 PENKETH

(a) Goodwill

	\$000
Deferred consideration (1.54 × 90,000 × $^{1}/_{1.1}$)	126,000
Non-controlling interest (1.25 × 60,000)	75,000
Less: Fair value of net assets at acquisition (W1)	(196,000)
Goodwill on acquisition	5,000

(b) Penketh – Consolidated statement of profit or loss and other comprehensive income for the year ended 31 March 20X4

	\$000
Revenue (620,000 + (310,000 × $^{6}/_{12}$) – 20,000 intra-group sales)	755,000
Cost of sales (W2)	(457,300)
Gross profit	297,700
Distribution costs (40,000 + (20,000 × $^{6}/_{12}$))	(50,000)
Administrative expenses (36,000 + (25,000 × $^{6}/_{12}$) + (5,000/5 × $^{6}/_{12}$ re customer list))	(49,000)
Investment income (5,000 + (1,600 × $^{6}/_{12}$))	5,800
Finance costs (2,000 + (5,600 × 6/12) + (126,000 × 10% × $^{6}/_{12}$ re deferred consideration))	(11,100)
Profit before tax	193,400
Income tax expense (45,000 + (31,000 × $^{6}/_{12}$))	(60,500)
Profit for the year	132,900
Other comprehensive income	
Loss on revaluation of land (2,200 – 1,000 gain for Sphere)	(1,200)
Total comprehensive income for the year	131,700
Profit attributable to:	
Owners of the parent (balance)	117,700
Non-controlling interest (W2)	15,200
	132,900
Total comprehensive income attributable to:	
Owners of the parent (balance)	116,100
Non-controlling interest (W3)	15,600
	131,700

Workings

(W1) Net assets of Sphere at acquisition

	$000
Share capital	75,000
Retained earnings (70,000 b/f + 40,000 pre-acquisition)	110,000
Fair value adjustment – plant	6,000
Fair value adjustment – customer relationships	5,000
	196,000

(W2) Cost of sales

	$000
Penketh	400,000
Sphere (150,000 × $^{6}/_{12}$)	75,000
Intra-group purchases	(20,000)
Additional depreciation of plant (6,000/2 years × $^{6}/_{12}$)	1,500
Unrealised profit in inventory (20,000 × $^{1}/_{5}$ × $^{25}/_{125}$)	800
	457,300

(W3) Non-controlling interest in profit for the year

	$000
Sphere's profit (80,000 × $^{6}/_{12}$)	40,000
Fair value depreciation – plant	(1,500)
Fair value amortisation – customer list	(500)
Sphere adjusted profit	38,000
Non-controlling interest at 40%	15,200

Non-controlling interest in total comprehensive income

	$000
Non-controlling interest in statement of profit or loss (above)	15,200
Other comprehensive income (1,000 × 40%)	400
	15,600

ACCA marking guide		
		Marks
(a)	Goodwill	
	Consideration paid	1
	NCI at acquisition	1
	Net assets at acquisition (½ share capital, 1½ RE, 1 FV adjustments)	3
(b)	Consolidated statement of profit or loss and other comprehensive income	
	Revenue	2
	Cost of sales	3
	Distribution costs	½
	Administrative expenses	1½
	Investment income	1
	Finance costs	1½
	Income tax expense	1
	Other comprehensive income	1½
	Non-controlling interest in profit for year	2
	Non-controlling interest in other comprehensive income	1
Total		**20**

427 PALISTAR

Palistar – Consolidated statement of financial position as at 30 June 20X5

Assets	$000
Non-current assets:	
Property, plant and equipment (55,000 + 28,600)	83,600
Goodwill (W3)	3,000
Game rights (12,000 – 1,200 (W2))	10,800
Financial asset equity investments (13,200 + 7,900)	21,100
	118,500
Current assets	
Inventory (17,000 + 15,400 + 800 GIT – 600 (W6))	32,600
Trade receivables (14,300 + 10,500 – 2,400 intra-group)	22,400
Bank (2,200 + 1,600)	3,800
	58,800
Total assets	177,300
Equity and liabilities	
Equity attributable to owners of the parent	
Equity shares of $1 each (20,000 + 6,000 (W3))	26,000
Other components of equity (share premium) (4,000 + 18,000 (W3))	22,000
Retained earnings (W5)	52,425
	100,425
Non-controlling interest (W4)	15,675

Total equity	116,100
Current liabilities	
Deferred consideration (18,000 + 900 finance cost (W5))	18,900
Other current liabilities (25,800 + 18,100 + 800 GIT – 2,400 intra-group)	42,300
	61,200
Total equity and liabilities	177,300

Workings

(W1) Group structure

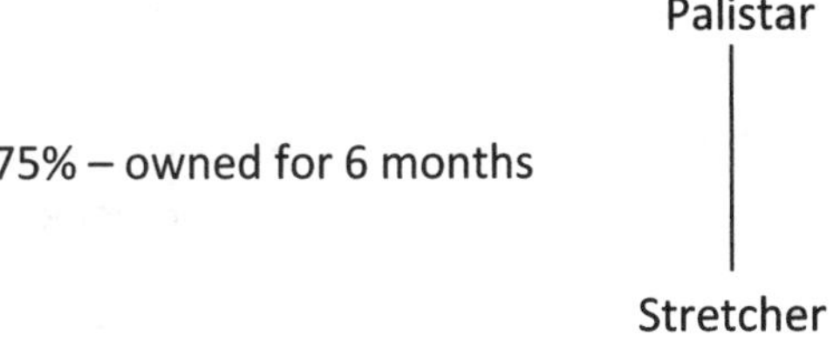

(W2) Net assets

	Acquisition	**Reporting date**	**Post-acquisition**
	$000	$000	$000
Share capital	20,000	20,000	–
Retained earnings (see below)	18,000	24,000	6,000
Fair value: game rights	12,000	12,000	–
Amortisation × $^1/_5$ × $^6/_{12}$		(1,200)	(1,200)
Fair value investments	1,000	1,900	900
	51,000	56,700	5,700
	W3		W4/W5

Stretcher makes 60% of its profit in the period from 1 June. Therefore the post-acquisition retained earnings is $6 million (60% × $10 million), making the retained earnings at acquisition $18 million ($24 million less $6 million).

(W3) Goodwill in Stretcher

	$000
Share exchange (20,000 × 75% × $^{2}/_{5}$) = (6,000 × $4)	24,000
Deferred consideration (20,000 × 75% × $^{\$1.32}/_{1.1}$)	18,000
Non-controlling interest (20,000 × 25% × $3)	15,000
	57,000
Net assets at acquisition	(51,000)
Goodwill on acquisition	6,000
Impairment	(3,000)
Goodwill at 30 June 20X5	3,000

The shares issued by Palistar (6 million at $4 – see above) would be recorded as share capital of $6 million (6,000 × $1) and share premium in other components of equity of $18 million (6,000 × $3).

(W4) Non-controlling interest

	$000
Fair value on acquisition (W3)	15,000
Post-acquisition profit (5,700 × 25% (W2))	1,425
NCI share of impairment (3,000 × 25%)	(750)
	15,675

(W5) Consolidated retained earnings:

	$000
Palistar's retained earnings (26,200 + 24,000)	50,200
Stretcher's adjusted post-acquisition profit (5,700 (W2) × 75%)	4,275
Palistar's share of impairment (3,000 × 75%)	(2,250)
Finance cost on deferred consideration (18,000 × 10% × $^{6}/_{12}$)	(900)
PUP in inventory (W6)	(600)
Gain on equity investments (13,200 – 11,500)	1,700
	52,425

(W6) Provision for unrealised profit (PUP)

The inventory of Stretcher at 30 June 20X5 (adjusted for goods-in-transit (GIT) sale of $800,000) is $2.6 million (1,800 + 800). The unrealised profit on this will be $600,000 ($2.6m × $^{30}/_{130}$).

ACCA marking guide	
	Marks
Consolidated statement of financial position:	
Property, plant and equipment	½
Goodwill	5
Game rights	1
Financial asset investments	1
Inventory	2
Receivables	1
Bank	½
Equity shares	1
Other component of equity	1
Retained earnings	4
Non-controlling interest	1
Deferred consideration	1
Other current liabilities	1
Total	**20**

428 LAUREL

(a) Laurel: Consolidated goodwill on acquisition of Rakewood

	$000	$000
Investment at cost		
Shares (15,000 × 60% × $^3/_5$ × $7.00)		37,800
Deferred consideration (9,000 × $1.62/1.08)		13,500
Non-controlling interest (15,000 × 40% × $2.00)		12,000
		63,300
Net assets (based on equity) of Rakewood as at 1 January 20X6		
Equity shares	15,000	
Retained earnings at 1 October 20X5	25,000	
Earnings 1 October 20X5 to acquisition (10,400 × $^3/_{12}$)	2,600	
Fair value adjustments:		
plant	4,000	
inventory	200	
Net assets at date of acquisition		(46,800)
Consolidated goodwill		16,500

(b) Laurel consolidated statement of profit or loss for the year ended 30 September 20X6

	\$000
Revenue (84,500 + (52,000 × $^9/_{12}$) – (1,200 × 9 months) intra-group sales)	112,700
Cost of sales (see working below)	(74,900)
Gross profit	37,800
Distribution costs (2,000 + (1,600 × $^9/_{12}$))	(3,200)
Administrative expenses (4,100 + (2,800 × $^9/_{12}$))	(6,200)
Investment income (400 × $^9/_{12}$)	300
Income from associate (2,400 × 25% based on underlying earnings)	600
Finance costs (300 + (13,500 × 8% × $^9/_{12}$ re deferred consideration))	(1,110)
Profit before tax	28,190
Income tax expense (4,800 + (3,600 × $^9/_{12}$))	(7,500)
Profit for the year	20,690
Profit for year attributable to:	
Equity holders of the parent	18,370
Non-controlling interest ((10,400 × $^9/_{12}$) – 200 re inventory – 1,500 depreciation – 300 PUP) × 40%))	2,320
	20,690

Working

Cost of sales

	\$000
Laurel	58,200
Rakewood (34,000 × $^9/_{12}$)	25,500
Intra-group purchases (1,200 × 9 months)	(10,800)
Fair value inventory adjustment	200
PUP in inventory at 30 September 20X6 (1,800 × $^{20}/_{120}$)	300
Additional depreciation (4,000/2 years × $^9/_{12}$)	1,500
	74,900

ACCA marking guide

		Marks
(a)	Consolidated goodwill:	
	Consideration – share exchange	1
	– deferred consideration	1
	– NCI	1
	Net assets – equity shares	½
	– retained earnings at acquisition	1½
	– fair value adjustments	2
		7
(b)	Consolidated statement of profit or loss:	
	Revenue	1½
	Cost of sales	4½
	Distribution costs	½
	Administrative expenses	½
	Investment income	1½
	Finance costs	1½
	Income tax expense	1
	NCI	2
		13
Total		**20**

429 DARGENT CO

Consolidated statement of financial position as at 31 March 20X6

Assets	$000	$000
Non-current assets:		
Property, plant and equipment		110,500
(75,200 + 31,500 + 4,000 mine – 200 dep)		
Goodwill (W3)		11,000
Investment in associate (4,500 + 1,200 (W5))		5,700
		127,200
Current assets		
Inventory (19,400 + 18,800 + 700 GIT – 800 PUP (W6))	38,100	
Trade receivables (14,700 + 12,500 – 3,000 intra group)	24,200	
Bank (1,200 + 600)	1,800	
		64,100
Total assets		191,300

Equity and liabilities		
Equity shares of $1 each (50,000 + 10,000 (W3))		60,000
Other equity reserves (share premium) (W3)		22,000
Retained earnings (W5)		37,390
		119,390
Non-controlling interest (W4)		9,430
Total equity		128,820
Non-current liabilities		
8% loan notes (5,000 + 15,000 consideration (W3))	20,000	
Accrued loan interest (W5)	300	
Environmental provision (4,000 + 80 interest (W2))	4,080	
		24,380
Current liabilities (24,000 + 16,400 + 700 GIT – 3,000 intra group)		38,100
Total equity and liabilities		191,300

Workings (figures in brackets are in $000)

(W1) Group structure

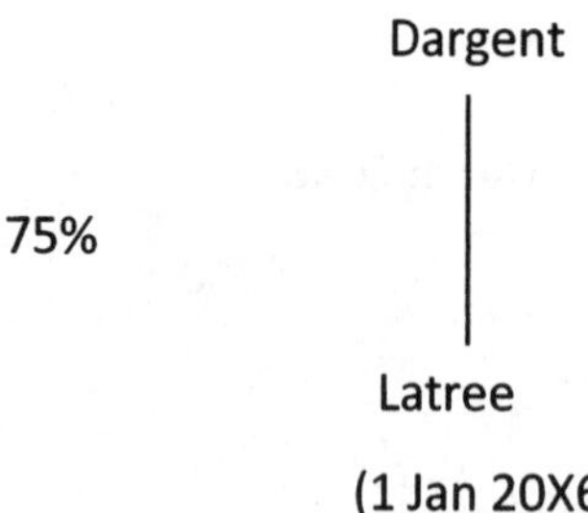

(W2) Net assets of Latree Co

	Acquisition	Reporting date	Post-acquisition
	$000	$000	$000
Equity shares	20,000	20,000	
Retained earnings at 1 April 20X5	19,000	19,000	
Earnings 1 April to acquisition (8,000 × 9/12)	6,000	8,000	2,000
Fair value adjustment: Mine asset	4,000	4,000	
Mine depreciation (4,000 × 1/5 × 3/12)		(200)	(200)
Mine provision	(4,000)	(4,000)	
Interest on provision (4,000 × 8% × 3/12)		(80)	(80)
	45,000	46,720	1,720

Applying the group policy to the environmental provision would mean adding $4 million to the carrying amount of the mine and the same amount recorded as a provision at the date of acquisition. This has no overall effect on the net assets at acquisition, but it does affect the consolidated statement of financial position and post-acquisition profit.

(W3) Goodwill in Latree Co

	$000
Controlling interest	
Share exchange (20,000 × 75% × 2/3 × $3.20)	32,000
8% loan notes (20,000 × 75% × $100/100)	15,000
Non-controlling interest (20,000 × 25% × $1.80)	9,000
	56,000
Net assets at acquisition (W2)	(45,000)
	11,000

The share exchange of $32 million would be recorded as share capital of $10 million (10,000 × $1) and share premium of $22 million (10,000 × ($3.20 – $1)).

(W4) Non-controlling interest

	$000
Value at acquisition (W3)	9,000
Post-acquisition profit (1,720 (W2) × 25%)	430
	9,430

(W5) Retained earnings

	$000
Dargent Co retained earnings	36,000
Latree Co post-acquisition profit (1,720 (W2) × 75%)	1,290
Amery unrecorded share of profit ((6,000 – 2,000) × 30%)	1,200
Unpaid loan interest (15,000 (W3) × 8% × $^3/_{12}$)	(300)
PUP (W6)	(800)
	37,390

(W6) Provision for Unrealised Profit (PUP)

	$000
Inventory held by Latree	2,100
Goods in transit	700
Total intra-group inventory held	2,800
Profit included (2,800 × 40/140)	800

ACCA marking guide	
	Marks
Property, plant and equipment	2
Goodwill: consideration	2½
Goodwill: fair value net assets	2
Investments in associate	1
Inventory	1½
Receivables	1
Bank	½
Equity shares and share premium	1
Retained earnings: post-acquisition sub	2
Retained earnings: other	2
Non-controlling interests	1½
8% loan notes	½
Environmental provision	1½
Current liabilities	1
Total	**20**

430 PARTY CO

(a) Consolidated statement of financial position for Party Co as at 30 September 20X5

		$000
Assets		
Non-current assets:		
Property, plant and equipment	(392,000 + 84,000)	476,000
Investments	(120,000 – 92,000 – 28,000)	0
Goodwill		32,396
		508,396
Current assets:	(94,700 + 44,650 + 60 FV – 250 PUP)	139,160
Total assets		647,556
Equity and liabilities		
Equity:		
Share capital		190,000
Retained earnings	(W5)	209,398
Revaluation surplus		41,400
		440,798
Non-controlling interest	(W4)	15,392
Total equity		456,190
Non-current liabilities:		
Deferred consideration	(23,996 + 1,920)	25,916
Current liabilities:	(137,300 + 28,150)	165,450
Total equity and liabilities		647,556

(W1) Group structure

Party Co owns 80% of Streamer Co.

Party Co has owned Streamer Co for one year.

(W2) Net assets

	Acquisition	**Year-end**	**Post acq'n**
	$000	$000	$000
Share capital	60,000	60,000	0
Retained earnings	34,000	36,500	2,500
Revaluation surplus	4,000	4,000	0
Fair value adj inventory	600	60	(540)
	98,600	100,560	1,960

(W3) Goodwill

	$000
Cash	92,000
Deferred cash (28m × 0.857)	23,996
NCI at acquisition	15,000
Less: Net assets at acquisition	(98,600)
Goodwill at acquisition	32,396

(W4) Non-controlling interest

	$000
NCI at acquisition (W3)	15,000
NCI % of Streamer post acquisition (1,960 (W2) × 20%)	392
	15,392

(W5) Retained earnings

	$000
Party Co	210,000
P's % of Streamer post acquisition RE (1,960 (W2) × 80%)	1,568
Unwinding discount on deferred consideration (23,996 (W3) × 8%)	(1,920)
Unrealised profit (1,000 × 25%)	(250)
	209,398

(b) The consolidated financial statements of the Party Group are of little value when trying to assess the performance and financial position of its subsidiary, Streamer Co. Therefore the main source of information on which to base any investment decision would be Streamer Co's individual financial statements. However, where a company is part of a group, there is the potential for the financial statements (of a subsidiary) to have been subject to the influence of related party transactions. In the case of Streamer Co, there has been a considerable amount of post-acquisition trading with Party Co and, because of the related party relationship, there is the possibility that this trading is not at arm's length (i.e. not at commercial rates). Indeed from the information in the question, Party Co sells goods to Streamer Co at a much lower margin than it does to other third parties. This gives Streamer Co a benefit which is likely to lead to higher profits (compared to what they would have been if it had paid the market value for the goods purchased from Party Co). Had the sales of $8m been priced at Party Co's normal prices, they would have been sold to Streamer Co for $10.9 million (at a margin of 25% these goods cost $6m, if sold at a normal margin of 45% they would have been sold at $6m/55% × 100). This gives Streamer Co a trading 'advantage' of $4.9 million ($10.9 million – $6 million).

There may also be other aspects of the relationship where Party Co gives Streamer Co a benefit which may not have happened had Streamer Co not been part of the group, e.g. access to technology/research, cheap finance, etc.

The main concern is that any information about the 'benefits' Party Co may have passed on to Streamer Co through related party transactions is difficult to obtain from published sources. It may be that Party Co has deliberately 'flattered' Streamer Co's financial statements specifically in order to obtain a high sale price and a prospective purchaser would not necessarily be able to determine that this had happened from either the consolidated or entity financial statements.

ACCA marking guide

		Marks
(a)	Property, plant and equipment	½
	Goodwill	4
	Current assets	2½
	Share capital	½
	Retained earnings	3½
	Revaluation surplus	½
	NCI	1½
	Deferred consideration	1½
	Current liabilities	½
		15
(b)	Limitations of interpretation using consolidated financial statements	**5**
Total		**20**

Examiners' report

Part (a) required the preparation of a consolidated statement of financial position with a series of routine adjustments supporting the consolidation process. The overall performance on this question, from a well-tried part of the syllabus, was very good. That said there were a **number of common errors and weaknesses**.

The fair value adjustment required at consolidation was $600,000 but this needed to be split by recognising that 90% of this had been sold since acquisition ($540,000 of this profit has been realised) and **only 10% ($60,000) should be adjusted for at the date of consolidation** by increasing the value of current assets.

Many candidates scored full marks for the goodwill calculation. Other than the fair value adjustment, the **deferred consideration was the most common problem**. The $28 million (payable on 1 July 20X8 – in two years' time) needed to be discounted at 8% to its present value at 1 July 20X6, for which the discount rate was given. Candidates who correctly made their own factor calculations and/or rounded the sum to $24 million were not penalised. **A few candidates omitted the NCI** (or tried to calculate the amount at acquisition for themselves) or tried to calculate the parent's share of goodwill only.

Some candidates **incorrectly included the pre-acquisition amount of the revaluation surplus** in the consolidated revaluation surplus – it should of course have been included in the goodwill calculation.

Most candidates, using the "own figure" rule, gained full marks for the NCI as this was the value at the date of acquisition plus 20% of post-acquisition profits (including the revaluation surplus).

The deferred consideration was also an issue for retained earnings and liabilities. As noted above, the amount needed to be discounted for the goodwill calculation as it was payable in two years' time. For the consolidated statement of financial position one year later the discount (at 8%) **needed to be "unwound" for a year** with a deduction from the parent's retained earnings and an increase in the discounted non-current liability. The majority of candidates who recognised this amount only adjusted retained earnings.

Although many candidates provided full and clear workings, the importance of **explaining where all numbers not already given in the question have come from cannot be over-emphasised**. This allows markers to determine whether an incorrect figure has been used in a calculation or whether the final total is wrong but the supporting figures are correct.

In part (b) of the question, most candidates were able to identify that the **individual financial statements of Streamer Co would be a better source of information** on which to base any investment decisions. However, the main point to be made was that the subsidiary's post-acquisition results had been improved due to **favourable pricing of the intra-group trading** originated by the parent based on the terms stated in the question. This is an example of the possible effect of related party transactions but **very little of this was mentioned by the vast majority of candidates**. Only a very small proportion of answers made reference to any numbers in this part of the question.

431 RUNNER CO

(a) Runner Co consolidated statement of financial position as at 31 March 20X5

	$000	$000
Assets		
Non-current assets		
Property plant and equipment (455,800 + 44,700 + 9,000 (W1))		509,500
Investment		12,500
Goodwill (W2)		20,446
		542,446
Current assets		
Inventory (22,000 + 16,000 – 720 (W4))	37,280	
Trade receivables (35,300 + 9,000 – 3,000 CIT – 3,400 inter-co)	37,900	
Bank (2,800 + 1,500 + 3,000 CIT)	7,300	
		82,480
Total assets		624,926
Equity and liabilities		
Equity attributable to the owners of the parent		
Equity shares of $1 each		202,500
Retained earnings (W5)		290,950
		493,450
Non-controlling interest (W3)		14,476
Total equity		507,926
Current liabilities (81,800 + 17,600 – 3,400 inter-co)	96,000	
Deferred consideration (19,446 + 1,554)	21,000	
		117,000
Total equity and liabilities		624,926

Workings

(W1) Net assets of Jogger Co

	Year-end	**Acquisition**	**Post-acquisition**
	$000	$000	$000
Share capital	25,000	25,000	
Retained earnings	28,600	19,500	9,100
Fair value adjustment	9,000	10,000	(1,000)
Unrealised profit	(720)		(720)
	61,880	54,500	7,380

(W2) Goodwill in Jogger Co

	$000
Cost of investment: Cash	42,500
Deferred consideration (21,000 × 0.926)	19,446
	61,946
Non-controlling interest	13,000
Less: Net assets acquired (W1)	(54,500)
Goodwill	20,446

(W3) Non-controlling interest

	$000
NCI at acquisition	13,000
NCI share of post-acquisition reserves (7,380 × 20%)	1,476
	14,476

(W4) Intercompany transaction

	$000
Inventory held at year end	4,800
Unrealised profit (4,800 × 15%)	720

(W5) Retained earnings

	$000
Runner Co	286,600
Runner Co's share of Jogger Co's post-acquisition retained earnings (7,380 (W1) × 80%)	5,904
Unwinding discount on deferred consideration (21,000 – 19,446 (W1))	(1,554)
	290,950

(b) Runner Co has significant influence over Walker Co, therefore Walker Co should be treated as an associate in the consolidated financial statements, using the equity method.

In the consolidated statement of financial position, the interest in the associate should be presented as 'investment in associate' as a single line under non-current assets. The associate should initially be recognised at cost and subsequently adjusted each period for the parent's share of the post-acquisition change in net assets (retained earnings). This figure should be reviewed for impairment at each year end which given the fall in value of the investment due to the loss would be most likely. Calculation:

	$000
Cost of investment	13,000
Share of post-acquisition change in net assets (30,000 × 30%)	(9,000)
	4,000

ACCA marking guide

		Marks
(a)	PPE and investments	2
	Goodwill	3
	Current assets	3½
	Share capital and NCI	1½
	Retained earnings	4
	Current liabilities	2
		16
(b)	Explanation of equity accounting	2
	Calculation of investment in associate	2
		4
Total		**20**

432 PLANK CO

(a) Consolidated statement of profit or loss and other comprehensive income for the year ended 31 December 20X8

	$000
Revenue (705,000 + ($^9/_{12}$ × 218,000) – 39,000)	829,500
Cost of sales **(W1)**	(348,100)
Gross profit	481,400
Distribution costs (58,000 + ($^9/_{12}$ × 16,000))	(70,000)
Administrative expenses (92,000 + ($^9/_{12}$ × 28,000))	(113,000)
Share of profit of associate **(W2)**	32,400
Other income (46,000 + ($^9/_{12}$ × 2,000) – 5,000 **(W5)** – 12,250 **(W4)** – 15,300 **(W4)**)	14,950
Finance costs (**W5**)	(18,750)
Profit before tax	327,000
Income tax expense (51,500 + ($^9/_{12}$ × 15,000))	(62,750)
Profit for the year	264,250
Other comprehensive income:	
Gain on revaluation of land (2,800 + 3,000)	5,800
Total comprehensive income for the year	270,050
Profit attributable to Parent (balance)	257,313
Profit attributable to NCI **(W3)**	6,937
	264,250
Total comprehensive income attributable to Parent (balance)	262,663
Total comprehensive income attributable to NCI **(W3)**	7,387
	270,050

(b) Investment in Associate

	$000
Carrying amount of investment at 31 December 20X7	145,000
Income from associate **(W2)**	32,400
Dividend received **(W4)**	(12,250)
Unrealised profit **(W1)**	(2,100)
Carrying amount at 31 December 20X8	**163,050**

Workings

(W1) Cost of sales

	$000
Plank Co	320,000
Strip Co (81,000 × $^{9}/_{12}$)	60,750
Intercompany purchases	(39,000)
Fair value depreciation (8,000 / 3 years × $^{9}/_{12}$)	2,000
Unrealised profit Strip (39,000 × $^{1}/_{4}$ × $^{30}/_{130}$)	2,250
Unrealised profit Arch (26,000 × 35% × $^{30}/_{130}$)	2,100
	348,100

(W2) Income from associate

	$000
Share of profit after tax (92,570 × 35%)	**32,400**

(W3) NCI Share of profit and total comprehensive income

	Strip	NCI @ 15%
	$000	$000
Strip profit for the year	66,000	
Add back: post-acquisition interest (see W5)	5,000	
	71,000	
Post-acquisition element (× $^{9}/_{12}$)	53,250	
Less: post-acquisition interest	(5,000)	
	48,250	
Less: Fair value depreciation (W1)	(2,000)	
Adjusted Strip profit	**46,250**	**6,937**
Other comprehensive income	3,000	
Strip total comprehensive income	**49,250**	**7,387**

(W4) Dividend income removed from SPL

	$000
Strip: 18,000 × 85%	**15,300**
Arch: 35,000 × 35%	**12,250**

(W5) Finance cost

	$000	$000
Plank		12,000
Strip: per SPL	14,000	
Less: post-acquisition payable to Plank Co	(5,000)	
	9,000	
Post-acquisition element (× $^9/_{12}$)		6,750
		18,750

Note that the loan from Plank to Strip was made on 1 April 20X8 so the interest payable to Plank of $5,000 must all relate to the post-acquisition period, and must be removed before time-apportioning the balance, then cancelled with $5,000 other income.

ACCA marking guide

		Marks
(a)	Revenue to admin expenses	6
	Investment income/associate	6
	Finance cost, tax, OCI, split	6
(b)	Investment in associate	2
Total		**20**

Examiners' report

Almost all candidates that attempted this question were able to complete the basic consolidation by adding the income and expenses of the parent and subsidiary together to show control. However, some candidates **failed to time apportion** the results of the subsidiary to represent the nine month post acquisition period. This continues to be a problem when this type of question is examined. A minority of candidates' time apportioned the subsidiary results by an incorrect number of months, for example eight months instead of nine. In this situation, the marking team were able to provide own figure marks providing workings were clearly shown.

Surprisingly, there continue to be a **minority of candidates that proportionately consolidate** the results of subsidiary (e.g. including 85% of Strip Co's income and expenses). As previously noted, this is a fundamental error and the basic consolidation marks will not be awarded when using this method.

This question required candidates to make adjustments for **common consolidation transactions**, including an adjustment for fair value depreciation and intra-group adjustments for sales and purchases, unrealised profit and internal dividends. On the whole these were generally dealt with well. The nine month post acquisition period continued to be a problem here, with some candidates forgetting to time apportion the fair value depreciation while others incorrectly time apportioned unrealised profit or the dividend.

It was pleasing to see that many candidates recognised that the dividend received from Strip Co was to be removed from investment income. However, there were a considerable number of candidates that **removed the entire $18 million**. As Plank Co only owns 85% of the shares in Strip Co it was necessary to adjust the dividend by this percentage before removing.

Note (iii) not only required candidates to adjust for the internal dividend discussed above, but it also required an **adjustment in respect of intra-group loan interest**. There were some candidates that seemingly missed this from the question and failed to deal with it at all. For those that did, a variety of answers were produced. To correctly adjust for this transaction, candidates needed to recognise that the loan **interest was both payable by Strip Co and receivable by Plank Co**. This interest therefore needed to be eliminated from both finance costs and investment income. The interest of $5 million did not need to be time apportioned as the loan to Strip Co was made on 1 April 20X8 (the same as the acquisition date).

It was noted in the opening paragraph that Plank Co had previously acquired 35% of Arch Co. Further detail in note (v) confirmed that Arch Co is **an associate of Plank Co and is therefore equity accounted** for in accordance with IAS 28 Investments in Associates and Joint Ventures. Only a minority of candidates correctly included the share of Arch Co in the consolidated statement of profit or loss.

The marking team noted that **this area of the consolidation had the largest variation in responses**. Firstly, the **dividend received from Arch Co needed to be eliminated** from Plank Co's investment income (e.g. 35% × $35 million) and then the **'income from associate' was to be included as a separate entry** within the consolidated profit or loss. Using the equity accounting method, candidates were required to include 35% of Arch Co's profit for the year and then adjust for the unrealised profit. Many candidates were able to calculate the unrealised profit as they would for a subsidiary ($26 million × 30/130), but the majority then failed to multiply this amount by the 35% influence that Plank Co had over Arch Co.

It was disappointing to note that a number of candidates attempted to **incorrectly consolidate the results of Arch Co** on a line-by-line basis. Again, this treatment is considered to be a fundamental error that does not follow the equity accounting method and should be discouraged.

When preparing a SPLOCI candidates must remember to **split both the profit for the year and total comprehensive income** between the amount attributable to the parent's shareholders and the amount attributable to the non-controlling interest. This continues to be the most commonly omitted part of the statement and often represents a significant portion of the total marks.

Part (b) to the question was well done with many of the candidates that attempted this part of the question able to score well. Markers were able to apply the own figure rule for the dividend and unrealised profit adjustment if previously adjusted for incorrectly in part (a).

433 GOLD CO

(a) Goodwill

	$000	$000
Consideration:		
Deferred cash (90% × 16,000 × $2.42 × 0.9091)		31,680
Shares (90% × 16,000 × 3/5 × $8.00)		69,120
		100,800
Non-controlling interest (NCI) (10% × 16,000 × $3.50)		5,600
		106,400
Less: fair value of net assets at acquisition		
Equity shares	16,000	
Retained earnings:		
At 1 October 20X1	56,000	
1 October 20X1–1 January 20X2 ($9,920 × 3/12)	2,480	
Fair value adjustments:		
Plant	2,600	
Contingent liability	(850)	
		(76,230)
Goodwill		**30,170**

(b) Consolidated statement of profit or loss for the year ended 30 September 20X2

		$000
Revenue	(103,360 + (60,800 × 9/12) – 5,400 (W1))	143,560
Cost of sales	(81,920 + (41,600 × 9/12) – 5,400 (W1) + 240 (W1) + 650 (W2))	(108,610)
Gross profit		34,950
Distribution costs	(2,560 + (2,980 × 9/12))	(4,795)
Administrative expenses	(6,080 + (3,740 × 9/12))	(8,885)
Share of profit from associate	(3,000 × 40%)	1,200
Finance costs	(672 + 136 (W3) + 2,376 (W4))	(3,184)
Profit before tax		19,286
Income tax expense	(4,480 + (2,560 × 9/12))	(6,400)
Profit for the year		12,886
Profit attributable to:		
Owners of the parent		12,207
NCI (W5)		679
		12,886

Workings

(W1) Intercompany and PUP

Post-acquisition sales ($600 × 9)	$5,400
PUP (1,200 × 25/125)	$240

(W2) Fair value depreciation on plant = ($2,600/3 × 9/12) = $650

(W3) Convertible loan — calculate liability component

Cashflow		$000	**DF 8%**	$000
Interest	(10,000 × 6%)	600	3.993	2,396
Principal		10,000	0.681	6,810
			Liability	9,206

Interest charge to SPL	($9,206 × 8%) =	736
Interest already charged		(600)
Additional charge		136

(W4) Deferred cash consideration

Unwinding of discount on deferred consideration (see goodwill calculation):

$31,680 × 10% × 9/12 = $2,376

(W5) Non-controlling interest

		$000
Silver Co profit for the year	($9,920 × 9/12)	7,440
Fair value depreciation (W2)		(650)
Silver Co adjusted profit		6,790
NCI share 10%		679

ACCA marking scheme		
		Marks
(a)	Goodwill	6
(b)	Revenue/COS	5½
	Other including NCI	8½
Total		**20**

Extract from examiners' report (for detailed report see ACCA website)

Gold Co is a fairly straightforward consolidated financial statements question from syllabus area D2. In this type of question, you may be asked to prepare a consolidated statement of profit or loss or a consolidated statement of financial position for a simple group (parent and up to two subsidiaries). This type of question may also require you to account for an associate company.

Overall, this question is worth 20 marks, giving you 36 minutes of your exam time to answer the entire question (180 minutes/100 marks = 1.8 minutes per mark × 20 marks). It is suggested that you break this down further into the component requirements of the question. For example, requirement (a) is worth 6 marks overall and therefore you should allocate 11 minutes of your exam time to this (10.8 minutes to be precise) and the remaining 25.2 minutes would be allocated to requirement (b).

Please note, you are not expected to answer the requirements in chronological order so if you wish to complete (b) first that is acceptable. However, this may not be possible for some questions, depending on the nature of the requirements.

In this type of question, it is absolutely vital that you present your workings clearly for the marking team. These can either be shown separately or can be included within a cell in the spreadsheet. If you calculate an amount on the calculator tool incorrectly and do not show the working, the marking team will not be able to award any own figure marks.

Requirement (a) – 6 marks

You are told in the question that Gold Co acquired 90% of Silver Co's 16 million $1 equity shares, therefore they have purchased 14.4 million equity shares.

Gold Co issued 8.64 million shares in the exchange (14.4 million shares × 3/5) and these must be measured at fair value. Many candidates incorrectly used the share price of $3.50 relating to the value of Silver Co's shares at acquisition. As Gold Co issues the shares as part of the acquisition, these shares must be valued using Gold Co's share price at acquisition of $8.00.

There were two net asset fair value adjustments in this question, and the adjustment to plant was generally dealt with well, although some candidates incorrectly tried to adjust fair value depreciation within the calculation of goodwill. Surprisingly, despite being tested before, many candidates omitted the fair value adjustment in respect of the contingent liability entirely. In accordance with IFRS 3 Business Combinations, the contingent liability was part of net assets acquired and should be included at fair value in the consolidated financial statements.

Requirement (b) – 14 marks

This requirement is fairly lengthy and would take up the majority of the time for this question. Candidate performance on a consolidated statement of profit or loss is usually weaker than when a consolidated statement of financial position is examined, and this question was no exception.

From an exam technique point of view, you may find it useful to layout the consolidated statement of profit or loss immediately. In doing this, it is highly recommended that you also head up the split between the profit that is attributable to the parent and that of the NCI at the bottom of the consolidation.

The split of profit and total comprehensive income between the parent company and NCI should be calculated in a separate working. You should spend time practising and revising this.

In Gold Co, many candidates failed to complete the split of profit for the period, with many omitting it altogether. By not completing the split, candidates immediately lost marks. If you spend a small amount of time laying out the split in the early part of your answer, this will act as a reminder to attempt to complete this later on and in doing so score valuable marks.

When completing the consolidated statement of profit or loss, ensure you get the 'easy' marks out of the question early on. These marks are earned in the initial consolidation process. You should add together all income and expenses (and other comprehensive income if there is any) for the parent and subsidiary. Be careful though, if control of the subsidiary was acquired mid-way through the period it will be necessary to time-apportion the subsidiary's income and expenses and in Gold Co the post-acquisition period is nine months. This is vital in a consolidated profit or loss question and is an area that many candidates often forget.

The fair value adjustment for plant will require an additional consolidation expense in respect of fair value depreciation. This was generally done well by the majority of candidates. However, some candidates omitted this adjustment all together, while others failed to time apportion the depreciation charge for the post acquisition period of 9 months.

Gold Co's investment income included a dividend from an investment in a 40% owned associate company, which should be removed and replaced with a 40% share of the associate's profit for the year of $1.2 million ($3 million × 40%).

Finally, note (6) contained an accounting adjustment in respect of a convertible loan note that was issued by Gold Co on 1 October 20X1. The marking team noted that this adjustment caused confusion for some candidates. This appeared to be because this was an individual company adjustment rather than a traditional group accounting adjustment. You must be prepared for adjustments such as this to be contained within a group accounting question.

Overall, consolidations are an integral part of the FR syllabus. Candidates spend most of their time, it would appear, preparing for a consolidated statement of financial position. There is an equal likelihood that a consolidated statement of profit or loss and other comprehensive income may be tested and therefore it is vital that you prepare for all aspects of the syllabus.

434 CHANG CO

(a) Goodwill

	$000	$000
Consideration:		
Deferred cash (80% × 8,000 × $2.20 × 0.9091)		12,800
Shares (80% × 8,000 × 3/5 × $9)		34,560
		47,360
Non-controlling interest (NCI) (20% × $38,640)		7,728
		55,088
Less: fair value of net assets at acquisition		
Equity shares	8,000	
Retained earnings:		
At 1 October 20X7	28,000	
1 October 20X7–1 January 20X8 ($4,960 × 3/12)	1,240	
Fair value adjustments:		
Plant	1,800	
Contingent liability	(400)	
		(38,640)
Goodwill		**16,448**

(b) Consolidated statement of profit or loss for the year ended 30 September 20X2

		$000
Revenue	(51,680 + (30,400 × 9/12) – 2,700 (**W1**))	71,780
Cost of sales	(30,960 + (20,800 × 9/12) – 2,700 (**W1**) + 150 (W1) + 450 (**W2**))	(44,460)
Gross profit		27,320
Distribution costs	(1,280 + (1,490 × 9/12))	(2,398)
Administrative expenses	(3,040 + (1,870 × 9/12) + 1,000 impair)	(5,442)
Share of profit from associate	(1,000 × 30%)	300
Finance costs	(336 + 68 (**W3**) + 960 (**W4**))	(1,364)
Profit before tax		18,416
Income tax expense	(2,240 + (1,280 × 9/12))	(3,200)
Profit for the year		15,216
Profit attributable to:		
Owners of the parent		14,592
NCI (W5)		624
		15,216

Workings

(W1) Intercompany and PUP

Post-acquisition sales ($300 × 9)	$2,700
PUP (600 × 25%)	$150

(W2) Fair value depreciation on plant = ($1,800/3 × 9/12) = $450

(W3) Convertible loan — calculate liability component

Cashflow		$000	DF 8%	$000
Interest	(5,000 × 6%)	300	3.993	1,198
Principal		5,000	0.681	3,405
			Liability	4,603

Interest charge to SPL	($4,603 × 8%) =	368
Interest already charged		(300)
Additional charge		**68**

(W4) Deferred cash consideration

Unwinding of discount on deferred consideration (see goodwill calculation):

$12,800 × 10% × 9/12 = **$960**

(W5) Non-controlling interest

		$000
Sing Co profit for the year	($4,960 × 9/12)	3,720
PUP (**W1**)		(150)
Fair value depreciation (**W2**)		(450)
Sing Co adjusted profit		3,120
NCI share 20%		**624**

ACCA marking guide

		Marks
(a)	Goodwill	5
(b)	Revenue/COS	5
	Other including NCI	10
Total		**20**

435 ZEFFER CO

Zeffer Group statement of profit or loss for the year ended 30 September 20X3

		$000
Continuing operations		
Revenue	(70,000 + 15,000 – 1,200)	83,800
Cost of sales	(34,000 + 8,800 – 1,200 + 80 (**W1**) + 90 (**W2**))	(41,770)
Gross profit		42,030
Operating expenses	(18,000 + 1,200)	(19,200)
Finance costs	(2,400 + 600)	(3,000)
Profit before tax		19,830
Income tax expense	(4,800 + 800)	(5,600)
Profit for the year from continuing operations		14,230
Profit for the year from discontinued operations (**W5**)		2,600
Total profit for the year		16,830
Profit for the year is attributable to:		
Owners of the parent (balancing figure)		15,544
Non-controlling interest (**W6**)		1,286
		16,830

(W1) Fair value depreciation

	$000
Fair value adjustment over 5 years (400 × $^1/_5$)	**80**

(W2) PUP adjustment

	$000
Remaining goods at 30% margin (300 × 30%)	**90**

(W3) Profit on disposal of subsidiary

	$000	$000
Sale proceeds		6,200
Values at disposal:		
Net assets (5,000 + (4,800 × $^6/_{12}$))	7,400	
Goodwill (**W4**)	450	
Non-controlling interest (7,400 × 25%))	(1,850)	
		(6,000)
Profit on disposal		**200**

(W4) Goodwill

	$000
Fair value of consideration	3,500
Add: NCI (3,800 × 25%)	950
Less: Net assets at acquisition	(3,800)
	650
Less: impairment	(200)
Goodwill at date of disposal	**450**

(W5) Profit from discontinued operation

	$000
Shem profit to date of disposal:	
$4,800 × $^{6}/_{12}$	2,400
Profit on disposal (**W3**)	200
Profit from discontinued operation	**2,600**

(W6) Non-controlling interest

	$000		$000
Shem profit to date of disposal:			
$4,800 × $^{6}/_{12}$	2,400	× 25%	600
Jaco profit for the year	3,600		
Fair value depreciation (**W1**)	(80)		
PUP adjustment (**W2**)	(90)		
	3,430	× 20%	686
Non-controlling interest			**1,286**

ACCA marking guide	
	Marks
Continuing operation	8
Discontinued operation, including profit on disposal	9
Non-controlling interest	3
Total	**20**

436 PERD CO

(a) Consolidated statement of profit or loss and other comprehensive income for Perd Co for the year ended 31 March 20X8

		$000
Revenue	(58,200 + 34,300 – 9,000 intra-group)	83,500
Cost of sales	(34,340 + 20,400 – 9,000 + 600 unrealised profit)	(46,340)
Gross profit		37,160
Operating expenses (**W1**)		(28,270)
Profit from operations		8,890
Investment income	(3,000 – 800 dividend from S Co ($1m × 80%))	2,200
Finance costs	(3,240 + 1,600 + 453 unwinding (**W2**))	(5,293)
Profit before tax		5,797
Tax	(1,560 + 1,480)	(3,040)
Profit for the year		**2,757**
Other comprehensive income		
Gain on revaluation (4,100 + 700)		4,800
Total comprehensive income		**7,557**
Profit attributable to:		
Shareholders of Perd Co		2,639
Non-controlling interests (**W3**)		118
		2,757
Total comprehensive income attributable to:		
Shareholders of Perd Co		7,299
Non-controlling interests (**W3**)		258
		7,557

(b) Total assets

	$000
Perd Co	297,310
Sebastian Co	110,540
Goodwill	3,200
Impairment (400 + 300)	(700)
Unrealised profit	(600)
Intra-group balance	(7,000)
Revaluation gain	4,800
	407,550

(W1) Operating expenses

	$000
Perd Co	18,040
Sebastian Co	7,130
Impairment	300
Fair value depreciation ($3m/15 years × $^{6}/_{12}$)	100
Removal of Sebastian profit on disposal (see below)	5,100
Group profit on disposal (see below)	(2,400)
	28,270

Sebastian Co would have recorded a profit on disposal based on historical cost. At 30 September 20X7, the property would have had a carrying amount of $9.9m, being $11m less 1½ years' depreciation ($11m/15 × 1½ = $1.1m). Therefore, the profit on disposal would have been $5.1m, being $15m less $9.9m.

The group profit on disposal would be based on the carrying amount to the group. The carrying amount of the property in the consolidated financial statements at 30 September 20X7 would have been $12.6m ($14m less 1½ years' depreciation). Therefore, the profit on disposal will be $2.4m ($15m less $12.6m).

(W2) Unwinding discount

	$000
$7.547m × 6%	453

(W3) Non-controlling interest

	Adjusted	**NCI @ 20%**
Sebastian Co adjusted performance	$000	$000
Profit for the year	3,690	
Adjusted profit on disposal ($5.1m – $2.4m)	(2,700)	
Fair value depreciation	(100)	
Goodwill impairment	(300)	
Adjusted profit for the year	590	**118**
Revaluation gain	700	
Total comprehensive income	1,290	**258**

ACCA marking guide		
		Marks
(a)	Revenue/Cost of sales	3½
	Other income and expenses	8
	Profit/OCI appropriation	3½
		15
(b)	Total assets	5
Total		**20**

Extract from examiners' report (for detailed report see ACCA website)

When asked to prepare a consolidated statement of profit or loss and other comprehensive income (SPLOCI) the FR examining team recommend that you set up the proforma for the consolidation immediately, and also include the split between the parent shareholders and NCI for both profit and total comprehensive income (TCI). The most common omission in a SPLOCI is this split of profit and this can often result in a significant number of marks being lost.

By not completing the split in Perd Co, candidates immediately lost marks. If you spend a small amount of time laying out the split in the early part of your answer, this will act as a reminder to attempt to complete this later and, in doing so, help score valuable marks.

For candidates that did attempt the split, many failed to split both the profit for the year and the TCI. Some candidates incorrectly took 80%:20% of the profit for the year and the total comprehensive income. As a simpler approach, NCI must be calculated and the parent share is always a balancing amount. This is an area that candidates must revise and practise.

You should add together all income and expenses and other comprehensive income for the parent and subsidiary. Be careful though, it is extremely important to establish how long you have had control over the subsidiary company. If control of the subsidiary was acquired mid-way through the period, it will be necessary to time apportion the subsidiary's income and expenses only. For Perd Co, however, the subsidiary was acquired two years ago and so the results of Sebastian Co did not need to be time apportioned.

Despite commentary in previous examiner reports, several candidates continue to use proportional consolidation, incorporating 80% of Sebastian Co's income, expenses and other comprehensive income. This is fundamentally incorrect and relates to the basic consolidation marks. Do not proportionately consolidate the results of the subsidiary based on ownership.

Unwinding of the discount

This transaction was relatively straightforward and candidates just needed to calculate 6% of the opening liability and include it as a finance cost. A small number of candidates attempted to discount the $7.547m incorrectly before unwinding. This wasted time and resulted in those candidates not achieving full marks for this part of the question.

Impairments

In the SPLOCI, candidates needed to include the $300,000 expense for the current year which most did correctly. However, there were several candidates that incorrectly included both impairments at $700,000 or the $400,000.

Fair value depreciation

Many candidates failed to time apportion the depreciation, despite specifically being told depreciation is charged on a pro-rata basis.

Property disposal

The examining team noted that many candidates did not attempt the disposal calculations and, for those that did, they simply calculated the subsidiary gain or the group gain (rather than both). Another common mistake when the gain(s) was/ were calculated was to include the adjustment the wrong way (i.e., as a loss).

Property revaluation

The examining team noted that many candidates are still unsure as to what should and shouldn't be included in other comprehensive income. Note (5) indicated that group assets were revalued at the reporting date and the gains were given for both Perd Co and Sebastian Co. A small number of candidates correctly included both the $4.1m and the $0.7m in other comprehensive income. There were many instances where the revaluation gains were omitted completely and several candidates incorrectly included 80% of Sebastian Co's gain only.

Dividend

The dividend paid by Sebastian Co in note (6) was $1m and Perd Co only received 80% of this, so $800,000 should be eliminated from investment income. A significant number of candidates removed the full $1m and, therefore, did not earn the full mark available. Some credit for elimination was still awarded.

Consolidations are an integral part of the FR syllabus. The examining team note that performance on a consolidated statement of financial position is generally better than a consolidated SPLOCI. There is an equal likelihood that a consolidated SPLOCI may be tested and, therefore, it is vital that you prepare for all aspects of the syllabus.

To answer part (b) of the question, candidates needed to determine which notes from the further information would have an impact on the consolidated assets. This included both current and non-current assets.

Performance on this part of the question was mixed. Disappointingly, many candidates did not attempt this part of the question and, for others that did, it was largely incomplete. This may indicate poor time management and so candidates are advised to spend the appropriate amount of time on each part of the question.

Working through the notes in order, candidates should consider if any of the information would adjust the consolidated total assets:

Note (1) simply required candidates to unwind the discount on the deferred consideration and this would have no impact on assets.

Note (2) required candidates to include the goodwill of $3.2m in total assets – this was generally done well. The impairment charge would reduce the goodwill asset and this, therefore, reduced total assets.

Most candidates attempted to adjust total assets for the fair value depreciation and the disposal outlined in note (3). This was not required as the disposal had taken place during the year and had already been accounted for in the financial statements of Sebastian Co.

The adjustment for unrealised profit in note (4) would reduce inventories in the consolidated statement of financial position and so this would be deducted from total assets. For candidates that did adjust for the unrealised profit, it was common to see it being added to total assets rather than deducted. Note (4) also contained an intra-group receivable and payable that needed to be eliminated from receivables.

Finally, many candidates did correctly adjust for the revaluation gains and added these onto the total consolidated assets. The marks were consistent with the adjustments made to other comprehensive income in part (a) and own figure marks were awarded for this adjustment.

437 DOBRY

	$
Non-current assets:	
Property, plant and equipment	508,000
(240,000 + 130,000 + 120,000 + 24,000 (**W2**) – 6,000 (**W2**))	
Goodwill (**W3**)	141,000
Current assets	756,500
(526,000 + 170,000 + 80,000 – 1,500 (**W2**) – 18,000 (inter-co))	
	1,405,500
Ordinary $1 share capital	500,000
Revaluation surplus (**W6**)	12,000
Retained earnings (**W5**)	270,700
	782,700
Non-controlling interest (**W4**)	87,600
Current liabilities	535,200
(308,000 + 90,000 + 68,000 – 18,000 (inter-co) + 80,000 (**W3**) + 7,200 (**W5**))	
	1,405,500

Workings

(W1) Group structure

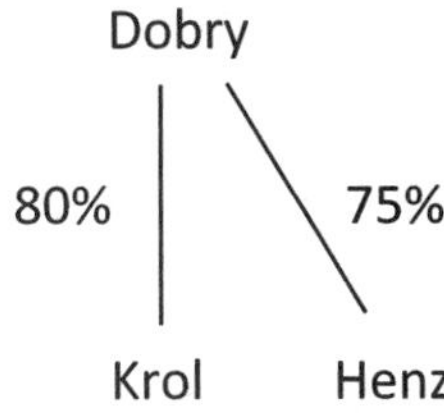

(W2) Net assets

Krol	**At acquisition**	**At reporting date**	**Post-acquisition**
	$	$	$
Share capital	100,000	100,000	
Revaluation surplus	15,000	30,000	15,000
Retained earnings	30,000	80,000	50,000
PUP adjustment		(1,500)	(1,500)
(18,000 × $^{20}/_{120}$ × ½)			
	145,000	208,500	63,500

Note that post-acquisition reserves are split between revaluation surplus of $15,000 and retained earnings of $48,500 ($50,000 – $1,500).

Henz	**At acquisition**	**At reporting date**	**Post-acquisition**
	$	$	$
Share capital	100,000	100,000	
Retained earnings	16,000	32,000	16,000
Fair value adjustment	24,000	24,000	
Fair value depreciation (24,000 × ¼)		(6,000)	(6000)
	140,000	150,000	10,000

(W3) Goodwill

	Krol	**Henz**
	$	$
Fair value of parent consideration:		
Cash	180,000	100,000
Deferred cash (87,200 × $^1/_{1.09}$)		80,000
Non-controlling interest	39,000	35,000
Fair value / $140,000 (**W2**) × 25%		
Net assets (**W2**)	(145,000)	(140,000)
Goodwill on acquisition	74,000	75,000
Impairment	(8,000)	–
	66,000	75,000

Total goodwill = $66,000 + $75,000 = **$141,000**

(W4) Non-controlling interest

	Krol	**Henz**
	$	$
Value on acquisition (**W3**)	39,000	35,000
Post-acquisition reserves:		
Krol $63,500 (**W2**) × 20%	12,700	
Henz $10,000 (**W2**) × 25%		2,500
Impairment: $8,000 × 20%	(1,600)	–
	50,100	37,500

Note that the goodwill for Henz Co may have been calculated as net assets × NCI%, $150,000 × 25% = **$37,500.**

Total non-controlling interest = $50,100 + $37,500 = **$87,600.**

(W5) Group retained earnings

	$
Dobry: 100%	238,000
Krol: $48,500 (**W2**) × 80%	38,800
Henz: $10,000 (**W2**) × 75%	7,500
Impairment: $8,000 × 80%	(6,400)
Unwind discount: $80,000 (**W3**) × 9%	(7,200)
	270,700

(W6) Group revaluation surplus

	$
Krol: $15,000 (**W2**) × 80%	**12,000**

ACCA marking guide	
	Marks
Property, plant and equipment	1½
Goodwill	6½
Current assets	1½
Equity share capital	½
Revaluation surplus	½
Retained earnings	4
Non-controlling interest	4
Current liabilities	2
Total	**20**

ANALYSING FINANCIAL STATEMENTS

438 WOODBANK

Key answer tips

This style of question is naturally time consuming – ensure you answer all parts of the question and do not spend too much time calculating ratios. When interpreting the results in part (b) be wary of making generalisations – you must ensure that you relate it to the information given in the question. Presentation is also crucial in part (b), so make it easy for the marker to read by using short paragraphs and spaces between paragraphs. The highlighted words are key phrases that markers are looking for.

(a) Note: Figures in the calculations of the ratios are in $million

	20X4 Excluding Shaw	**20X3**	**20X4**
Return on capital employed (ROCE)	13%	10.5%	12.0%
(profit before interest and tax/year-end total assets less current liabilities)	(13/100)		
Net asset (equal to capital employed) turnover	1.2 times (120/100)	1.16 times	1.0 times
Gross profit margin	20% (24/120)	22.0%	22.0%
Profit before interest and tax margin	10.8% (13/120)	9.1%	12.0%
Current ratio	–	1.7:1	1.08:1
Gearing (debt/(debt + equity))	–	5.3%	36.7%

(b) Analysis of the comparative financial performance and position of Woodbank for the year ended 31 March 20X4

Introduction

When comparing current performance and position with the previous year (or years), using trend analysis, it is necessary to take into account the effect of any circumstances which may create an inconsistency in the comparison. In the case of Woodbank, the purchase of Shaw is an example of such an inconsistency.

20X4's figures include, for a three-month period, the operating results of Shaw, and Woodbank's statement of financial position includes all of Shaw's net assets (including goodwill) together with the additional 10% loan notes used to finance the purchase of Shaw. None of these items were included in the 20X3 financial statements.

The net assets of Shaw when purchased were $50 million, which represents one third of Woodbank's net assets (capital employed) as at 31 March 20X4. It therefore represents a major investment for Woodbank and any analysis necessitates careful consideration of its impact.

Profitability

ROCE is considered by many analysts to be the most important profitability ratio. A ROCE of 12.0% in 20X4, compared to 10.5% in 20X3, represents a creditable 14.3% (12.0 – 10.5)/10.5) improvement in profitability.

When ROCE is calculated excluding the contribution from Shaw, at 13.0%, it shows an even more favourable performance. Although this comparison (13.0% from 10.5%) is valid, it would seem to imply that the purchase of Shaw has had a detrimental effect on Woodbank's ROCE.

However, caution is needed when interpreting this information as ROCE compares the return (profit for a period) to the capital employed (equivalent to net assets at a single point in time).

In the case of Woodbank, the statement of profit or loss only includes three months' results from Shaw whereas the statement of financial position includes all of Shaw's net assets, which is inconsistent.

It would be fair to speculate that in future years, when a full year's results from Shaw are reported, the ROCE effect of Shaw will be favourable.

Indeed, assuming a continuation of Shaw's current level of performance, profit in a full year could be \$20 million. On an investment of \$50 million, this represents a ROCE of 40% (based on the initial capital employed) which is much higher than Woodbank's pre-existing business.

The cause of the improvement in ROCE is revealed by consideration of the secondary profitability ratios: asset turnover and profit margins. For Woodbank this reveals a complicated picture.

Woodbank's results, as reported, show that it is the increase in the profit before interest and tax margin (12.0% from 9.1%) which is responsible for the improvement in ROCE, as the asset turnover has actually decreased (1.0 times from 1.16 times) and gross profit is exactly the same in both years (at 22.0%).

When the effect of the purchase of Shaw is excluded the position changes. The overall improvement in ROCE (13.0% from 10.5%) is caused by both an increase in profit margin (at the before interest and tax level, at 10.8% from 9.1 %), despite a fall in gross profit (20.0% from 22.0%) and a very slight improvement in asset turnover (1.2 times from 1.16 times). This means that the purchase of Shaw has improved Woodbank's overall profit margins, but caused a fall in asset turnover.

Again, as with the ROCE, this is misleading because the calculation of asset turnover only includes three months' revenue from Shaw, but all of its net assets. When a full year of Shaw's results is reported, asset turnover will be much improved (assuming its three-month performance is continued).

Liquidity

The liquidity position, as measured by the current ratio, has fallen considerably in 20X4 and is a cause for concern.

At 1.67:1 in 20X3, it was within the acceptable range (normally between 1.5:1 and 2.0:1) but the 20X4 ratio of 1.08:1 is very low, indeed it is more like that which would be expected for the quick ratio (acid test).

Without needing to calculate the component ratios of the current ratio (for inventory, receivables and payables), it can be seen from the statements of financial position that the main causes of the deterioration in the liquidity position are the reduction in the cash (bank) position and the dramatic increase in trade payables. The bank balance has fallen by $4.5 million (5,000 – 500) and the trade payables have increased by $8 million.

An analysis of the movement in the retained earnings shows that Woodbank paid a dividend of $5.5 million (10,000 + 10,500 – 15,000) or 6.88 cents per share. It could be argued that during a period of expansion, with demands on cash flow, dividends could be suspended or heavily curtailed.

Had no dividend been paid, the 20X4 bank balance would be $6.0 million and the current ratio would have been 1.3:1 ((27,000 + 5,500):25,000). This would be still on the low side, but much more reassuring to credit suppliers than the reported ratio of 1.08:1.

Gearing

Woodbank has gone from a position of very modest gearing at 5.3% in 20X3 to 36.7% in 20X4. This has largely been caused by the issue of the additional 10% loan notes to finance the purchase of Shaw.

Arguably, it might have been better if some of the finance had been raised from a share issue, but the level of gearing is still acceptable and the financing cost of 10% should be more than covered by the prospect of future high returns from Shaw, thus benefiting shareholders overall.

Conclusion

The overall operating performance of Woodbank has improved during the period (although the gross profit margin on sales other than those made by Shaw has fallen) and this should be even more marked next year when a full year's results from Shaw will be reported (assuming that Shaw can maintain its current performance). The changes in the financial position, particularly liquidity, are less favourable and call into question the current dividend policy. Gearing has increased substantially, due to the financing of the purchase of Shaw but it is still acceptable and has benefited shareholders. It is interesting to note that of the $50 million purchase price, $30 million of this is represented by goodwill. Although this may seem high, Shaw is certainly delivering in terms of generating revenue with good profit margins.

(c) Below are a number of issues/items of information in relation to the acquisition of Shaw which would be useful in producing a better analysis of Woodbank.

- Did the acquisition of Shaw include any consideration payable dependent on Shaw's results? If so, this should be recorded as a liability at its fair value.
- Shaw's statement of financial position would be useful. This would be useful in assessing the working capital cycle of Shaw compared to Woodbank, as the Woodbank group has a low cash balance as at 31 March 20X4.
- Shaw's statement of cash flows would be useful (as would the statement of cash flow for Woodbank). This would help assess the reasons for the significant fall in cash during the year.
- Any one-off costs associated with the acquisition of Shaw, such as professional fees. These will have been expensed and will have affected the profit margins in the year.

- Whether there are any potential savings to be made following the acquisition of Shaw, such as reduction in staff costs or shared properties. These may involve one-off costs such as redundancies or lease termination costs but could lead to improved margins in future periods.
- The nature of Shaw's business should be looked at in comparison to Woodbank. It will be useful to know if Shaw was a competitor of Woodbank, or maybe a supplier of goods to Woodbank. This would help with further analysis regarding market share or the potential future cost of goods if Shaw was either of these.
- A breakdown of Shaw's major customers would be useful, to see if any have left following the change of ownership in Shaw.

ACCA marking guide

			Marks
(a)	1 mark per ratio	**Maximum**	**4**
(b)	1 mark per relevant point to maximum		12
(c)	1 mark per relevant point to maximum		4
Total			**20**

439 HYDAN

(a) For comparison

	Hydan adjusted	Hydan as reported	Sector average
Return on equity (ROE)	21.7%	47.1%	22.0%
Net asset turnover	1.75 times	2.36 times	1.67 times
Gross profit margin	28.6%	35.7%	30.0%
Net profit margin	9.3%	20.0%	12.0%

Hydan's adjusted ratios

On the assumption that after the purchase of Hydan, the favourable effects of the transactions with other businesses owned by the family would not occur, the following adjustments to the statement of profit or loss should be made:

	$000
Cost of sales (45,000/0.9)	50,000
Directors' remuneration	2,500
Loan interest (10% × 10,000)	1,000
These adjustments would give a revised statement of profit or loss:	
Revenue	70,000
Cost of sales	(50,000)
Gross profit	20,000
Operating costs	(7,000)
Directors' remuneration	(2,500)
Loan interest	(1,000)
Profit before tax	9,500
Income tax expense	(3,000)

Profit for the year		6,500

In the statement of financial position:

Equity would be the purchase price of Hydan (per question)		30,000
The commercial loan (replacing the directors' loan) would now be debt		10,000
From these figures the adjusted ratios above are calculated as:		
Return on equity	((6,500 /30,000) × 100)	21.7%
Net asset turnover	(70,000/(30,000 + 10,000))	1.75 times
Gross profit margin	((20,000)/70,000) × 100)	28.6%
Net profit margin	((6,500/70,000) × 100)	9.30%

(b) An analysis of Hydan's ratios based on the financial statements provided reveals a strong position, particularly in relation to profitability when compared to other businesses in this retail sector. Hydan has a very high ROE which is a product of higher-than-average profit margins (at both the gross and net profit level) and a significantly higher net asset turnover. Thus, on the face of it, Hydan is managing to achieve higher prices (or reduced cost of sales), has better control of overheads and is using its net assets more efficiently in terms of generating revenue.

However, when adjustments are made for the effects of its favourable transactions with other businesses owned by the family, the position changes somewhat. The effect of purchasing its inventory from another family-owned supplier at favourable market prices means that its reported gross profit percentage of 35.7% is flattering. Had these purchases been made at market prices, it would fall to 28.6% which is below the sector average of 30.0%. The effects of the favourable inventory purchases carry through to net profit. Based on Xpand's estimate of future directors' remuneration, it would seem the existing directors of Hydan are not charging commercial rates for their remuneration. When Xpand replaces the board of Hydan, it will have to increase directors' remuneration by $1.5 million. Additionally, when the interest free directors' loans are replaced with a commercial loan, with interest at 10% per annum, this would reduce net profit by a further $1 million. The accumulation of these adjustments means that the ROE which Xpand should expect would be 21.7% (rather than the reported 47.1%) which is almost exactly in line with the sector average of 22.0%.

In a similar vein, when the asset turnover is calculated based on the equity purchase price and the commercial loan (equating to net assets), it falls from 2.36 times to 1.75 times which is above, but much closer to, the sector average of 1.67 times. In summary, Hydan's adjusted results would still be slightly ahead of the sector averages in most areas and may well justify the anticipated purchase price of $30 million. However, Hydan will be nowhere near the excellently performing business suggested by the reported figures and Xpand needs to exercise a degree of caution in its negotiations.

(c) The consolidated financial statements of Lodan are of little value when trying to assess the performance and financial position of its subsidiary, Hydan. Therefore the main source of information on which to base any investment decision would be Hydan's own entity financial statements. However, where an entity is part of a group, there is the potential for the financial statements to have been subject to the influence of related-party transactions. In the case of Hydan, there has been a considerable amount of post-acquisition trading with Lodan and, because of the related-party relationship, it appears that this trading is not at arm's length (i.e. not at commercial rates).

There may be other aspects of the relationship where Lodan gives Hydan a benefit that may not have happened had Hydan not been part of the group, e.g. access to technology/research, cheap finance.

The operations of Hydan may now be centralised and run by Lodan. If Lodan doesn't allocate some of these costs to Hydan then Hydan's expenses will be understated. It could also be difficult for a purchaser to assess whether additional property would be required if Hydan share this with other group entities.

The main concern is that any information about the 'benefits' Lodan may have passed on to Hydan through related party transactions is difficult to obtain from published sources. It may be that Lodan would deliberately 'flatter' Hydan's financial statements specifically in order to obtain a high sale price and a prospective purchaser would not necessarily be able to determine that this had happened from either the consolidated or entity financial statements. There are suggestions of this in the fact that Hydan's directors are not charging market rates for their remuneration and are giving interest-free loans.

ACCA marking guide		
		Marks
(a)	1½ marks per ratio	6
(b)	1 mark per valid point. A good answer must emphasise the different interpretation when using adjusted figures	9
(c)	1 mark per valid point, emphasising potential distortion of true trading performance	5
Total		**20**

440 YOGI

Note: References to 20X5 and 20X4 refer to the periods ended 31 March 20X5 and 20X4 respectively.

(a) Calculation of equivalent ratios (figures in $000):

	(i) 20X4 excluding division	**(ii) 20X5 as reported**	**20X4 per question**
Gross profit margin ((20,000 – 8,000)/(50,000 – 18,000) × 100)	37.5%	33.3%	40.0%
Operating profit margin ((11,800 – 5,800)/32,000 × 100)	18.8%	10.3%	23.6%
Return on capital employed (ROCE) ((11,800 – 5,800)/(29,200 – 7,200 – 7,000 see below) × 100)	40.0%	21.8%	53.6%
Net asset turnover (32,000/15,000)	2.13 times	2.12 times	2.27 times

Note: The capital employed in the division sold at 31 March 20X4 was $7 million ($8 million sale proceeds less $1 million profit on sale).

The figures for the calculations of 20X4's adjusted ratios (i.e. excluding the effects of the sale of the division) are given in brackets, the figures for 20X5 are derived from the equivalent figures in the question. However, the operating profit margin and ROCE calculations exclude the profit from the sale of the division (as stated in the requirement) as it is a 'one-off' item.

(b) The most relevant comparison is the 20X5 results (excluding the profit on disposal of the division) with the results of 20X4 (excluding the results of the division), otherwise like is not being compared with like.

Profitability

Although comparative sales have increased (excluding the effect of the sale of the division) by $4 million (36,000 – 32,000), equivalent to 12.5%, the gross profit margin has fallen considerably (from 37.5% in 20X4 down to 33.3% in 20X5) and this deterioration has been compounded by the sale of the division, which was the most profitable part of the business (which earned a gross profit margin of 44.4% (8/18)). The deterioration of the operating profit margin (from 18.8% in 20X4 down to 10.3% in 20X5) is largely due to poor gross profit margins, but operating expenses are proportionately higher (as a percentage of sales) in 20X5 (23.0% compared to 18.8%) which has further reduced profitability. This is due to higher administrative expenses (as distribution costs have fallen), perhaps relating to the sale of the division.

Yogi's performance as measured by ROCE has deteriorated dramatically from 40.0% in 20X4 (as adjusted) to only 21.8% in 20X5. As the net asset turnover has remained broadly the same at 2.1 times (rounded), it is the fall in the operating profit which is responsible for the overall deterioration in performance. Whilst it is true that Yogi has sold the most profitable part of its business, this does not explain why the 20X5 results have deteriorated so much (by definition the adjusted 20X4 figures exclude the favourable results of the division). Consequently, Yogi's management need to investigate why profit margins have fallen in 20X5. It may be that customers of the sold division also bought (more profitable) goods from Yogi's remaining business and they have taken their custom to the new owners of the division, or it may be related to external issues which are also being experienced by other businesses such as an economic recession. A study of industry sector average ratios could reveal this.

Other issues

It is very questionable to have offered shareholders such a high dividend (half of the disposal proceeds) to persuade them to vote for the disposal. At $4 million (4,000 + 3,000 – 3,000, i.e. the movement on retained earnings or 10 million shares at 40 cents) the dividend represents double the profit for the year of $2 million (3,000 – 1,000) if the gain on the disposal is excluded. Another effect of the disposal is that Yogi appears to have used the other $4 million (after paying the dividend) from the disposal proceeds to pay down half of the 10% loan notes. This has reduced finance costs and interest cover, but, as the finance cost at 10% is much lower than the 20X5 ROCE of 21.8%, it will have had a detrimental effect on overall profit available to shareholders.

Summary

In retrospect, it may have been unwise for Yogi to sell the most profitable part of its business at what appears to be a very low price. It has coincided with a remarkable deterioration in profitability (not solely due to the sale) and the proceeds of the disposal have not been used to replace capacity or improve long-term prospects. By returning a substantial proportion of the sale proceeds to shareholders, it represents a downsizing of the business.

(c) Although the sports club is a not-for-profit organisation, the request for a loan is a commercial activity that should be decided on according to similar criteria as would be used for other profit-orientated entities.

The main aspect of granting a loan is how secure the loan would be. To this extent a form of capital gearing ratio should be calculated, say existing long-term borrowings to net assets (i.e. total assets less current liabilities). Clearly if this ratio is high, further borrowing would be at an increased risk. The secondary aspect is to measure the sports club's ability to repay the interest (and ultimately the principal) on the loan. This may be determined from information in the statement of comprehensive income. A form of interest cover should be calculated, say the excess of income over expenditure (broadly the equivalent of profit) compared to (the forecast) interest payments. The higher this ratio the less risk of interest default. The calculations would be made for all four years to ascertain any trends that may indicate a deterioration or improvement in these ratios. As with other profit-oriented entities the nature and trend of the income should be investigated: for example, are the club's sources of income increasing or decreasing, does the reported income contain 'one-off' donations (which may not be recurring) etc? Also matters such as the market value of, and existing prior charges against, any assets intended to be used as security for the loan would be relevant to the lender's decision-making process. It may also be possible that the sports club's governing body (perhaps the trustees) may be willing to give a personal guarantee for the loan.

ACCA marking guide			
			Marks
(a)	(i) and (ii)	Gross profit margin	1
		Operating profit margin	1½
		Return on capital employed	1½
		Net asset turnover	1
			5
(b)	1 mark per point (a good answer must consider the effect of the sale of the division)		**10**
(c)	1 mark per point		**5**
Total			**20**

441 XPAND

(a) Missing ratios for Kovert:

Return on year-end capital employed (ROCE) (4,900/(5,600 + 9,200 + 1,000 × 100)	31.0%
Profit margin (before interest and tax) (4,900/40,000 × 100)	12.3%
Trade payables' payment period (2,100/32,800 × 365)	23 days
Gearing (debt/(debt + equity)) (10,200/15,800 × 100)	64.6%

(b) Assessment of the comparative performance and financial position of Kandid and Kovert for the year ended 30 September 20X5

Introduction

This assessment of the two entities will look at the areas of profitability, liquidity and gearing with reference to some differences which may make the comparison of the reported figures potentially invalid.

Profitability

ROCE is usually considered as the most important measure of profitability and is often described as a measure of management's overall efficiency in the use of the assets at its disposal. The ROCE of 62.5% of Kandid is far superior (more than double) to the 31.0% return achieved by Kovert. This superior return of Kandid can be analysed into its component parts of profit margin and asset turnover and in both of these areas Kandid's performance is better than that of Kovert. Kandid is generating $3.30 for every dollar invested, compared to only $2.50 per dollar invested in Kovert and earning a profit margin of 19.0% compared to just 12.3% by Kovert. Additionally, Kandid's gross profit margin at 24% is a third (6%/18%) higher than the 18% of Kovert. This may be, at least in part, due to marketing policy. Kovert may be deliberately charging lower selling prices in order to generate greater revenue. This is evidenced by Kovert's turnover of $40 million compared to only $25 million for Kandid. The superior gross margin of Kandid continues into the operating profit level indicating that Kandid has better control of its overheads.

There are, however, a number of areas relating to the capital employed which may bring this superiority into question. Kandid has deducted the receipt of a government grant directly from the carrying amount of the related plant, which is allowed but is rather unusual. Normally, plant is shown gross less accumulated depreciation and related government grants are shown as a separate deferred credit. It also appears that Kandid rents its property whereas Kovert has purchased its property (and indeed revalued it which has increased its capital employed). Kandid also holds proportionately less inventory and receivables than Kovert. Whilst these factors may not necessarily result in a higher profit for Kandid (e.g. property rental may be higher than the equivalent depreciation of property), they would act to give Kandid lower net assets, and thus lower capital employed and in turn a higher ROCE than Kovert.

Bearing in mind these differences, it may be more helpful if Xpand were to calculate a return on its potential equity investment (ROE) of $12 million as this would be more relevant should it acquire either of the entities. Using profit after tax, Kandid's ROE would be 30% (3,600/12,000 × 100) whereas Kovert's ROE would be 25% (3,000/12,000). This still supports Kandid's superior return, but this introduces further differences. Both entities have $5 million in loan notes but the interest rate on Kandid's loan is only 5% compared to 10% for Kovert, presumably this reflects the difference in the creditworthiness of the two entities which is something that Xpand should take note of. There also appears to be a favourable tax discrepancy with Kandid paying a nominal rate of tax on its profit of 20% compared with 25% paid by Kovert. This may be due to be adjustments relating to previous years' profits or other tax issues. If Kandid had a comparable finance cost and tax rate to Kovert, its ROE would be nearer that of Kovert.

Liquidity

The given ratios show that both entities have healthy liquidity positions. Kandid's current ratio is slightly higher than Kovert's, perhaps too high. This seems to be down to holding more cash than Kovert as it has better inventory and receivables control, though arguably the current lease liability of Kovert should not be included in this ratio for comparative purposes. The individual components of the current ratio could suggest that Kovert holds a greater range of inventory, perhaps enabling it to achieve more sales, and the relatively high receivables collection period could be indicative of an uncollectable customer balance which should have been written off, or may just be due to poor credit control.

Gearing

At around 65%, both entities are highly geared. The relatively low equity, particularly retained earnings, may be due to the entities having a policy of paying most of their earnings as dividends. Kovert's high gearing is in part due to its policy of using leases to acquire its plant. Xpand should be aware that, for both entities, the $5 million loans are due for repayment in the near future which will represent a substantial further cash outlay on top of the purchase price it may pay.

Summary

Although both entities operate in a same industry sector and have a similar level of after-tax profits, and indeed have the same indicative valuation, they would represent very different investments. Kovert's revenue is over 60% (15,000/25,000 × 100) higher than that of Kandid, it is financed by high levels of debt (loans and leases), and it also owns, rather than rents, its property. Another point of note is that Kovert's plant is 80% depreciated and will need replacement in the near future, with consequent financing implications. Ultimately, the investment decision may be determined by Xpand's attitude to risk and how well each investment would fit in with existing activities and management structure.

(c) Basing an investment decision solely on one year's summarised financial statements is fraught with danger. Below are a number of issues and items of information to which Xpand may wish to seek clarification before making an offer.

General:

- in addition to using different strategies (e.g. buying property or renting it, targeting low mark-up/high volume sales), the two entities may use different accounting policies
- the availability of non-published forward-looking information such as profit forecasts, capital commitments and the size of orders on the books (providing this information should not be unreasonable if the shareholders are receptive to a takeover)
- is either entity established or a relatively young and growing entity, with more risk, but potentially more reward?

Specific:

- as noted above, the owned assets of Kovert are nearing the end of their useful life. Will these need replacing soon, or have they already been replaced by the leased assets?
- how much of the profit is due to the reputation or contacts of the current management and would they continue in their role after a takeover (and indeed would Xpand want this or would it prefer to use its own managers)?
- the fair value of the assets, compared to their carrying amounts, which will impact on the calculation of goodwill.

ACCA marking guide		
		Marks
(a)	1 mark per ratio	4
(b)	1 mark per value point up to	12
(c)	1 mark per valid point up to	4
Total		**20**

442 PITCARN

(a) Ratios for the year ended 31 March 20X6

Gross profit margin	30%	(28,200/94,000) × 100
Operating margin	6%	(5,600/94,000) × 100
Interest cover	2.9 times	(5,600/(1,900)

In producing the consolidated information, Sitor must be added in for the year, with adjustments made to remove the intra-group sale, rent, interest and dividend.

	20X6
	$000
Revenue (86,000 + 16,000 – 8,000 intra-group)	94,000
Cost of sales (63,400 + 10,400 – 8,000 intra-group)	(65,800)
Gross profit	28,200
Other income (3,400 – 300 rent – 1,000 dividend – 500 interest)	1,600
Operating expenses (21,300 + 3,200 – 300 rent)	(24,200)
Profit from operations	5,600
Finance costs (1,500 + 900 – 500 intra-group)	(1,900)

(b) Looking at the figures calculated for the Pitcarn group, it seems that performance has deteriorated in terms of revenue, margins and interest cover.

This would suggest that the disposal of Sitor is a mistake, as the group appear to be performing worse without Sitor than when Sitor was included as a subsidiary.

Looking at Sitor's individual results appears to confirm this, as Sitor has profit margins which are higher than the rest of the group, both in terms of gross and operating margin.

A closer examination of Sitor's results highlights an issue to be aware of. Half of Sitor's revenue is made by selling to Pitcarn, and this is done at an extremely high margin of 40%. This is much higher than the margin of 35% made overall, and means that the other half of Sitor's sales must be made at a margin of 30%. This means that the external sales of Sitor are actually made at the same gross margin as the rest of the group.

It is possible that Pitcarn deliberately purchased goods from Sitor at an inflated price in order to demonstrate a stronger performance in Sitor in order to achieve a good selling price.

While this allowed, it highlights the problem with analysing an entity's performance based on its individual financial statements if it is part of a group, as prices can be manipulated within the group to artificially inflate the performance of one part.

A similar fear arises in respect of the operating margin. Sitor uses Pitcarn's properties, and is paying a lower rate than the market rate of rent. This will again artificially inflate the margin made by Sitor, as Pitcarn bear the majority of the property costs without recharging an accurate rate of rent.

It appears that Pitcarn have suffered lower margins in order to make the margins look better in Sitor by paying a high price for goods and not charging a market rate of rent. Pitcarn has taken a further $1.5 million cash out of Sitor during the year, through the receipt of a $1 million dividend and $500,000 interest. The loan agreement should be investigated further in order to assess if the interest charged was at market rates or not.

Following the disposal of Sitor, Pitcarn will lose at least $1.3 million of income through no longer obtaining a dividend or rent from the properties. For a more detailed analysis of future prospects, it will be important to speak to Pitcarn regarding the excess office space and whether there are plans to utilise it themselves or to rent it to a third party. The loan agreement with Sitor should also be examined to see if this will change following the sale. It may be that the interest rate increases now Sitor is no longer in the group, or the loan may need repaying by the new Sitor owners.

The one area where Sitor underperformed relative to the rest of the Pitcarn group is in terms of interest cover, with profits able to cover interest less times. Again, a review of the loan agreement with Pitcarn will be able to assess if this interest rate is at market rate, as Pitcarn may be charging a higher rate of interest than market rates in exchange for the cheaper rent and higher priced goods.

Examination should also be made as to whether Pitcarn will still need Sitor to supply goods. If so, supplies may be harder to obtain now that Sitor is no longer in the group.

Overall, the sale of Sitor appears to be a reasonable move. Whilst Sitor does appear to be making good profits, when the goods and rent with Pitcarn are adjusted to market values it is likely that Sitor would not be making significant profits. As long as Pitcarn is not reliant on Sitor as a supplier, this seems to be a reasonable move and one which may free up space in the premises to pursue more lucrative options.

(c) Gain/loss on disposal

	$000	$000
Proceeds		25,000
Net assets at disposal	17,000	
(10,000 share capital + 7,000 retained earnings)		
Goodwill at disposal (W1)	7,000	
Non-controlling interest at disposal (W2)	(3,800)	
		(20,200)
Gain on disposal		**4,800**

Workings

(W1) Goodwill

	$000
Consideration	17,000
NCI at acquisition	3,000
Net assets at acquisition	(13,000)
(10,000 share capital + 3,000 retained earnings)	
Goodwill at acquisition	7,000

(W2) Non-controlling interest at disposal

	$000
NCI at acquisition	3,000
NCI share of Sitor's post acquisition retained earnings (20% × (7,000 – 3,000))	800
Non-controlling interest at disposal	3,800

443 GREGORY

(a) Note: References to 20X6 and 20X5 are to the years ending 31 March 20X6 and 20X5 respectively.

Comment (1)

"I see the profit for the year has increased by $1m which is up 20% on last year, but I thought it would be more as Tamsin was supposed to be very profitable."

There are two issues with this statement: first, last year's profit is not comparable with the current year's profit because in 20X5 Gregory was a single entity and in 20X6 it is now a group with a subsidiary. A second issue is that the consolidated statement of profit or loss for the year ended 31 March 20X6 only includes six months of the results of Tamsin, and, assuming Tamsin is profitable, future results will include a full year's profit. This latter point may, at least in part, mitigate the CEO's disappointment.

Comment (2)

"I have calculated the EPS for 20X6 at 13 cents (6, 000/46, 000 × 100 shares) and at 12.5 cents for 20X5 (5,000/40, 000 × 100) and, although the profit has increased 20%, our EPS has barely changed."

The stated EPS calculation for 20X6 is incorrect for two reasons: first, it is the profit attributable to only the equity shareholders of the parent which should be used and second the 6 million new shares were only in issue for six months and should be weighted by $^6/_{12}$. Thus, the correct EPS for 20X6 is 13.3 cents (5,700/43,000 × 100). This gives an increase of 6% (13.3 – 12.5)/12.5) on 20X5 EPS which is still less than the increase in profit. The reason why the EPS may not have increased in line with reported profit is that the acquisition was financed by a share exchange which increased the number of shares in issue. Thus the EPS takes account of the additional consideration used to generate profit, whereas the trend of absolute profit does not take additional consideration into account. This is why the EPS is often said to be a more accurate reflection of performance than the trend of profits.

Comment (3)

"I am worried that the low price at which we are selling goods to Tamsin is undermining our group's overall profitability."

Assuming the consolidated financial statements have been correctly prepared, all intra-group trading has been eliminated, thus the pricing policy will have had no effect on these financial statements. The comment is incorrect and reflects a misunderstanding of the consolidation process.

Comment (4)

"I note that our share price is now $2.30, how does this compare with our share price immediately before we bought Tamsin?"

The increase in share capital is 6 million shares, the increase in the share premium is $6m, thus the total proceeds for the 6 million shares was $12m giving a share price of $2 at the date of acquisition of Tamsin. The current price of $2.30 presumably reflects the market's favourable view of Gregory's current and future performance.

(b)

		20X6	**20X5**
(i)	Return on capital employed (ROCE) (7,500/74,300 × 100)	10.1%	11.3%
(ii)	Net asset turnover (46,500/74,300)	0.63 times	0.53 times
(iii)	Gross profit margin (9,300/46,500 × 100)	20.0%	25.7%
(iv)	Operating profit margin (7,500/46,500 × 100)	16.1%	21.4%

Looking at the above ratios, it appears that the overall performance of Gregory has declined marginally. The ROCE has fallen from 11.3% to 10.1%, which has been caused by a substantial fall in the gross profit margin (down from 25.7% in 20X5 to 20% in 20X6), over a 22% (5.7%/25.7%) decrease. The group have relatively low operating expenses (at around 4% of revenue), so the poor gross profit margin feeds through to the operating profit margin. The overall decline in the ROCE due to the weaker profit margins has been mitigated by an improvement in net asset turnover, increasing from 0.53 times to 0.63 times. Despite the improvement in net asset turnover, it still seems very low, with only 63 cents of sales generated from every $1 invested in the business, although this will depend on the type of business Gregory and Tamsin are engaged in.

On this analysis, the effect of the acquisition of Tamsin seems to have had a detrimental effect on overall performance, but this may not necessarily be the case, as there could be some distorting factors in the analysis. As mentioned above, the 20X6 results include only six months of Tamsin's results, but the statement of financial position includes the full amount of the consideration for Tamsin. [The consideration has been calculated (see comment (4) above) as $12m for the parent's 75% share plus $3.3m (3,600 – 300 share of post-acquisition profit) for the non-controlling interest's 25%, giving total consideration of $15.3m.] The above factors disproportionately increase the denominator of ROCE which has the effect of worsening the calculated ROCE. This distortion should be corrected in 20X7 when a full year's results for Tamsin will be included in group profit. Another factor is that it could take time to fully integrate the activities of the two entities and more savings and other synergies may be forthcoming such as bulk buying discounts.

The non-controlling interest share in the profit for the year in 20X6 of $300,000 allows a rough calculation of the full year's profit of Tamsin at $2.4m (300,000/25% × $^{12}/_{6}$, i.e. the $300,000 represents 25% of $^{6}/_{12}$ of the annual profit). This figure is subject to some uncertainty such as the effect of probable increased post-acquisition depreciation charges. However, a profit of $2.4m on the investment of $15.3m represents a return of 16% (and would be higher if the profit was adjusted to a pre-tax figure) which is much higher than the current year ROCE (at 10.1%) of the group. This implies that the performance of Tamsin is much better than that of Gregory as a separate entity, and that Gregory's performance in 20X6 must have deteriorated considerably from that in 20X5 and this is the real cause of the deteriorating performance of the group.

Another issue potentially affecting the ROCE is that, as a result of the consolidation process, Tamsin's net assets, including goodwill, are included in the statement of financial position at fair value, whereas Gregory's net assets appear to be based on historical cost, as there is no revaluation surplus. As the values of property, plant and equipment have been rising, this effect favourably flatters the 20X5 ratios. This is because the statement of financial position of 20X5 only contains Gregory's assets which, at historical cost, may considerably understate their fair value and, on a comparative basis, overstate 20X5 ROCE.

In summary, although on first impression the acquisition of Tamsin appears to have caused a marginal worsening of the group's performance, the distorting factors and imputation of the non-controlling interest's profit in 20X6 indicate the underlying performance may be better than the ratios portray and the contribution from Tamsin is a very significant positive. Future performance may be even better.

Without information on the separate financial statements of Tamsin, it is difficult to form a more definite view.

ACCA marking guide		
		Marks
(a)	2 marks for each reply to the CEO's observations	8
(b)	1 mark for each pair of ratios	4
	1 mark per relevant comment on performance up to	8
		12
Total		**20**

Examiners' report

This is the first time a question combining interpretation with an element of consolidation has been examined and candidates did find this a challenging question.

For part (a) the comments required in response to the Chief Executive Officer (CEO)'s observations were not at the expected standard. Most candidates launched into irrelevant detail regarding ratio movements and did not consider the reason for the difference between the two years' financial statements, specifically that the **statement of profit or loss for the second year included the consolidated results of the newly-acquired subsidiary but, crucially, only for six months**.

The low margin on intra-group sales was seen by many candidates as, correctly, not affecting the consolidated financial statements or the overall profitability of the group. Some candidates did mention the impact of any unrealised profit on inventories held from such trading, but this was not likely to have a material effect.

For part (b) the four ratio calculations were generally well done although for ROCE, capital employed should include the non-controlling interest as this is part of equity (those who took total assets less current liabilities had no problem with this) and the calculation of net asset turnover (revenue/capital employed) was either omitted or the figures inverted. A minority of candidates attempted to adjust for the intra-group transactions before calculating ratios which was not required as we must assume that intra-group transactions had already been correctly eliminated on consolidation.

For the comments on comparative performance, the usual observations on past papers continue to apply. **To suggest ratios have increased or decreased does not qualify as analysis**. Suggesting the change is better or worse begins to show understanding, but more than this is required. In many cases the impact of the acquisition (as answered in part (a)) was completely ignored and candidates compared this year and last year results as if they were directly comparing like with like.

The relationship between gross and operating profit margin was often misunderstood. Many candidates stated that the decrease in the operating margin was caused by increased operating costs when in fact operating costs were a lower % of revenue in the second year (despite any one-off costs of the acquisition) and the cause of the decrease was the reduction in the gross profit margin. **Very few candidates used the information in the question** regarding the non-controlling interest in the subsidiary's profit to determine the subsidiary's possible contribution to the group's profit for the year and thus determine that there could have been a decline in the profit earned by the parent alone in the second year.

444 LANDING

(a) Archway's restated figures

On the assumption that Landing purchases Archway, the following adjustments relate to the effects of notes (i) to (iii) in the question and the property revaluation:

	$000
Revenue (94,000 × 95%)	89,300
Cost of sales (see below)	76,000
Loan interest (10,000 × 8%)	800
Equity (10,000 + 2,300 RE + 3,000 revaluation)	15,300
Non-current liabilities: 8% loan notes	10,000

The cost of sales should be first adjusted for the annual licence fee of $1m, reducing this to $mom. Half of these, $36m, are net of a discount of 10% which equates to $4m (36,000/90% – 36,000). Adjusted cost of sales is $76m (73,000 – 1,000 + 4,000).

(b) These figures would give the following ratios:

Annual sales per square metre of floor space	(89,300/12,000)	$7,442
ROCE	(13,300 – 10,000)/(15,300 + 10,000) × 100)	13%
Net asset turnover	(89,300/(15,300 + 10,000))	3.5 times
Gross profit margin	((89,300 – 76,000)/89,300 × 100)	15%
Operating profit margin	((13,300 – 10,000)/89,300 × 100)	3.7 %
Gearing (debt/equity)	(10,000/15,300)	65.4%

(c) Performance

	Archway as reported	**Archway as adjusted**	**Sector average**
Annual sales per square metre of floor space	$7,833	$7,442	$8,000
ROCE	58.5%	13%	18.0%
Net asset turnover	5.0 times	3.5 times	2.7 times
Gross profit margin	22.3%	15%	22.0%
Operating profit margin	11.7%	3.7%	6.7%
Gearing (debt/equity)	nil	65.4%	30.0%

A comparison of Archway's ratios based upon the reported results compares very favourably to the sector average ratios in almost every instance. ROCE is particularly impressive at 58.5% compared to a sector average of 18%, representing a return of more than three times the sector average. The superior secondary ratios of profit margin and asset utilisation (net asset turnover) appear to confirm Archway's above average performance. It is only sales per square metre of floor space which is below the sector average. The unadjusted figure is very close to the sector average, as too is the gross profit margin, implying a comparable sales volume performance. However, the reduction in selling prices caused by the removal of the brand premium causes sales per square metre to fall marginally.

As indicated in the question, should Archway be acquired by Landing, many figures particularly related to the statement of profit or loss would be unfavourably impacted as shown above in the workings for Archway's adjusted ratios. When these effects are taken into account and the ratios are recalculated, a very different picture emerges.

All the performance ratios, with the exception of net asset turnover, are significantly reduced due to the assumed cessation of the favourable trading arrangements. The most dramatic effect is on the ROCE, which, having been more than three times the sector average, would be 27.8% (18.0 – 13.0)/18.0 × 100) below the sector average (at 13% compared to 18.0%). Analysing the component parts of the ROCE (net asset turnover and profit margins), both aspects are lower when the reported figures are adjusted.

The net asset turnover (although adjusted to a lower multiple) is still considerably higher than the sector average. The fall in this ratio is due to a combination of lower revenues (caused by the loss of the branding) and the increase in capital employed (equal to net assets) due to classifying the loan notes as debt (non-current). Gross margin deteriorates from 22.3% to only 15.0% caused by a combination of lower revenues (referred to above) and the loss of the discount on purchases. The distribution costs and administrative expenses for Archway are less than those of its retail sector in terms of the percentage of sales revenue (at 11.3% compared to 15.3%), which mitigates (slightly) the dramatic reduction in the profit before interest and tax. The reduction in sales per square metre of floor space is caused only by the reduced (5%) volume from the removal of the branded sales.

Gearing

The gearing ratio of nil based on the unadjusted figures is not meaningful due to previous debt being classified as a current liability because of its imminent redemption. When this debt is replaced by the 8% loan notes and (more realistically) classified as a non-current liability, Archway's gearing is much higher than the sector average. There is no information as to how the increased interest payable at 8% (double the previous 4%) compares to the sector's average finance cost. If such a figure were available, it may give an indication of Archway's credit status although the doubling of the rate does imply a greater degree of risk in Archway seen by the lender.

Summary and advice

Based upon Archway's reported figures, its purchase by Landing would appear to be a good investment. However, when Archway's performance is assessed based on the results and financial position which might be expected under Landing's ownership, the recalculated ratios are generally inferior to Archway's retail sector averages. In an investment decision such as this, an important projected ratio would be the return on the investment (ROI) which Landing might expect. The expected net profit after tax can be calculated as $2m ((3,300 before interest and tax – 800 interest) × 80% post-tax), however, there is no information in the question as to what the purchase consideration of Archway would be. That said, at a (probable) minimum purchase price based on Archway's net asset value (with no goodwill premium), the ROI would only be 7.9% (2,000/25,300 × 100) which is very modest and should be compared to Landing's existing ROI. A purchase price exceeding $25.3m would obviously result in an even lower expected ROI. It is possible that under Landing's management, Archway's profit margins could be improved, perhaps coming to a similar arrangement regarding access to branded sales (or franchising) as currently exists with Cardol, but with a different entity. If so, the purchase of Archway may still be a reasonable acquisition.

ACCA marking guide		
		Marks
(a)	Revenue	½
	Cost of sales	2
	Loan interest	½
	Equity	1½
	Non-current liabilities	½
		5
(b)	1 mark per ratio	**6**
(c)	1 mark per relevant comment up to	**9**
Total		**20**

445 FUNJECT CO

(a) Restated financial information

Statement of profit or loss

	20X4 original	**Adjustments**	**20X4 restated**
	$000		$000
Revenue (note (i))	54,200	(2,100)	52,100
Cost of sales (note (i))	(21,500)	1,200	(20,300)
Gross profit	32,700		31,800
Operating expenses (W1)	(11,700)	(512)	(12,212)
Profit before tax	21,000		19,588

(W1) Adjustments to operating expenses

	20X4
	$000
Expenses relating to non-core division	(700)
Loss on disposal of non-core division	(1,500)
Gamilton management charge (54,200 × 1%)	(542)
Funject management charge (31,800 × 10%)	3,180
Rent charged by Gamilton	(46)
Commercial rent	120
Net increase to operating expenses	512

(b) Profit has decreased from $21,000,000 to $19,588,000 and the resulting journal entry will be:

	$000
Dr Retained earnings (21,000 – 19,588)	1,412
Cr Cash	1,412

Ratio calculations		**20X4**
Gross profit margin	31,800/52,100 × 100	61%
Operating profit margin	19,588/52,100 × 100	38%
Receivables collection period (days)	(5,700/52,100) × 365	40 days
Current ratio	(12,900 – 1,412)/(11600)	1:1
Acid test (quick)ratio	(12,900 – 4,900 – 1,412)/(11,600)	0.57:1
Gearing (debt/equity)	16,700/(9,000 – 1,412)	220%

(c) **Commentary on performance**

Profitability

The discontinued operation had a gross profit % (GP%) of 43% (900/2,100 × 100) and an operating profit % (OP %) of 10% (200/2,100 × 100). Before adjusting for the disposal, Aspect Co had a GP% of 60%. After an adjustment has been made to reflect the disposal, Aspect Co's GP% is 61%, which is higher than the industry average of 45%. Thus, it would appear that the disposal of the non-core division has had a positive impact on the GP% of Aspect Co. Such a positive comparison of the GP% to the industry average would suggest that Aspect Co has negotiated a very good deal with its suppliers for the cost of goods in comparison to its competitors, as the GP% is 16% (61 – 45) higher than the industry average.

However, when considering the OP%, the financial statements have been adjusted to reflect: (i) the disposal of the discontinued operation, (ii) a new management charge which would be imposed by Funject Co, and (iii) commercial rent charges. These adjustments result in an OP% of 38%. So, although the OP% is still 10% (38 – 28) higher than the industry average, it would appear that some of the advantage of having such a good deal with its suppliers is lost when operating costs are incurred. The OP% does not outperform the industry average to the same extent that GP% did. Although the management charge will be eliminated as an intra-group transaction on consolidation, it will still have an impact in the individual financial statements of Aspect Co. However, there is no indication of what this charge represents, and whether or not it reflects a market value for these costs. The rent of $120,000 is deemed to be a fair market value which would indicate that the previous rent charge of $46,000 was artificially low. If Funject Co acquires Aspect Co, it may wish to capitalise on the relationship which Aspect Co has with its supplier of goods but it might also need to investigate the composition of operating costs other than those described above to see if any of these can be avoided or reduced.

Liquidity

Aspect Co's receivables collection period appears to be comparable with the KPIs provided (40 days in comparison to 41 days). Terms of trade of 30 days are quite reasonable (though this usually depends on the type of business) and so there appear to be no causes for concern here.

Given that Aspect Co's receivables collection period is comparable to the industry average, the difference in the current ratio (1:1 in comparison to 1.6:1) can only be explained by either lower current assets other than receivables (for example, cash) or higher current liabilities. As Aspect Co's cash balance does not appear to be low ($2.3m), this suggests that its liabilities might be higher than average. Perhaps Aspect Co's favourable relationship with its suppliers also extends to longer than average credit terms. As Aspect Co's acid (quick) ratio (0.57:1) is much less than the industry average (1.4:1), this would also suggest that Aspect Co is holding a higher than average level of inventory. This may raise a concern about Aspect Co's ability to sell its inventory. There is also a current tax bill to consider. Indeed, if Aspect Co were asked to settle its current liabilities from merely its receivables and bank, it would be unable to do so. Perhaps Funject Co may wish to further investigate the procedures associated with the purchase and holding of Aspect Co's inventory prior to a takeover. As a parent company, Funject Co should be able to influence these procedures and have more control over the levels of inventory held.

Gearing

Aspect Co appears to be highly-geared but perhaps this is not a huge cause for concern because it appears to be a highly-geared industry (220% compared to 240%). It may be that the proceeds from the sale of the non-core division can be or perhaps were used to repay loans. As the gearing for the industry is higher than that of Aspect Co, it may be that Aspect Co could still increase borrowings in future. If so, Aspect Co may need to increase working capital efficiency and reduce costs in order to generate enough cash to service higher borrowings.

Conclusion

Overall, Aspect's statement of financial position gives little cause for concern: the profit margins appear to be healthy, although further investigation of operating costs and working capital efficiency may be required. More information also needs to be obtained about the nature of the business and perhaps the financial statements of several years (as opposed to one) would also be beneficial.

ACCA marking guide

		Marks
(a)	Adjustment to revenue and cost of sales	1
	Disposal of non-core division	1
	Management charge (remove old, add new)	2
	Rent expense (remove current, add commercial)	1
		5
(b)	1 mark per ratio	**5**
(c)	1 mark per relevant comment:	
	Profitability	5
	Liquidity	3
	Gearing	1
	Conclusion	1
		10
Total		**20**

446 FLASH CO

(a)

		20X4		**20X3**
Gross profit margin	(37,000/92,600)	40%	(29,400/81,700)	36%
Operating profit margin	(22,600/92,600)	24.4%	(17,100/81,700)	20.9%
Interest cover	(22,600/5,100)	4.4 times	(17,100/4,200)	4.1 times
Cash generated from operations/profit from operations	(29,900/22,600)	132.3%	(18,000/17,100)	105.3%

(b) Performance

Flash Co's revenue has increased significantly in 20X4. This increase is likely to be due to Flash's geographical expansion during 20X4.

The loss of a competitor during the year will have benefitted Flash Co, as the competitor's customers seek alternative supply. There is likely to be much less impact in 20X4 from the new stores, as these only opened in February 20X4, but we would expect that the effect of the new stores will prove much more significant in future years, once a full year's income is recognised from the new locations.

Flash Co's gross profit margin has increased from 36% to 40%, and there may be a number of reasons for this. Flash Co is likely to have been able to charge higher prices for solar panels following the increased demand for that product.

Secondly the improved terms with major suppliers are also likely to have contributed to lower purchase prices. This will also have improved the gross profit margin.

The operating margin has also increased, although slightly less than the increase in gross profit, which suggests that operating costs have increased. A quick analysis shows that operating costs have increased by 17% compared to an increase in revenue of 13%. This increase is likely to incorporate various one-off costs associated with the geographical expansion and acquisition of new stores. In the year of acquisition and opening, there would be expected to be numerous set-up and marketing costs, but these have not led to an excessive increase in costs. In future years these costs will not be repeated and we should see an improvement in operating margins.

Interest cover has improved in the year, despite the increase in finance costs which will have arisen as a result of the new loan notes. This demonstrates that Flash Co is generating sufficiently robust profits to meet its interest obligations.

It is likely that the 8% loan notes were issued to fund the acquisition of the new stores, and may therefore not have been in existence for the entire period. The annual interest payable on these new loan notes will be $0.8m, so Flash Co will easily be able to cover this based on 20X4's performance.

Cash flow

Flash Co is generating excellent cash from operations in comparison to the profit from operations in both years, and there is a significant improvement in this from 20X3 to 20X4. The cash generated in 20X4 easily covers the interest and tax payments, as well as a dividend. This shows that sufficient cash exists for the expansion of the business.

In addition to this, Flash Co's working capital management seems to be strong. Inventories have fallen during the year despite the increased sales level. This is likely to be due to the high demand for solar panels.

There is a significant increase in trade receivables, which is likely to be as a result of acquiring new customers following the demise of the competitor.

The increase in trade payables is likely to result from the increased trading levels, together with an increased payment period following the negotiated improved terms with major suppliers.

The major reason for the net cash outflow during the year is the large amount spent on the purchase of property, plant and equipment. This is likely to be linked to the acquisition of the new stores, and related geographical expansion.

Of the $31.6m spend on new assets, $22.5m is funded from the cash generated from Flash Co's operating activity, demonstrating the sustainable strength of Flash Co's performance.

Flash Co has raised $10m through the issue of 8% loan notes in the year. These are likely to have been issued to fund the acquisition of the new stores, which is an appropriate use of long-term financing. As stated previously, Flash Co is easily capable of covering the interest payments on this, although it is worth noting that the finance costs are greater than the interest paid. This suggests that the effective rate of interest on their overall funding is above that being paid, and may mean that a redemption premium will be payable in the future.

Conclusion

To reassure the sales director it is worth pointing out that cash inflows and outflows arise as a result of the three different activities that an entity undertakes: operating, investing and financing. The increased levels of profit mentioned by the sales director are reflected within the cash generated from operating activities. The net reduction in cash balances during the year is due to significant levels of investing activity as a result of the business expansion, but this should lead to increased levels of revenue and profits in the future.

ACCA marking guide		
		Marks
(a)	Ratios	**4**
(b)	Revenue and margins	7
	Interest cover	2
	Cash flow	6
	Conclusion	1
		16
Total		**20**

447 MOWAIR CO

(a)

	20X7	**Workings**	**20X6**	**Workings**
Operating profit margin	8.0%	12,300/154,000	11.7%	18,600/159,000
Return on capital employed	3.6%	12,300/(192,100 + 130,960 +19,440)	8.7%	18,600/(44,800 + 150,400 +19,440)
Net asset turnover	0.45 times	154,000/(192,100 + 130,960 +19,440)	0.74 times	159,000/(44,800 + 150,400 +19,440)
Current ratio	0.53:1	15,980/29,920	1.22:1	28,890/23,690
Interest cover	1.3 times	12,300/9200	1.8 times	18,600/10,200
Gearing (Debt/Equity)	78.3%	(130,960+19,440)/ 192,100	379.1%	(150,400 + 19,440)/44,800

(b) Performance

Mowair Co's revenue has declined in the year. As Mowair Co has had exactly the same number of flights in the year, the decline must be due to either lower numbers of passengers or from Mowair Co reducing the price on certain flights. To substantiate this, it would be helpful to see the number of passengers who have flown on Mowair Co flights during the year.

In addition to the decline in revenue, there has been a decline in the operating profit margin in the year. As the number of flights operated by Mowair Co has remained the same, it would appear that a number of the costs incurred by Mowair Co on operating the airline will be relatively fixed and may not have changed significantly during the year. It has been noted that there has been an increase in cost of licences charged by airports during the year, which would again cause the operating profit margin to fall as amortisation would be higher. This only occurred in April 20X7, so the full impact will not actually be felt until next year.

In addition to this, it important to note that there are numerous contracts up for renewal in the next year. This could lead to higher prices for using the airports, and may even result in Mowair Co being unable to use those airports in future. If this was the case, it may have a significant impact on the revenue for the business, as these are described as major airports, which will have the higher levels of demand.

Return on capital employed has declined significantly in the year. There are two major reasons for this. First, there has been a decline in the profit from operations, as discussed above. In addition to this, Mowair Co has revalued its non-current assets in the year. This means that there is a large revaluation surplus in 20X7 which was not present in 20X6. This will have the effect of reducing the return on capital employed due to there being a much larger total balance in equity. If the return on capital employed is calculated without this, it would be 6.2%, which still represents a decline in performance.

Looking at the net asset turnover, this has declined dramatically from 0.74 times to 0.45 times. This will again be affected by the revaluation surplus, making the two years incomparable. If this is removed from the calculation, the net asset turnover increases to 0.78 times. This is a slight increase in performance. This increase has not come from increased revenue, as it can be seen that revenue has fallen by $5 million. Rather, this increase has come from the decrease in capital employed. This arises from the reduction in the loan notes, which appear to have a significant amount repaid annually.

Position

The value of non-current assets has risen sharply in the year, by $147 million. A large proportion of that will be due to the revaluation which has taken place, leading to an increase of $145 million. This suggests that Mowair Co has acquired some new assets in the year, but it is unclear what these are. They may be replacement components on aircraft, as it is unlikely to be significant enough to be an actual new aircraft itself.

The level of debt in the business is a concern, as this makes up a significant portion of the entity's financing, and appears to incur a large annual repayment. The reduction in the current ratio can be attributed to the large decrease in cash, which is likely to be due to the debt repayments made.

It is worth noting that Mowair Co is almost completely funded by debt, with a relatively small amount held in share capital. Therefore, there is an opportunity for a new investor to consider putting more money into the business in the form of shares and the company then repaying some of the loans held by Mowair Co. As Mowair Co is currently repaying $19 million a year on the loans, it may be more sensible to repay these if possible, freeing up a lot more cash for growing the business or to be returned annually in the form of dividends, also saving $9 million a year in interest.

Areas of concern for the future

There are a number of things to consider regarding the future performance of Mowair Co. The first of these is the ten major licences which are due for renegotiation with airports. If the price is raised on these, then this will lead to reduced profits being made by Mowair Co in future periods.

The debt appears to be being repaid in annual instalments of $19 million, meaning that Mowair Co needs to generate sufficient cash to repay that each year, before returning any profit to the owner. In addition to this, the $9 million interest means that the business appears currently unable to return any cash to investors.

Finally, Mowair Co's business model is heavily dependent on large, expensive items of non-current assets. It has been noted that there has been criticism of under-investment in these, so this could lead to large potential outlays in the near future to replace assets.

Conclusion

Mowair Co has not shown a weakened performance in the current year, but appears to be a profitable business at its core. The major issue with the business is the level of debt, which is resulting in $19 million annual repayments and $9 million annual interest. Any new investor who was able to reduce these amounts as part of any future purchase, would put the business in a much stronger cash position.

ACCA marking guide		
		Marks
(a)	Ratio calculations	**6**
(b)	Performance	6
	Position	4
	Future issues of concern	3
	Conclusion	1
		14
Total		**20**

Examiners' report

This was a standard ratios and analysis question built around summary financial statements and a brief scenario for an airline. As in many previous diets, the majority of **answers provided for the interpretation were superficial and lacked depth**. This commentary shows how these answers might have been improved.

Candidates are reminded to **provide workings to support all ratio calculations** as these are helpful to markers. Appropriate workings allow markers to see what adjustments have been made, and to ensure that any obvious arithmetic errors are not penalised. This approach also allows markers to easily apply the "own figure" rule where candidates have interpreted ratios that have been calculated incorrectly.

For part (b), the structure of candidates' responses could have been **improved had they been presented in three (headed) sections**: performance, position and conclusion. This approach was consistent with the requirements of the question and the marking grid. Additionally, there was a specific requirement to highlight issues that the company should consider in the near future. **Few candidates gave any separate consideration to these issues** at all. Very good scripts identified this as a separate heading and reflected on their analysis of the company's recent past and looked forward.

Candidates were **expected to use the information provided in the scenario** which gave useful clues as to why the company's performance in 20X7 was weaker than in 20X6. (A few candidates got the years the wrong way round, however, markers continued to give due credit in such circumstances)

Many candidates noted if the ratios in part (a) were higher or lower, the percentage increase or decrease from the past year and whether they represented an improvement or a worsening of the financial performance or position. Whilst this approach is acceptable as an introductory sentence, it **does not answer the question and does not comment on the company's performance or position using of all the information available.**

A key criticism of the company was its under-investment in its non-current assets. However, there was a substantial increase in the carrying amount of its property, plant and equipment (PPE) which led many candidates to say that such investment had taken place without appreciating that these assets had been revalued, for the first time, by almost the same amount as the increase in carrying amount. Removing the effect of the revaluation from the 20X7 carrying amount shows a small reduction in PPE, thus confirming (subject to depreciation charges) that no substantial investment had taken place. Well-prepared candidates pointed out that this distorted comparison between the two years (particularly for key ratios such as ROCE, net asset turnover and gearing).

Revenue and operating profit margin had both declined (one is not an inevitable consequence of the other) although the number of flights and destinations remained the same. This invited comments as to the company's pricing policies, number of passengers carried, cost control, the incidence of fixed costs (for an airline these would be significant) and the part-year effect of increased licence costs.

ROCE declined significantly but was, as noted above, materially influenced by the impact of the PPE revaluation and the decline in profit from operations in both absolute and relative terms. Candidates were given credit if their answer included a revised 20X7 ROCE calculation, excluding the effect of the revaluation, for a better comparison between the two years. In this case, this showed a decline but not as significant as the initial calculations. A similar approach could have been taken to net asset turnover which showed a very slight increase in 20X7. This was caused by a combination of the decline in revenue and a decrease in capital employed evidenced by the decrease in cash and cash equivalents and/or non-current liabilities.

The cost of the licences acquired late in the financial year was responsible for the increase in intangible assets. It was not possible for candidates to assess the impact of increased depreciation charges caused by the revaluation of PPE or amortisation of the intangible assets, but a good answer referred to these charges having a further impact on 20X7 margins and thereby limiting a valid comparison between the two years.

With respect to the current ratio, many candidates insisted that as this ratio was below 2:1, this was a significant financial problem. **There are no "ideal" ratios** and no sector averages were provided on this occasion so answers should have concentrated on the reasons for the decline which were a combination of the increase in trade payables and the decrease in cash and cash equivalents (influenced by the repayment of loan notes).

Interest cover had declined, even though finance costs had decreased (because of the repayment of some loan notes). This was primarily because of the decline in the profit from operations noted earlier. The decline in cash flow from operations provided further evidence of potential liquidity problems for the company.

Unless the revaluation surplus was excluded from the 20X7 equity, the decrease in gearing was not a valid comparison or evidence of a stronger financial position. The main reason for the decrease was the impact of the revaluation. If this was removed it shows that gearing was still worryingly high – especially for a company that will need to invest in new non-current assets in the near future (to address the issue of recent under-investment).

The above commentary on performance and position is intended to offer those working through the question an insight into the sort of issues that should be taken from the question (especially the written narrative and candidate's own ratios) and applied to support analysis of the company's (in this case) financial weaknesses.

The question asked candidates to "highlight any issues that Mowair Co should be considering in the near future". As this was specifically asked, markers were looking for responses – ideally as a separately headed section in answers. **Very few candidates made any reasonable attempt** at this although observations from the question were repeated in different parts of answers. Good answers could have mentioned, under one heading, such impending issues as: the impact of the negotiations with airports for more new licences which will put further strain on profitability and cash flow and may even prevent the company from using those airports if renewal costs are prohibitive, the high levels of existing debt and the company's limited ability to continue to pay this off, the possible difficulties of paying dividends with little available profit and cash and the need to invest in non-current assets and how this investment will be financed.

A conclusion, drawing together key issues (present and future in this case) in a short final paragraph was expected.

448 PERKINS

(a) Gain on disposal in Perkins group consolidated statement of profit or loss (SPL)

	$000
Proceeds	28,640
Less: Goodwill (W1)	(4,300)
Less: Net assets at disposal	(26,100)
Add: NCI at disposal (W2)	6,160
	4,400

(W1) Goodwill

	$000
Consideration	19,200
NCI at acquisition	4,900
Less: Net assets at acquisition	(19,800)
	4,300

(W2) NCI at disposal

	$000
NCI at acquisition	4,900
NCI% × S post acquisition	
20% × (26,100 – 19,800)	1,260
	6,160

(b) Adjusted SPL extracts:

	$000
Revenue (46,220 – 9,000 (S × 8/12) + 1,000 (intra-group))	38,220
Cost of sales (23,980 – 4,400 (S × 8/12)) [see note]	(19,580)
Gross profit	18,640
Operating expenses (3,300 – 1,673 (S × 8/12) + 9,440 profit on disposal)	(11,067)
Profit from operations	7,573
Finance costs (960 – 800 (S × 8/12))	(160)

Note: Originally, the intra-group sale resulted in $1m turnover and $0.7m costs of sales. These amounts were recorded in the individual financial statements of Perkins Co. On consolidation, the $1m turnover was eliminated – this needs to be added back. The corresponding $1 m COS consolidation adjustment is technically made to Swanson Co's financial statements and so can be ignored here.

(c) Ratios of Perkins Co, eliminating impact of Swanson Co and the disposal during the year

	20X7 recalculated	Working (see SPL above)	20X7 original	20X6
Gross profit margin	48.8%	18,640/38,220	48.1%	44.8%
Operating margin	19.8%	7,573/38,220	41%	16.8%
Interest cover	47.3 times	7,573/160	19.7 times	3.5 times

(d) Analysis of Perkins Co

Gross profit margin

In looking at the gross margin of Perkins Co, the underlying margin made by Perkins Co is higher than in 20X6.

After the removal of Swanson Co's results, this continues to increase, despite Swanson Co having a gross margin of over 50%. It is possible that Swanson Co's gross profit margin was artificially inflated by obtaining cheap supplies from Perkins Co. Perkins Co makes a margin of 48.8%, but only sold goods to Swanson at 30%.

Operating margin

The operating margin appears to have increased significantly on the prior year. It must be noted that this contains the profit on disposal of Swanson Co, which increases this significantly.

Removing the impact of the Swanson Co disposal still shows that the margin is improved on the prior year, but it is much more in line.

Swanson Co's operating margin is 32.6%, significantly higher than the margin earned by Perkins Co, again suggesting that a profitable business has been sold. This is likely to be due to the fact that Swanson Co was able to use Perkins Co's facilities with no charge, meaning its operating expenses were understated compared to the market prices.

It is likely that the rental income earned from the new tenant has helped to improve the operating margin, and this should increase further once the tenant has been in for a full year.

Interest cover

Initially, the interest cover has shown good improvement in 20X7 compared to 20X6, as there has been a significant increase in profits. Even with the profit on disposal stripped out, the interest cover would still be very healthy.

Following the removal of Swanson Co, the interest cover is improved further. This may be because the disposal of Swanson Co has allowed Perkins Co to repay debt and reduce the interest expense incurred.

Conclusion

Swanson Co seems to have been a profitable company, which raises questions over the disposal. However, some of these profits may have been derived from favourable terms with Perkins Co, such as cheap supplies and free rental. It is worth noting that Perkins Co now has rental income in the year. This should grow in future periods, as this is likely to be a full year's income in future periods.

ACCA marking guide		
		Marks
(a)	Proceeds	½
	Goodwill	2½
	Net assets	½
	NCI	1½
		5
(b)	Revenue and COS	2
	Other costs	2
		4
(c)	Ratios	2
(d)	Gross profit margin	2
	Operating profit margin	5
	Interest cover	1
	Conclusion	1
		9
Total		**20**

449 DUKE CO

(a) Calculation of NCI and retained earnings:

	$000
Non-controlling interest (W1)	3,740
Retained earnings (W2)	14,060

(W1) Non-controlling interest

	$000	
NCI at acquisition	3,400	
NCI% × S post acq	700	20% × ($7m × 6/12)
NCI% × FV depn	(60)	20% × ($3m/5 × 6/12)
NCI% × URP	(300)	20% × $1.5m
Total	3,740	

Alternative presentation:

		$000	
NCI at acquisition		3,400	
Profit	3,500		($7m × 6/12)
FV depn	(300)		($3m/5 × 6/12)
URP	(1,500)		($4,500 – $2,500 = $1.5m)
	1,700		
	× 20%	340	
		3,740	

(W2) Retained earnings

	$000	
100% × P RE	13,200	
P% × S post acq	2,800	80% × ($7m × 6/12)
P% × FV depn	(240)	80% × ($3m/5 × 6/12)
P% × URP	(1,200)	80% × $1.5m
Professional fees	(500)	
Total	14,060	

Alternative presentation:

		$000	
NCI at acquisition		13,200	
Professional fees		(500)	
Profit	3,500		($7m × 6/12)
FV depn	(300)		($3m/5 × 6/12)
URP	(1,500)		($4,500 – $2,500 = $1.5m)
	1,700		
	× 80%	1,360	
		14,060	

(b) Ratios:

	20X8	Working	20X7	Working
Current	1.4:1	30,400/21,300	1.8:1	28,750/15,600
ROCE	31.3%	14,500/(11,000 + 6,000 + 14,060 + 3,740 + 11,500)	48.1%	12,700/(19,400 + 7,000)
Gearing	33%	(11,500/11,000 + 6,000 + 14,060 + 3,740)	36.1%	(7,000/19,400)

(c) Analysis

Performance

The ROCE has declined significantly from 20X7. However, rather than being due to a reduction in profit from operations which has increased slightly ($14.5m from $12.7m), it is due to a significant increase in capital employed which has gone from $26.4m to nearly $50m. This will be partly due to the fact that Smooth Co was acquired through the issue of shares in Duke Co.

The ROCE will look worse in the current period as it will only contain six months' profit from Smooth, but the entire liabilities and non-controlling interest at the reporting period.

As Smooth Co made a profit after tax of $7m in the year, six months of this would have made a significant increase in the overall profit from operations. If excluded from the consolidated SPL, it suggests that there is a potential decline (or stagnation) in the profits made by Duke Co.

Position

The current ratio has decreased in the year from 1.8:1 to 1.4:1. Some of this will be due to the fact that Smooth Co is based in the service industry and so is likely to hold very little inventory. The large fall in inventory holding period would also support this.

An increase in trade receivables is perhaps expected given that Smooth Co is a service based company. This is likely to be due to Smooth Co's customers having significant payment terms, due to their size.

This increase in receivables collection period could mean that Smooth Co has a weaker cash position than Duke Co. While the size of the customers may mean that there is little risk of irrecoverable debts, Smooth Co may have a small, or even overdrawn, cash balance due to this long collection period.

The gearing has reduced in the year from 36.1% to 33%. This is not due to reduced levels of debt, as these have actually increased during the year. This is likely to be due to the consolidation of the debt held by Smooth Co, as Duke Co has not taken out additional loans in the year.

This increase in debt has been offset by a significant increase in equity, which has resulted from the share consideration given for the acquisition of Smooth Co.

Conclusion

Smooth Co is a profitable company and is likely to have boosted Duke Co profits, which may be slightly in decline. Smooth Co may have more debt and have potentially put pressure on the cash flow of the group, but Duke Co seems in a stable enough position to cope with this.

ACCA marking guide		
		Marks
(a)	Non-controlling interests	3
	Retained earnings	3
		6
(b)	Ratios	**4**
(c)	Performance	4
	Position	5
	Conclusion	1
		10
Total		**20**

Examiners' report

This question required three tasks to be completed with most of the marks being awarded for the **calculation of some standard ratios** and an analysis of financial statement extracts for a newly formed, two company group.

Part (a) required a calculation of non-controlling interests and group retained earnings to complete the financial statement extracts. Overall, **this section of the question was well received** by most candidates with some achieving full marks. For those who did not achieve full marks, this was generally due to some common mistakes noted below.

Many candidates treated the professional fees incurred by Duke Co as an expense in Smooth Co's calculation of profit. Professional fees (acquisition costs) per IFRS 3 are **not to be included within the calculation of goodwill** but should instead be expensed as incurred. This cost would need to be deducted from Duke Co's profit within the retained earnings working.

When looking at the detail in the question, Duke Co acquired Smooth Co on 1 January 20X8. The acquisition therefore took place **six months into the accounting year**. As a result, when looking to identify Smooth Co's post-acquisition profit, the profit for the year of $7 million **needed to be time apportioned 6/12**. Similarly, fair value depreciation on the brand also needed to be time apportioned and this was often omitted by candidates.

Finally, for those candidates who calculated unrealised profit on the non-current asset transfer correctly, many included this as a deduction against Duke Co. It was Smooth Co that transferred the asset and made the profit on disposal and therefore the unrealised profit needed to be split between both non-controlling interests and retained earnings according to the percentage of ownership.

For part (b) candidates were asked to calculate three ratios for both 20X7 and 20X8 using some of the information that been calculated in part (a). Most candidates correctly calculated current ratio for both 20X7 and 20X8, but for many **calculating return on capital employed and gearing correctly proved to be more challenging**.

Candidates, as always, are reminded to **provide workings for their ratio calculations**. This is because an incorrect answer that has no supporting workings will be awarded no marks. However, the same response may have been awarded full marks if the incorrect balance was found using the candidates 'own figures' from part (a).

Finally, part (c) to this question required candidates to comment on the comparative performance and position over the two-year period and to specifically comment on the impact that the acquisition had on the analysis. Despite the requirement being very clear, **many candidates failed to refer to the acquisition at all**. This was disappointing for the marking team as group interpretation is no longer a new area to the syllabus and there are numerous examiner commentaries and several past practice questions that have similar requirements.

For some candidates, the **analysis was very weak with many simply noting that a ratio had increased or decreased** in the year. This approach will continue to secure limited marks as it is not providing an analysis of why there was a change in performance during the year.

Well-prepared candidates discussed liquidity and noted that the change in current ratio was likely to be due to Smooth Co being in the service industry and therefore holding limited (if any) inventory. Few candidates went on to support this comment with evidence from the decrease in the inventory holding period. Only a few candidates noted that Duke Co's liquidity would have reduced due to the acquisition of Smooth Co in part being due to a cash element.

Many candidates stated that the current ratio was very poor, and that the company faced going concern issues as the ratio was below the 'norm' of 2:1. These comments received few, if any marks, and **candidates are discouraged from making statements such as this**. Instead, candidates are encouraged to use the scenario to suggest possible reasons for the change in the ratio.

Return on capital employed (ROCE) had deteriorated significantly in 20X8. Indeed, the scenario provided candidates with **clues as to why ROCE may have deteriorated** which included an increase in share capital and share premium because of the share exchange on acquisition of Smooth Co. Also, there had been an increase in long-term loans which must have been due to the acquisition, given that the scenario said that Duke Co had no new loans during the year. In addition, it was worth noting that Smooth Co's profit had only been consolidated for six months and therefore ROCE may improve in the following year. Very few candidates discussed all of these issues.

There had been very little change in gearing during the year with a small decrease in gearing being recognised. Many candidates suggested that this was due to a reduction in loans, when in fact long-term loans had increased following the acquisition (as previously mentioned this was solely due to the acquisition of Smooth Co). Well-prepared candidates were able to identify that the **fall in gearing was due to the increase in equity** following the acquisition of Smooth Co resulting in increased share capital and share premium.

Candidates are **encouraged to provide a conclusion** for any analysis requirement, pulling together the key findings from the scenario and the analysis performed.

450 PIRLO

(a) Gain/loss on disposal

(i) Individual financial statements of Pirlo Co

	$000
Sales proceeds	300,000
Cost of investment	(210,000)
Gain on disposal	90,000

(ii) Consolidated financial statements of the Pirlo group

	$000
Sales proceeds	300,000
Less: goodwill	(70,000)
Less: net assets ($260m + $50m FV)	(310,000)
Add: NCI	66,000
Loss on disposal	(14,000)

(b) Key ratios

	20X9	**20X8**
Gross profit margin	45.8%	44.9%
	(97,860/213,480) × 100%	(97,310/216,820) × 100%
Operating margin	11.9%	13.5%
	(25,500/213,480) × 100%	(29,170/216,820) × 100%
Interest cover	1.43	1.8
	(25,500/17,800)	(29,170/16,200)

(c) Comment on the performance

The revenue for the group for the year has actually declined in the year. The scenario states that the Samba Co revenue has remained the same in both years, so this decrease appears to represent a decline from the remaining companies in the group.

Whilst there has been an overall decline in revenue, the gross profit margin has improved in 20X9 (44.9% increased to 45.8%). Samba Co has a significantly higher gross profit margin (81%) in relation to the rest of the group, suggesting that the rest of the Pirlo group operates at a lower gross profit margin.

The operating profit margin of the group has deteriorated in 20X9 (13.5% has decreased to 11.9%). This is initially surprising due to the significant increase in the operating profit margin of Samba Co (41% has increased to 66%). However, the increase in Samba Co's operating profit margin may not represent a true increase in performance in Samba Co due to the following:

– Samba Co has recorded a $2m profit on disposal of its properties, which will inflate its profit from operations in 20X9.

– In addition to this, Samba Co has been charged a lower rate of rent by Pirlo Co, which may also have the impact of making the profit from operations in 20X9 higher than the previous period if the rent is lower than the depreciation Samba Co would have recorded.

This concern is further enhanced when the share of the profit of the associate is considered. This has contributed $4.6m to the profit for the year, which is nearly 40% of the overall profit of the group.

The combination of these factors raises concerns over the profitability of Pirlo Co and any other subsidiaries in the group, as it appears to be loss making. Some of these losses will have been made through the loss of rental income through the new arrangement.

The joining fee paid to Samba Co's previous directors is a one-off cost paid by Pirlo Co. Consequently, it is included in the consolidated statement of profit or loss for the year ended 31 December 20X9. A similar amount was paid by Samba Co in the form of an annual bonus in the year ended 20X8. Therefore, 20X8 and 20X9 are comparable but the joining fee represents a cost saving for Pirlo Co in future years.

The decline in interest cover appears to be driven by both the decrease in profit from operations and an increase in finance costs. As Samba Co has a large amount of debt, and much lower interest cover than the group, this should increase in future periods.

The disposal of Samba Co appears to be surprising, given that it generates the high margins compared to the rest of the group. The loss on disposal of Samba Co should be brought into the consolidated statement of profit or loss. This would reduce profit from operations by a further $14m and would reduce the operating profit margin further to 5.4%.

The sale of Samba Co at a loss is very surprising given that it appears to contribute good results and has a history of strong performance.

Whilst selling Samba Co at a loss may be a strange move, Pirlo Co may believe that the real value of the Samba Co business has been secured by employing the two founding directors.

Conclusion

The disposal of Samba Co does not appear to be a good move, as the Pirlo group seem to be losing its most profitable element. The Pirlo Co directors seem to have made a risky decision to move into the software development industry as a competitor of Samba Co.

ACCA marking guide		
		Marks
(a)	Disposal	**5**
(b)	Ratios	**3**
	Revenue/margins	6
	Other and conclusion	6
		12
Total		**20**

Examiners' report

This question required candidates to complete three tasks. The majority of the marks available were for the calculation of standard ratios and analysis of financial statement extracts for a group company following a disposal of a subsidiary during the year.

Part (a) required a calculation of a gain/loss on disposal for both the parent's individual financial statements and the group financial statements. On the whole candidates demonstrated a sound knowledge of calculating a group gain/loss but often struggled with the relatively straightforward calculation for the parent company gain.

A common mistake was the inclusion of goodwill in the disposal calculation at its closing value. This was disappointing to see as goodwill should be valued at acquisition then reviewed annually for impairment. Increases in goodwill are not recorded in the group financial statements.

Part (b) required candidates to calculate three relatively straightforward ratios for a two-year period. Candidates who **did not score full marks were those who did not follow the question instruction**. Candidates were specifically told not to adjust for the disposal calculation in part (a), yet many still attempted to adjust the profit figures. This resulted in incorrect ratio calculations.

Marks **cannot be awarded to incorrect calculations if workings cannot be seen** and it continues to be a problem that many candidates do not provide the marking team with supportive workings.

Other errors in the calculation of ratios included some candidates **using profit before tax when calculating operating profit margin** and the inverse of the fraction was often used for interest cover. You will almost certainly be required to perform some ratio calculations in the financial reporting exam so you must ensure that you are familiar with the formulae.

Finally, part (c) asked candidates to comment on the performance and interest cover of the Pirlo group for the comparative two-year period. The requirement asked candidates to consider three specific areas including how the disposal of the subsidiary would impact your current analysis and what implications this may have for the future.

Those candidates who used the requirements to give their analysis structure, or used the requirements as headings in their analysis generally tended to score well with sensible comments being made. However many candidates overlooked this prompt in the requirement and as a result provided superficial analysis. This was disappointing as the importance of using the requirement to structure an answer has been highlighted in previous examiners' commentary.

Again, disappointingly, many candidates **continue to provide a weak analysis by simply stating that one ratio is bigger or smaller than another**. These types of comments are likely to score relatively few marks as there is no actual analysis of the company being provided. Candidates are encouraged to use the scenario to add substance (and therefore marks) to an answer.

For example, at first glance, the Pirlo group appears to be disposing of a company which is performing particularly well when looking at the increase in their operating profit margin. However, the scenario indicated that property was being rented to Samba Co at a reduced rent, which would in part be a reason for Samba's superior profit margins. In addition to this, the profit on disposal of Samba's properties in the year will have artificially inflated the profit from operations this year. In following accounting periods, these **one-off gains on disposal would not be included and Samba's individual margins are likely to fall**.

An increasing number of candidates attempted to provide a conclusion to their analysis which was **particularly pleasing to see**, and something that candidates should be encouraged to continue to do.

451 BUN CO

(a) Inventory adjustment

The disposal of the inventory at a discounted price would be classified as an adjusting event in accordance with IAS® 10 Events After the Reporting Period.

Retail price of inventory	\$1.5 million
GP margin 20%	\$0.3 million
Closing inventory (currently credited to SPL)	\$1.2 million

A write down to NRV would require a \$0.6m charge to cost of sales thereby increasing it to \$70.6 million and reducing profit from operations to \$12.56 million.

In the statement of financial position, inventory is written down to \$3.36 million and equity will be adjusted to \$32.28 million.

	Bun Co	**Sector average**
Return on year-end capital employed (12,560/(32,280 + 14,400) × 100)	26.9%	18.6%
Operating profit margin (12,560/100,800 × 100%)	12.5%	8.6%
Inventory holding period (days) (3,360/70,600 × 365)	17.4 days	4 days
Debt to equity (debt/equity) (14,400/32,280 × 100)	44.6%	80%
Asset turnover (100,800/46,680)	2.16	2.01

(b) Analysis of financial performance

Profitability

The primary measure of profitability is the return on capital employed (ROCE) and this shows that Bun Co (26.9%) is outperforming the sector (18.6%). The ROCE measures the operating profit relative to the net assets employed in the business. As a percentage, it would appear that Bun Co is 31% ((26.9 – 18.6)/26.9) more efficient that its competitors. However, this ratio should be treated with caution because Bun Co's capital employed includes its revaluation surplus associated with the property. If Bun Co's competitors did not revalue their property, then the ratio is not directly comparable. For example, if Bun Co's revaluation surplus were to be excluded from capital employed, it would increase ROCE to be even higher than the sector average.

As there is little difference between the asset turnover of Bun Co and that of the sector, it would appear that the main cause of ROCE over-performance is due to a significantly higher operating profit margin (12.5% compared to 8.6%). Offering meal deals is advisable, as the company can still afford to reduce its prices and still make a high operating profit margin compared to the industry sector average. By offering meal deals at reduced prices, Bun Co would look to increase their sales volume and therefore this may help them to control and reduce inventory days.

Alternatively, it may be that Bun Co has better control over its costs (either direct, indirect or both) than its competitors. For example, Bun Co may have lower operating costs. As Bun Co owns 80% of its non-current assets in the form of property, this means that it is not paying any rent, whereas its competitors may be. Bun Co's competitors may prefer to lease premises which could be a more flexible basis on which to run a business, but often more costly.

Financial position (limited to inventory and gearing)

In a company like Bun Co, it is expected that inventory would be turned into cash in a relatively short period of time. Bun Co is taking significantly longer than its competitors to sell its inventory which is being held on average for 17 days instead of four days as per the sector average. The main worry is that the inventory is largely perishable. It may be that, since the acquisition of the brand, Bun Co pursued a higher pricing strategy but this may be having a detrimental impact on the company's ability to move its inventory.

Bun Co's debt to equity at 44.6% is lower than the sector average of 80%. This could be because Bun Co acquired its property which has no associated finance. This also means that there will be smaller amounts of interest charged to the statement of profit or loss but this is difficult to confirm as the extract provided is only to profit from operations. There is a bank loan of $14.4m and, although the bank loan interest rate of 10% might appear quite high, it is lower than the ROCE of 26.9% (which means shareholders are benefiting from the borrowings). Finally, Bun Co also has sufficient tangible non-current assets to give more than adequate security on any future borrowings. Therefore there appear to be no adverse issues in relation to gearing.

Conclusion

Bun Co is right to be concerned about its declining profitability compared to previous years, but from the analysis compared to the industry sector averages, it seems that Bun Co may be in a strong position. The information shows that Bun Co has a much better profitability compared to the industry, but the worrying issue which could become a long-term problem is the length of time Bun Co is holding inventory. Bun Co should seriously consider the strategy of reducing their prices to enable them to sell more inventory and reduce wastage. Should Bun Co wish to raise finance in the future, it seems to be in a strong position to do so.

(c) Factors which may limit the usefulness of the comparison with business sector averages

It is unlikely that all the companies which have been included in the sector averages will use the same accounting policies. In the example of Bun Co, it is apparent that it has revalued its property. This will increase its capital employed and (probably) lower its gearing (compared to if it did not revalue). Other companies in the sector may carry their property at historical cost.

There could also be differences as Bun Co owns the shop, and yet other companies in the sector may not own the freehold and may just rent the shop space. Dependent on how the depreciation compares to the equivalent rate would lead to differences in the margins experienced by each company.

The accounting dates may not be the same for all the companies. In this example the sector averages are for the year ended 30 June 20X7, whereas Bun Co's are for the year ended 30 December 20X7. If the sector is exposed to seasonal trading (which could be likely if there are cakes made for Christmas orders, large bread orders for Christmas and New Year parties), this could have a significant impact on many ratios, in particular working capital based ratios. To allow for this, perhaps Bun Co could prepare a form of adjusted financial statements to 30 June 20X7.

It may be that the definitions of the ratios have not been consistent across all the companies included in the sector averages (and for Bun Co). This may be a particular problem with ratios like gearing as there are alternative methods used to calculate it (inventory days used costs of sales in the calculation, but industry could use purchases). Often agencies issue guidance on how the ratios should be calculated to minimise these possible inconsistencies. Of particular relevance in this example is that it is unlikely that other bakery stores will have a purchased trademark.

Sector averages are just that: averages. Many of the companies included in the sector may not be a good match to the type of business and strategy of Bun Co. This company not only has bakery stores but cafés too and this may cause distortions if comparing to companies within the sector who do not have the same facilities. Also, some companies may adopt a strategy of high-end specialist loaves, cakes and patisserie goods which have high mark-ups, but usually lower inventory turnover, whereas other companies may adopt a strategy of selling more affordable bread and cakes with lower margins in the expectation of higher volumes.

ACCA marking guide		
		Marks
(a)	Inventory adjustment	2
	Ratios	5
		7
(b)	Profitability	5
	Financial position	4
	Conclusion	1
		10
(c)	Sector comparison limitations	**3**
Total		**20**

452 PARUL CO

(a) Statement of profit or loss

	As given	Adjustments	As restated
	$000		$000
Revenue	267,920	– ($^4/_{12}$ × 87,600) + 1,600	240,320
Cost of sales	(165,840)	– ($^4/_{12}$ × 30,780)	(155,580)
Gross profit	102,080		84,740
Net operating expenses	(44,920)	– ($^4/_{12}$ × 8,020) + 1,600	(43,847)
Operating profit	57,160		40,893

Statement of financial position

	As given	Adjustments	As restated
	$000	$000	$000
Inventories	151,920	– 4,240	147,680
Cash and cash equivalents	15,120	– 14,680	440

Note: The adjustments represent the removal of Saachi's figures plus the reversal of the intra-group adjustment in respect of four months' consultancy fees.

(b)

	20X8 (restated)	**20X7**
Gross profit margin	35.3%	38.2%
	(84,740/240,320)	(97,320/254,680)
Operating profit margin	17.0%	22.0%
	(40,893/240,320)	(56,080/254,680)
Inventory days	346 days	283 days
	(147,680/155,580 × 365)	(121,800/157,360 × 365

(c) **Revenue and gross margin**

Although 20X8's gross margin as given in the question is almost identical to 20X7, the restated gross margin has fallen by 3%. Saachi Co's gross margin is almost double that of the rest of the Parul Group at 64.9% and the acquisition of Saachi Co has helped to mask the Parul Group's deteriorating performance.

The restated revenue for 20X8 is 5.6% lower than the previous year, which could be due to falls in sales volume or prices or both.

Restated cost of sales has fallen by around 1%, so it would appear that the reason for the fall in the Parul Group's gross margin is primarily a fall in sales prices.

Operating profit margin

The fall in the restated operating profit margin from 22% to 17% is partly caused by the fall in gross profit margin, but would also be affected by movements in net operating expenses. Again, the Parul Group's operating profit margin has been boosted by the inclusion of Saachi Co, which has an operating profit margin of 55.7%.

The operating margin may also have decreased due to potential one-off costs arising as a result of the acquisition of Saachi. These costs will not be repeated in the future and the operating profit margin should improve.

The inter-company charge for the consultancy service had been removed on consolidation, and adding this back worsens the Parul Group's operating expenses and operating profit margin.

Statement of financial position

The Parul Group has very slow inventory turnover, with 283 days in 20X7 worsening further in 20X8 to a restated 346 days. We are not told the industry in which the Parul Group operates and further investigation would be advisable to determine how typical this is of that industry. Given the fall in revenue and gross margin, it seems likely that the Parul Group is experiencing falling demand and is struggling to sell its inventory.

If, as suggested above, selling prices are being reduced, it is possible that some of the inventory may be overvalued, and it may be necessary to reduce the value down to net realisable value. The resulting reduction in inventory value (and increase in cost of sales) would improve calculated inventory days, but the impact of the charge to the statement of profit or loss would worsen profitability margins still further.

The restated amount for cash and cash equivalents shows that the inclusion of Saachi Co's cash balances in the consolidated accounts masked a large drop in the underlying cash balances of the Parul Group. However it should be noted that the acquisition of Saachi Co may have been wholly or partly financed by cash and so the fall in the Parul Group's cash balances might be due to the acquisition.

We also do not know how much of the increase in loans relates to Saachi Co. Saachi Co may have high levels of borrowings (and interest) or the loans may have been taken out by the Parul Group in order to finance the acquisition of Saachi Co.

Caution must be exercised when interpreting the unadjusted consolidated financial statements of the Parul Group as these include only four months of the items on Saachi Co's statement of profit or loss yet 100% of the values from Saachi Co's statement of financial position and ratios may be distorted.

Conclusion

The concern that the acquisition of Saachi is obscuring Parul's underlying performance seems justified.

Overall, the underlying performance in 20X8 is markedly worse than 20X7, and Parul may have acquired Saachi in order to bolster its own results.

ACCA marking guide		
		Marks
(a)	Restatement – profit or loss	4
	– inventory and cash	2
		6
(b)	Ratios (½ mark each)	**3**
(c)	Performance	5
	Position and conclusion	6
		11
Total		**20**

453 FIT CO

(a) Ratio calculations

	Fit Co	**Sporty Co**
Gross profit	24.0%	31.8%
	(60,000/250,000)	(70,000/220,000)
Operating profit	10.0%	14.5%
	(25,000/250,000)	(32,000/220,000)
Trade payables days	67 days	29 days
	((35,000/190,000)×365)	((12,000/150,000) × 365)
Return on capital employed	18.5%	42.7%
	(25,000/(90,000+45,000))	(32,000/(60,000+15,000))
Gearing	50%	25%
	(45,000/90,000)	(15,000/60,000)

(b) Performance and position

Performance

As can be seen from the ratio calculations, Sporty Co has a higher gross profit margin than Fit Co, even though it has lower revenue overall. The reason for this could be that Sporty Co sources its items direct from the manufacturer, and so does not incur manufacturing costs.

Indeed, it is surprising that Fit Co has a lower GPM than Sporty Co given that it is selling premium branded goods – it would be expected that such goods would be sold at a higher margin.

The difference could also be a result of the competition suffered by Fit Co in the year, which may have led Fit Co to decrease its selling prices.

The gross profit margin of Fit Co may also fall further, as the gross profit margin of the Active division is 40%, which is much higher than Fit Co overall. Therefore, the underlying gross profit margin of the remaining Fit Co business would be expected to be lower than that shown for the current year.

The operating profit for Sporty Co is 4% higher than Fit Co. This is not surprising given that Sporty Co's GPM is higher than that of Fit Co. On closer inspection, Fit Co's OPM is inflated because of the non–recurring $5m gain on disposal. In addition to this, Fit Co profit for 31 December 20X0 includes central services income of $1.2m which will not recur following the disposal of the Active division. It is also worth noting that Fit Co will have a higher cost base, which would be expected as it operates its own stores, whereas Sporty Co uses department stores.

Sporty Co has a much higher return on capital employed than Fit Co, as it has a higher operating profit, and lower long–term debt and equity.

Position

Fit Co has a gearing ratio twice that of Sporty Co, as it has much higher long–term debt. This makes Fit Co a riskier business than Sporty Co, as it must meet these debt repayments or would face insolvency.

As the gearing for Sporty Co is much lower than that of Fit Co, Sporty Co should be able to secure debt finance if needed for its planned international expansion.

Fit Co will incur much higher finance costs on its debt than Sporty Co, which is equity financed. Both companies can currently cover interest payments from operating profits however the cash balance for Fit Co is much lower than Sporty Co, which applies further pressure to Fit Co as it must meet high interest payments. The current year interest payments for Fit Co exceed the cash balance at year–end, therefore Fit Co must ensure that its cash interest payments are sustainable in the long term.

Trade payables days are 67 for Fit Co and 29 for Sporty Co. This is consistent with the fact that Fit Co has a much lower cash balance than Sporty Co and shows that Fit Co is unable to pay suppliers quickly. This could lead to future problems with suppliers and shows that Fit Co needs to monitor its cash balance to ensure it can continue to trade in the long term.

Conclusion

Overall, it would appear that Sporty Co is in a better financial position than Fit Co, as it is more profitable, has lower debt, and should be able to access additional resources for its planned expansion.

ACCA marking guide		
		Marks
(a)	Ratio calculations	6
(b)	Performance	9
	Position and conclusion	5
Total		**20**

Examiners' report

This was considered to be a relatively straightforward performance appraisal question that required candidates to calculate some financial ratios and provide a commentary on the performance and position of two companies operating in the same sector.

Part (a) required the calculation of five standard financial ratios for both companies. It was pleasing to note that **many candidates were able to score full marks** on this part of the question. There were some common errors made in the calculation of some these ratios such as profit before tax being incorrectly used in both operating margin and return on capital employed. Also, many candidates used the **wrong capital employed figure** to arrive at the return on capital employed (this should be debt + equity). It was surprising that despite previous guidance from the examining team there continues to be a number of candidates that calculate gearing using the formula of debt to debt + equity **despite the question specifically asking** for debt to equity. While the former is acceptable in some questions, if you are given specific guidance in the question requirement ensure you calculate the ratio as instructed to achieve the mark available.

The quality of the commentary provided to part (b) of this question was particularly disappointing. The trend continues where many candidates provide either **little or no analysis or the analysis provided is superficial** and does not attempt to use the information in the scenario to guide the commentary. Those candidates that link their commentary to the scenario tend to score very well.

There was **plenty of information in the scenario** of this question that could act as a prompt for a more detailed commentary. For example, both companies operate in the same sector. However, one company is a manufacturer and retailer of premium branded sportswear, while the other sources mid-market sportswear from its suppliers and retails them separately. Based on this information it is likely that both sales prices, costs etc. will be significantly different for each company and could be used to explain the differences in performance. Both companies sell online, but one sells through its own branded stores and one sells through department stores. Again, this would give rise to differences not only in the costs incurred by each business but the structure of the statement of financial position is likely to be different (Fit would be expected to have more assets due to its manufacturing facilities and premises for its stores) and this in turn would impact return on capital employed. These are not the only prompts given in the question!

Candidates are encouraged to **look at the information provided** in the scenario and to use it to add depth and meaning to their analysis. The marking guide to this and other published FR questions can be used to give you further ideas of the commentary required to score well on a performance appraisal question.

The marking team continues to encourage candidates to **provide a conclusion** to their analysis/commentary. Whilst some candidates did attempt to provide a conclusion on this question, there were many that did not. In this particular question for example, candidates could summarise their findings to determine which company is considered to be the best performing based on the limited information available.

454 KARL CO

(a) Loss on disposal

The loss on disposal in the consolidated financial statements is:

	$m
Proceeds	20.0
Less: net assets	(29.0)
Less: carrying amount of goodwill **(W1)**	(2.1)
Loss on disposal	(11.1)

(W1) Goodwill

	$m
Fair value of investment	35.0
Less net assets at acquisition	(28.0)
Goodwill at acquisition	7.0
Goodwill impairment (70%)	(4.9)
Carrying amount of goodwill	2.1

(b) Ratios and commentary

	20X8	**20X7**
Profitability ratios		
Gross profit margin	42.9%	48.5%
	((124/289) × 100)	((132/272) × 100)
Operating profit margin	22.1%	35.3%
	((64/289) × 100)	((96/272) × 100)
Return on capital employed	8.9%	13.2%
(operating profit / equity + NCL)	(64/(621 + 100))	(96/(578 + 150))
Liquidity ratios		
Current ratio	3.1:1	0.8:1
	(112/36)	(125/161)
Gearing (debt/ debt + equity)	13.9%	20.6%
	(100/(621 + 100))	(150/(578 + 150))

Financial performance

Consolidated revenue has increased from 20X7 to 20X8, despite the loss of Sinker Co's significant customer contract three months into the financial year. This might suggest that an increase in the revenue of Karl (or its other subsidiary, or both) has more than compensated for Sinker Co's lost revenue. However, even though the group revenue has increased, the gross profit margin has fallen by 5.6% and the group cost of sales is higher than 20X7. This is likely to have been impacted by the poor financial performance of Sinker Co. Alternatively, it may be that the sales mix of the group has changed.

As sales of Sinker Co represent 14% of the total group sales, this poor performance will also have impacted on the group operating margin. Operating profit margin has dropped significantly from 35.3% to 22.1%. Administrative expenses have almost doubled from $23m for the year ended 31 December 20X7 to $45m for the year ended 31 December 20X8. Part of this increase will be due to the $11.1m loss on disposal of Sinker Co. The administrative expenses will also have increased as a result of the $15m staff redundancy costs and impairment of goodwill.

ROCE has fallen from 13.2% to 8.9%, but this figure is hard to interpret, as the return includes the results of Sinker Co (including the loss on disposal and impairment of goodwill) but the capital employed does not include the capital of Sinker Co due to the disposal at the year end. The operating loss made by Sinker Co of $17m, plus the loss on disposal of $11.1m and impairment of $4.9m will have reduced operating profit. Although it is a simplification, removing these balances would result in a group ROCE of 12.9% ($64m + ($17m + $11.1m + $4.9m))/(($621m + $17m + $11.1m + $4.9m) + $100m) which is more in line with the 20X7 figure.

Financial position

The current ratio shows considerable improvement for the year ended 20X8, following the disposal of Sinker Co. The group was in a net current liability position at the end of 20X7.

This would suggest that Sinker Co may have had a large bank overdraft balance or high levels of payables at 31 December 20X8. It would appear that the sale of Sinker Co has improved the liquidity of the group.

It should be noted that 20X8 group current assets of $112m will include the $20m consideration for Sinker Co. This could be used to settle some of the long-term debt. Bank loans have already decreased by at least $50m. There is no information about the long-term loans of Sinker Co.

Gearing has been reduced during the year from 20.6% to 13.9% but, without further information on Sinker Co's non-current liabilities, it is very difficult to tell if this is a result of the disposal or whether Karl Co has simply repaid debt during the year.

Conclusion

The inclusion of Sinker Co in the consolidated statement of profit or loss does not appear to have had an adverse impact on revenue generation but, now that Karl Co has disposed of the poorly performing subsidiary, it might be able to better control costs, thereby improving gross and operating profit margins. Sinker Co appears to have been a drain on the liquidity of the group, and the position of the group appears to be much healthier following the disposal of Sinker Co.

(c) Comparability

As the sale of Sinker Co took place on 31 December 20X8, both 20X7 and 20X8 include a full year's trading for Sinker Co so profitability would appear to be comparable. However, we need to remember that the consolidated administration expenses for 20X8 includes the loss on disposal of $11.1 million, so this will need to be adjusted before comparison is possible.

The main area where comparability will be affected is within the statement of financial position, because the 20X8 consolidated statement of financial position (CSFP) will exclude the assets and liabilities of Sinker Co. Any ratios for 20X8 which use CSFP figures will not be directly comparable with those for 20X7. This will include return on capital employed, current ratio and gearing ratio.

This lack of comparability is one of the reasons that IFRS 5 *Non-current Assets Held for Sale and Discontinued Operations* was introduced, to show the discontinued operation separately in order to better measure the performance and position of the continuing business. Despite the fact that, according to the question, the sale did not meet the necessary definition, comparability would have been improved by applying the IFRS 5 treatment.

ACCA marking guide		
		Marks
(a)	Disposal loss	4
(b)	Ratio calculations	5
	Analysis	8
(c)	Comparability	3
Total		**20**

455 PASTRY CO

(a) Adjusted financial statement extracts and ratios for Dough Co

	As per question	**Adjustment**	**Adjusted**
	$000	$000	$000
Statement of profit or loss			
Revenue	16,300		16,300
Cost of sales	(8,350)	(2,500)	(10,850)
Gross profit	7,950		5,450
Operating expenses	(4,725)	(1,000) (2,500)	(1,225)
Profit from operation	3,225		4,225
Statement of financial position			
Property	68,500	(30,000) 1,000	39,500
Equity shares	1,000		1,000
Revaluation surplus	30,000	(30,000)	–
Retained earnings	2,600	1,000	3,600
Loan notes	5,200		5,200

	Cook Co	**Dough Co (original)**	**Workings**	**Dough Co (restated)**
Gross profit margin	32.3%	48.8%	5,450/16,300 × 100	33.4%
Operating profit margin	23.3%	19.8%	4,225/16,300 × 100	25.9%
ROCE	18.8%	8.3%	4,225/(4,600 + 5,200) × 100	43.1%

Tutorial note: The explanations below were not part of the requirement but are included to assist candidates in understanding how the adjustments were determined.

If Dough Co accounted for properties under the cost model:

- Depreciation would reduce by $1 million ($30 million/30 years), reducing operating expenses and increasing profit from operations to $4.225 million.
- Retained earnings would increase by $1 million to $3.6 million.
- Revaluation surplus of $30 million would be removed.
- Property would decrease by $29 million ($30 million less extra depreciation).

If Dough Co accounted for amortisation in cost of sales:

- Cost of sales would increase by $2.5 million, making gross profit $5.45 million.
- Operating expenses would decrease by $2.5 million, but profit from operations would remain at $4.225 million.

(b) Margins

Cook co may be a slightly larger company, having made more sales and profits during the year. Initially, it appears that Dough Co makes a significantly higher margin than Cook Co (48.8% compared to 32.3%), which suggests that it is much more profitable to sell as a retailer rather than wholesale.

However, this is misleading as the higher gross profit margin is largely due to the accounting policy of where amortisation is charged. Once the figures are adjusted to make the two companies comparable, the two gross profit margins are much closer (33.4% and 32.3%).

Even with this adjustment, Dough Co still makes a higher gross profit margin, suggesting that the relatively high cost properties are still producing a good return.

Looking at the operating profit margin, it appears that Cook Co makes a significantly higher margin, suggesting a greater cost control (23.3% compared to 19.8%). Once the adjustments for the different accounting policies are taken into account, it can be seen that the margins are much more comparable (23.3% and 25.9%).

Without further information on the operating expenses, it is difficult to draw too many conclusions about the cost management of the two companies.

The one thing which can be noted is the higher payment of salaries in Dough Co compared to Cook Co. As both companies are owner-managed, it may be that Cook Co's management are taking a lower level of salaries in order to show increased profits.

Alternatively, it could be that the Dough Co management are taking salaries which are too high, at the expense of the growth of the business. The low level of retained earnings suggests that Dough Co's owners may not leave much money in the business for growing the company.

ROCE

When looking at the return on capital employed, the initial calculations show that Cook Co is making a much more impressive return from its long-term funding (18.8% compared to 8.3%). This is completely reversed when the revaluation surplus is removed from Dough Co's figures, as Dough Co makes a return of more than twice that of Cook Co (18.8% and 43.1%).

This return is not due to high operating profits, as the margins of the two companies are similar, with Dough Co actually making lower profits from operations.

The reason for the high return on capital employed is that Dough Co has a much better asset turnover than Cook Co. This is not because Dough Co is generating more sales, as these are lower than Cook Co. The reason is that Dough Co has a significantly lower equity balance, due to having extremely low retained earnings relative to Cook Co.

Difficulties

Without examining the market value of Cook Co's properties, it will be difficult to assess which company is likely to cost more to purchase.

Basing any investment decision on a single year's financial statements is difficult, as the impact of different accounting policies is difficult to assess.

From the information provided, it is unclear whether Cook Co's directors are taking an unrealistically low salary, or whether Dough Co's directors are taking vastly greater salaries than average.

Conclusion (marks awarded for sensible conclusion)

Overall, both companies appear to be profitable and have performed well. Looking at previous years' financial statements of both entities will enable us to make a much clearer investment decision, as will looking at the notes to the accounts to assess the accounting policies applied by each company.

Other comments which candidates may produce which could be given credit

Comments that Cook Co's operating profit margin would be lower if equivalent salaries to Dough Co were paid.

Comment on the relative size or cost of premises of the two companies.

Discussion of potential reasons for low retained earnings in Dough Co.

Discussion of the relative level of debt and relative interest charges.

Dough Co being highly geared but owning property.

Dough Co having much lower rate of interest with sensible suggestion of why this may be the case (e.g. possibly due to loan being new or from parent).

Lack of prior year financial statements included as a difficulty.

ACCA marking guide		
		Marks
(a)	Restated ratios	6
(b)	Margins discussion	6
	ROCE discussion	4
	Difficulties and conclusion	4
Total		**20**

Extract from examiners' report (for detailed report see ACCA website)

Pastry Co shares similarities with recent questions examined on the syllabus area of analysis and interpretation of the financial statements (syllabus section C). The question contained both numerical information and additional information relating to two companies, Cook Co and Dough Co that are potential acquisition targets for Pastry Co.

Analysis and interpretation is an important area of the syllabus and will continue to be examined. As in previous examination sessions, most candidates failed to score high marks on this question. The reason for this seemed to be poor exam technique by not addressing the requirements or **not adequately using the information in the scenario**.

Candidates were required to recalculate ratios based on their adjustments in (a). As always, the 'own figure' rule was applied here. This means that if candidates had made errors on the earlier adjustments of their financial statements they were given the marks for using their own adjusted figures, even if they were incorrect.

As an example, a candidate may have added $30 million to the revaluation surplus, rather than deducting it as they should have done. As long as they showed their working in their return on capital employed (ROCE) calculation, they would get the full follow through marks, even though their capital employed figure was $60m higher than it should have been.

The use of the 'own figure' rule means that the only candidates who would not score full marks on the ratio calculations were those who either did not know the formulae for those ratios or those who did not provide workings. If a candidate made an error in adjusting their figures and then did not provide a working for their adjusted ratio, it was difficult to see how they had arrived at the calculations. Markers will not try to guess or assume what the candidate has done, so it is **essential that detailed workings are shown**.

The FR examinations team have mentioned this in most of the examiners' reports which have been written, but it is absolutely **essential that candidates use the information in the scenario** in answering the question. Far too many candidates are still trying to answer analysis questions with explanations rote-learned from a textbook.

This means that answers are often generic and bear no relevance to the scenario in front of them. It is important that candidates understand possible reasons for the movements in ratios but then use the scenario to fully explain the performance of the entities.

Candidates can approach this in any way they see fit, although **candidates working their way from top to bottom generally seem to score higher**. These candidates discuss movements in revenue, gross profit margin, operating profit margin and then go on to ROCE.

Weaker candidates start with ROCE, explaining how ROCE is made up. This is not needed in the exam, as we are looking for candidates to explain the reasons for movements rather than explaining the definitions of ratios.

Overall, the standard of narrative was disappointing in responses to this question.

Answers were either too brief or too generic. The golden rules for candidates to think about to produce a good answer are:

– **Use the scenario** – any answer not based on this will not score well
– One mark per well explained point
– Talk about all key areas (revenue in particular), even if it's not in a ratio calculation
– **Always say WHY** ratios or figures have changed or are different

If a candidate follows these rules, they will be able to score well in this type of question. Unfortunately, far **too many candidates seem to be content with learning ratio definitions** and trying to repeat these in the exam.

456 PINARDI CO  Walk in the footsteps of a top tutor

Key answer tips

This style of question with a number of requirements is naturally time consuming – ensure you answer all parts of the question and do not spend too much time on the calculations. Part (b) offers easy marks if you have a decent knowledge of IFRS 5 *Non-current Assets Held for Sale and Discontinued Operations*, and are independent of the rest of the question so you could do part (b) first to avoid missing out on 'easy' marks. When interpreting the results in part (d) is sure to link your response to the additional information given in the question. Presentation is also important in part (d), so make it easy for the marker to read by using short paragraphs and spaces between paragraphs. The highlighted words are key phrases that markers are looking for.

(a) Gain on disposal:

	$000
Proceeds	42,000
Less: Net assets at disposal	(35,000)
Less: Goodwill at disposal (W1)	(4,200)
Gain on disposal	**2,800**

(W1) Goodwill at disposal

	$000
Goodwill at acquisition	6,000
Less impairment	(1,800)
Unimpaired goodwill at disposal	**4,200**

(b) Explanation of Silva Co disposal

Silva Co is likely to meet the criteria as it is a separate major line of operations that has been disposed of during the year.

As a discontinued operation the results would be removed and presented separately at the bottom of the statement of profit or loss together with the gain (post-tax) on disposal of $2.8 million.

As Silva Co was sold on 1 January 20X7, there are no results to incorporate for the current year. However, the results of 20X6 should be shown as a discontinued operation for comparative purposes.

(c) Ratio calculations

Ratio	**Working**	**20X7**	**Working**	**20X6**
Gross profit margin	(50,700/98,300)	51.6%	(50,600/122,400)	41.3%
Operating profit margin	(17,000/98,300)	17.3%	(13,200/122,400)	10.8%
Interest cover	(17,000/3,200)	5.3 times	(13,200/5,500)	2.4 times
Inventory turnover days	(13,300/47,600 × 365)	102 days	(22,400/71,800 × 365)	114 days

(d) Analysis

Performance

The overall revenue is down by $24.1m, which may be largely due to the disposal of Silva Co which is in the 20X6 results but contributed no revenue in 20X7.

Last year, Silva Co contributed $36m in revenue. Removing this from the 20X6 results shows that there has been a like for like increase of $11.9m (($122.4m – $36m) – $98.3m) from the fragrance and cosmetics divisions.

The gross profit margin is up significantly from 20X6 to 20X7, from 41% to 52%. We can see that the gross profit margin of Silva Co in 20X6 was only 35% ($12.6m/$36m), so the other parts of the group were able to generate higher gross margins historically.

The operating margin has increased, although not quite as dramatically as the increase in gross profit margin. In fact, the operating expenses have only decreased by $3.7m, despite the $24.1m decrease in revenue. There are some factors to consider within the operating expenses for 20X7. There is a one-off exit fee of $3m for the cosmetics division to exit the lease. While this is expensive, the division would have been paying $25m over 10 years, so will ultimately save a significant amount of money.

In addition to this, the effects of foreign exchange gains and losses are included in the operating expenses line. In 20X6 there was a gain of $3m but in 20X7 there was a loss of $1m which will have reduced operating profit. This shows that the Pinardi group have quite large exposure to foreign currency risk.

The interest cover has increased from 2.4 to 5.3 during the year, which is a combination of both an increase in operating profits and a decrease in finance costs. The finance costs are likely to have decreased due to the exit from the lease.

Position

The decrease in non-current liabilities is likely to be partly due to the removal of the lease liability for the cosmetics decision, which had 10 years remaining.

Some of the non-current liabilities may also have been paid off from the proceeds from the sale of Silva Co. Silva Co was sold for $42m, but cash has only increased by around $17m. Therefore the Pinardi group may have used some of the cash to reduce the non-current liabilities in the group.

It is also worth noting that in 20X6 the assets and liabilities would have included the Silva Co figures. It may have been that Silva Co had significant non-current liabilities which were removed when it was sold.

The inventory turnover figure shows that the Pinardi group is able to turn over inventory more quickly than previously. The inventory days are high, but the nature of the Pinardi group products will mean that they are not immediately perishable so this is unlikely to be a significant concern.

In 20X6 the Pinardi group inventory turnover period will include the figures relating to Silva Co. The removal of this seems to show that the inventory turnover period relating to cosmetics and fragrance is lower than that of the jewellery sector.

Conclusion (marks awarded for sensible conclusion)

Whilst Silva Co does generate profits, the disposal seems to have been a good move. Silva Co's results have actually improved since disposal, showing it is not a struggling business. The additional focus on the remaining divisions has generated more profits for the Pinardi group, particularly now the cosmetics division is utilising the group property and no longer requiring leased premises.

Other comments which candidates may produce which could be given credit

It should be noted that there is now $2m revenue relating to the use of the Silva Co name which will be there each year. Removing this for comparability shows that the like for like increase in revenue is $10m.

The inclusion of the $2m income from Silva Co with no cost of sales will have increased the gross margin. Even removing this reduces it to 50.6% so has not accounted for a significant movement.

Whilst cash has only increased by $17m despite the $42m sale, it may have been that Silva Co had a significant amount of cash in the bank, which was removed from the group when Silva Co is disposed of.

The exclusion of the $36m revenue and $6.6m operating expenses of Silva Co from the 'continuing operations' consolidated statement of profit or loss for 20X6 suggest operating expenses as a % of revenue in 20X6 were (30,800 (37,400 – 6,600)/86,400 (122,400 – 36,000) 35.6% which is actually higher than that for 20X7 (34.2%). On a like-for-like basis this, along with the improvement in the gross margin, suggests a better financial performance for the Pinardi group without Silva Co.

ACCA marking guide		
		Marks
(a)	Calculations	2
(b)	Explanation	3
(c)	Ratios	4
(d)	Analysis	11
Total		**20**

Extract from examiners' report (for detailed report see ACCA website)

Pinardi Co shares similarities with recent questions examined on the syllabus area of analysis and interpretation of the financial statements. The analysis and interpretation of a group is an important area of the syllabus and will continue to be examined. As in previous examination sessions, most candidates failed to score high marks on this question. The reason for this seemed to be poor exam technique such as not addressing the requirements or not adequately using the information in the scenario.

Calculating a gain or loss on the disposal of a subsidiary has been part of the FR syllabus for many years now. The information on the disposal of Silva Co, a 100% owned subsidiary, was mostly straightforward. Many candidates were able to score full marks on this requirement. However, there were some candidates who omitted this part of the answer entirely and others who demonstrated a lack of knowledge of this syllabus area.

Part (b) of the question required candidates to apply their knowledge of IFRS 5 *Non-current Assets Held for Sale and Discontinued Operations*. Numerous candidates ignored this part of the question altogether which was both surprising and disappointing.

It was pleasing to see that many candidates were able to score full marks on part (c) of the question. The examining team continue to recommend that candidates show not only the relevant formula for the ratios, but also fully show their workings. An incorrect answer without workings will not be awarded any marks, but where workings are provided markers are able to award marks despite any 'calculation errors' where relevant. This is an integral part of the syllabus and features at every examination sitting and as such candidates should have a working knowledge of financial ratios.

For part (d) the examinations team noted that many scripts continue to provide superficial, 'textbook' answers that do not draw on any of the information from the scenario. Candidates should note that these types of answers will attract little, if any, marks.

To earn marks in this type of question it is essential that candidates use the scenario to provide a rationale for the changes in the performance and position. This scenario was not short of clues, one of the biggest being the disposal of Silva Co, so it was surprising that many answers failed to consider this at all.

A good answer would discuss the immediate impact of the disposal such as the reduction in both revenue and costs, but then would aim to develop this further. For example, despite the reduction in revenue following the disposal of Silva Co, gross profit and operating margins improved. If candidates calculated the gross profit and operating profit margins for Silva Co using the information provided in note (4), candidates could go on to explain that Silva Co has good results on a standalone basis, but these were below group results, suggesting that better margins are earned in the fragrance and cosmetics industry compared to jewellery manufacturing.

The highest-level candidates would then develop their answers further by drawing on the information that has been included in the scenario. For example, operating expenses include a one-off payment as a result of exiting the lease, which distorts the current year profit. By excluding this one-off cost, operating profit margin would improve, and this would continue to be expected in 20X8.

Overall, the analysis on these questions continues to be disappointing with only a minority of candidates using the scenario to form their answer. Answers were either far too brief or too generic.

457 VENUS CO

(a) Ratios

	Workings	**20X8**	**Workings**	**20X7**
Gross profit %	12,500/39,000 × 100	32.1%	11,000/32,000 × 100	34.4%
Net profit %	9,800/39,000 × 100	25.1%	8,900/32,000 × 100	27.8%
Return on equity %	9,800/87,500 × 100	11.2%	8,900/42,000 × 100	21.2%

(b) (i) Adjusted profit:

	$000
Venus Co consolidated profit for the year	9,800
Deduct Luto Co post-acquisition profit – note (1)	(2,000)
Deduct savings due to discounts received from Luto Co – note (2)	(500)
Add back unwinding of discount on deferred consideration (W1) – note (3)	185
Add back fair value adjustment depreciation (900/3 × $^6/_{12}$) – note (4)	150
Venus Co single entity net profit	7,635

Net profit % working: 22.5%

7,635/(39,000 – 5,000 Luto Co post-acquisition revenue) × 100

Workings

(W1)

	$000
Discount unwound (5m × 0.926 × 8% × $^6/_{12}$)	185
Alternatively:	
Discount unwound ((5m/1.08) × 8% × $^6/_{12}$)	185

(ii) Comparability

It is not possible to compare consolidated financial statements with those of a single entity for a number of reasons which include:

The results in a consolidated statement of profit or loss include not only the income and expenses of the parent, but also the income and expenses of any subsidiaries for the period during the year that they are controlled by the parent.

Transactions between the parent and its subsidiaries, such as intra-group sales, will be eliminated on consolidation but will remain in the single entity statement of profit or loss.

The consolidated statement of financial position includes all of the assets and liabilities controlled by the parent at the year end, including those of its subsidiaries.

Equity in consolidated financial statements will be increased by the addition of the non-controlling interest and the post-acquisition retained earnings from subsidiaries, less any impairment of goodwill.

Intra-group balances are removed on consolidation, but the single entity financial statements will include items like intra-group loans, intra-group receivables and intra-group payables.

(c) Performance

Despite the increase in revenue, profit attributable to the owners of Venus Co has increased by only $0.3m ($9.2m – $8.9m) following the acquisition.

As Luto Co has made a profit of $2m, this suggests that Venus Co has made a smaller profit than in the previous year.

The disappointing gross profit noted by the managing director and the resulting fall in the gross profit % will be partly due to a reduction in Venus Co's profitability.

Venus Co's 20X8 net profit without Luto Co would have been down on 20X7 by $1.265m ($8.9m – $7.635m (part (b))) and the net profit % would have fallen to 22.5% (part (b)) from 27.8% (part (a)). Venus Co has maintained its profit at a comparable level to the previous year only through the contribution of its subsidiary. This shows that the profits of Luto Co have had a positive impact on the group.

The acquisition has led to a significant deterioration in the return on equity (ROE) (11.2% compared to 21.2%). This is not so much due to the reduction in net profit percentage, which is down by less than three percentage points (27.8% – 25.1%), but to the significant increase in equity ($87.5m compared to $42m).

The acquisition has increased share capital and share premium, as a result of the share exchange, and brought in non-controlling interests (NCI). The financial statements show the entire share issue and NCI but only six months' group trading which will have a negative impact on ROE.

Managing director's (MD's) comments

The MD is incorrect to be disappointed in the performance of the subsidiary as it has had an overall positive impact on group performance (see performance comments above) which should increase when a full year's results are consolidated in 20X9.

The MD was expecting to see a favourable effect on gross profit due to the new discount from Luto Co. This has no effect on the consolidated financial statements, or the ratios based on the consolidated financial statements, as intra-group trading is eliminated on consolidation.

Conclusion

It does not appear that the disappointing results for the year to 30 June 20X8 can be attributed to the acquisition, as the results of Venus Co would have been down on the previous year if the acquisition had not taken place.

Additional points which could have been made:

There may also be synergies arising from the acquisition which will reduce operating costs in future years but have not yet had time to fully emerge.

It is also relevant to note that, while Luto Co's assets have undergone a fair value uplift, the non-current assets of Venus Co are carried at historical cost, which can have the effect of inflating ROE. If Venus Co's assets were recognised at fair value, this would probably increase equity and also reduce earnings through a higher depreciation charge.

ACCA marking guide		
		Marks
(a)	Ratios	3
(b)	(i) Venus Co profit	5
	(ii) Comparability	3
(c)	Performance and conclusion	9
Total		**20**

Extract from examiners' report (for detailed report see ACCA website)

As in previous examination sessions, most candidates failed to score high marks on this question. The reason for this seemed to be poor exam technique by not addressing the requirement or not adequately using the information in the scenario.

Requirement (a) was generally well received by candidates, with many earning full marks. This demonstrated that the ratio calculations had been well revised. The candidates who did not score well on this part of the question typically produced incorrect ratios without providing any workings, or there were some candidates who attempted to adjust the draft financial statement extracts before calculating the ratios. This was not asked for and candidates are reminded to read the requirements carefully before answering the question.

Requirement (b) (i) is one that candidates found challenging. In order to assess the true performance of the parent company, candidates were asked to remove the impact of the acquisition from the consolidated draft financial statement extracts. This is another way of testing if candidates know how the acquisition of a subsidiary will affect the figures in a consolidated statement of profit or loss.

To perform well on this section, candidates needed to demonstrate that they were comfortable with some core accounting entries relating to consolidations including depreciation on assets following a fair value adjustment at acquisition and the unwinding of a discount on deferred consideration. This part of the question should have been straightforward as these adjustments are common in a group scenario. However, outside the context of actually preparing consolidated financial statements, many candidates struggled.

It is important to note that Venus Co acquired its controlling interest in Luto Co six months ago and therefore the fair value depreciation and the unwinding of the discount needed to be time apportioned. This was often overlooked by candidates in their calculations.

Requirement (b) (ii) was looking for candidates to demonstrate a good understanding of the topic matter. The requirement specifically asks for an explanation as to why consolidated financial statements are not comparable to single entity financial statements, so it was surprising to see many answers stating generic limitations of ratio analysis that were not group related. These comments did not attract any marks.

The performance on part (c) of the question remained broadly consistent with previous years. The best candidates attempted to use the scenario and assess how the points given could have affected the numbers in the financial statements. Weaker candidates appear to have grasped the message about the importance of using the scenario but now copy out sections of the requirement into the answer. This repetition of the scenario will not gain marks as the examination team are looking for individuals to use that information to explain the impact on the entity.

The lowest performing candidates continue to make the same mistakes, either ignoring the scenario completely and giving 'textbook' answers about what the movements in the ratios could mean or simply putting extremely brief answers.

458 TREATS CO

(a) Ratios

Ratio	**Working**	**Treats Co**	**Sector**
Return on capital employed (ROCE)	7,466/(25,968 + 33,621)	12.5%	28.8%
Net asset turnover	214,553/(25,968 + 33,621)	3.6 times	2.4 times
Gross profit margin	106,544/214,553	49.7%	55%
Operating profit margin	7,466/214,553	3.5%	12%
Current ratio	47,996/50,391	0.95:1	1.8:1
Inventory turnover period	(30,393/108,009) x 365	103 days	25 days
Gearing (debt/equity)	33,621/25,968	129%	43%
Receivables collection period	17,603/214,553 x 365	30 days	15 days

(b) Performance

Treats Co's gross profit margin is slightly below the market average. This is not surprising as Treats Co sells goods to supermarkets which are likely at lower margins than goods sold directly to the public.

However, Treats Co's operating profit margin is significantly below the industry average. It is unclear what the cause of this is but it does suggest cost control issues as this is much worse than the sector average, compared to the difference in gross profit margin.

The fact that the assets held by the company are old and may need replacing may mean there have been large repairs and maintenance expenses in the year or have had impairment charges applied to them.

ROCE is much lower than the industry average. This is as a direct result of the low operating profit margin as the net asset turnover is above the sector average.

The fact that the ROCE is low in comparison to the industry average is concerning as this figure would drop further following an investment in property, plant and equipment (PPE). Currently Treats Co does not have the cash to acquire assets, so replacements are likely to lead to an increase in debt (whether due to loans or leasing assets), which would further reduce the ROCE.

The net asset turnover is higher than the industry average. Again, it must be noted that once the PPE is replaced, this figure will be significantly reduced.

Position

The current ratio is significantly lower than the industry average. This is likely to be due to the significant overdraft which Treats Co uses for working capital management.

It appears that a lot of cash is tied up in inventories. This could be due to the need to hold large volumes of goods to meet the supermarket contracts but could also signify issues over demand for Treats Co's products.

The inventory holding period is more than four times longer than the industry average. Considering that Treats Co sells perishable food products, this is of concern as items may require to be written down/off.

Treats Co's receivables collection period is not particularly high at 30 days but is still twice that of the industry average. This is likely to be due to the supermarket contract which will demand much longer payment terms.

Most of the sector sells goods solely through their own stores and so these are likely to be cash sales. As a result, the receivables days ratio is not comparable with many companies in the sector.

The gearing ratio is significantly higher than the industry average, which is a significant concern, particularly in the light of Treats Co's cash position. Treats Co is likely to need investment in non-current assets; it is doubtful whether it will be possible to raise debt finance to do this.

The large dividend payment is questionable as $7.14m has been paid despite the entity being overdrawn and in need of investment.

Conclusion

Overall, the results are mixed and further information is required to fully investigate the performance and financial position of Treats Co. Further investigation is required of the composition of operating expenses. Neither the inventory nor the cash position looks very strong in comparison to the industry averages; however, the receivables is reasonable – further aged analysis of inventory and the classification of receivables would also be useful to explain these positions. Finally, gearing is high and so more information relating to the terms of borrowings would also be useful.

Other points which could be made:

Gross margin – Treats Co still makes a 50% margin. This may be because Treats Co is a larger company (as shown in the supermarket contract) and can exercise economies of scale in managing costs or negotiating purchase discounts.

Gross margin – It is unclear what proportion of goods are sold to the supermarkets versus direct to the public. More information on this would help to further understand Treats Co's margin compared to the sector average.

Operating margin – This may get worse if assets are replaced or if impairments are needed. New assets are likely to have higher depreciation, which will further reduce the margin (as will impairment charges).

ACCA marking guide		
		Marks
(a)	Ratio analysis	5
		——
(b)	Performance	6
	Position and conclusion	9
		——
		15
		——
Total		**20**
		——

Extract from examiners' report (for detailed report see ACCA website)

Part (a) of the question required candidates to calculate eight ratios for Treats Co and was generally well answered. Many candidates were able to score full marks.

The examining team continue to remind candidates to **show both the formula for the relevant ratio and all workings** so that markers can allocate marks accordingly.

For example, where candidates had the incorrect denominator for return on capital employed (ROCE), if workings were shown, when this error followed through to the denominator for net asset turnover, markers were able to award the marks for net asset turnover in full. If no workings were shown for either ratio, candidates would lose the mark not only for ROCE but also for asset turnover.

The question specifically stated 'debt to equity' for the gearing ratio. Many candidates calculated gearing as 'debt to debt + equity'. Even though this is a valid way to calculate gearing, it was incorrect within the requirement of this question and, therefore, was not awarded any marks.

Some candidates included the overdraft as part of debt. Note (3) in the additional information told candidates that the overdraft did not form part of long-term financing and, therefore, the overdraft should not have been included in the calculation of gearing.

Many candidates did not allocate sufficient time to part (b) of the question with some only providing short sentences or bullet points, and others omitting this part entirely.

Under 'performance', candidates would typically discuss the profitability ratios (e.g., ROCE, net asset turnover and margins) and under 'position' the efficiency and solvency ratios (e.g. current ratio, working capital ratios and gearing). By using headings to structure discussion, candidates should be encouraged to explore the possible reasons for the ratio results.

Many candidates continue to answer these questions with explanations that are rote learnt from a textbook and bear no resemblance to the question scenario. This results in weak, largely generic, analysis, and scores few marks.

For example, a typical comment on the reason that the current ratio for Treats Co is lower was due to either "smaller assets or bigger liabilities" and no rationale was provided as to why this may be the case, such as the large overdraft held by Treats Co.

Several candidates simply copied out information from the question. This would appear to be because of reading previous examiner reports where candidates have been advised to use the scenario, however, to score marks this information must be used in the context of the scenario and ratio results rather than just copy and paste.

Weaker candidates sometimes misunderstood the scenario and provided commentary which was consistent with a year-on-year analysis rather than providing an explanation between the potential differences between Treats Co and the rest of the sector.

A good answer covered the range of ratios and attempted to provide possible, plausible reasons for the differences between Treats Co and the rest of the sector.

For example, it was pleasing to see that some candidates were able to recognise that most of Treats Co's profitability ratios were worse than the rest of the sector except for asset turnover. Many candidates were able to use note (4) to identify that Treats Co's products were sold both via its own stores and through supermarket chains and, therefore, margins were likely to be lower.

Very few candidates picked up on the information in note (1) where a low carrying amount on property, plant and equipment, when compared to its original cost, likely meant that the assets were old and may need replacing soon. This information meant that asset turnover is likely to be artificially high and will fall in the future if/when these assets are replaced. For those candidates that did recognise this, some were able to explore this further when analysing gearing.

Overall, the standard of the narrative on this question was disappointing, with many candidates missing the obvious clues in the question scenario. As discussed above, answers were generally too brief or too generic and lacked focus.

To produce an answer that scores well, candidates should consider the following:

Use the scenario – when discussing the differences in the ratios, this should be supported with information from the scenario. One mark will be awarded for a well-explained point.

Talk about **all areas in the scenario** – for Treats Co this means coverage of both performance and financial position.

Always consider **why results are different** and do not simply state that a result has increased/decreased.

Always **provide a conclusion** that is relevant to the requirement – for Treats Co, following your analysis, comment on whether Treats Co is performing better or worse that the sector average.

If a candidate follows these rules, they will be able to score well in this question.

459 SOUTTAR

(a) Ratios

	Working	**20X3**	**Working**	**20X2**
Operating profit margin	(120/630) × 100	19%	(90/450) × 100	20%
Interest cover	120/24	5.0	90/9	10.0
Dividend cover	82/25	3.3	69/20	3.5
Cash generated from operations / profit from operations	(108/120) × 100	90%	(75/90) × 100	83%

(b) Performance

Souttar Co's revenue has increased by 40% in 20X3. This increase is likely to be the result of increased grant work and the geographical expansion during 20X3.

The operating margin has fallen, which means that operating costs have increased relative to revenue. There are a number of possible explanations for this:

- Operating costs in this type of service business includes the employee costs, which have been subject to overtime payments this year.
- The use of freelancers, who are likely to charge a premium above the level of pay for Souttar Co's own staff, will also have increased operating costs.
- The expansion into new offices will may have resulted in a number of one-off costs linked to the new premises, such as set-up and marketing costs. In future, these costs will not be repeated and we should see a relative reduction in operating costs.
- The purchase of property, plant and equipment (including the new offices) will have resulted in additional depreciation costs.

However, the improved terms negotiated with major suppliers are likely to have resulted in lower purchase prices, reducing operating costs, offsetting some of these increases.

Interest cover has declined significantly in the year. Finance costs have almost trebled, primarily due to the issue of 9% loan notes during the year. However, interest cover of 5.0 is still healthy, and demonstrates that Souttar Co is generating sufficiently robust profits to meet its interest obligations.

It is likely that the 9% loan notes were issued to fund the expansion. The annual interest payable on these new loan notes will be $12,600, so Souttar Co will easily be able to cover this based on 20X3's performance.

Cash flow

The amount of cash generated from operations relative to the profit from operations has significantly improved in 20X3. The cash generated in 20X3 also easily covers a dividend as well as the interest and tax payments. This shows that sufficient cash is being generated to cover the cost of financing the business, which has increased due to the expansion. We should note that the increased dividend is a discretionary payment, so must have been deemed affordable when it was paid.

There is a significant increase in trade receivables, which is likely to be a result of acquiring new clients following the geographical expansion. In addition to this Souttar Co will have acquired new clients as a result of the government grant scheme. It is important that Souttar Co maintains strong credit control over these new clients, especially as most are likely to be new businesses (given the purpose of the government grant scheme).

The managing director has expressed concern that the business may have expanded too quickly. However, it is typical that expansion results in an increase in cash outflows due to the increased working capital requirement resulting from new customers taking credit and investment in property, plant and equipment. However, it is clear that the company has been able to easily finance this expenditure through:

- issuing new debt
- operating cash inflows this year
- opening cash balances

The increase in trade payables is likely to result from the increased trading levels and an increased payment period following the improved terms negotiated with major suppliers.

Souttar Co has raised $140,000 through the issue of 9% loan notes in the year. These have been issued to fund the expansion, which is an appropriate use of long-term financing. As stated previously, Souttar Co is easily capable of covering the interest payments on this new finance. It is worth noting that the finance costs in the statement of profit or loss are greater than the interest paid in the statement of cash flows. This suggests that the effective rate of interest on Souttar Co's overall funding is above the coupon payment made, meaning that a redemption premium may be payable in the future.

Conclusion

To reassure the managing director it is worth pointing out that cash inflows and outflows arise as a result of three activities that an entity undertakes: operating, investing and financing. The increased levels of profit mentioned by the marketing director are reflected within the cash generated from operating activities. The net reduction in cash balances during the year is due to significant levels of investing activity as a result of the business expansion, but this should lead to increased levels of revenue and profits in the future.

Overall the profit levels and cash generated appear to be sustainable, although care must be taken to ensure that receivables are collected on a timely basis and recovery does not become a problem.

ACCA marking guide		
		Marks
(a)	Ratio calculation	4
(b)	Performance	8
	Cash flow and conclusion	8
		16
Total		**20**

460 MARVELL CO

(a) Gain/loss on disposal of Bilston Co:

	$000
Sale proceeds	22,000
Less: Net assets at disposal (**W1**)	(18,200)
Less: Goodwill at disposal (**W2**)	(1,500)
Gain on disposal	2,300

Note: NCI is nil as Bilston Co was a wholly owned subsidiary.

(W1) Net assets at disposal date

	$000
Share capital	20,000
Revaluation surplus	3,200
Retained earnings	(5,000)
	18,200

(W2) Goodwill at disposal date

	$000
Fair value of consideration paid	25,000
Net assets at acquisition (20,000 + 3,000)	(23,000)
	2,000
Impairment to date (25%)	(500)
	1,500

(b) Ratio calculations (workings in $000):

	20X7		20X6	
Gross margin	21.8 %	(60,000/275,000) × 100	21.3%	(80,000/375,000) × 100
Operating margin	8.5%	(23,500/275,000) × 100	11.5%	(43,000/375,000) × 100
Return on capital employed	9.8%	(23,500/226,000 + 15,000) × 100	11.4%	(43,000/238,000 + 140,000) × 100
Net asset turnover	1.14	(275,000 /(226,000 + 15,000))	0.99	(375,000/(238,000 + 140,000))

Note: capital employed includes non-controlling interest

(c) Analysis of the performance of Marvell group for the year ended 31 December 20X7.

Impact of Bilston Co disposal:

The performance of Bilston Co is only included in the group results for the first six months of the year. Therefore, the results in the current period would be expected to show lower levels of income and expenditure, as 20X6 would include a full year of Bilston Co's figures.

The slight improvement in the group's gross margin suggests that Bilston Co was making a slightly lower gross margin than the rest of the Marvell group. Although not significantly different, this may have been a factor in the disposal decision. As Bilston Co was only included for the six months prior to its disposal, most of the gross margin would have been made from the remaining group companies.

The gain on disposal of $2.3m would have increased the operating margin. Without this gain on disposal, profit from operations would have been $21.2m ($23.5m – $2.3m), resulting in an operating margin of 7.7% ($21.2m/$275m).

Goodwill fell from $8m in 20X6 to nil in 20X7, of which $1.5m was the goodwill disposed with Bilston Co. The balance of the reduction in goodwill must be due to impairment of other subsidiaries in the current year due to the difficult trading conditions faced by the group. This $6.5m of impairment will have had a major impact on both administration expenses and operating margin, representing 2.4% of revenue.

A revised operating margin for 20X7, removing the effect of both the profit on disposal and the impairment would be 5.3% (($23.5m – $2.3m – $6.5m)/$275m).

Revenue and margins

There has been a significant decline in the revenue of the Marvell group in 20X7. This will be partly due to the disposal of Bilston Co, as mentioned above. We are also told that the Marvell group encountered difficulties in trading, which is likely to have led to a fall in revenue.

Despite the fall revenue and the difficult trading conditions, the gross profit margin is relatively unaffected. Increasing slightly from 21.3% to 21.8%. It would seem that Marvell Co has not responded to difficult conditions by reducing its prices.

The operating margin has fallen significantly, despite the inclusion of the gain on the disposal of Bilston Co. A large element of the fall will be due to the goodwill impairment discussed above, but there are clearly other problems. Distribution costs have not fallen as much as might have been expected from the decline in revenue, possibly due to some fixed element included such as wages or depreciation. There are also likely to have been expenses incurred during the disposal of Bilston Co, although these are one-off costs and will not be repeated in future years.

Return on capital employed

The primary measure of profitability is the return on capital employed (ROCE) and Marvell group's ROCE of 9.8% in the current year is lower than the previous year. The main cause of this fall seems to be the drop in operating margin, which has deteriorated from 11.5% to 8.5%.

In addition to the goodwill impairment and disposal costs discussed above, this decline in the operating margin may be linked to the difficulty in trading conditions.

This measure is somewhat distorted as six months of Bilston Co's operating profits are included in the consolidated statement of profit or loss, whereas none of its capital employed is reflected in the year end consolidated statement of financial position.

Asset turnover

While the operating margin has declined, the net asset turnover has actually increased, which would initially indicate that the Marvell group have become more efficient at generating better revenue from its capital employed. However, a closer look reveals that the improvement in net asset turnover is not due to increased revenue (as revenue has declined dramatically), but due to the significant decline in capital employed.

The decrease in capital employed can be seen in a number of areas, which could all be linked to the disposal of Bilston Co. First, the loan notes have decreased by $125m. Although some of these may have been repaid from the sale proceeds of Bilston Co, it would seem more likely that the loan notes were held by Bilston Co, and have now been removed from the group following Bilston Co's disposal.

In addition to the loan notes, in total, the net assets (equity) of Bilston Co at disposal was $18.2m (W1). This is reflected in the reduction in intangible assets, which had a value of $120m in 20X6. Furthermore, the revaluation surplus has fallen by $3.5 million which is largely due to the disposal of Bilston Co which had a revaluation surplus of $3.2 million atthe date of the disposal.

Dividends and finance

The retained earnings have decreased, despite the Marvell group making $9.3m profit during the year. This would suggest that a significant dividend has been paid by the parent company, possibly funded by the sale proceeds on disposal of Bilston Co. This would not seem to be sensible, given the current trading difficulties.

Finance costs have reduced significantly from $11.5m in 20X6 to $6.2m in 20X7. This is linked to the decrease in 8% loan notes on the statement of financial position. The loan notes may have been part of Bilston Co's liabilities which were extinguished as a result of the disposal of that company.

Conclusion

Overall, the disposal of Bilston Co has had a positive effect on group profitability due to the profit on disposal and the likelihood that Bilston Co was loss-making (shown by its negative retained earnings balance). However, the difficult trading conditions faced by all the companies in the group have resulted in decreased levels of reported profits for the group as a whole.

ACCA marking guide		
		Marks
(a)	Gain on disposal	4
(b)	Ratio calculation	4
(c)	Impact of Bilston	4
	Performance and conclusion	8
		12
Total		**20**

Section 7

SPECIMEN EXAM QUESTIONS

F7 Financial Reporting - Specimen Exam

This exam is divided into three sections:

Section A

- 15 objective test (OT) questions, each worth 2 marks.
- 30 marks in total.

Section B

- Three OT cases, each containing a scenario which relates to five OT questions, each worth 2 marks.
- 30 marks in total.

Section C

- Two constructed response questions, each containing a scenario which relates to one or more requirement(s).
- Each constructed response question is worth 20 marks in total.
- 40 marks in total.

Please note that the live exam is worth a total of 110 marks, 10 marks of which are for questions that do not count towards your final result and are included for quality assurance purposes. This specimen exam is worth a total of 100 marks, reflecting the element of the live exam on which your result will be based.

All questions are compulsory.

Click **Next** to start your exam.

F7 Financial Reporting - Specimen Exam

Section A

This section of the exam contains **15 objective test (OT) questions**.

Each question is worth **2 marks** and is compulsory.

This exam section is worth **30 marks** in total.

Select **Next** to continue.

Q1

Match the tokens to the appropriate category based on whether or not the costs should be capitalised in the initial carrying amount of an item of plant.

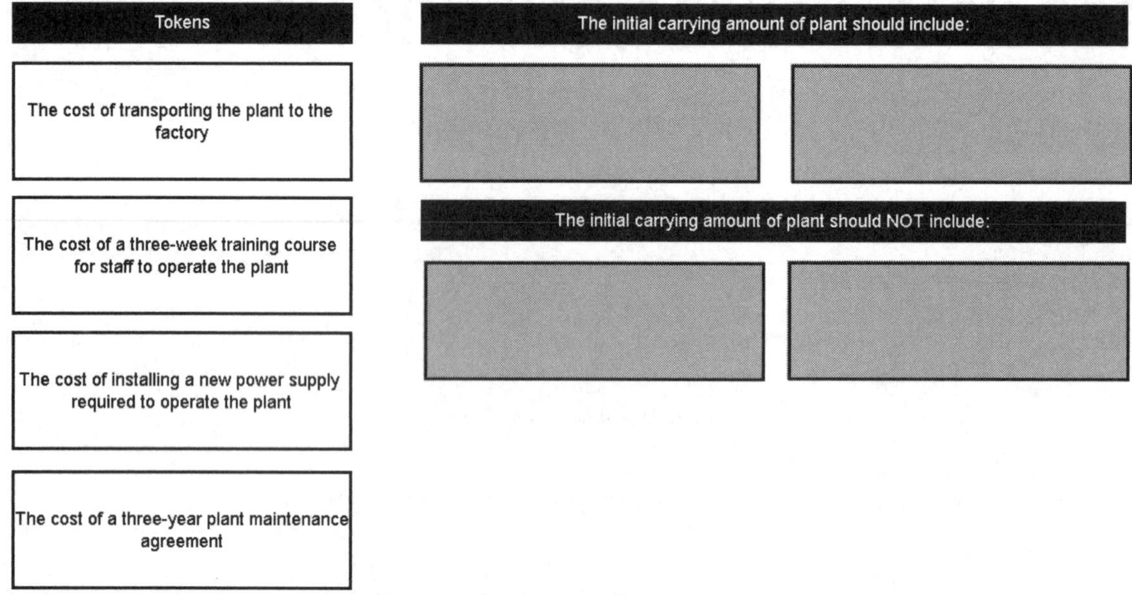

Q2

When a parent is evaluating the assets of a potential subsidiary, certain intangible assets can be recognised separately from goodwill, even though they have not been recognised in the subsidiary's own statement of financial position.

Which of the following is an example of an intangible asset of the subsidiary that may be recognised separately from goodwill when preparing consolidated financial statements?

- A new research project which the subsidiary has correctly expensed to profit or loss but the directors of the parent have reliably assessed to have a substantial fair value
- A global advertising campaign which was concluded in the previous financial year and from which benefits are expected to flow in the future
- A contingent asset of the subsidiary from which the parent believes a flow of future economic benefits is possible
- A customer list which the directors are unable to value reliably

Q3

On 1 October 20X4, Flash Co acquired an item of plant under a five-year lease agreement. The present value of the total lease payments was $25m. The agreement had an implicit finance cost of 10% per annum and required an immediate deposit of $2m and annual rentals of $6m paid on the 30 September each year for five years.

Calculate the current liability of the lease in Flash Co's statement of financial position as at 30 September 20X5.

$ [ ]

Q4

Financial statements represent transactions in words and numbers. To be useful, financial information must represent faithfully these transactions in terms of how they are reported.

Only one of the following four statements regarding faithful representation is true. Identify that statement, by clicking on the relevant box in the table below, and mark all of the others as false.

Charging the rental payments for an item of plant to profit or loss where the rental agreement meets the criteria for a right of use asset is an example of faithful representation	TRUE	FALSE
Including a convertible loan note in equity on the basis that the holders are likely to choose the equity option on conversion is an example of faithful representation	TRUE	FALSE
Derecognising factored trade receivables sold without recourse is an example of faithful representation	TRUE	FALSE
Treating redeemable preference shares as part of equity in the statement of financial position is an example of faithful representation	TRUE	FALSE

Q5

On 1 October 20X4, Kalatra Co commenced drilling for oil from an undersea oilfield. Kalatra Co is required to dismantle the drilling equipment at the end of its five-year licence. This has an estimated cost of $30m on 30 September 20X9. Kalatra Co's cost of capital is 8% per annum and $1 in five years' time has a present value of $0.68.

What is the provision which Kalatra Co would report in its statement of financial position as at 30 September 20X5 in respect of its oil operations?

- $32,400,000
- $22,032,000
- $20,400,000
- $1,632,000

Q6

When a single entity makes purchases or sales in a foreign currency, it will be necessary to translate the transactions into its functional currency before the transactions can be included in its financial records.

In accordance with IAS 21 The Effect of Changes in Foreign Currency Exchange Rates, which TWO of the following foreign currency exchange rates may be used to translate the foreign currency purchases and sales?

- The rate that existed on the day that the purchase or sale took place
- The rate that existed at the beginning of the accounting period
- An average rate for the year, provided there have been no significant fluctuations throughout the year
- The rate that existed at the end of the accounting period

Q7

On 1 October 20X4, Hoy Co had $2.5m of equity share capital (shares of $0.50 each) in issue. No new shares were issued during the year ended 30 September 20X5, but on that date, there were outstanding share options which had a dilutive effect equivalent to issuing 1.2 million shares for no consideration.

Hoy Co's profit after tax for the year ended 30 September 20X5 was $1,550,000.

The graph below represents a trend in both basic and diluted earnings per share (EPS) since 20X3. Complete the EPS trend analysis by calculating the diluted EPS for the year ended 30 September 20X5 for Hoy Co and click on the graph to identify its position.

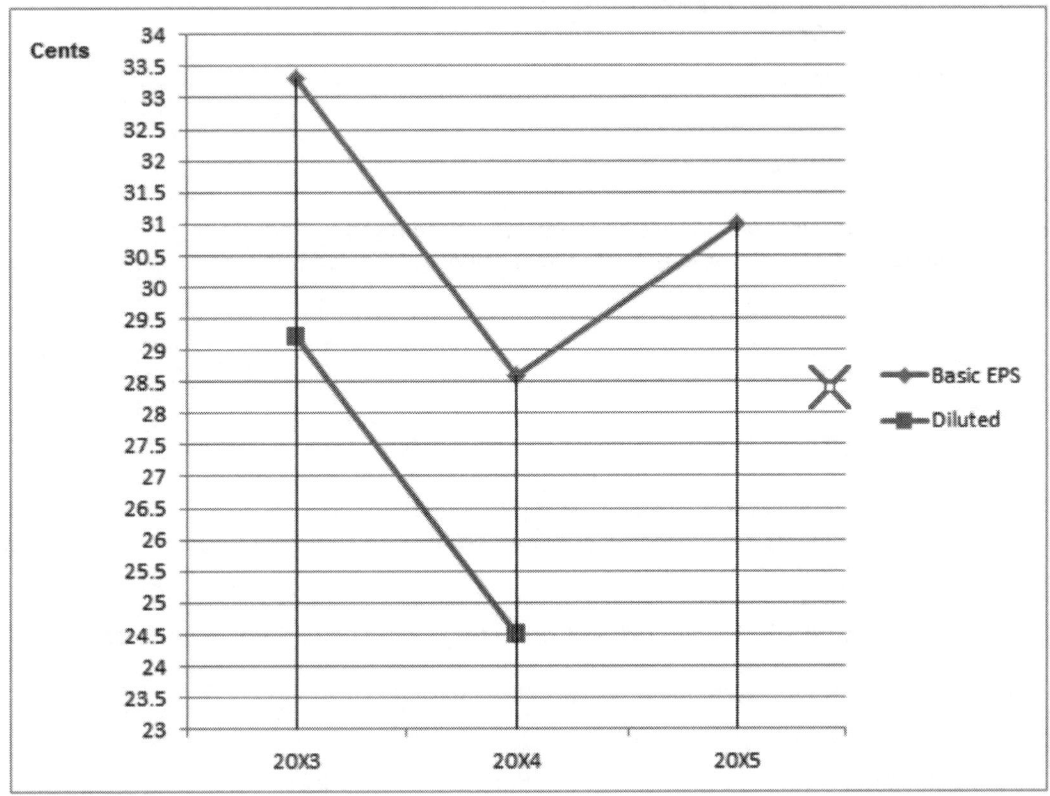

Q8

Fork Co owns an 80% investment in Spoon Co which it purchased several years ago. The goodwill on acquisition was valued at $1,674,000 and there has been no impairment of that goodwill since the date of acquisition.

On 30 September 20X4, Fork Co disposed of its entire investment in Spoon Co details of which are as follows:

	$'000
Sales proceeds of Fork Co's entire investment in Spoon Co	5,580
Cost of Fork Co's entire investment in Spoon Co	3,720

Immediately before the disposal, the consolidated financial statements of Fork Co included the following amounts in respect of Spoon Co:

	$'000
Carrying amount of the net assets (excluding goodwill)	4,464
Carrying amount of the non-controlling interests	900

Calculate the profit/loss on disposal (before tax) that will be recorded in Fork Co's CONSOLIDATED statement of profit or loss for the year ended 30 September 20X4.

$ [ ]

Q9

Consolidated financial statements are presented on the basis that the companies within the group are treated as if they are a single economic entity.

Which TWO of the following are requirements of preparing consolidated financial statements?

- ☐ All subsidiaries must adopt the accounting policies of the parent in their individual financial statements
- ☐ Subsidiaries with activities which are substantially different to the activities of other members of the group should not be consolidated
- ☐ All entity financial statements within a group should normally be prepared to the same accounting year end prior to consolidation
- ☐ Unrealised profits within the group must be eliminated from the consolidated financial statements

Q10

A parent sells goods to its 80% owned subsidiary during the financial year, some of which remains in inventory at the year end.

Match the tokens to the appropriate item in the statement of financial position (SOFP) to reflect the adjustment required in the consolidated statement of financial position to eliminate any unrealised profit in inventory.

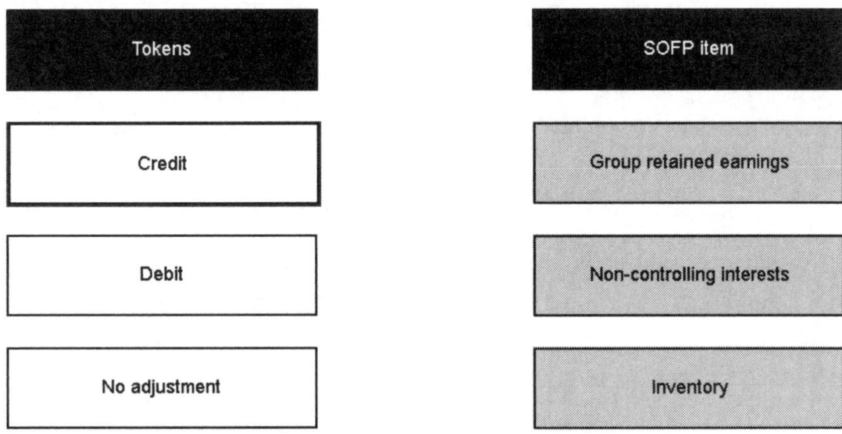

Q11

Caddy Co acquired 240,000 of Ambel Co's 800,000 equity shares for $6 per share on 1 October 20X4. Ambel Co's profit after tax for the year ended 30 September 20X5 was $400,000 and it paid an equity dividend on 20 September 20X5 of $150,000.

On the assumption that Ambel Co is an associate of Caddy Co, what would be the carrying amount of the investment in Ambel Co in the consolidated statement of financial position of Caddy Co as at 30 September 20X5?

- $1,515,000
- $1,560,000
- $1,395,000
- $1,690,000

Q12

Quartile Co is in the jewellery retail business which can be assumed to be highly seasonal. For the year ended 30 September 20X5, Quartile Co assessed its operating performance by comparing selected accounting ratios with those of its business sector average as provided by an agency.

Assume that the business sector used by the agency is a meaningful representation of Quartile Co's business.

Which TWO of the following circumstances may invalidate the comparison of Quartile Co's ratios with those of the sector average?

- In the current year, Quartile Co has experienced significant rising costs for its purchases
- The sector average figures are compiled from companies whose year ends are between 1 July 20X5 and 30 September 20X5
- Quartile Co does not revalue its properties, but is aware that other entities in this sector do
- During the year, Quartile Co discovered an error relating to the inventory count at 30 September 20X4. This error was correctly accounted for in the financial statements for the current year ended 30 September 20X5

Q13

Which of the following criticisms does NOT apply to historical cost financial statements during a period of rising prices?

- They contain mixed values; some items are at current values and some are at out of date values
- They are difficult to verify because transactions could have happened many years ago
- They understate assets and overstate profit
- They overstate gearing in the statement of financial position

Q14

The following information has been taken or calculated from Fowler Co's financial statements for the year ended 30 September 20X5:

Cash cycle as at 30 September 20X5	70 days
Inventory turnover	6 times
Year-end payables at 30 September 20X5	$230,000
Credit purchases for the year ended 30 September 20X5	$2,000,000
Cost of sales for the year ended 30 September 20X5	$1,800,000

Complete the following table, by dragging and dropping the tokens into the appropriate place, in order to reflect the correct calculation for Fowler Co's cash cycle at 30 September 20X5.

Tokens	Add/subtract		Days
Subtract			
		Inventory turnover days	C
Add			
42 days	A	Receivables collection period	D
51 days			
	B	Trade payables period	E
61 days			
		Fowler Co's cash cycle at 30 September 20X5	70

Q15

On 1 October 20X4, Pyramid Co acquired 80% of Square Co's 9 million ($1) equity shares. At the date of acquisition, Square Co had an item of plant which had a fair value of $3m in excess of its carrying amount. At the date of acquisition it had a remaining life of five years.

Pyramid Co's policy is to value non-controlling interests at fair value at the date of acquisition. For this purpose, Square Co's shares had a value of $3.50 each at that date. In the year ended 30 September 20X5, Square Co reported a profit of $8m.

At what amount should the non-controlling interests of Square Co be valued in the consolidated statement of financial position of Pyramid Co as at 30 September 20X5?

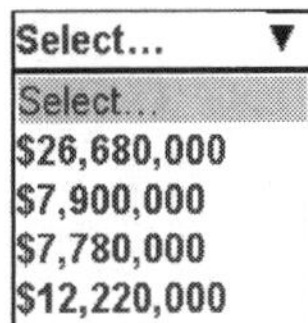

Section B

This section of the exam contains **three OT cases**.

Each OT case contains a scenario which relates to **five OT questions**.

Each question is worth **2 marks** and is compulsory.

This exam section is worth **30 marks** in total.

Select **Next** to continue.

Telepath Co has a year end of 30 September and owns an item of plant that it uses to produce and package pharmaceuticals. The plant cost $750,000 on 1 October 20X0 and, at that date, had an estimated useful life of five years. A review of the plant on 1 April 20X3 concluded that the plant would last for a further three and a half years and that its fair value was $560,000. Telepath Co adopts the policy of revaluing its non-current assets to their fair value but does not make an annual transfer from the revaluation surplus to retained earnings to represent the additional depreciation charged due to the revaluation.

On 30 September 20X3, Telepath Co was informed by a major customer that it would no longer be placing orders with Telepath Co. As a result, Telepath Co revised its estimates that net cash inflows earned from the plant for the next three years will be:

Year ended 30 September:	**$'000**
20X4	220
20X5	180
20X6	200

Telepath Co's cost of capital is 10% which results in the following discount factors:

Value of $1 at 30 September:	**$**
20X4	0.91
20X5	0.83
20X6	0.75

Telepath Co also owns Rilda Co, a 100% subsidiary, which is treated as a cash generating unit. On 30 September 20X3, there was an impairment to Rilda Co's assets of $3,500,000. The carrying amount of the assets of Rilda Co immediately before the impairment were:

	$'000
Goodwill	2,000
Factory building	4,000
Plant	3,500
Receivables and cash (at recoverable amount)	2,500
	12,000

Q16

Use the tokens to complete the following definitions in accordance with IAS 36 Impairment of Assets.

An asset is impaired if its [ ] is [ ]

than its recoverable amount. In turn, the recoverable amount

of an asset is defined as the higher of its fair value less costs

of disposal and its [ ]

TOKENS		
carrying amount	historical cost	less
replacement cost	greater	value in use

Q17

Prior to considering any impairment, what is the carrying amount of Telepath Co's plant and the balance on the revaluation surplus at 30 September 20X3?

- The carrying amount of the plant is $480,000 and the balance on the revaluation surplus is $185,000
- The carrying amount of the plant is $300,000 and the balance on the revaluation surplus is $0
- The carrying amount of the plant is $480,000 and the balance on the revaluation surplus is $0
- The carrying amount of the plant is $300,000 and the balance on the revaluation surplus is $185,000

Q18

Calculate the value in use of Telepath Co's plant at 30 September 20X3.

$ [ ]

Q19

Which of the following are TRUE in accordance with IAS 36 Impairment of Assets?

(1) A cash generating unit is the smallest identifiable group of assets for which individual cash flows can be identified and measured

(2) When considering the impairment of a cash generating unit, the calculation of the carrying amount and the recoverable amount does not need to be based on exactly the same group of net assets

(3) When it is not possible to calculate the recoverable amount of a single asset then that of its cash generating unit should be measured instead

- 1 only
- 2 and 3
- 3 only
- 1 and 3

Q20

Calculate the carrying amount of Rilda Co's plant at 30 September 20X3 after the impairment loss has been correctly allocated to its assets.

$ [ ]

At a board meeting in June 20X3, Neutron Co's directors made a decision to close down one of its factories by 30 September 20X3 and market both the building and the plant for sale. The decision had been made public, was communicated to all affected parties and was fully implemented by 30 September 20X3.

The directors of Neutron Co have provided the following information relating to the closure:

(1) Of the factory's 250 employees, 50 will be retrained and deployed to other subsidiaries within the Neutron group during the year ended 30 September 20X4, at a cost of $125,000. The remainder accepted redundancy at an average cost of $5,000 each.

(2) The factory's plant had a carrying amount of $2.2m, but is only expected to sell for $500,000, incurring $50,000 of selling costs. The factory itself is expected to sell for a profit of $1.2m.

(3) The company also rented a number of machines in the factory under operating leases which have an average of three years to run after 30 September 20X3. The present value of these future lease payments at 30 September 20X3 was $1m, however, the lessor has stated that they will accept $850,000 if paid on 30 October 20X3 as full settlement.

(4) Penalty payments, due to the non-completion of supply contracts, are estimated to be $200,000, 50% of which is expected to be recovered from Neutron Co's insurers.

Q21

Which TWO of the following must exist for an operation to be classified as a discontinued operation in accordance with IFRS 5 Non-current Assets Held for Sale and Discontinued Operations?

- ☐ It represents a separate major line of business or geographical area
- ☐ It is a subsidiary
- ☐ It has been sold or is classified as held for sale
- ☐ It is considered not to be capable of making a future profit following a period of losses

Q22

IFRS 5 Non-current Assets Held for Sale and Discontinued Operations prescribes the recognition criteria for non-current assets held for sale. For an asset or a disposal group to be classified as held for sale, the sale must be highly probable.

Which TWO of the following must apply for the sale to be considered highly probable?

- ☐ A buyer must have been located
- ☐ The asset must be marketed at a reasonable price
- ☐ Management must be committed to a plan to sell the asset
- ☐ The sale must be expected to take place within the next six months

Q23

Calculate the employee cost associated with the closure and sale of Neutron Co's factory that should be charged to profit or loss for the year ended 30 September 20X3.

$ [ ]

Q24

What is the profit or loss on discontinued operations relating to property, plant and equipment for the year ended 30 September 20X3?

- $1.75m loss
- $1.75m profit
- $550,000 loss
- $550,000 profit

Q25

In respect of the operating leases and penalty payments, what provision is required in the statement of financial position of Neutron Co as at 30 September 20X3?

- $1,100,000
- $1,050,000
- $1,200,000
- $950,000

Speculate Co is preparing its financial statements for the year ended 30 September 20X3. The following issues are relevant:

(1) Financial assets

Shareholding A - a long-term investment in 10,000 of the equity shares of another company. These shares were acquired on 1 October 20X2 at a cost of $3.50 each. Transaction costs of 1% of the purchase price were incurred. On 30 September 20X3 the fair value of these shares is $4.50 each.

Shareholding B – a short-term speculative investment in 2,000 of the equity shares of another company. These shares were acquired on 1 December 20X2 at a cost of $2.50 each. Transaction costs of 1% of the purchase price were incurred. On 30 September 20X3 the fair value of these shares is $3.00 each.

Where possible, Speculate Co makes an irrevocable election for the fair value movements on financial assets to be reported in other comprehensive income.

(2) Taxation

The existing debit balance on the current tax account of $2.4m represents the under/over provision of the tax liability for the year ended 30 September 20X2. A provision of $28m is required for income tax for the year ended 30 September 20X3.

The existing credit balance on the deferred tax account is $2.5m and the provision required at 30 September 20X3 is $4.4m.

(3) Revenue

On 1 October 20X2, Speculate Co sold one of its products for $10m. As part of the sale agreement, Speculate Co is committed to the ongoing servicing of its product until 30 September 20X5 (ie three years after the sale). The sale value of this service has been included in the selling price of $10m. The estimated cost to Speculate Co of the servicing is $600,000 per annum and Speculate Co's gross profit margin on this type of servicing is 25%. Ignore discounting.

Q26

Match the financial instrument to its appropriate classification in accordance with IFRS 9 Financial Instruments.

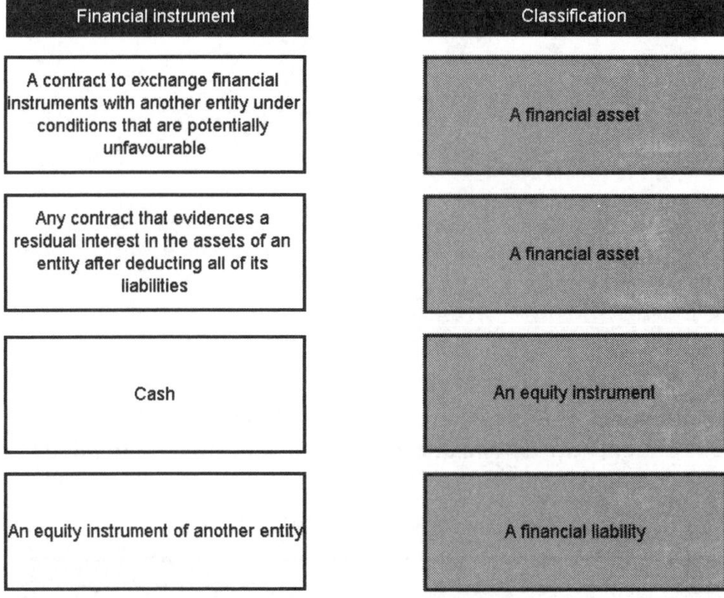

Q27

In respect of the financial assets of Speculate Co, what amount will be included in other comprehensive income for the year ended 30 September 20X3?

- $9,650
- $10,600
- $10,000
- $0

Q28

Calculate the total amount that will be charged to the statement of profit or loss for the year ended 30 September 20X3 in respect of taxation.

$ [ ]

Q29

What is the amount of deferred income which Speculate Co should recognise in its statement of financial position as at 30 September 20X3 relating to the contract for supply and servicing of products?

- $1.2 million
- $0.6 million
- $1.5 million
- $1.6 million

Q30

Only two of the following statements in respect of Speculate Co's deferred income at 30 September 20X3 are true. Identify these statements, by clicking on the relevant box in the table below and mark all the others as false.

The deferred income will be split evenly between the current and non-current liabilities in Speculate Co's statement of financial position as at 30 September 20X3	**TRUE**	**FALSE**
The costs associated with the deferred income of Speculate Co should be recognised in the statement of profit or loss at the same time as the revenue is recognised	**TRUE**	**FALSE**
The deferred income can only be recognised as revenue by Speculate Co when there is a signed written contract of service with its customer	**TRUE**	**FALSE**
When recognising the revenue associated with the service contract of Speculate Co, the stage of its completion is irrelevant	**TRUE**	**FALSE**

Section C

This section of the exam contains **two constructed response questions**.

Each question contains a scenario which relates to one or more requirement(s) which may be split over multiple question screens.

Each question is worth **20 marks** and is compulsory.

This exam section is worth **40 marks** in total.

Important: In your live exam please show all notes/workings that you want the marker to see within the spreadsheet or word processing answer areas. Remember, any notes/workings made on the Scratch Pad or on your workings paper will not be marked.

Select **Next** to continue.

Q31

This scenario relates to three requirements.

After preparing a draft statement of profit or loss for the year ended 30 September 20X5 and adding the current year's draft profit (before any adjustments required by notes (1) to (3) below) to retained earnings, the summarised trial balance of Kandy Co as at 30 September 20X5 is:

	$'000	$'000
Equity shares of $1 each		20,000
Retained earnings as at 30 September 20X5		15,500
Proceeds of 6% loan note (note (1))		30,000
Investment properties at fair value (note (2))	20,000	
Land ($5 million) and buildings – at cost (note (2))	35,000	
Plant and equipment – at cost (note (2))	58,500	
Accumulated depreciation at 1 October 20X4:		
buildings		20,000
plant and equipment		34,500
Current assets	68,700	
Current liabilities		43,400
Deferred tax (notes (2) and (3))		2,500
Interest paid (note (1))	1,800	
Current tax (note (3))		1,100
Suspense account (note 2)		17,000
	184,000	**184,000**

The following notes are relevant:

(1) The loan note was issued on 1 October 20X4 and incurred issue costs of $1 million which were charged to profit or loss. Interest of $1·8 million ($30 million at 6%) was paid on 30 September 20X5. The loan is redeemable on 30 September 20X9 at a substantial premium which gives an effective interest rate of 9% per annum. No other repayments are due until 30 September 20X9.

(2) Non-current assets:
On 1 October 20X4, Kandy Co owned two investment properties. The first property had a carrying amount of $15 million and was sold on 1 December 20X4 for $17 million. The disposal proceeds have been credited to a suspense account in the trial balance above. On 31 December 20X4, the second property became owner occupied and so was transferred to land and buildings at its fair value of $6 million. Its remaining useful life on 31 December 20X4 was considered to be 20 years. Ignore any deferred tax implications of this fair value.

The price of property has increased significantly in recent years and so the directors decided to revalue the land and buildings. The directors accepted the report of an independent surveyor who, on 1 October 20X4, valued the land at $8 million and the buildings at $39 million on that date. This revaluation specifically excludes the transferred investment property described above. The remaining life of these buildings at 1 October 20X4 was 15 years. Kandy Co does not make an annual transfer to retained profits to reflect the realisation of the revaluation gain; however, the revaluation will give rise to a deferred tax liability. The income tax rate applicable to Kandy Co is 20%.

Plant and equipment is depreciated at 12.5% per annum using the reducing balance method. No depreciation has yet been charged on any non-current asset for the year ended 30 September 20X5.

Plant and equipment is depreciated at 12.5% per annum using the reducing balance method. No depreciation has yet been charged on any non-current asset for the year ended 30 September 20X5.

(3) A provision of $2·4 million is required for income tax on the profit for the year to 30 September 20X5. The balance on current tax in the trial balance is the under/over provision of tax for the previous year. In addition to the temporary differences relating to the information in note (2), Kandy Co has further taxable temporary differences of $10 million as at 30 September 20X5.

Required:

(a) Prepare a schedule of adjustments required to the retained earnings of Kandy Co as at 30 September 20X5 as a result of the information in notes (1) to (3).

(8 marks)

(b) Prepare the statement of financial position of Kandy Co as at 30 September 20X5.

Note: The notes to the statement of financial position are not required

(9 marks)

(c) Prepare the extracts from Kandy Co's statement of cash flows for operating and investing activities for the year ended 30 September 20X5 which relate to property, plant and equipment.

(3 marks)

(20 marks)

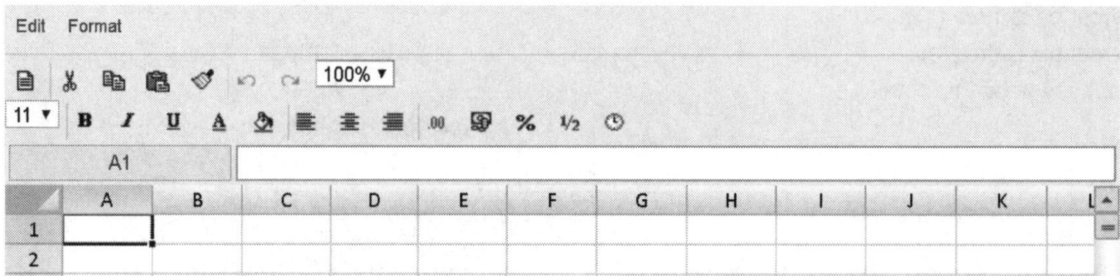

Q32

This scenario relates to three requirements.

The summarised consolidated financial statements for the year ended 30 September 20X5 (and the comparative figures) for the Tangier group are shown below.

Consolidated statements of profit or loss for the year ended 30 September:

	20X5	**20X4**
	$m	**$m**
Revenue	2,700	1,820
Cost of sales	(1,890)	(1,092)
Gross profit	**810**	**728**
Administrative expense	(345)	(200)
Distribution costs	(230)	(130)
Finance costs	(40)	(5)
Profit before taxation	**195**	**393**
Income tax expense	(60)	(113)
Profit for the year	**135**	**280**

Consolidated statements of financial position as at 30 September:

	20X5	20X5	20X4	20X4
	$m	$m	$m	$m
Non-current assets				
Property, plant and equipment		680		310
Intangible asset: manufacturing licence		300		100
goodwill		230		200
		1,210		**610**
Current assets				
Inventory	200		110	
Trade receivables	195		75	
Bank	0	**395**	120	**305**
Total assets		**1,605**		**915**
Equity and liabilities				
Equity shares of $1 each		330		250
Other components of equity		100		0
Retained earnings		375		295
		805		**545**
Non-current liabilities				
5% secured loan notes	100		100	
10% secured loan notes	300	**400**	0	**100**
Current liabilities				
Bank overdraft	110		0	
Trade payables	210		160	
Current tax payable	80	**400**	110	**270**
Total equity and liabilities		**1,605**		**915**

At 1 October 20X4, the Tangier group consisted of the parent, Tangier Co, and two wholly owned subsidiaries which had been owned for many years. On 1 January 20X5, Tangier Co purchased a third 100% owned investment in a subsidiary called Raremetal Co. The consideration paid for Raremetal Co was a combination of cash and shares. The cash payment was partly funded by the issue of 10% loan notes. On 1 January 20X5, Tangier Co also won a tender for a new contract to supply aircraft engines which Tangier Co manufactures under a recently acquired long-term licence. Raremetal Co was purchased with a view to securing the supply of specialised materials used in the manufacture of these engines. The bidding process had been very competitive and Tangier Co had to increase its manufacturing capacity to fulfil the contract.

Required:

(a) Comment on how the new contract and the purchase of Raremetal Co may have affected the comparability of the consolidated financial statements of Tangier Co for the years ended 30 September 20X4 and 20X5.

(5 marks)

(b) Calculate appropriate ratios and comment on Tangier Co's profitability and gearing. Your analysis should identify where the new contract and the purchase of Raremetal Co have limited the usefulness of the ratios and your analysis.

Note: Your ratios should be based on the consolidated financial statements provided and you should not attempt to adjust for the effects of the new contract or the consolidation. Working capital and liquidity ratios are not required.

(12 marks)

(c) Explain what further information you might require to make your analysis more meaningful.

(3 marks)

(20 marks)

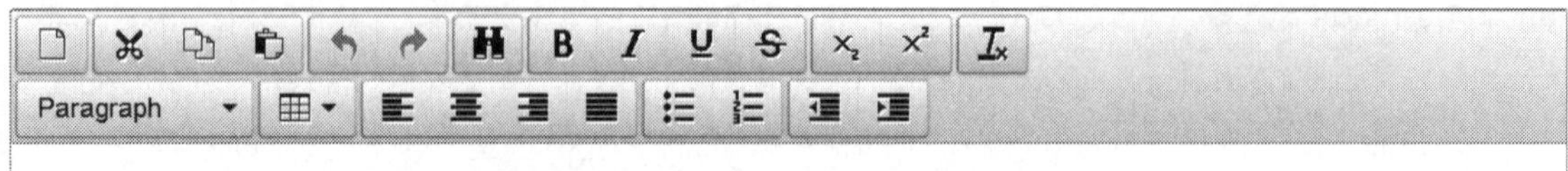

Section 8

ANSWERS TO SPECIMEN EXAM QUESTIONS

SECTION A

Q1

The correct answer is that the initial carrying amount of plant should include:
(1) the cost of transporting the plant to the factory; and
(2) the cost of installing a new power supply required to operate the plant.

Q2

The correct answer is the new research project.

Q3

Current liability = 19,300,000-15,230,000 = $4,070,000

	$'000s
FV 1 Oct 20X4	25,000
Deposit	(2,000)
	23,000
Interest 10%	2,300
Payment 30 Sep 20X5	(6,000)
	19,300
Interest 10%	1,930
Payment 30 Sep 20X6	(6,000)
Liability at 30 Sep 20X6	15,230

Q4

The correct answer is:
Derecognising factored trade receivables sold without recourse to the seller is an example of faithful representation.

Q5

Dismantling provision at 1 October is $20.4 million (30,000 x 0.68) discounted. This will increase by an 8% finance cost by 30 September 20X5 = $22,032,000

Q6

The correct answer is the rate that existed on the day that the purchase or sale took place or an average rate for the year may be used.

Q7

(1,550/(2,500 x 2 + 1,200)) = $0.25

Q8

		$'000
Sales proceeds		5,580
Net assets at disposal	4,464	
Goodwill at disposal	1,674	
Less: carrying amount of NCI	(900)	(5,238)
		342

Q9

The correct answer is that all entity financial statements within a group should normally be prepared to the same accounting year end prior to consolidation and unrealised profits within the group must be eliminated.

Q10

The correct answer is:
DEBIT Group retained earnings
CREDIT Inventory

Q11

	$'000
Cost (240,000 x $6)	1,440
Share of associate's profit (400 x 240/800)	120
Less dividend received (150 x 240/800)	(45)
	1,515

Q12

The correct answers are:

- The sector average figures are compiled from companies whose year ends are between 1 July 20X5 and 30 September 20X5
- Quartile Co does not revalue its properties, but is aware that other entities in this sector do

Q13

The correct answer is:
They are difficult to verify because transactions could have happened many years ago - this is not a vald criticism of historic cost financial statements

Q14

Inventory turnover is 61 days (365/6)
Trade payables period is 42 days (230,000 x 365/2)
Therefore, receivables collection period is 51 days (70-61 +42)

Q15

	$'000s
FV NCI at 1/10/14 (9000 x 20% x $3.50)	6,300
Post acq'n profit (8000-(3000/5)) = 7,400@20%	1,480
	7,780

Q16

The correct answer is:
An asset is impaired if its carrying amount is greater than its recoverable amount. In turn, the recoverable amount of an asset is defined as the higher of its fair value less costs of disposal and its value in use.

Q17

Annual depreciation prior to the revaluation is $150,000 (750/5). At the date of revaluation (1 April 20X3) the carrying amount is $375,000 (750-(150x2.5yrs)). Revalued to $560,000 with a remaining life of 3.5 years results in a depreciation charge of $160,000 per annum which means $80,000 for 6 mths. The carrying amount at 30 September 20X3 is therefore $480,000 (560-80). An alternative calculation is $560,000 - ($560,000/3.5 x 6/12) = $480,000 Revaluation surplus : $560,000-$375,000=$185,000

Q18

	cflow	10%discount	present value
	$'000	$'000	$'000
30-Sep-X4	220	0.91	200.2
30-Sep-X5	180	0.83	149.4
30-Sep-X6	200	0.75	150
			499.6

Q19

The correct answers are:

- A cash generating unit is the smallest identifiable group of assets for which individual cash flows can be identified and measured; and
- When it is not possible to calculate the recoverable amount of a single asset then that of its cash generating unit should be measured instead

Q20

	Carrying amt before	Impairment loss	Carrying amt after
Goodwill	2,000	2,000	Nil
Property	4,000	800	3,200
Plant	3,500	700	2,800
Cash and receivables	2,500	nil	2,500
	12,000	3,500	8,500

Q21

The correct answers are:

- It represents a separate major line of business or geographical area
- It has been sold or is classified as held for sale

Q22

The correct answers are:

- The asset must be marketed at a reasonable price
- Management must be committed to a plan to sell the asset

Q23

The correct answer is:
200 employees at $5,000 = $1,000,000 redundancy costs. The retraining costs are a future cost.

Q24

The impairment loss on plant is $1,750,000 (2,200,000 - (500,000 - 50,000))

Q25

Onerous contract $850,000 + penalty payments $200,000 = $1,050,000. The possible insurance receipt should be ignored as there is no certainty that it would be received and it would not be netted off against the provision anyway.

Q26

The correct answer is:

- Cash = a financial asset
- An equity instrument of another entity = a finacial asset
- A contract to exchange financial instruments with another entity under conditions that are potentially unfavourable = a financial liability
- Any contract that evidences a residual interest in the assets of an entity after deducting all of its liabilities = an equity instrument

Q27

The correct answer is:
Shareholding A is not held for trading as an election made - FVTOCI
Shareholding B is held for trading and so FVTPL (transaction costs are not included in carrying amount)
Cost of shareholding A is 10,000 x $3.50 x 1.01 = $35,350
FV at 30 September 20X3 10,000 x $4.50 = $45,000
Gain - 45,000 - 35,350 = $9,650

Q28

	$'000s
DT provision required at 30 Sep 20X3	4,400
DT provision at 1 October 20X2	(2,500)
	1,900
Underprovision for the y/e 30 Sep 20X2	2,400
Income tax for the year ended 30 Sep 20X3	28,000
Charge for the year ended 30 Sep 20X3	32,300

Q29

At 30 September 20X3 there are two more years of servicing work, thus $1.6 million ((600,000 x 2) x 100/75) must be treated as deferred income

Q30

The correct answers are:

- the deferred income will be split evenly between the current and non-current liabilities in Speculate Co's statement of financial position as at 30 September 20X3; and
- The costs associated with the deferred income of Speculate Co should be recognised in the statement of profit or loss at the same time as the revenue is recognised

Q31

Note: this spreadsheet is preformatted so that all numbers use a comma separator for $'000s and all negatives are expressed in

Kandy Co – Schedule of adjustments to retained earnings as at 30 September 20X5

	$'000
Retained earnings per trial balance	15,500
Adjustments re:	
Issue costs of loan note (w(i))	1,000
Loan finance costs [(30,000-1,000)@9%] (w(i))	(2,610)
Gain on disposal of investment property (17,000-15,000)	2,000
Gain on revaluation of investment property prior to transfer (6,000-5,000)	1,000
Depreciation of buildings (w (ii))	(2,825)
Depreciation of plant and equipment(w(ii))	(3,000)
Income tax expense (w(iii))	(800)
Adjusted retained earnings	10,265

Kandy Co – Statement of Financial Position as at 30 September 20X5

	$'000	$'000
ASSETS		
Non-current assets		
Property, Plant and Equipment(50,175 + 21,000) (w(ii))		71,175
Current assets		
Per trial balance		68,700
Total Assets		139,875

EQUITY AND LIABILITIES		
Equity		
Equity Shares of $1 each		20,000
Revaluation Surplus(32,000 - 6,400) (w (ii) and (iii))		25,600
Retained Earnings Part (a)		10,265
		55,865
Non-current liabilities		
6% loan note (w(i))	29,810	
Deferred Tax (w(iii))	8,400	38,210
Current liabilities		
Per trial balance	43,400	
Current Tax	2,400	45,800
Total Equity and Liabilities		**139,875**

Kandy Co – Extracts from the Cash Flow Statement for the year ended 30 September 20X5

	$'000
Cash flows from operating activities:	
Add back depreciation	5,825
Deduct gain on revaluation of investment property	(1,000)
Deduct gain on disposal of investment property	(2,000)
Cash flows from investing activities:	
Investment property disposal proceeds	17,000

Workings (monetary figures in brackets in $'000)

w(i) Loan note

The issue costs should be deducted from the proceeds of the loan note and not charged as an expense. The finance cost of the loan note, at the effective rate of 9% applied to the carrying amount of the loan note of $29 million (30,000 - 1,000) is $2,610,000. The interest actually paid is $1.8 million. The difference between these amounts of $810,000 (2,610 - 1,800) is added to the carrying amount of the loan note to give $29,810,000 (29,000 + 810) for inclusion as a non-current liability in the statement of financial position.

w(ii) Non-current assets

Land and Buildings

The gain on revaluation and carrying amount of the land and buildings will be:

	$'000
Carrying amount at 1 October 20X4 (35,000 - 20,000)	15,000
Revaluation at that date (8,000 + 39,000)	47,000
Gain on revaluation	32,000

Buildings depreciation for the year ended 30 September 20X5:	
L&B existing at 1 October 20X4 (39,000/15 years)	2,600
Transferred investment property (6,000/20 x 9/12)	225
	2,825
Carrying amount at 30 September 20X5 (47,000 + 6,000 - 2,825)	50,175

Plant and Equipment

Carrying amount at 1 October 20X4 (58,500 - 34,500)	24,000
Depreciation for the year ended 30 September 20X5 (12.5% reducing balance	(3,000)
	21,000

w(iii) Taxation

Income Tax Expense

Provision for year ended 30 September 20X5	2,400
Over-provision in previous year	(1,100)
Deferred tax (see below)	(500)
	800

Deferred Tax

Provision required at 30 September 20X5 ((10,000 + 32,000) x 20%)	8,400
Provision at 1 October 20X4	(2,500)
Movement in provision	5,900
Charge to revaluation of land and buildings (32,000 x 20%) - SOCIE	(6,400)
Balance – credit to profit or loss	(500)

Marking scheme		
Part (a) Schedule of adjustments to retained earnings at 30 Sep 20X5		
	Maximum Ma	**Awarded**
retained earnings per trial balance	½	
issue costs	1	
loan finance costs	1	
gains on investment properties	1	
depreciation charges	3	
income tax expense	1½	
	8	
Part (b) Statement of financial position as at 30 September 20X5		
property, plant and equipment	2	
current assets	½	
equity shares	½	
revaluation surplus	2	
deferred tax	1	
6% loan note	1½	
current liabilities (per trial balance)	½	
current tax payable	1	
	9	
Part (c) Extracts from the statement of cash flows for the year ended 30 September 20X5		
Cash flows from operating activities:		
add back depreciation	1	
less gain on revaluation of investment property	½	
less gain on disposal of investment prop	½	
Cash flows from investing activities:		
Investment property disposal proceeds	1	
	3	

Q32

(a) Note: References to '20X5' are in respect of the year ended 30 September 20X5 and '20X4' refers to the year ended 30 September 20X4.

The key matter to note is that the ratios for 20X4 and 20X5 will not be directly comparable because two significant events, the acquisition of Raremetal Co and securing the new contract, have occurred between these dates. This means that the underlying financial statements are not comparable. For example, the 20X4 statement of profit or loss (SOPL) will not include the results of Raremetal Co or the effect of the new contract. However, the 20X5 SOPL will contain nine months of the results of Raremetal Co (although intra-group transactions will have been eliminated) and nine months of the effects of the new contract (which may have resulted in either a net profit or loss). Likewise, the 20X4 statement of financial position does not contain any of Raremetal Co's assets and liabilities, whereas that of 20X5 contains all of the net assets of Raremetal Co and the cost of the licence. This does not mean that comparisons between the two years are not worthwhile, just that they need to be treated with caution. For some ratios, it may be necessary to exclude all of the subsidiaries from the analysis and use the single entity financial statements of Tangier Co as a basis for comparison with the performance of previous years. Similarly, it may still be possible to compare some of the ratios of the Tangier group with those of other groups in the same sector although not all groups will have experienced similar acquisitions.

Assuming there has been no impairment of goodwill, the investment in Raremetal Co has resulted in additional goodwill of $30 million which means that the investment has cost more than the carrying amount of Raremetal Co's net assets. Although there is no indication of the precise cost, it is known to have been achieved by a combination of a share exchange (hence the $180 million new issue of shares) and a cash element (funded from the proceeds of the loan issue and the decrease in the bank balance). Any intra-group sales have been eliminated on consolidation and it is not possible to determine in which individual company any profit on these intra-group sales will be reported; it is therefore difficult to measure any benefits of the investment. Indeed, the benefit of the investment might not be a financial one but merely to secure the supply of raw materials. It would be useful to establish the cost of the investment and the profit (if any) contributed by Raremetal Co so that an assessment of the benefit of the investment might be made.

(b)

Relevant ratios:	**20X5**	**20X4**
Gross profit margin % (810/2,700 x 100)	30·0%	40·0%
Operating profit margin (235/2,700 x 100)	8·7%	21·9%
ROCE (235/(805 + 400))	19·5%	61·7%
Net asset turnover 2,700/(805 + 400)	2·24 times	2·82 times
Debt/equity (400/805)	49·7%	18·3%
Interest cover (235/40)	5·9 times	79·6 times

All of the issues identified in (a) make a comparison of ratios difficult and, if more information was available, then some adjustments may be required. For example, if it is established that the investment is not generating any benefits, then it might be argued that the inclusion of the goodwill in the ROCE and asset turnover is unjustified (it may be impaired and be written off). Goodwill has not been excluded from any of the following ratios.

The increase in revenues of 48·4% (880/1,820 x 100) in 20X5 will be partly due to the consolidation of Raremetal Co and the revenues associated with the new contract. Yet, despite these increased revenues, the company has suffered a dramatic fall in its profitability. This has been caused by a combination of a falling gross profit margin (from 40% in 20X4 to only 30% in 20X5) and markedly higher operating overheads (operating profit margin has fallen from 21.9% in 20X4 to 8.7% in 20X5). Again it is important to note that some of these costs will be attributable to the consolidation of Raremetal Co and some to the new contract. It could be speculated that the 73% increase in administrative expenses may be due to one-off costs associated with the tendering process (consultancy fees, etc) and the acquisition of Raremetal Co and the 77% increase in higher distribution costs could be due to additional freight/packing/insurance cost of the engines, delivery distances may also be longer (even to foreign countries) (although some of this increase may also be due to consolidation).

This is all reflected in the ROCE falling from an impressive 61·7% in 20X4 to only 19·5% in 20X5 (though even this figure is respectable). The fall in the ROCE is attributable to a dramatic fall in profit margin at operating level (from 21·9% in 20X4 to only 8·7% in 20X5) which has been compounded by a reduction in the asset turnover, with only $2·24 being generated from every $1 invested in net assets in 20X5 (from $2·82 in 20X4).

The information in the question points strongly to the possibility (even probability) that the new contract may be responsible for much of the deterioration in Tangier Co's operating performance. For example, it is likely that the new contract may account for some of the increased revenue; however, the bidding process was 'very competitive' which may imply that Tangier Co had to cut its prices (and therefore its profit margin) in order to win the contract.

The costs of fulfilling the contract have also been heavy: investment in property, plant and equipment has increased by $370 million (at carrying amount), representing an increase of 61% (no doubt some of this increase will be due to the acquisition of Raremetal Co). The increase in licence costs to manufacture the new engines has cost $200 million plus any amortisation (which is not identified in the question) and there is also the additional goodwill of $30 million.

An eight-fold increase in finance cost caused by the increased borrowing at double the interest rate of the borrowing in 20X4 and (presumably) some overdraft interest has led to the dramatic fall in the company's interest cover (from 79·6 in 20X4 to only 5·9 in 20X5). The finance cost of the new $300 million 10% loan notes to partly fund the investment in Raremetal Co and any other non-current assets has also increased debt/equity (one form of gearing measure) from 18·3% in 20X4 to 49·7% in 20X5 despite also issuing $180 million in new equity shares. At this level, particularly in view of its large increase from 20X4, it may give debt holders (and others) cause for concern as there is increased risk for all Tangier Co's lenders. If it could be demonstrated that the overdraft could not be cleared for some time, this would be an argument for including it in the calculation of debt/equity, making the 20X5 gearing level even worse. It is also apparent from the movement in the retained earnings that Tangier Co paid a dividend during 20X5 of $55 million (295,000 + 135,000 – 375,000) which may be a questionable policy when the company is raising additional finance through borrowings and leaves Tangier Co with a substantial overdraft.

Overall, the acquisition of Raremetal Co to secure supplies appears to have been an expensive strategy, perhaps a less expensive one might have been to enter into a long-term supply contract with Raremetal Co.

(c) Further information which would be useful to obtain would therefore include:

(i) The cost of the investment in Raremetal Co, the carrying amount of the assets acquired and whether Tangier Co has carried out a goodwill impairment test as required under IFRS.
(ii) The benefits generated from the investment; for example, Raremetals Co's individual financial statements and details of sales to external customers (not all of these will be measurable in financial terms).
(iii) The above two pieces of information would demonstrate the investment in Raremetal Co had been worthwhile.
(iv) The amount of intra-group sales made during the year and those expected to be made in the short to medium term.
(v) The pricing strategy agreed with Raremetal Co so that the effects on the profits reported in the individual financial statements of Raremetal Co and Tangier Co can be more readily determined.
(vi) More information is needed to establish if the new contract has been detrimental to Tangier Co's performance. The contract was won sometime between 1 October 20X4 and 1 January 20X5 and there is no information of when production/sales started, but clearly there has not been a full year's revenue from the contract. Also there is no information on the length or total value of the contract.

Marking Scheme		
	Maximum Marks	**Awarded**
Part (a) comparability		
A like for like comparison taking account of the consolidation and the contract	**5**	
Part (b) Analysis of results		
up to 5 marks for ratio calculations	5	
Profitability	4½	
Gearing and interest cover	2½	
	12	
Part (c) additional information		
Any three of the six suggestions provided	**3**	

Section 9

REFERENCES

The Board (2022) *Conceptual Framework for Financial Reporting*. London: IFRS Foundation.

The Board (2022) *IAS 1 Presentation of Financial Statements*. London: IFRS Foundation.

The Board (2022) *IAS 2 Inventories*. London: IFRS Foundation.

The Board (2022) *IAS 7 Statement of Cash Flows*. London: IFRS Foundation.

The Board (2022) *IAS 8 Accounting Policies, Changes in Accounting Estimates and Errors*. London: IFRS Foundation.

The Board (2022) *IAS 10 Events after the Reporting Period*. London: IFRS Foundation.

The Board (2022) *IAS 12 Income Taxes*. London: IFRS Foundation.

The Board (2022) *IAS 16 Property, Plant and Equipment*. London: IFRS Foundation.

The Board (2022) *IAS 20 Accounting for Government Grants and Disclosure of Government Assistance*. London: IFRS Foundation.

The Board (2022) *IAS 21 The Effects of Changes in Foreign Exchange Rates.* London: IFRS Foundation.

The Board (2022) *IAS 23 Borrowing Costs*. London: IFRS Foundation.

The Board (2022) *IAS 27 Separate Financial Statements*. London: IFRS Foundation.

The Board (2022) *IAS 28 Investments in Associates and Joint Ventures*. London: IFRS Foundation.

The Board (2022) *IAS 32 Financial Instruments: Presentation*. London: IFRS Foundation.

The Board (2022) *IAS 33 Earnings per Share*. London: IFRS Foundation.

The Board (2022) *IAS 36 Impairment of Assets*. London: IFRS Foundation.

The Board (2022) *IAS 37 Provisions, Contingent Liabilities and Contingent Assets*. London: IFRS Foundation.

The Board (2022) *IAS 38 Intangible Assets*. London: IFRS Foundation.

The Board (2022) *IAS 40 Investment Property*. London: IFRS Foundation.

The Board (2022) *IAS 41 Agriculture*. London: IFRS Foundation.

The Board (2022) *IFRS 3 Business Combinations*. London: IFRS Foundation.

The Board (2022) *IFRS 5 Non-current Assets Held for Sale and Discontinued Operations*. London: IFRS Foundation.

The Board (2022) *IFRS 7 Financial Instruments: Disclosure*. London: IFRS Foundation.

The Board (2022) *IFRS 9 Financial Instruments*. London: IFRS Foundation.

The Board (2022) *IFRS 10 Consolidated Financial Statements*. London: IFRS Foundation.

The Board (2022) *IFRS 13 Fair Value Measurement*. London: IFRS Foundation.

The Board (2022) *IFRS 15 Revenue from Contracts with Customers*. London: IFRS Foundation.

The Board (2022) *IFRS 16 Leases*. London: IFRS Foundation.